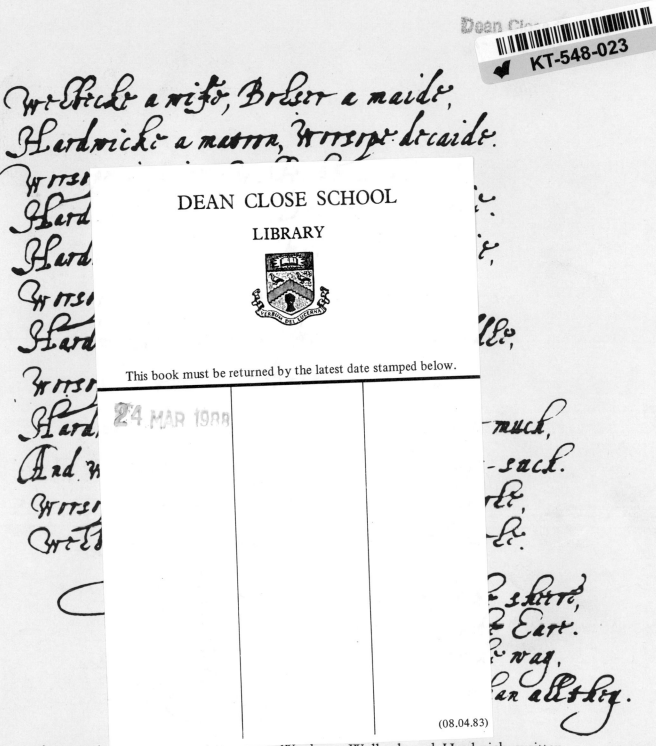

A poem in celebration of Bolsover, Worksop, Welbeck and Hardwick, written in about 1640 by Dr Francis Andrewes. (British Museum Harl. Mss. 4955, f.67v)

Robert Smythson

ROBERT SMYTHSON
& The Elizabethan Country House

Mark Girouard

Yale University Press
New Haven & London 1983

FOR MY FATHER

Title page: Bolsover Castle in the snow.

Designed by Dorothy Girouard and set in Monophoto Bembo.
Calligraphy by Anne Moring
Printed in Great Britain by Butler & Tanner Ltd, Frome, Somerset.

Library of Congress Cataloging in Publication Data
Girouard, Mark, 1931—
   Robert Smythson and the Elizabethan country house.

   Updated ed. of: Robert Smythson and the architecture
of the Elizabethan era. 1967.
   Includes bibliographical references and index.
   1. Smythson, Robert, 1534 or 5-1614.
2. Architecture, Elizabethan – England. 3. Country
homes – England.   I. Title.
NA997.S6G5 1983   720'.92'4   83-50004
ISBN 0-300-03134-3

PREFACE

AN EARLIER edition of this book appeared in 1966, under the title *Robert Smythson and the Architecture of the Elizabethan Era*. It was my first book and has long been out of print. Enough has come to light or been published in the intervening years to make a new edition seem desirable, and I have incorporated considerable additions, corrections and alterations throughout the text, though the form and structure of the book remain substantially unchanged.

The book was originally written in two years under the impetus of great enthusiasm for the subject, which I hope can still be felt in the new edition. The enthusiasm was generated by the extraordinary nature of the buildings with which I was concerned. It has been an experience both enjoyable and exciting to go back to them, and, for instance, to visit in one day Hardwick, Bolsover, Manor Lodge, Barlborough, and Shireoaks, five houses within a few miles of each other which are collectively as strange, exciting and original as any group of buildings in England or Europe. Since the first edition came out the fate of many of the buildings with which it dealt has not been an especially encouraging one. Heath Old Hall has, unforgivably, been demolished; the ruins of Thorpe Salvin and Slingsby Castle have seriously deteriorated; Barlborough has lost its lantern and chimneystacks, although there are hopes of re-erecting the former; Pontefract New Hall has been demolished. Other buildings have suffered from too much attention rather than too little. The black and battered splendour of Hardwick, brilliantly captured by Edwin Smith in his photograph of the west front, has vanished under a bland re-facing which must leave one questioning whether it need have been so drastic; the magic of the Little Castle at Bolsover has been adulterated by well-intentioned but not always sensitive restoration and redecoration; and much of the money lavished on Wootton Lodge, once one of the most beautiful houses in England, would have been better unspent.

The book deals with the buildings which can be connected with Robert Smythson, his son, John, and his grandson, Huntingdon, and tries to place these in the context of their time. The central source of evidence for their work is the large collection of Smythson drawings now belonging to the Royal Institute of British Architects. My catalogue of these was published in 1962 as Volume V of *Architectural History*, the journal of the Society of Architectural Historians; numbers in brackets in the text of *Robert Smythson* refer to the drawings as numbered in the catalogue. The drawings combine with documentary evidence from accounts or letters to produce a hard core of buildings with which the Smythsons were definitely involved. Others can be added on stylistic grounds, or grounds of family connection, but it should be emphasised that there is an especially high degree of surmise in linking buildings of this period to individuals, owing to the organisation of the Elizabethan building world, in which the

v

concept of an architect had scarcely yet emerged. Interiors feature comparatively little, because there are only a few houses in which there is evidence or likelihood of Smythson involvement in the design of internal detail, and most of these have been destroyed, remodelled or redecorated.

Elizabethan and Jacobean architecture remains somewhat out of fashion, and in recent years has been far less written about than the architecture of the eighteenth and nineteenth centuries. There are encouraging signs of growing interest, however; and I hope the new edition of this book may help to make people look more closely at Elizabethan and Jacobean buildings, and encourage more architectural historians to investigate a rewarding, fascinating and still relatively unexplored period. For help in my revision I must record my thanks to my fellow enthusiasts: David Durant, for hospitality, shared information and the light he has shed on Bess of Hardwick; Anthony Wells-Cole, for generously sharing the first-fruits of his researches into sixteenth-century pattern books; Leo Godlewski, who has rescued Shireoaks from decay and probably from demolition, for help, suggestions, and plans; and Douglas Blain, for the pleasure of his company and ideas at Bolsover and elsewhere. Among many others I would like to acknowledge the help, information, or ideas which I have had from J. R. Arundell, Alan Bemrose, Lady Anne Cavendish-Bentinck, Howard Colvin, Miranda Davies, Jane Fowles, Alice Friedman, John Harris, Anthony Jarvis, John Kenworthy-Browne, F. J. Ladd, Rosamund Meredith, John Newman and Reresby Sitwell, David Thompson and Martin Wakelin.

ONTENTS

Introduction   I

I   Longleat   39

II   Wardour & Wollaton   77

III Worksop & Related Houses   109

IV   Hardwick   143

V   Robert Smythson:
     The Later Houses   165

VI   Bolsover Castle & the
     Revival of Chivalry   205

VII The Buildings of John Smythson   233

VIII Robert Smythson:
     A Summing Up   285

     Appendix I. The Letter from
     Smythson & Maynard to
     Thynne   295

Appendix II. The Building
    Chronology of Bolsover
    Castle   297

Appendix III. The Smythson
    Family Tree & the Later
    Smithsons   303

Notes to the Text   305

List of Illustrations   319

Index of Names and Places   323

Subject Index   328

1. (right) Drawing of a summer house in Chelsea, by Robert or John Smythson (I/9).

A Summer house at Chealsea

Introduction

DURING three generations and over seventy years Robert Smythson, his son John and his grandson Huntingdon built some of the most magnificent, romantic or ingenious houses in England. Yet they spent their lives in obscurity, ignored by the writers and historians of their time; and for the next three centuries they failed to obtain any but perfunctory recognition. It is only in recent years that Robert Smythson, by far the most important of the three, has begun to receive his due as a figure of the first rank in the history of English architecture.

This long neglect was due to the circumstances under which they worked; and, in order to explain it, some account has to be given of the general architectural scene in the time of Elizabeth and the early Stuarts. English architecture of this period has been called Renaissance. The term is a confusing one, for the period saw the birth of a style to a considerable extent independent of, and even hostile to, the classical architecture of the Continent; it drew its strength as much from native Gothic roots. The story of its development is a curious one, for the style when it did come was in the highest degree original and exciting, yet at the start the odds seemed to lie heavily against its birth ever taking place.

The obscurity in which the Smythsons worked was not peculiar to them. The period as a whole is particularly baffling for the architectural historian. The Elizabethans themselves reveal almost nothing about their own buildings or the men who built them. Apart from drawings made by masons and surveyors only a handful of contemporary illustrations of Elizabethan houses survive.[1] In 1576 du Cerceau published his *Plus excellents bastiments de France*, a magnificent series of engravings of the most important buildings of the time. England was to have nothing anywhere near approaching this until *Britannia Illustrata*, two volumes of country-house views by Kip and Knyff, appeared in 1707 and 1715.

Written or printed comments and description are nearly as rare, and when they do occur are often very meagre. Topographers like Camden and Norden pay more attention to the family trees of the gentry than to their houses. Except when letters to or from the actual artificers or surveyors survive, it is very seldom that one finds references to buildings in Elizabethan correspondence. When Burghley wrote to the Earl of Rutland, and Philip Sidney to his brother, giving them advice on what to do while touring the Continent, they recommended them to study the manners, form of government, agriculture, and industries of the countries through which they passed, but said nothing about looking at buildings or works of art.[2] In the reign of Elizabeth only one book on architecture was published in England, John Shute's *The First and Chief Groundes of Architecture* of 1563; whereas the equivalent period in France saw the works of de l'Orme, Goujon, Lescot, Bullant, Sambin and du Cerceau.[3] The very large number of translations published under Elizabeth did not include a single architectural book.

As a result any historian who tries to go beyond an examination and classification of surviving Elizabethan buildings is forced into a tedious and often unrewarding search: for building accounts and contracts; for stray references in letters and literary scraps; for descriptions and drawings made by artists or antiquaries in the seventeenth or eighteenth centuries.

This Elizabethan silence was nothing new. It was an inheritance from the Middle Ages. The publicity which architecture was receiving in Italy and beginning to receive in France was a direct result of the Renaissance, and the Renaissance, as far as the visual arts were concerned, had failed to establish itself in England. The reasons for this are not very hard to find.

At the beginning of the sixteenth century the architecture of Italy, the result of a sudden and passionate rediscovery of that of ancient Rome, began to spread over the rest of Europe. In England the King and Church were ready and eager to receive it. The few ripples and trickles that had already arrived seemed the advance guard of a more comprehensive flood. But in 1533 the church in England separated from Rome and for the next hundred years had no longer the inclination to erect magnificent buildings or the money to pay for them. A little later, and for quite different reasons, the Crown abandoned almost entirely the rôle of patron of the arts. By two sharp blows English architecture had lost its main supports and the main links which would have connected it with the architecture of the Continent. For fifty years it remained provincial, a backwater in which there were only faint or distorted echoes of developments over the Channel.

It is worth comparing England with France. In the early years of the sixteenth century they develop on roughly parallel lines; England was a little more remote, and so less able to get the best talent. The French kings brought Leonardo de Vinci, Fra Giocondo, and Boccador from Italy; Henry VIII failed to tempt Raphael to England, but obtained the services of Torrigiano and owned a palace in Rome designed by Bramante. Wolsey, his ecclesiastical counterpart, had his tomb carved by a Florentine and employed Italians on the details of Hampton Court. But after the break with Rome Henry, though still an enthusiastic patron, was at a disadvantage. Italians of the first rank were unlikely to risk Papal disapproval by coming to England. François I acquired, in the second half of his reign, the services of Serlio, Rosso, and Primaticcio, men of international reputation. But Henry had to be content with dim figures such as John of Padua, Nicholas Bellin and Toto del Nunziata. The great palace of Nonsuch, though decorated with much detail of high quality, was as a whole barbarous in comparison with contemporary buildings in Italy or even France.

When Henry died, Edward VI was too young and his sister Mary too insecure to embark on ambitious building schemes. But Elizabeth, throughout the forty-five years of her reign, deliberately abstained from building on a large scale, as a matter of policy. Sir Nicholas Bacon, speaking as a minister of the crown, could boast that she did not construct 'gorgeous sumptuous superfluous buildings'.[4] This was not only meanness: she knew that the situation was different in England from what it was abroad, that only by delicately walking the financial tightrope could she keep her power and her popularity. But as a result England got no Fontainebleau, no Louvre, no Tuileries, no Charleval, with all the

3

incentives to architects, painters and sculptors that such buildings would have provided.

The Stuarts were not so wise. Not only did they buy up the great houses of the Elizabethan courtiers, Theobalds in 1607, Holdenby in 1608, Wimbledon in 1638; they themselves built on a considerable scale and planned more extravagantly than they built. They patronised foreign artists of the first reputation – Rubens, Bernini, Van Dyck – and in Inigo Jones found the first Englishman who had a true understanding of Renaissance architecture. This encouragement of the arts brought England back into the main current of European culture. But it was highly unpopular with a large and vocal section of the country, who contrasted angrily the splendour and extravagance of the new court with the frugality of the great Elizabeth. It was one of the elements that greatly increased Crown expenditure; the consequent efforts to raise money led to the new and unpopular taxes, or the recourse to disgruntled and belligerent Parliaments, that ultimately resulted in the Civil War. It was appropriate but ironical that Charles I stepped on to the scaffold out of the window of Inigo Jones's Banqueting House.

THE ELIZABETHAN RULING CLASSES

The fact that under the Tudors Church and Crown stopped building on any extensive scale meant that, as in the eighteenth century, the initiative passed to the nobility and gentry. These were well prepared to demand and pay for new standards of splendour and of comfort. Or at any rate a section of them were. Increasingly, in dealing with the reign of Elizabeth, one becomes aware of a cohesive group, those who had accepted (and been accepted by) the new régime and become part of the machinery of government. These were the judges, the justices of the peace, the members of the various Councils, the rich merchants who invested their fortune in land and took their part in local government. The Catholic families, or those who were without ambition, or inefficient, or simply decadent, or those who disliked the government or were disliked by it, lived on in their old manor houses, or built new ones of unpretentious design. With a few exceptions, it was the families in the swing, proud to be the leaders of a Protestant élite and eager to demonstrate their pride, who built the great Elizabethan and Jacobean houses.[5] Many of them were self-made men, little bound by precedent and eager patrons of the latest fashions. Monastery lands, law profits, successful adventures in commerce, privateering, or industry, and the endless perquisites and bribes of office, gave them the means to build. As a result, as William Harrison commented at the time, the old wood and plaster manors were being replaced or supplemented all over England by new houses of brick and cut stone 'so magnificent and stately as the basest house of a baron doth often match in our days with some honours of princes in old time'.[6]

This process was actively encouraged by Elizabeth. During the summer months she liked to live at her subjects' expense. With an enormous retinue she moved from house to house; and these were altered or rebuilt to receive her.

4

Hatton and Burghley built their great palaces at Holdenby and Theobalds expressly as alternative residences for their queen.

But the Elizabethan ruling classes were very different from, for instance, the Whig aristocracy of the eighteenth century. They were, on the whole, a philistine crew. A lot of them were only lately rich; none of them felt secure. It was not an age in which it was easy to relax, to cultivate leisure. The correspondence of the time is uncomfortable: bristling, in interminable and artificial prose, with the screams, the struggles, the squabbles, of the new rich fighting to consolidate, the old rich fighting to keep from going under. The typical figure of the age is not the country gentleman, at ease in his study among books and busts of the philosophers, but the lawyer on the make, the dangerous and magnificent courtier, on whom no man could rely, the landowner increasing his income by lending money to his neighbours. Moreover the whole bias of the time was Protestant; the puritans, though numerically a minority, were a fashionable and powerful one; puritanism was the religion of young, ambitious and up-to-date men. The visual arts were papish, and therefore suspect. Those members of the upper classes with intellectual interests, the circle of Sidney, Greville, Raleigh and Spenser, were all deeply involved in the Protestant crusade; which is perhaps why they took only a marginal interest in painting, sculpture or architecture. Most of the great Elizabethan houses were built, not because their owners had a passion for architecture, but because they wished to demonstrate their wealth and their position.

George Whetstone in his *Heptameron of Civil Discourse* published in 1582, after a lavish description of the palace of Philoxenus, ends thus:

> And to be briefe, this Pallace, with all her conveinces, as well necessarie as of pleasure, fully matched the statelynesse of Cardinall Farneses Pallace, buylded and beautified with the various Monumentes of Rome, in her pride: so that the curiousness thereof, was of power to have enchanted my eyes with an immodest gase, had I not remembered, that it belongeth unto a Gentleman to see, and not to stare upon, the straungest Novell that is: for bace is his mynde whose spirit hourely beholdeth not greater matters than either beautie, buylding, or braverie. And certenly, at this instant, I delighted more to contemplate of Segnior Phyloxenus virtues than to regarde his sumptuous buyldings.[7]

And in 1615 Sir George Buck could write of the art of painting:

> In the art called of Aristojle γραφιχη (Graphice) and in English painting; There be in this citie cunning masters, for either shaddowing, pourtraying, counterfetting, tricking, painting, enlumining, or limming. But this is an art now not accounted ingenuous or fit for a Gentleman, by reason that it is much fallen from the reputation which it had aunciently which whether it be for the unworthiness or unskilfulnesse of the persons exercising it and practising it in this age, or for the abuses and deceipts used by paynters, or for the scandall of

5

images and idols (for the which Philo condemneth it) or for the foul devise of the faire cosmetica or for what other cause I know not well, but sure I am, it is now accounted base and mechanicall, and a mere mestier of an artificer, and handy craftsman. In so much as fewe or no Gentleman or generous and liberall person will adventure the practising this art.[8]

It is interesting to compare this extract with the advice given by Sir Thomas Eliot to an earlier and perhaps more visually-conscious generation. In his *Boke named the Gouernour* (1530-1), when discussing the education of a nobleman's son, he says: 'If the childe be of nature inclined (as many have been), to paint with a penne, or to fourme images in stone or tree: he shulde not be therfrom withdrawen . . . in vacant tymes from other more serious lernynge, he shulde be, in the moste pure wise, enstructed in painting or kervinge.'[9]

THE IDEA OF THE ARCHITECT

This lack of enlightened patronage of the visual arts, and the small estimation in which they were held, meant that there were no Elizabethan architects. In England at the time 'architect' both as a word and a concept was so alien and unfamiliar as to be meaningless. The architect was a revival or product of the Renaissance.

In the Middle Ages a distinction had been made between the liberal and the mechanical arts: the former purely or mainly intellectual, the latter involving work with the hands, to do with making rather than knowing, and therefore held to be inferior. 'Arts that respect the mind were ever reputed nobler than those that serve the body.'[10] The liberal arts were Grammar, Dialectic, Rhetoric, Geometry, Arithmetic, Astrology, and Music or Harmony. The mechanical arts included, along with tillage, spinning, cooking, and so on, painting, carving, and building. These were the provinces of hereditary groups of artificers, of painters, carvers, carpenters, and masons, organised in guilds, and working their way up their guilds, from the lowest rank of apprentice to the highest of master.

A master-artificer was a person of some accomplishment and position. A master-mason, for instance, often no longer worked in stone but confined himself to organising, supervising, contracting and making plans. The old notion of a Gothic cathedral as the anonymous product of groups of craftsmen has had to be abandoned, or at any rate greatly modified. There were without doubt medieval master-masons who could and did make detailed drawings for every inch of a building.[11]

Even so the status of a master-artificer was well below that of a professor of a liberal art. Not only was his skill considered less intellectual, but there was a definite stigma, of inferiority and 'ungentleness', attached to an occupation that involved, at any time, working with the hands.

During the Renaissance a great and successful campaign took place to raise painting, carving and building to the level of liberal arts. The strategy of this campaign was to emphasise their intellectual and theoretical basis. Vitruvius had said that to be good at building a man should also be an accomplished lawyer, astronomer, musician, orator and mathematician. Even if this was thought by some Renaissance theorists to be carrying the attack to the point of absurdity, it was generally agreed that he should have a knowledge of mathematics and geometry, in order to build strongly, of harmony, in order to build according to the right proportion, and of the monuments of ancient Rome, in order to build after the right models.

An architect was a man who had this theoretical knowledge, and acquaintance with antiquity. His training was quite different from that of an artificer; and as a result a new distinction, and ultimately a social barrier, grew up between architecture and building, between the architect, who designed, and the artificer, who carried out his designs.

The difference in status between this new class of architects and the old master-craftsmen was very great. Among the latter there had been men of character and genius; but even they had lived relatively in the shadows, and now can be traced only in such accounts, leases or contracts as have survived. But the architect was a figure of standing in the society of his time; dealt more or less on an equality with his employers; was written about, commented on, praised or satirised, and himself published books expounding the theory of his art or describing the buildings he had designed. As a result people became conscious to a far greater degree than they had been in the Middle Ages of particular buildings as being the work of a particular individual.

No such consciousness existed in Elizabethan England. Although both John Shute in *The First and Chief Groundes of Architecture* (1563), and John Dee, in his preface to Euclid's *The Elements of Geometrie* (1570), expounded the Renaissance and Vitruvian ideal of the architect,[12] the concept remained an alien one. The medieval system continued with little alteration, so that it is seldom possible to ascribe an English building to one man with anything like the certainty with which in France or Italy one can say that a particular building is by Vignola or San Gallo, Lescot or de l'Orme. A description of how the Elizabethan building world was organised will make this clear.

BUILDERS AND DESIGNERS

The most obvious and the most ambitious building organisation in England was the Royal Works.[13] This had its main centre in the building-yard at Whitehall. Its head was the Surveyor, in supreme charge of all building operations and nearly always a professional mason or carpenter. Next came the Comptroller, who ran the administrative and financial side, but was also by origin an artificer, waiting to succeed to the Surveyorship. Under him worked a staff of administrative clerks. But the fighting troops of the organisation were the working artificers, the various divisions of which were commanded by the Master Mason, the Master Carpenter, the Master Joiner, the Sergeant Plumber, and the Master Glazier.

Outside London, at Windsor or Berwick for instance, similar organisations existed, each with their own Surveyor, though the London Surveyor seems to have had precedence, and perhaps some sort of control, over the others.

The Royal Works was a permanent organisation, the members of which received regular salaries and frequently stayed in it for life. But wherever in England a private person started building operations on any scale, there arose for the time being a miniature version of the Works. For instance, in the reign of Edward VI the Duke of Somerset had separate staffs of Surveyor, Comptroller and Master Artificer at his two great houses at Syon and in the Strand.[14] But he was building on a very large scale; more often either there was no Surveyor, and building operations were run by a partnership of the chief artificers, or one of the chief artificers was made Surveyor as well. The former was the case at Longleat; whereas Sir Edward Pytts, building at Kyre in Worcestershire, appointed John Chaunce 'chief mason, workman, and surveyor of the work'.[15] And in many cases the duties of Comptroller were taken on by the employer's bailiff, steward, or one of the other household officials, who was made responsible for organisation, co-ordination and the payment of the workmen.

As in the Middle Ages there were two principal methods of payment, for day-work and for piece- or task-work – that is to say by time or by quantity. On the whole, a daily wage tended to be paid mostly to the labourers and the less important craftsmen, or for the less skilled work. In the case of mouldings, carved work, chimney-pieces, panelling and so on, the normal procedure was to pay by results; a fixed price was agreed on and the completed work was measured up by the Surveyor or one of the senior craftsmen. Very often an artificer entered into a specific contract to supply a particular piece of work, or even an entire portion of the building: in such a case a lump sum was agreed upon, and it was left to the contractor, if the work was beyond his individual capacity, to arrange for the hiring and paying of additional workmen.[16]

So much for the machinery of building a house; but who designed it? This is an unreal question, because the average Elizabethan building emerged from the interaction of a number of different people. The plan might come from one source, the details from a number of others. Designs could be supplied by one or more of the craftsmen actually employed on the building; or by an outside craftsman; or by the employer; or by a friend of the employer; or by a professional with an intellectual rather than craft background – that is to say, someone approaching an architect in the modern sense. The last are the most intangible class. There are a few individuals in the sixteenth century who were neither amateurs with a penchant for design nor masons who had worked their way up the social scale, but something in between the two. Several of the Queen's Surveyors, for instance, were exceptions to the general rule, and were brought into the works from outside the artificer class. Thomas Graves, Surveyor from 1578 to 1587, was certainly not a craftsman by training, though it is a mystery what his origins were. He designed the first Banqueting Hall in Whitehall in

8

1581 and is mentioned in that connection by Holinshed[17] the only such an attribution in the whole of Elizabethan literature. His successor, Thomas Blagrave, Surveyor from 1587–94, started his career in the household of a courtier and then became an official in the Revels, the department that organised the royal masques and entertainments. He held the Surveyorship jointly with the clerkship of the Revels, but possibly as a sinecure, for he cannot be connected with the design of a single building. His successor (1594–5), Robert Adams, was best known as a map-maker and expert on fortifications.[18]

Outside the Works there is the interesting figure of Leonard Digges, a gentleman by birth, and a mathematician and land surveyor of European reputation, who wrote two treatises on mensuration and anticipated the invention of the telescope; in addition to which, according to Fuller, he 'was the best architect of that age, for all manner of buildings, for conveniency, pleasure, state, strength, being excellent in fortifications'.[19] But no one has yet discovered which these buildings were.

In contrast to this shadowy group, the employers and their friends form a more tangible and formidable body. It is reasonable enough to suppose that dealing as they were, not with architects of authority and repute but with comparatively uneducated and obscure artificers, their influence was greater than in the eighteenth or nineteenth centuries; and that they were more ready to dictate features of the design or to alter it once it had been made. But there are some patrons whose claims go further than this and who are worth considering as their own designers. Henry VIII had a reputation in this way. Harrison talks of the palaces 'such as he erected after his own devise; for he was nothing inferior in this trade to Adrian the emperour and Justinian the law-giver'.[20]

Sir John Thynne produced at least two designs for houses, in 1559 and 1570, one for himself at Longleat and one for a friend, the Earl of Hertford.[21] In 1612 Sir John Strode employed for his house at Chantmarle in Dorset a mason, Gabriel Moore, 'to survey and direct the building to the form I conceived and plotted it'.[22] The complex design of Richard Carew's little fishing lodge in the middle of the fishpond at Antony in Cornwall was 'devised for me by that perfectly accomplished gentleman, the late Sir Arthur Champernowne'.[23] Sir Charles Cavendish was described by his son as a 'good architect'; in 1607 he sent plans of a house, apparently of his own devising, to the Earl of Salisbury, who was collecting ideas for Hatfield.[24] John Aubrey, when describing the ingenious house built by Francis Bacon for himself at Verulam, says that there was 'no question but his lordship was the chiefest architect', though he employed William Dobson (father of the painter) to assist him.[25] More generally, Harrison remarks how 'divers men being bent to buildinge, and having a delectable view in spending of their goodes by that trade, doo dailie imagine new devises of their owne to guide their workmen withall'.[26]

It is unlikely that these amateur designers got beyond an idea or at best a rough preliminary sketch; certainly, no single drawing survives which can definitely be

9

ascribed to them. Of St George's Chapel at Windsor it is recorded that Henry VIII 'signed the platte that he will have of his chapel, which is the platte that was made according to his first device',[27] which makes it clear that the final drawings were not drawn by the king. Both of Thynne's plans were produced jointly with masons; Bacon had a co-adjutor; Sir Charles Cavendish used a professional to draw up his ideas. The evidence is lacking that would enable us to call any of these amateurs architects in the same way as Alberti in Italy or, later, Sir Robert Pratt and Lord Burlington in England.

It is the professional artificer class to whom all known architectural drawings of the period can be attributed, and which most often appears in surviving documentary evidence as providing designs for buildings. Very often the Surveyor himself did so: this was the case with Robert Smythson at Wollaton, as his tombstone tells us; or if there was no Surveyor, the master-mason: for example, Sir Thomas Tresham's mason, William Grombald, made drawings for the market-house at Rothwell in Northamptonshire, in 1578.[28] This was the normal medieval procedure. But perhaps equally often a design was obtained from outside the regular building staff, from some other surveyor or artificer who had a reputation for providing good plans. The officials of the Royal Works were much called on in this way. For the Works, though creatively torpid under Elizabeth, gave its members both a fixed income and a certain social status, not very high, but higher than that of the normal run of artificers. As a result many of the more prominent English masons went into royal service, though once in it they may have provided as many designs for private persons as for the Queen. Lord Burghley obtained plans for portions of Theobalds from Hawthorne, the Queen's Surveyor at Windsor;[29] and Sir Thomas Tresham's New Bield at Lyveden appears to have been designed by Robert Stickelles, the Clerk of the Works at Richmond (Plate 2).[30]

But apart from the members of the Works, there were other men, of no official position, who had a reputation for the providing of designs. Walter Hancock, for instance, a Shropshire mason, is described in the register which records his burial in 1599 as being, among other things, 'a very skilful man in the art of masonry, in setting of plottes for buildings and performing the same . . . as doth appear by his works which may be seen in divers parts of England and Wales'.[31] Several buildings on the Welsh border can be connected with him, notably Condover Hall in Shropshire. A similar regional reputation was enjoyed in Somerset and Dorset by William Arnold; he was concerned with a number of buildings in those counties, including Montacute and Cranborne Manor, and (on the strength of a Somerset connection) designed Wadham College in Oxford.[32]

To make a secure living out of designing or even supervising the erection of buildings was not easy, outside the Royal Works. Many of those who gained a reputation for designing combined it with other and more profitable intellectual or managerial skills. Some entered the service of great families. William Spicer, who dominated the building work at Longleat from 1555 to 1563 (and was later to become Surveyor of the Royal Works) was also bailiff and rent collector at one of Sir John Thynne's manors.[33] There is some evidence that Bernard Dinninghof, a German whose skills included making heraldic stained glass and providing platts of houses, was in the household of the Earl of Northumberland.[34] John Thorpe made his main income as a land surveyor. Robert Smythson spent the second half of his life in the service of the Willoughbys of Wollaton; once Wollaton itself was built he was employed on anything that came to hand, from collecting coal rents to making lists of bedding. John and Huntingdon Smythson were employed by the Cavendishes, as bailiffs of their manors or surveyors of their lands.[35]

ARCHITECTURAL DRAWINGS: THE THORPE AND SMYTHSON COLLECTIONS

Both Thorpe and the Smythsons were able to combine such activities with something not so very far removed from an architectural practice; and they are most fortunate than Hancock and Arnold in that large collections of their drawings have survived. Of these Thorpe's book of drawings, now in the Soane Museum, is the more famous, for it includes plans of many of the best-known Elizabethan and Jacobean houses. On the strength of this Thorpe was long considered to be the one great name in the architecture of the period. It has gradually been realised, however, that many of his plans are of houses designed before he was born, or while he was a child, or of houses documented as by others: that is to say, they must be surveys rather than original designs. Thorpe was, in fact, a Northamptonshire mason who entered the Royal Works in 1582, failed to get promotion, left the royal service in 1601 for a more profitable career as a land-surveyor, but continued to provide 'plottes' as a side-line. Although many of the drawings in the book are certainly surveys of the work of others, a considerable proportion are undoubtedly his own design. It seems likely, for instance, that the wings and possibly the central block of Holland House, the neighbouring Campden House, the porches and forecourt at Audley End, and a number of fancifully ingenious designs which were probably never executed were by Thorpe, and that he was one of the creators of the Jacobean style.[36]

The other great collection is that of the drawings of the Smythson family, now in the Royal Institute of British Architects in London. The history of the two collections is very different and this difference explains why Thorpe's reputation was for long so much greater than that of the Smythsons. Thorpe's book was first made known to the general public by Horace Walpole in his *Anecdotes of Painting* (1780). It was then in the library of the Earl of Warwick; Sir John Soane acquired it in 1810, and it has been much publicised ever since. The equally important Smythson drawings were almost unknown until this century. They were first mentioned in 1725, in a notebook of Vertue's where, in discussing John Smythson, he says: 'Many of Smithson's designs in possession of Lord Byron, who got

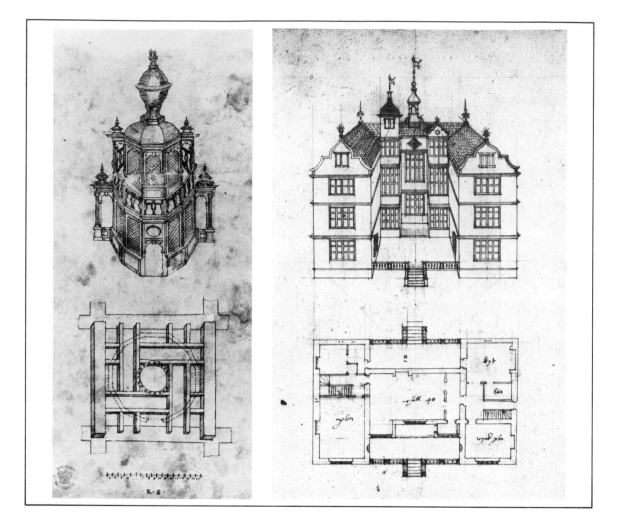

them from the family who lived at Bolsover'. At the fifth Lord Byron's sale, held at Newstead Abbey in June, 1778, they were bought by the Rev. D'Ewes Coke, of Broke-hill Hall, Pinxton, Derbyshire. But they remained in obscurity until lent by the Coke family to the R.I.B.A. to be shown at the President's 'At Home' on 25 February 1907.

Two articles in the *R.I.B.A. Journal* of that and the following years introduced them to a wider audience. They were exhibited again in 1922, and afterwards first loaned and then given by the Coke family to the R.I.B.A.[37] As with Thorpe, a number of the Smythson drawings are only surveys, but a great many are certainly original designs. There is no doubt that among the independent artificers one of the most prolific and proficient in the drawing of plans was Robert Smythson, and that in addition to making plans for the buildings which he personally supervised, he was called on for plans from the whole of the Midlands and North of England. So, on a smaller scale and in a more localised area, were his son John and possibly his grandson Huntingdon.

The Smythson collection includes not only original plans and elevations, but

12

2. (top left) Design by Robert Stickelles for a lantern for Lyveden New Bield, Northampton-shire.

3. (top right) Design by John Thorpe for an unidentified house.

designs for tombs, screens, fountains, details of all sorts, and even beds, tools and horse-training apparatus. Two visits to London provided material for a series of drawings and plans of buildings that interested them; and in addition there are copies of, or adaptations from, designs published in the books of Serlio, Dietterlin and Vredeman de Vries. The Thorpe collection is less varied, but it also includes surveys, original designs and adaptations from Palladio, Serlio, du Cerceau and de Vries. All masons, artificers and surveyors of any pretension must have formed similar collections of their own designs and the designs of others, although those of the Smythsons and Thorpe are the only examples known to survive. These collections belong to the same class as the famous sketch-book of Villard de Honnecourt; they are in the medieval tradition.

A quite different sort of collection, that of a patron not a craftsman, was accumulated by William Cecil, Lord Burghley, and his son Robert; it was bound, perhaps by Robert, into two large folio volumes and is now in the library at Hatfield.[38] There are one or two designs in the collection which can be connected with the Cecils' own buildings; but most designs of this sort are to be found elsewhere in the Cecil archives, and these two volumes are filled mainly with miscellaneous drawings. These include, for instance, a design for Trinity College, Dublin (with the foundation of which Burghley was connected); a drawing of the Escorial; survey plans of a number of royal places; one late Gothic design; drawings connected with water-supplies and drainage; designs for a garden, a ceiling, and a fountain; a curious design for a house on the plan of a cross; and two plans of Longleat. The presence of the latter in Burghley's collection is significant. There was undoubtedly a certain amount of collecting or exchanging of plans by patrons interested in building in this period; in 1577, for instance, the sixth Earl of Shrewsbury sent Burghley the elevation of a lodge he was then engaged in building and asked for his advice on it; unfortunately the drawing does not survive in the Hatfield collection.[39]

But by far the largest part of these two books at Hatfield is filled with drawings connected with war and fortification: plans of battles, of sieges, of forts, of towns and their defences. This emphasis is the result of the particular position of the Cecils; but generally speaking there is no doubt that in this period more expert interest was taken by the upper class in the art of military engineering than of architecture, and correspondingly that a competent military engineer enjoyed more prestige than a surveyor of buildings.

In addition to these three collections a certain number of much smaller groups, or individual designs, of the period have survived, so that the total amount of existing Elizabethan and Jacobean architectural drawings is big enough to make generalisations. The great majority of the drawings are plans, generally known at the time as 'plotts' or 'platts'. There are also a considerable number of elevations; these were sometimes called 'uprights', though on occasions 'platt' was used to cover both plans and elevations. The plans are usually competent; the elevations vary a great deal in quality. At their worst they are crude little drawings, with the detail shown roughly and out of scale, and often with an element of perspective; at their best they are reasonably informative and accurate. Proper perspective drawings begin to appear towards the end of the century, although almost invariably with one façade shown full frontal. In addition to plans, perspectives and elevations a number of designs for detail exist, especially in the Smythson collection; but these never approach the comprehensiveness of a modern working drawing. Taken as a whole the designs of the period give the impression that a good deal, and often a great deal, of scope was left to the executive craftsmen.

Indeed, the idea of a building as the product of one controlling mind, which was to become increasingly important in the next three centuries, meant little or nothing to the Elizabethans. One must visualise the plans and elevations, if provided from outside, being often sketchy and liable to every degree of alteration by the employer and the executive craftsmen; and a mass of individual features, such as panelling, chimney-pieces, staircases, porches, arcades and plasterwork, being normally designed by the craftsmen who carried them out.

FOREIGN CRAFTSMEN AND PATTERN BOOKS

Where these features involved the use of classical ornament, the craftsmen engaged to supply them were often foreigners. A Frenchman, Alan Maynard, carved the chimney-pieces at Longleat in the 1560s and 1570s.[40] At Cobham the elaborate three-storey porches and several of the chimney-pieces were carved in the 1590s by Giles de Witt, a craftsman presumably from the Low Countries.[41] In 1592 the Flemish sculptor, Gerard Holleman, supplied a chimney-piece at Kyre Park in Worcestershire, though the 'platts' for the house itself were obtained from an English official of the Works, John Symondes.[42] Another Fleming, Maximilian Colt, was responsible for the splendid chimney-pieces at Hatfield, though here again the general design of the house can probably be attributed to an English artificer, Robert Lyming.[43]

On other occasions these individual features were derived from the pattern books in circulation at the time, sometimes supplied to the craftsman by his employer. A good many such derivations have been identified, and there were undoubtedly many more which have not. Fireplaces from Serlio's *Architecture* are to be found at Wollaton, Hardwick and Burghley. Detail copied from Vredeman de Vries appears profusely at Wollaton and Montacute,[44] and some of the ornaments at Kirby comes straight from the title pages of John Shute's *The First and Chief Groundes of Architecture*.[45] Derivations of this kind appear in the plans, as well as the details of houses. John Thorpe actually traced two plans straight out of Palladio;[35] but by altering partitions and windows, and combining the plans with totally un-Palladian façades, he effectively disguised his sources.[46]

In a rather similar manner the craftsmen of the period tended to be either too inventive or too clumsy to keep close to their originals, and the sources of their details are often elusive. This elusiveness should not disguise the importance of the pattern-book in the period; and one of the most decisive ways in which patrons exerted their influence must have been in supplying their craftsmen with particular patterns to copy.

A certain amount is known about the architectural libraries of Elizabethan and Jacobean patrons.[47] In at least four cases they were remarkably comprehensive. Sir Thomas Tresham, whose building activities in Northamptonshire produced results as inventive and delightful as anything in England, owned the standard treatises by Alberti, Vignola, Bullant, Cataneo, du Cerceau, Labacco, de L'Orme, Palladio, Serlio and de Vries, in addition to Shute's *First and Chief Groundes* and a number of works on perspective. The collections of Sir Thomas Knyvett at Aswellthorpe, the sixth Earl of Northumberland at Petworth, and Sir Francis and Sir Percival Willoughby at Wollaton were almost as impressive. The more prosperous artificers and surveyors may have acquired their own pattern-books, but little evidence for this has come to light. John Smythson left an unspecified 'Library and Books' in his will;[48] but with the important exception of Inigo Jones, no example is known of a specific architectural or related book belonging to a member of this class.

There was much variety in the Elizabethan building scene, and the general picture of the great Elizabethan house as the joint product, in its design, of a considerable number of people is not the invariable one. Robert Smythson, for instance, is called on his monument the 'architector and survayor' of Wollaton; the building accounts show that he supervised its erection from start to finish; and we have his own drawings for its plan and portions of its elevation, and outside and inside detail. Here is an example of someone approaching the position of an architect; and if more contemporary documents survived no doubt other examples could be found.

But generally speaking the plan and appearance of Elizabethan and Jacobean houses are due to the interaction of three forces: the patrons and their friends; foreign craftsmen; and English craftsmen. The influence of the first two cannot be dismissed; but the patrons were often ambitious rather than knowledgeable, and the foreigners of third-rate quality. By far the largest class was the last one, and by sheer weight it exerted perhaps more influence than the other two, though it absorbed ideas from, and was stimulated by them. The men of whom it was composed, masons, carvers, joiners, and carpenters, were of little education and low social standing; in many cases they inherited a tradition of design and craftsmanship from their fathers and grandfathers; they had never been to Italy or France, and had only a superficial knowledge of Renaissance architecture. But among them were men of independent and original ideas; and it is probably largely due to this class that Elizabethan architecture is, at its best, more than a provincial shake-up of ill-digested foreign ideas. From our point of vantage the men who composed it work like moles, in obscurity underground; they never emerge into polite society or contemporary literature; they are known to us only from burial entries, or accounts, or stray references in letters; as human beings they are, and seem likely to remain, only cardboard figures.

THE USE OF THE TERM 'ARCHITECT'

It is not surprising that the idea of 'the architect' failed to take root in this scheme of things, and that the word remained for a long time an *outré* and unfamiliar one. Shakespeare, for instance, uses it only once, and then in a metaphorical sense. There are only two occasions on which it is known to have been applied to specific people in sixteenth-century England. John Shute, in *The First and Chief Groundes of Architecture*, published in 1563, calls himself on the title page 'architect and painter'. But Shute was a unique case; the only sixteenth-century Englishman who went to Italy specifically, as he himself says, 'to confer with the doings of the skilful masters in architecture, and also to view such ancient monuments thereof as are yet extant': the only sixteenth-century Englishman to write and get published a treatise on architecture. Moreover he did not come from the traditional class of masons and carpenters: he was a painter-stainer by training, and is known to have drawn miniatures.[49] In his background and his travels he was the prototype of Inigo Jones. It is in the light of his knowledge of antiquity, and emboldened by the status of architecture as he had seen it in Italy, that he calls himself an architect. But he was a barren prototype, who, perhaps, through lack of patronage, achieved little; he died in the year his book came out, and no single building can be linked with his name.

The same kind of classical allusion appears in a different way in the case of Sir Thomas Smith,[50] who left £25 to his 'architect', Richard Kirby in his will. Thomas Smith was as much in touch with Renaissance architecture as any Englishman of the time; had been ambassador in France, had sent French architectural books over to Burghley, introduced a giant order into his house in Essex and had copies of Vitruvius in his library. In addition he was a good classical scholar, a protagonist in the great Cambridge quarrel over the pronunciation of Greek. He kept a Latin diary in which he referred to his home at Mount Hall as 'Montaula'. It was probably in the same somewhat pedantic way that he called his master-mason an architect.

In 1580 James Baret published his *Alvearie or quadruple dictionarie* of Latin, Greek, French and English, a book which shows clearly that the word 'architect' had not yet been assimilated into the English language. Instead Baret fumbles and fails to find an English equivalent to it, never translating the Latin and Greek Architectus, Architector, αρχιτέκτων as 'architect', but variously as 'a deviser in building', 'the maister mason, the maister carpenter, or the principall overseer and contriver of any work', and 'a chiefe deviser of building, maister of the workes'.

Under the Stuarts, and without doubt due mainly to their patronage of the arts, the situation began to change. Of this change the chief exemplar was Inigo

Jones, a protégé of the Stuarts who had studied in Italy and who rose up a different ladder from that of the artificers to a position of far more eminence than theirs. His epic and successful battle against Ben Jonson was in fact one for the new status of architect. Jonson's tactics were to make fun of that status; he referred to Jones scornfully as a joiner and parodied Vitruvius's list of the accomplishments of an architect, by applying it to a cook.[51]

Along with Jones other men not coming from the artificer class became figures in the building world. In 1611 Prince Henry, the eldest son of James I, acquired the services of an Italian, Constantino de Servi, described by Thomas Campion in 1614 as 'an Italian, Architect to our late Prince Henry', perhaps the first Italian artist to come to England since John of Padua departed and died in the reign of Mary.[52] Bernard Dinninghof, a German, who was contracting to build houses in 1618, if not before, was not a mason or carpenter but a glass painter by origin.[53] Balthaser Gerbier, the Dutch courtier and diplomatist, was designing buildings for the Duke of Buckingham in 1626-7.[54]

At the same time the English artificers had begun to travel, to increase in pretension, and more and more often to be called, however unjustifiably, architects. Nicholas Stone was in Amsterdam, working under the Dutch sculptor-architect Hendrick de Keyser (whose daughter he married) from 1606 until 1613.[55] Sir Roger Townshend took his mason, William Edge, abroad with him in 1620, probably to the Low Countries.[56] William Arnold, who in 1610 was 'Arnold the freemason', had become 'William Arnold, Gentleman' by 1617.[57] At Cambridge Ralph Symons (1585-1605), who seems always to have called himself 'freemason', was entitled 'architectus sua aetate peretissimus' on his portrait in Emmanuel College.[58] Similarly, the Yorkshire carpenter and masons, Thomas Holt, John Akroyd and John Bentley, who came south to work at Oxford in 1609, were all at one time or another described as 'architect'. When Robert Smythson died in 1614, he was called 'architector'[59] on his monument, probably for the first time. When the carpenter Robert Lyminge died in 1628 he was entered as 'the architect and builder of Blickling Hall' in the Blickling parish register.

Abroad, Coryat in his *Crudities* of 1611 was perhaps the first Englishman to give fairly detailed accounts of foreign buildings and to compare them with those in England. That familiar figure of the seventeenth, eighteenth and nineteenth centuries, the English gentleman abroad with his sketch-book, first appears in a charming illustration in George Sandys's *Relation of a Journey* (1615), showing tourists sketching on the shores of Lake Avernus. At the same time writings on architecture by Englishmen began to appear: Peake's translation of Serlio in 1611: the chapter on architecture in Peacham's *Compleat Gentleman* of 1622; Bacon's Essay on architecture, first published in 1623; Sir Henry Wotton's *Element's of Architecture* in 1624; a series which should have culminated in Inigo Jones's own treatise, unpublished and unfinished owing to the Civil War.[60]

THE ELIZABETHANS AND THE RENAISSANCE

From the foregoing pages some picture of the Elizabethan attitude to the architecture of Renaissance and Antiquity is perhaps beginning to emerge. It would be a mistake to underrate the continual influence exerted on the buildings of the time by foreign craftsmen and foreign publications. Although the most obvious result of this is in ormanental detail, the almost inevitable symmetry, and the frequent compactness, of larger Elizabethan houses is to a considerable extent due to the the compact and symmetrical designs which their builders saw in the pages of Serlio and others. But the Elizabethans approached the classical treasury in the spirit of pirates rather than disciples. As Sir John Summerson says: 'Although foreign fashions in ornament, and sometimes in plan, were excitedly adopted, they were adopted for the intrinsic pleasure they gave rather than any sense of apprenticeship to foreign achievement greater than their own.'[61] There was no attitude of reverence, no feeling that the classical style was a discipline to be learnt, or that it expressed principles of absolute validity.

Correspondingly, a man who had studied its monuments, and was prepared to expound its principles, could expect none of the prestige that accrued to him on the Continent. This particular expertise was an essential quality of the Renaissance architect; the low value given to it in England was one of the reasons why the concept of the architect failed to emerge. It is scarcely surprising, in view of this, that no artist or architect of more than third-rate reputation in his country was tempted to England under Elizabeth. Although the Elizabethans built profusely and on a palatial scale, their attitude to their houses was much the same as to their clothes. They thought a great deal about dress and spent extravagant sums on it. But they did not write or read books on the theory of costume; they seldom discussed clothes in letters to their friends; and they did not ask their tailor to dinner.

This subordination and isolation of building was far from being a complete disaster. English architecture preserved its independence.

At the same time the few drops of Renaissance influence were enough to set up a fermentation in the stagnant waters of Tudor Gothic, and when the cloudiness had cleared away it emerged transmuted into a new style. The aberrations and provincialisms of Elizabethan detail are unimportant in comparison to the novelty, daring and unity of the architecture as a whole that emerged in the last twenty years of the reign and ran on well into the seventeenth century; an architecture which would have been impossible if England had been exposed to the full blast of the Renaissance, and which is one of the curiosities and the triumphs of European art.

ELIZABETHAN TASTE

Before giving some account of this transmutation it is perhaps worth treating of the general preferences of the Elizabethans which conditioned it. These can to some extent be gathered from their own writings; but they are on the whole very simple and most of them become clear after the shortest study of their buildings.

They wanted above all to impress: private houses have always been to some extent status symbols, but never so blatantly and nakedly as under Elizabeth and James I. They admired size and symmetry, the two qualities most certain to produce an impressive effect. They had a passion for brightness, thinking of buildings as lanterns, light within and glittering without. Brought up for the most part in houses of timber and plaster, they were always impressed by cut stone. They appreciated space, not only internally, as in the tunnel vistas of their long galleries, but externally in broad prospects from their houses of the country around. They were conscious of the lines of communication: a stately approach to a house, a dignified move from floor to floor and room to room.

One of the most enthusiastic and charming of the few Elizabethan descriptions of buildings is that of Kenilworth, given by Laneham in his account of the Queen's reception there in 1575.[62] He describes 'the stately seat of Kenelwoorth Castle, the rare beauty of bilding that his Honor hath avaunced; all of the hard quarry-stone: every room so spacious, so well belighted, and so hy roofed within: so seemly too sight by du proportion without: a day tyme, on every syde so glittering by glasse; a nights, by continuall brightnesse of candel, fyre, and torch-light, transparent thro the lyghtsome wyndz, az it wear the Egiptian Pharos reluctent untoo all the Alexandrian coast: or els (too talk merily with my mery frend) thus radiant az though Phoebus for his eaz woold rest him in the Castl, and not every night so travel doooun unto the Antipodes'.

Laneham's delight in the glitter of Kenilworth is reflected in George Whetstone's description of an imaginary palace in his *Heptameron of Civill Discourses* of 1562.[63] 'After I had journeyed the space of an hower in a sweete Groave of Pyne Apple trees, mine eye fastened upon a stately pallace, ye brightnes whereof glimmered through the branches of the younger woodde, not unlyke the Beames of the Sonne through the Crannelles of a walle.'

In 1579 Lord Burghley went to see Sir Christopher Hatton's as yet unfinished house at Holdenby, Northamptonshire, and commented on it in a letter to Hatton: 'But approaching to the house, being led by a large, long, straight fairway, I found a great magnificence in the front or front pieces of the house, and so every part answerable to other, to allure liking. I found no one thing of greater grace than your stately ascent from your hall to your great chamber; and your chamber answerable with largeness and lightsomeness, that truly a Momus could find no fault. I visited all your rooms, high and low, and only the contentation of mine eyes made me forget the infirmity of my legs.'[64]

George Chaworth's description of the Earl of Dunbar's house at Berwick, though written in 1607, is still in much the same vein: 'What is sayde of the famous house my Lo: Dunbar ys building at Barwick I cannot heare subscribe; but surely (admiranda cano) yt ys, as they saye, the greatest squadron by much in England; and of that exceeding heyght, and yet magnificent turrets above that heyght, a goodly front, and a brave prospect open to the meanest and most distant roome, and that uniforme proportion everye waye generally, as wold stodye a good architector to describe.'[65]

Chaworth's 'brave propsect' is pleasantly expanded by Philip Sidney, in his account of Basilius's lodge in the *Arcadia*: 'Truly a place for pleasantness, not unfit to flatter solitariness, for, it being set upon such an insensible rising of the ground as you are come to a pretty height before almost you perceive that you ascend, it gives the eye lordship over a good large circuit, which according to the nature of the country, being diversified between hills and dales, woods and plains, one place more clear, another more darksome, it seems a pleasant picture of nature, with lovely lightsomeness and artificial shadows.'[66]

Finally Harrison neatly sums up the Elizabethan house, arrogant and splendid on its hill-top: 'Each one desireth to set his house aloft on the hill, to be seen afar off, and cast forth his beames of stately and curious workmanship into every quarter of the country.'[67]

One quality of Elizabethan architecture and indeed of Elizabethan design as a whole forcibly strikes anyone who studies the period today, but is scarcely mentioned in the literature of the time. It is, however, hinted at in a passage of Harrison. The buildings of his day, he says, are very magnificent, but those built by Henry VIII were more solid; contemporary buildings are 'like cut paper-work'.[68]

Elizabethan buildings show an avoidance of deep surface relief, and a fondness for linear pattern. A Gothic window, for instance, almost invariably has a deep, or fairly deep, reveal on the exterior; Elizabethan windows are commonly set flush to the outside wall. When an applied order is used the preference tends to be for pilasters rather than columns. The Elizabethans seldom employed buttresses. As a result, although Elizabethan houses can exhibit very complex groupings and considerable recession and projection in their plans, the actual wall surface tends to look flat and insubstantial, two rather than three-dimensional. This linear quality is to be found throughout Elizabethan buildings: in the complex patterns of window-leading; in the lozenges and squares of panelling; in the diapers and network of plasterwork. More generally, it constantly appears in the intricate patterns used for flower-beds, for the chasing of silver, for fabrics and for clothes. In the world of painting the full Renaissance modelling and light and shade introduced into England by Holbein was abandoned for the delicate linear style associated with Hilliard. The Elizabethan had a passion and a genius for pattern.

This quality of Elizabethan design might be classified as an unclassical and Gothic characteristic, but although the former epithet is correct enough, the latter is an over-simplification. As Harrison observed, Elizabethan buildings were more two-dimensional than Perpendicular ones. Elizabethan ribbed plaster ceilings derive from Gothic vaulting, but develop a combination of structure and pattern into pattern pure and simple. Even Elizabethan open-timber roofs are,

20

on the whole, much flimsier in appearance than medieval roofs. The linear preoccupation of the Elizabethans, though deriving from Gothic sources, was a feature peculiar to the age.

A PARADISE OF DAINTY DEVICES

There remains another characteristic of the Elizabethans which coloured their whole life and insinuated itself into everything they wrote or made: that is their fascinated and unremitting pursuit of what they called the 'conceit', or 'invention' or above all the 'device'.[69] The following poem attributed to Ralegh (which can be read both downwards and across) is typical of the kind of composition in which they delighted:

Hir face	*Hir tong*	*Hir wit*
So faire	*So sweete*	*So sharpe*
First bent	*Then drew*	*Then hit*
Mine eie	*Mine eare*	*My heart*
Mine eie	*Mine eare*	*My heart*
To like	*To learne*	*To love*
Her face	*Hir tong*	*Hir wit*
Doth lead	*Doth teach*	*Doth move*
Oh face	*Oh tong*	*Oh wit*
With frownes	*With cheeke*	*With smarte*
Wrong not	*Vex not*	*Wound not*
Mine eie	*Mine eare*	*My heart*
Mine eie	*Mine eare*	*My heart*
To learne	*To knowe*	*To feare*
Hir face	*Hir tong*	*Hir wet*
Doth lead	*Doth teach*	*Doth sweare*[70]

Such toys were produced, on occasions, by every poet of the age, and in every sort of form: acrostic poems, for instance, in which the first line read the same as the combination of the first letters of each line, or poems like those in George Puttenham's *Art of English Poesy*, printed in the shape of a diamond, a circle, an egg or an Ionic column (Plate 4). These were the extreme expressions of the tendency. But whenever an Elizabethan wrote a poem or a romance, his first aim was seldom to communicate an emotion, still less to tell a story, but rather to produce something novel or ingenious, in form, expression or treatment. That is why the Elizabethans loved the sonnet sequence: its form was at once so neat and so exquisitely adapted for the display of endless pretty conceits, hung upon the pegs of love or despair. The prose romance, too, allowed several hundred pages for ingenious, if purely decorative, metaphors, antithesis and plays upon words: 'A strange encounter of love's affects and effects that he by an affection

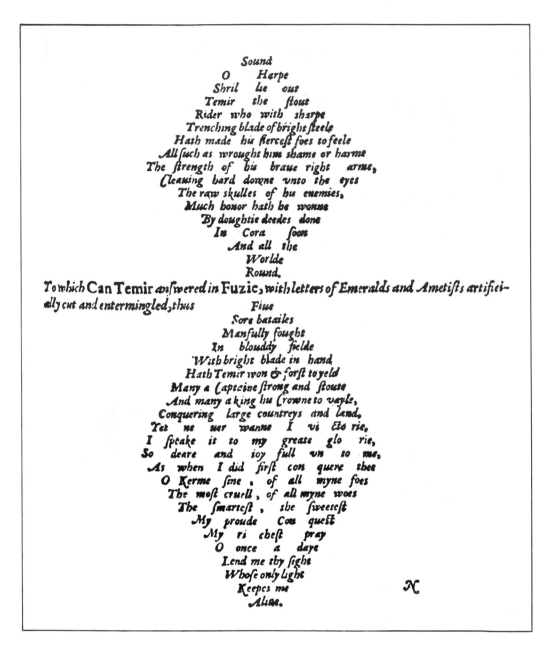

sprung from excessive beauty should delight in horrible foulness, and she of a vehement desire to have him should kindly build a resolution never to have him.'[71]

In Elizabethan England any witty or ingenious invention was called a 'device'. The *Paradise of Dainty Devices*, for instance, first published in 1576, was an immensely popular anthology of short witty poems, and went into five editions by the end of the century. But 'device' had a specialised sense as well, as the translation of the Italian *impresa*. In a device in this sense of the word the substance of a sonnet was melted down to an allegorical picture and a cryptic motto: as, for instance, Cupid shooting arrows at a breastplate, with the motto 'amour passe

22

4. Diamond-shaped poem, from George Puttenham's *Art of English Poesy* (1589).

5. (right) An emblem from Geoffrey Whitney's *A Choice of Emblemes* (1586).

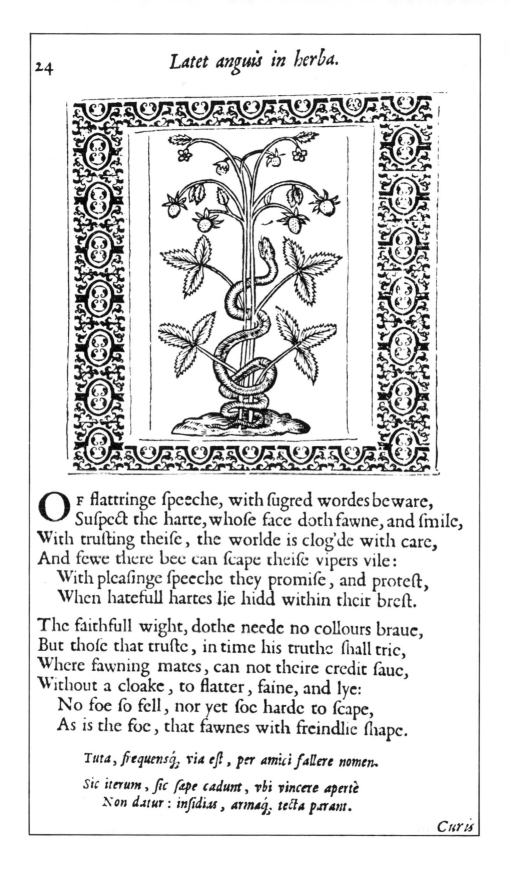

OF flattringe ſpeeche, with ſugred wordes beware,
Suſpect the harte, whoſe face doth fawne, and ſmile,
With truſting theiſe, the worlde is clog'de with care,
And fewe there bee can ſcape theiſe vipers vile:
  With pleaſinge ſpeeche they promiſe, and proteſt,
  When hatefull hartes lie hidd within their breſt.

The faithfull wight, dothe neede no collours braue,
But thoſe that truſte, in time his truthe ſhall trie,
Where fawning mates, can not theire credit ſaue,
Without a cloake, to flatter, faine, and lye:
  No foe ſo fell, nor yet ſoe harde to ſcape,
  As is the foe, that fawnes with freindlie ſhape.

Tuta, frequenſq́; via eſt, per amici fallere nomen.

Sic iterum, ſic ſæpe cadunt, vbi vincere apertè
Non datur : inſidias, armaq́; tecta parant.

Curis

tout', or a butterfly burning itself in a flame, with the motto 'I would rather die than live without it'. Similar to the *impresa*-device was what was known as the emblem. In this the picture was more elaborate, and supported by a set of verses and, sometimes, a motto as well (Plate 5). Strictly speaking, an emblem expressed a general truth, a device an intention or line of conduct adopted by an individual. But the distinction between them was a subtle one, and the two terms were often used interchangeably.

Devices had been introduced into Italy by the French invasions of the late fifteenth and early sixteenth centuries: the French knights carried them on their shields for they were, indeed, no more than the medieval crest and motto, a form that has survived in heraldry until this day. In Italy the device and its brother the emblem became exceedingly fashionable and they soon returned to Northern Europe enriched with much philosophical interpretation. The *Emblematum Liber* (1531) of Andrea Alciati was the first product of a truly gigantic literature of emblems and devices. In England foreign emblem books were in circulation from early days, though the first English one to be published was Geoffrey Whitney's *A Choice of Emblemes* of 1586. Emblems and devices are frequently described in Elizabethan romances; they were expressed in bright enamels and made into jewels or were embroidered on bed hangings or decorated the shields in the tourneys at court.

Used in these ways they can be very charming. So can the numerous other visual expressions of the same frame of mind – 'devices' in the more general sense of the word. Such, for instance, are the allegorical pictures of the sixteenth century: Sir John Luttrell naked to his waist in the sea with a background of shipwreck and epitaphs and storms; Hillard's young men silhouetted against the flames or clasping a hand from the clouds. Such, in a less extreme form, is the whole range of miniatures, themselves a variety of jewel, hanging from the neck or elbow in cases of turned ivory and enamel. Such were the show pieces of the Elizabethan plate cupboard, the salt cellars in the shape of ships in full sail, the cups disguised as cocks or eagles or pumpkins.

Even so it is difficult to understand the vivid and enchanted joy which the Elizabethans took in this jewelled toy-shop world, in the fresh and innocent colours of ivory and enamel, in the click-clack and the Chinese puzzle of thesis and antithesis, pun and counterpun, in all that was contained for them in the words 'dainty' or 'curiose' or 'ingeniose'.

THE DEVICE IN ARCHITECTURE

This characteristic of the Elizabethans can be traced as much in their architecture as elsewhere, and appears there in many different forms. Just as a poem could be written in the shape of a column, a house could be built in the shape of a letter or letters. Such was John Thorpe's design for a house on the plan of his initials, or Sir John Strode's house at Chantmarle: 'Constructa est in forma de littera E, scilicet Emanuel, id est, Deus nobiscum in aeternum.'[72] Or the plan of a house could express a visual rather than verbal symbol: of the Trinity in the triangular house at Longford and the Triangular Lodge at Rushton; of the cross, at Lyveden New Bield, and in a plan among those collected by Burghley, and now at Hatfield.

There are also a great number of ingenious geometrical plans which probably had no such literary or religious *raison d'être* (Plates 6-9). Nor (with one or two exceptions) do they seem to be connected with the complex plans of Renaissance centralised churches, to which in certain cases they have a resemblance. These are the result of philosophical theories about the harmonious structure of the Universe, and the supremacy of the circle and square. It is hard to find any theory or scheme of proportion behind the English plans; on the whole they express only a simple pleasure in the shapes themselves – another manifestation of the Elizabethan's delight in pattern.

They are for buildings of all sizes. The combination of quatrefoil and square appears in the tiny forecourt pavilion at Montacute, and, on a far larger scale, embedded on the centre-piece of the north front of Burghley. A square imposed on a Greek cross was used for the banqueting house in the garden at Wimbledon,[73] for Lord Exeter's lodge at Wothorpe,[74] for a house at Kiplin in Yorkshire, and, doubled, for the great mansion at Hardwick. Miniature alms-houses and chapels are grouped into a circle at Beamsley.[75] There are houses of considerable size, in the shape of a pentagon, at Chilham, and of a Y, at Warmwell, and two houses both called New House in Wiltshire and Herefordshire.[76] Both the Smythson and the Thorpe drawings are rich in ingenious combinations of the circle, the square, and the polygon, culminating in Thorpe's circular house, which is not as simple as it sounds, for within the circle a Y is entangled with a triangle, or alternatively, three rectangles and three circles are grouped around a hexagonal court.

A few quotations showing the attitude of mind behind the device may perhaps help to illuminate its expression in architectural form. Daniello Bartoli in his *De' Simboli trasportati al morale* tried to explain the significance of emblems by comparing them to designs in mosaic or inlay (from which, etymologically, the word emblem was derived): 'Is not the source of wonder, and therefore of delight in such works, the fact that one sees one thing used to express another.'[77] And wonder and delight was always readily evoked by these means in the sixteenth century, because this correspondence between apparently unrelated objects seemed to hint at an underlying unity in nature.

Puttenham, in dealing with his geometrical poems, talks of 'your meeters being by good symmetrie reduced into certaine Geometricall figures, whereby the maker is restrained to keepe him within his bounds, and sheweth not only more art, but serveth also much better for briefness and subtiltie of device'.[78] The concepts of 'briefeness and subtiltie' and of difficulty overcome were equally

The Elizabethans and the 'Ingenious Device'

present in the device in its specialist sense. One of its chief charms in the eyes of its admirers was its compactness: they could never get over their wonder that so much could be expressed so simply. As a Jesuit, Père le Moine wrote in 1666: '*Il ne faut a la Devise que deux traits et trois sillabes: et avec ces trois sillabes, et ces deux traits, elle fait en un clin d'oeil ce que le Poème et l'Histoire ne peuvent faire qu'après un long temps, avec tout leur attirail, et toute leur suite.*'[79]

To effect this compression required considerable ingenuity in the inventor of the device: but equally ingenuity was required to interpret it. In Paolo Giovio's *Dialogo delle Imprese militaire e amorose* (Rome, 1555) one of the five requisites given for a good *impresa* was that it 'should not be so obscure as to need the Sybil for its interpreter, nor so transparent that every mean mechanic might understand it'.[80] The pleasure to be derived from interpretation is expressed by Whitney in the introduction to his *Choice of Emblemes* when he defines an emblem as 'having some wittie devise expressed with cunning woorkemanship, something obscure to be perceived at the first, whereby, when with further consideration it is understood, it maie the greater delighte the behoulder'. But to the intellectual satisfaction of interpretation must be added the personal satisfaction of feeling superior not only to the 'mean mechanic' but to other gentlemen of less knowledge and sophistication.

The wonder evoked by the compactness of the device was often increased by the strangeness of the visual symbols used. The salamander, the phoenix, and the unicorn, and all the strange beasts and their strange habits described in the bestiaries were liberally drawn on to underline by their behaviour a moral for humans.

Armed with these quotations, let us try to understand the feelings of an educated Elizabethan when faced with a symbolic building such as Longford, or a house of ingenious geometric plan but (probably) no symbolic content, such as Hardwick. His reaction to Longford can perhaps be analysed as a mixture of wonder at the first sight of so unusual a building, of delight when its symbolism was explained to him, of self-satisfaction if he was able to interpret it without explanation. His reactions to Hardwick would have been much the same. What an extraordinary building. How unlike the rambling houses he had known as a boy. Who had ever seen a house like that before? What was the explanation of it? Ah yes, it was based on the combination of one large and six small rectangles. How witty to think of transforming a piece of geometry into a house. How ingenious to fit so many different rooms of different uses and sizes into so regular and compact a shape. How clever he himself was to understand what it was all about.

The idea of the device could be applied not only in the plan but in the treatment: obvious examples of this are the houses treated as castles, but for effect not defence; there are a number of such Elizabethan and Jacobean sham-castles, and they must have been considered very witty by contemporaries.[81] Details, too, could be devices: centrepieces of novel and elaborate design; bay windows

6. (top left) John Thorpe's design for a circular house.
7. (top right) A geometric plan in the Smythson Collection (II/10).
8. (bottom left) One of a book of designs, probably for garden layouts (British Museum, Harl. MS 5308).
9. (bottom right) A Smythson design for a round window (II/34).

constructed on complex geometric plans; ingenious internal features like the ceiling in imitation of the heavens at Theobalds and the vaulted pendant room at Longford.

To quote again from Harrison: 'divers men . . . doo dailie imagine new devises of their owne to guide their workmen withal'. As described earlier, St George's Chapel at Windsor and various lesser palaces were built according to the 'device' of Henry VIII. Sir Arthur Champernowne 'devised' a fishing lodge for Richard Carew. The concept of the device as a witty invention helps to explain the part played by many patrons in the design of Elizabethan and Jacobean houses. To think up a novel outline, or a novel theme, for a building needed no specialist training, and left a wide field of initiative to the executive craftsmen. It was probably in this sense that certain patrons were the 'devisers' of their houses, or the houses of their friends, and if so a 'deviser' was by no means equivalent to an architect.

The pursuit of the device led inevitably to the pursuit of variety: one of the essentials of a device was that it should provoke amazement, and it could not achieve this if it was too familiar. Hence the great variations in the plan and treatment among the houses of the period. This approach was basically different from the classical one, which always had in the background the Platonic concept of the ideal – resulting in the constant re-emergence and sophistication of a comparatively small number of themes. Inigo Jones was the first Englishman to break away from the pursuit of variety and turn to the classical tradition. Inevitably he was misunderstood at first. The Queen's House was welcomed as just another novelty: as Chamberlain wrote to Sir Dudley Carleton, 'yt is said to be some curious device of Inigo Jones'.[82]

The desire for size, for space, for symmetry, for great windows and the grand approach, and for the ingenious device, can be traced, in a varying degree, throughout Elizabethan and much of Jacobean architecture. But apart from these general characteristics it is possible to distinguish several stages in its evolution.

STAGES IN THE EVOLUTION OF A STYLE

From the death of Henry VIII until about 1570 English architecture is on the whole hesitant, confused and dull. There was anyway too much uncertainty, religious, social and political, to encourage extensive building. The general framework remained a rather lifeless Tudor Gothic; the interest is provided almost entirely by the occasional Renaissance detail, in the way of porches, pediments, chimney-pieces and so on. This detail is always French in character and reflects, sometimes with a considerable time-lag, the various developments in France: the arabesque and baluster columns of the early François Ier style, the pure classicism brought in by Serlio, the grotesque style that was popularised by du Cerceau. The English work (much of it undoubtedly carved by French craftsmen) varies a good deal in quality. At its best it is extremely good; perhaps

28

the most startling and splendid examples are the tombs of Bishop Gardiner at Winchester (Plate 11) and Sir Robert Dormer at Wing, works of an untainted and vigorous classicism that it would not be an absurd mistake to post-date by over a hundred years.

But this detail, good or bad, was never properly integrated into the buildings where it occurred. The first attempt, and not a very successful one, to produce a complete classical façade was in the Strand front of Somerset House, started in 1547 by the Protector Somerset, who undertook at any rate some of the functions of royal patron in the reign of Edward VI. He almost certainly employed French craftsmen on Somerset House; he built another great palace at Syon and projected a third in Wiltshire.[83] But his status is rather hard to assess. He was only in power for five years, and his buildings, including Somerset House, have vanished or been remodelled. It is difficult to say how discriminating or enthusiastic a patron he was, or how different the history of English architecture would have been had he survived. His usurper, the Duke of Northumberland, had scarcely time to send John Shute to Italy before he too came to a sudden and bloody end. Both Mary and Elizabeth, as has been remarked, were architecturally unimportant. Somerset's position as a patron of the new architecture was taken on, if by

29

10. Bachegraig.

anyone, by his protégé, William Cecil, whose work at Theobalds and Burghley in the 1560s was a by no-means unimpressive achievement in the French classical style.

But some of the detail at Burghley was imported ready-carved from Antwerp; for in the 1560s the influence of Flanders became, perhaps for the first time, a serious rival to that of France. One agent for its introduction was Sir Thomas Gresham, Elizabeth's financier, who was busy in the early years of her reign raising loans in Germany and the Low Countries. The Royal Exchange, built at his instigation in 1566, was a close copy of the Antwerp Teutonic Hanse; as at Burghley many of the details were carved in Antwerp and shipped over to London. In 1567 Gresham's agent, Richard Clough, built, with Flemish work-men, a little Flemish château at Bachegraig in a remote part of Denbighshire.[84]

These two buildings were in the simple somewhat provincial classical style of Flemish early Renaissance architecture. But in 1563 Vredeman de Vries published the first of a series of books in which the classical orders were twisted into heavy, intricate, and extravagant forms and enriched with gables and strap-work. This style of decoration was soon to become dominant in England and the whole of Northern Europe.

In the fifteen years between 1570 and 1585 English architecture begins to command respect. All over England buildings were put up which were no longer direct transplantations from Flanders or weak shake-ups of French and Tudor detail, but had their own original and individual flavour. This period, if any, could be called the false dawn of an English Renaissance, for nearly all these buildings were the result of a reaction, expressed in a multitude of different and personal ways, not only to classical detail, but above all to the classical applied order.

An early example, naïve but with a wonderful freshness, is Kirby Hall in Northamptonshire, put up between 1570 and 1573, with a giant order at either end of its courtyard. In 1573 Sir John Thynne began to remodel his house at Longleat using three orders of pilasters, of great precision and correctness (Plate 15). Sir Thomas Smith's courtyard house at Hill Hall, built around 1575, had a giant order of columns without and a two-storey order within. About 1577 Sir Christopher Hatton began the most splendid of Elizabethan palaces, at Holdenby, in which a triple order provided the framework for a great acreage of glass. In 1578 Sir Thomas Tresham built his market-hall at Rothwell, Northamptonshire, a toy-like building adorned with delicate and decorated pilasters. At much the same time Robert Corbett, fresh back from Italy, began to build a very provincial Ionic and Corinthian *palazzo* in Shropshire 'after the Italians modell',[85] but died of the plague before it was completed.

In all these buildings the decoration, though sometimes rich, was restrained and often exceedingly correct: it was derived from Serlio, or carved by or under the inspiration of French craftsmen. But around 1580, Flemish Mannerism arrived in England, in the pillared frontispiece of Longford, with its scrolls, blocks and

30

11. (top right) Bishop Gardiner's chantry, Winchester Cathedral (*c.* 1550).

12. (bottom right) A chimney-piece at Longleat (*c.* 1575).

The Classical Tradition in Sixteenth-Century England

gables, and above all in the rollicking orders and strapwork of Wollaton. Such Flemish adornment and torturing of the orders seem now one of the signs of a reaction to and counter-attack on the Renaissance. But it is unlikely that Sir Francis Willoughby of Wollaton, as he looked on his new house rich with pilasters and studded with statues of the gods and philosophers, thought that he was being anything but classical, in a new and appetising way.[86]

Then, quite suddenly, this holiday among the orders was over, and English architecture veered off on a different course. For twenty-five years it turned its back upon classic ornament and went for inspiration to its own Gothic past.

This is somewhat of an over-simplification. Few if any of the Elizabethans thought of Gothic and Classic as we tend to think of them, as opposed and naturally exclusive systems: if they had, their architecture would have been very different. Features of classical origin continued to be used in the last decades of Elizabeth, as they had in the first. But the nature of the mixture had changed. There is a striking contrast between the grand buildings of the 1570s and early 1580s, which are elaborately and classically decorated, and the grand buildings of the late 1580s and 1590s, which obtain their effects of magnificence in a quite different way, through height, huge windows, distinctive plans and vivid sky-lines. There are exceptions and overlappings, but the contrast remains remarkable enough.

Much of the inspiration of this later Elizabethan architecture seems to have come from the last, the Perpendicular, period of medieval architecture, with its squareness and high proportion of window to wall; above all from the court architecture of Henry VII and the young Henry VIII, from high and romantic buildings such as Richmond Palace and Thornbury Castle with their towers and turrets and many-shaped bay windows (Plate 13) or soaring gatehouses, such as Layer Marney.[87] The tower, the bay window, the grid of glass, sometimes the gable, were the main elements of the new Elizabethan style. These underwent certain modifications. They were stripped of Gothic detail such as buttresses, panelling and tracery; their string-courses and battlements were sometimes replaced by entablatures and balustrades; and they were arranged with a strict symmetry, which was perhaps a contribution of the Renaissance, and a feeling for dramatic massing and recession, which was a discovery of the Elizabethans themselves.

The style came to maturity with the suddenness and drama of an explosion, but in fact its arrival was by no means unheralded. The native Perpendicular Gothic tradition had been too strong to succumb altogether to the new style. The Somerset-Cecil circle introduced classical architecture, which was for a time taken up enthusiastically by many of the gentry and aristocracy; but in the end their enthusiasm lessened because their own Gothic tradition was better adapted to provide the particular kind of magnificence that they wanted.

Meanwhile, right through the classical period, large houses in the Court Gothic tradition were still being built in England. The old house at Chatsworth, started

13. (top right) Richmond Palace, Surrey (completed 1501).

14. (bottom right) Burghley House, Northants., as remodelled in the 1570s and 1580s.

The Gothic Tradition in Sixteenth-Century England

by William Cavendish in 1551 and carried on over the next twenty years, derived, in its great height and its towers, from buildings such as Richmond Palace, even though it was arid and undemonstrative in a way rather typical of the architecture of the mid-century. The amazing south front of Melford Hall, in Suffolk, built about 1560, with its four towers and its bold recession, was a much more exciting development of the Richmond Palace type. A new wing was built at Kenilworth in the 1570s plain and high with two soaring bay windows, to balance and match the medieval keep. In 1577 Burghley himself added on to his classical courtyard at Burghley a new front with towers and a gatehouse that were unmistakably in the old Tudor tradition (Plate 14). Even the classical buildings of the time often have very un-Renaissance features and owe much of their character to them. The grid of glass appeared at Kirby, Longleat and Holdenby. Three-sided bay windows projected from between the columns at Holdenby and in the classical gatehouses of Burghley courtyard and Tixall, in Staffordshire.

What was new in later Elizabethan architecture was not so much the use of individual features as a sudden understanding of their possibilities, and their use with a new intensity, confidence and skill. For fifteen or twenty years, in every part of England, it seemed as though the Elizabethans could do no wrong, as with wonderful fertility and resourcefulness they experimented with endless and exciting combinations of window, gable and tower. Yet if one surveys the whole galaxy of buildings of this date, the impression that remains is one of gravity and restraint, of quiet outlines and broad expanses of plain wall; an impression quite at variance with the accepted notion of Elizabethan architecture, but surely a true one.

To explain this relative desertion of the orders and development of a native style is not easy; it is a movement about which the literature and letters of the time are almost, if not completely, silent. But there are a few suggestions which are perhaps worth making.

In the second half of Elizabeth's reign a new generation of young men were coming to maturity, who unlike their fathers had had no experience of the political and religious disturbances of the mid-century. As a result they were less secret, less wary, able to indulge in chivalrous gestures which would have seemed absurd a generation before. To such men the knights of the Middle Ages, especially as idealised in the literature of Chivalry, had a glamour and an aura of romance that contrasted violently with the caution and self-interest of their fathers' circle, of the men that Ascham admired, 'grave, stedfast, silent of tongue, secret of heart';[88] men who had done well out of the monasteries and had held on to what they had got. Ascham hated all medieval romances and wrote off the *Morte d'Arthur* in a sentence: 'in which booke those be counted the noblest knights that do kill most men without quarrel, and commit fowlest adulteries by subtlest shiftes'.[89] But Arthur and the knights are back in strength in the *Arcadia* and *Faerie Queene*; Sidney confessed 'I never heard the olde song of Percy and Duglas, that I found not my heart moved more than with a trumpet';[90] Lords Cumberland, Arundel and Herbert, and Sir Anthony Mildmay, were painted in complete armour, ready for jousting;[91] and Essex, the darling of England in the 1590s, as he thrust a pike into the city gates of Lisbon and challenged any Spaniard to come out and break a lance in favour of his mistress, or kissed the blade of his sword on the beaches of France, was as romantic and impractical as any Arthurian knight.[92]

It would be a mistake, however, to paint the distinction between the two generations too strongly, for the older generation was changing too. The circle of Protestant humanists of which Burghley became the leader may have been accustomed in their youth to make fun of Gothic barbarity and the romances. But as they grew older tradition became more important to them: governments tend to grow more conservative and in addition they realised that romantic impulses could be harnessed to the service of the state. As a result one finds for instance, Burghley's own houses growing more, rather than less, Gothic as the years went on;[93] and elaborate tournaments and chivalric pageantry became a prominent feature of the second half of Elizabeth's reign, with complete government approval, for they were used to glorify Elizabeth herself.

It is true that the Elizabethan knight was only a fantasy version of the knight of the Middle Ages, and that the Elizabethans themselves thought of their new romanticism as an infinite improvement on the Gothic world; so that Sidney adds, after his praise just quoted, of the Chevy Chase: 'Which being so evil apparrelled in the dust and cobwebbs of that uncivill age, what would it worke trymmed in the gorgeous eloquence of Pindar.' Yet a new sympathy with the Gothic past had come into existence and appeared in buildings as well as literature and behaviour: buildings with their roots in the Gothic world and yet far removed from it, purged of what the Elizabethans might have considered barbarity and informed with a new feeling for order and compactness.

Quite apart from, but supporting this neo-medievalism there seems to have been something of a reaction against the decorated architecture which had been produced with so much brio and richness for the last fifteen years. The evidence for this is slight, but there is an interesting and relevant passage by Sidney in his description of the house of Kalander, in Book I of the *Arcadia*: 'The house itself was built of fair and strong stone, not affecting so much any extraordinary kind of fineness as an honourable representing of a firm stateliness; the lights, doors, and stairs rather directed to the use of the guest than to the eye of the artificer and yet as the one chiefly heeded, so the other not neglected; each place handsome without curiosity, and homely without loathsomeness; not so dainty as not to be trod on, nor yet slubbered up with good fellowship; all more lasting than beautiful, but that the consideration of the exceeding lastingness made the eye believe it was exceeding beautiful.'[94]

These two distinct attitudes both helped the movement toward a style more independent of the Renaissance. But there is no doubt that this movement was supported and stimulated, and the spirit behind it blown white-hot, by the great upsurge of national feeling, the purge of danger and endeavour, the triumph of success, that was the consequence of the struggle with Spain; a struggle which made the last years of the sixteenth century into a heroic age, in which every aspect of the country's life suddenly burst into flame. This extraordinary trans-figuration, the age of gold and coming of the spring, has been commented on often enough in so far as it affected literature and history. An exactly parallel development took place in architecture; and the style which emerged, naturally enough in view of the fighting Protestant and nationalist spirit behind it, was completely different from the architecture of Italy and France, even though it undeniably absorbed some elements from them.

Lord Exeter's long-demolished house at Wimbledon (Plate 16) can act as a convenient symbol: dramatic in its situation and grouping, but ornamentally of the utmost restraint and plainness; built on a late Gothic plan, adorned with towers and bay windows, but approached by a concertina of terraces and steps reminiscent of Caprarola; a building at once splendid and serious, and as a whole unique to England and its date, which, as an inscription[95] over the door proudly recorded, was the year of the Armada.

This new style, which had come into being in the war years of the reign of Elizabeth, continued with unlessened vigour well into that of James and was still surviving under Charles. But it developed according to a pattern of sophistication common, in one form or another, to many styles. Instead of the strong and simple masses of high Elizabethan style, the Jacobeans experimented with new, more complicated or more subtle combinations. Great houses like Hatfield, Holland House, Aston, Blickling and Audley End supply an almost endless repertory of picturesque groupings (Plate 17). Ornamentally they were much more profuse than the Elizabethans; at their worst capable of an almost monstrous elaboration, at their best, as at Cranborne or in the fireplaces at Knole and Bolsover, of a delicate and enchanting fantasy. A Jacobean house, 'a romantic pile, full of incident and surprise from every point of view',[96] can be rich and exciting food. But there is always the danger that the outlines will become too fantastic, the detail too overpowering. It is not altogether surprising that, in spite of its many originalities, Jacobean architecture sank through its own weight, and that there was a reaction towards a plainer style.

The buildings designed by Inigo Jones, with their restrained and carefully placed ornament and simple rectangular shapes, were in sharp and sudden contrast to these Jacobean fantasies. They were, of course, a great deal more: the first truly and intellectually Renaissance buildings in England. But in this they were excep-tional. Jones was the protégé of the court, an influential but not a typical figure, whose sensitive Italian architecture was restricted to a small circle. Building remained for the most part in the hands of the artificer class. Their works were very different from, and on a lower level to, those of Jones. But they did have two elements in common with them, which were characteristic of the architecture

36

15. (top right) Classical. Longleat, Wiltshire, 1572–80.
16. (centre right) Heroic. Wimbledon House, Surrey, 1588.
17. (bottom right) Fantastic. Holland House, London, c. 1606–7.

*Three Stages of the Country House:
Classical, Heroic, and Fantastic*

of the period as a whole. Their masses tended to be simple and block-like, with none of the complex groupings of the traditional Jacobean house, and their detail was consistently classical. For this detail, however, they went not to the subtle and cautious mannerism of Palladio, but to the mannerism of the Low Countries, with its lugged architraves, broken pediments, and heavy mouldings. Nevertheless, in however provincial a way, this 'Artisan Mannerism' along with the style of Jones did mark the opening up of England to continental influence and the end of the independent movement of the previous generations.

The decorated classical style of the middle of Elizabeth's reign, the unique and national architecture that followed, its development and enrichment under James, the pure Renaissance of Inigo Jones, the contemporary mannerism of the artificers; all these various movements of a complicated, obscure and fascinating period are expressed in the architecture of the Smythson family. Robert was a pioneer, a man of vigorous and enquiring mind, without doubt one of the heroes of the national Elizabethan and Jacobean style, whose buildings, though largely confined to the Midlands and North of England, were known and admired in the South. He first appears working at Longleat in Wiltshire; and to him are perhaps due the unclassic elements of what is otherwise the most refined and remarkable example of the classical style of the 1570s. In the full strength of his middle age he produced the splendid trinity of Wollaton, Worksop and Hardwick, houses which sum up the arrogance, romance and inventiveness of the last years of Elizabeth. Towards the end of his life he can be connected with a group of houses less ambitious in scale and less epic in conception, but fascinating to study because they show him varying and sophisticating the motifs of his middle period.

John and Huntingdon were less monumental figures, transmitters rather than originators, to some extent living on their inheritance from Robert, but also among those who brought the Artisan and, in a mangled form, the Jonesian style to the provinces. They had none of Robert's feeling for the management of mass; yet, in a less formidable and important way, John at any rate had an insinuating and even haunting personality, a certain genius for transmutation which makes his Bolsover chimney-pieces into unique and enchanting creations and gives a curious and eccentric flavour to his versions of Flemish and German mannerism.

Taken by themselves the Smythsons, in their lives and buildings, deserve a comprehensive study. Such a study is made still more worthwhile because, by a piece of great good fortune, a wide range of their own drawings survive to fill out and illuminate our knowledge of them. But they have also a particular interest taken together as a family, an architectural dynasty spanning three reigns, during which both buildings and the building world underwent momentous changes; whom we can watch rising and decaying, working their way up the social scale, influencing and beng influenced; in whom we can discern intriguing hereditary resemblances between the works of the three generations and equally intriguing differences, due to the different requirements they had to answer, and the different forces to which they were exposed.

38

18. Design for a chimney-piece in the Smythson collection, perhaps for Longleat.

1 Longleat

IN March 1568, Robert Smythson, then a comparatively young man of thirty-one, arrived at Longleat in Wiltshire to work as chief mason for Sir John Thynne, who had just begun to rebuild his house after its devastation by fire. He came with his gang of skilled masons, five men in all, and carried the following letter to Thynne from Humphrey Lovell, the Queen's Master Mason:

> Accordenge to my promes I have sent unto yowe this bearer Robert Smytheson, freemason, who of laytt was with Master Vice Chamberlaine, not dowting hem but to be a man fett for youre worshepe, and with these covenantes: fyrste he to have XVId a daye holle, that ys to saye VIIIs a weke and a nage kepte in your worshepes charges, and the rest of his men XIId a day. Seconde his men to have dayes wages for theare travel whiles they are in cominge, and the cariage of theare towles paid for. Hemselfe ys contented to stand to your worshepes benevolence trowsting you welle conseder of hem.[1]

The 'Master Vice Chamberlaine' was Queen Elizabeth's cousin, Sir Francis Knollys, and Smythson had probably been working on his great house at Caversham, across the river from Reading.[2] In 1613 Thomas Campion described the house as 'fairly built of brick',[3] but it was falling into ruin when Evelyn visited it in 1654[4] and seems to have disappeared soon afterwards; as in the case of many great Tudor houses, no picture or drawing of it is known to survive. Apart from this nebulous period of employment nothing is known about Smythson's early works or antecedents,[5] although the existence among the Smythson drawings of three rare late Gothic architectural designs,[6] one of them for part of Bishop Fox's chantry at Winchester, suggests that his forbears may also have been masons.

For all practical purposes he makes his first appearance at Longleat, that is, in the centre of the Elizabethan building world. For Sir John Thynne[7] was architecturally the most interesting of the body of Protestant reformers who grouped themselves round, in turn, the Duke of Somerset and William Cecil, and were the significant figures of the mid-century in architecture as in every other sphere. Thynne came of a family that had been obscure till his father's generation. His uncle, William Thynne, had entered the royal service, attracted the favour of Henry VIII, and pursued a successful career, ending up as clerk comptroller of the royal household. It was probably through his help that John Thynne was taken into the household of Edward Seymour, Earl of Hertford and ultimately Duke of Somerset. He became his steward and confidential man of business. He took full financial advantage of his position, not always with the maximum honesty. As his employer rose steadily to the splendid heights of Lord Protector of England, his own fortune rose accordingly. Thynne, like so many men of his generation, had a talent for survival: he survived Somerset's disgrace and execution, and the uncertainties of Mary's reign, and carried unscathed into the next reign his broad estates in Wiltshire, Somerset and Gloucestershire.

His position under Elizabeth was a strong one. Apart from his great wealth William Cecil and Thomas Smith, his old friends and fellow servants under

Somerset, were now the two Secretaries of State, and Cecil gradually became the most powerful man in England. His brother-in-law was Sir Thomas Gresham, the genius who manipulated the national finances. Thynne was an able if unattractive man, consumed with a restless and at times almost frenzied energy. If he had had the inclination, he could have risen with his friends to become one of the leaders of Elizabethan England.

But his interests, both in Somerset's day and later, were limited. He never took much part in politics, though he sat for some years as a member of Parliament. He was a Protestant, but not a very dynamic one. His uncle, William, had been a cultured man, a passionate admirer of Chaucer, whose work he edited; his cousin, Francis Thynne, was an antiquary of some distinction. He himself had few, if any, intellectual interests. Two passions seem to have dominated his life – making money and building.

In the 1540s he was intimately connected with the organisation of Somerset's grandiose building schemes: the great houses by the Thames, Somerset House in London, and Syon House outside it; and the equally ambitious house at Bedwyn in Wiltshire, which was abandoned at foundation level following Somerset's fall from power. Thynne's enthusiasm for these buildings was as great as, and perhaps greater than, his master's; he is described in a contemporary satire as 'infesting his Master's head with plattes and forms and many a subtle thing'.[8] As soon as he had a property of his own at Longleat he diverted an increasing proportion of his energy into first creating, and then improving, his house there. For thirty-five years there was scarcely a year in which the builder's gangs were not at work. The house spread upwards and outwards, and underwent a bewildering series of changes and reverses. Through all this period it was his original patron Somerset, in spite of his disgrace and execution, who remained his model and ideal; and during his long building career it was Somerset's house in the Strand which he endeavoured first to equal and ultimately to excel.

Longleat as he left it at his death in 1580 probably came as near as anything in England in the sixteenth century to a truly Renaissance house. The exterior remains today little altered, although the interior, other than the hall, was almost completely redecorated in the nineteenth century. It is perhaps the first Elizabethan house to have more than the charm of naïvity or freshness. It is a work of art, noble, delicate and intelligent.

Robert Smythson spent twelve years at Longleat, during which time the house was radically transformed into its final and most perfect form. The accounts show that he carved much of its exterior detail, but it is not easy to discover his exact share in its design. The building history of Longleat, better documented than that of any other Elizabethan house, is long and immensely complicated; a great number of people may have contributed towards its design at all its various stages. Sorting out Robert Smythson's share involves a kind of architectural chemistry. First one must try to discover what type of buildings existed at Longleat before he came, and to estimate the knowledge and capabilities of his employer and fellow craftsmen; on that basis it may be possible to isolate the new elements which appeared along with him, and to decide how far he was responsible for introducing them.

LONGLEAT BEFORE SMYTHSON[9]

Longleat grew like a pearl, the grit in the oyster being in its case the group of insignificant monastery buildings, an obscure house of the Carthusians, which Sir John Horsey had acquired at the Dissolution in 1539 and sold to Thynne the next year. In all probability one of the two small internal courtyards (now amalgamated) on the east side of the house was the original cloister garth of the monastic buildings. A late sixteenth century plan of Longleat (Plates 18 and 19), now at Hatfield, gives a good idea of the inner layers, growing smaller and smaller in scale and more confused in plan, round which the present smooth and unruffled outer skin eventually formed.

In fact it is possible, by careful examination of the surviving letters and building accounts, to distinguish four quite different Longleats, which over some thirty years were superimposed in turn on the same site. The first Longleat, which appeared between 1547 and 1553, was the result of Thynne's adaptation of the old monastery buildings as a dwelling-house for himself. There was nothing very ambitious about this work; it involved little except patching and alteration of the existing buildings. The original church for instance, which probably never consisted of more than a chancel and nave without a tower, seems to have had an extra floor inserted and been turned into two storeys of apartments, with a hall, buttery and chapel on the ground floor, and a great chamber and various other rooms on the floor above. A tower was built in front, with a turret containing a newel staircase. The buildings after adaptation provided accommodation of some twenty-seven rooms, all on a much smaller scale than in the later Longleats; the hall, for instance, was about one-third of the size of the present hall. The masons employed were probably local men, and there is no evidence of any Renaissance detail being used. But the old church windows were altered, perhaps to make them symmetrical, and the buttresses were cleared away. A house which gives some idea of what Longleat may have looked like at this stage is Buckland Abbey in Devon, where, in the 1570s, Sir Richard Grenville provided himself with a commodious house inside the shell of a Premonstratensian abbey church, the tower and main walls of which still survive, along with numerous fragments of detail.

The first Longleat was in fact a modest house (compared with what was to come) which still bore the marks of its monastic origins. The second Longleat, the result of another fourteen years of steady building, was more ambitious. Between 1553 and 1558 a new wing containing at least six rooms was added, probably on the west. At the same time either a new hall was built or the old one was remodelled; it may have been on the south front, as the hall at Longleat is now, and it was entered by a porch of some elaboration. Then, in 1559, an extensive piece of building or rebuilding was undertaken on the east and north

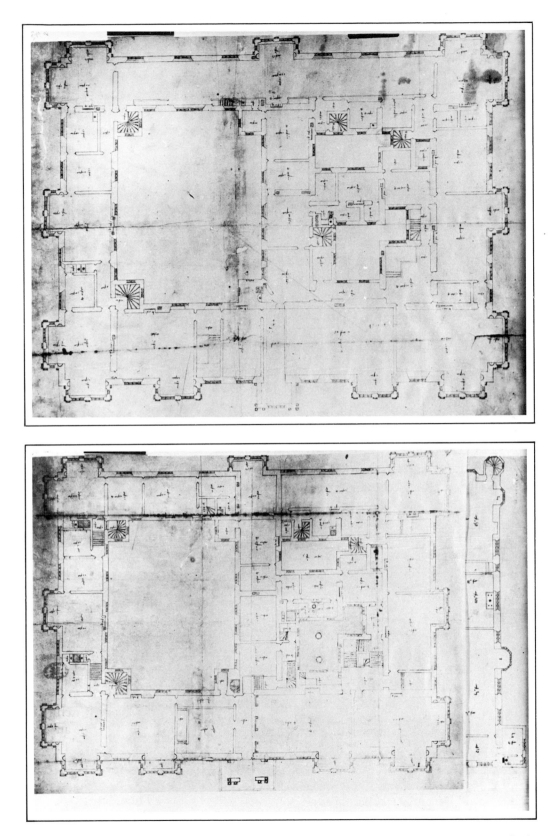

19. The ground and (top) first-floor plans of Longleat, from plans at Hatfield House, Hertford-shire.

sides. This new work was built to contain new and grander living rooms, including a great chamber, a dining chamber, and a long gallery. The shell was largely completed by about 1562, but work on fitting up the interior went on until 1567.

For this second and grander reconstruction Thynne employed a more high-powered body of craftsmen. His chief decorative stone-carver was John Chapman, who had worked for Henry VIII and who carved some, at any rate, of the exquisite early Renaissance detail at Lacock Abbey, on the other side of Wiltshire. At Longleat he worked on the hall screen and porch and carved a set of animals for the gable ends. John Lewis, who arrived as head carpenter in 1552 and stayed at Longleat until Thynne's death and after, had been employed by the Duke of Somerset, probably at Syon House, and his reputation was such that in 1562 he was forcibly impressed into the Queen's Works; he was diverted with her permission to work on the new Middle Temple Hall and was back at Longleat by the end of 1565. Arnold Gonerson, the chief joiner from 1555 to 1559, was probably the father of William Gonerson, better known by his alias of William Arnold, who was to become one of the most successful and interesting of Jacobean mason-architects.

But undoubtedly the dynamic new figure as Longleat was the mason William Spicer. He was a local man from the village of Nunney and when he first came to Longleat in 1555 he was, as his rates of pay show, only a junior craftsman. But he quickly increased in importance until in 1559 Thynne gave him the contract to build the whole of the considerable new work begun in that year, at the same time appointing him bailiff and rent-collector of his Somerset manor of Lullington. During the next four years, however, their relations steadily deteriorated and in 1563, after a series of rows, Spicer decamped leaving much of his contract unfinished and taking with him £34 of the Lullington rent money. This was by no means the end of his career; in the 1570s he was working for the Earl of Leicester in charge of the new building at Kenilworth Castle; in 1584, probably as a result of Leicester's influence, he was made Surveyor of the Queen's works at Berwick; and in 1596 he captured the plum of the Elizabethan building world, the Surveyorship of the Royal Works in London. He seems, in his own quite different sphere, to have been as tough and as much on the make as Thynne.

Spicer left the new work at Longleat an unfinished shell, and to fit up the interior Thynne engaged, in 1563, two new craftsmen, a sculptor, Alan Maynard, and a joiner, Adrian Gaunt. Over the next four years they were busy providing woodwork and chimney-pieces of some elaboration for the new rooms. Gaunt and Maynard introduced a new element at Longleat; they were both Frenchmen. Their knowledge of the classical style was greater than that possessed by anyone who had so far been employed at Longleat; Maynard's influence, in particular, on the ultimate design of the house was to be very considerable.

But at the time of their first appearance the exterior of the second Longleat had been largely completed. Its design was probably due as much to Thynne as to any of the workmen he employed; the new work of 1559, according to the surviving contract between Thynne and Spicer, was to be built 'accordinge to a platt thereof made and signed by the said Sir John Thynne and William Spicer'. What did it look like? The new work in the first Longleat seems to have been purely traditional; the second Longleat, like many buildings of its time, was a traditional building enlivened by a certain amount of classical ornament. Its predominant feature was its skyline, bristling with gables and an occasional battlemented tower; and the mouldings employed seem to have been Gothic rather than classical. But the façades were symmetrical; the windows were square-headed; and here and there, inside and out, were pieces of Renaissance detail. On the north front, for instance, Spicer covenanted to build 'a wyndowe of fyftene foote wyde in the gallery of freestone with Colompnes', and this window, as appears elsewhere in the accounts, was pedimented. Windows of this type, decorated with pediments and columns, and 14 feet wide, were to be found on the Strand façade of Somerset House (Plate 25), and the Longleat gallery was probably modelled on them. There were pedimented windows on other portions of the façades, and the great porch, on which Chapman was working for a very considerable time, would almost certainly have had much classical ornament. Inside there was even more classical work; the chimney-pieces which Spicer contracted (but largely failed) to supply were to be 'with colompnes or termes', and Maynard was supplying chimney-pieces of this type from 1563 onwards. At the same time Gaunt fitted the rooms with joinery of a very classical character, including a portal (that is, an interior porch) decorated with columns and terms, doors of marquetry, and doorcases framed by pilasters.

Longleat at this stage was a kind of degenerate Gothic cake, enriched with occasional classical cherries. Some idea of the mixture can be gained at Corsley, a few miles from Longleat, where at the same time as Thynne was remodelling his main house, he was building himself a secondary and smaller residence, employing the same craftsmen as at Longleat. A portion, at any rate, of this survives as a farmhouse. Its plain and unassuming gabled façades are the cake; and one cherry survives, a pedimented and pilastered stone door, now used as an archway into the forecourt, but not in its original position. The house is a pleasant but not very inspiring building; and Longleat at this period, although bigger and more elaborate, was probably not essentially so very different.

SMYTHSON AT LONGLEAT

On 21 April 1567 the second Longleat was largely consumed by fire. There are various pieces of evidence to show how great the damage was. In the 1568 building accounts the workmen are paid for 'workinge in New Buildinge of Longleate house . . . after the burning of the said house which was burnt Monday the XXIst Aprill 1567 about three of the clock and between that and seven of the clock or eight in the afternoon'. Sir Thomas Smith wrote from Paris, where he was ambassador, to condole with Thynne on his 'great misfortune', and for the next five years Thynne moved out of Longleat and went to live at Corsley. Meanwhile, at Longleat the wreckage was slowly removed. On 22 May a steward wrote to Thynne: 'The west side of Longleate hous ys almost taken down to the corbell.' From then till September there are payments for the pulling down of gables and carrying out of rubble; and in September Fosbery pulled down thirty gable ends, the 'peryments' of two windows, the hall porch and ten chimney-pieces.[10] The hall, then, was certainly gutted, the rest of the house at any rate partially and perhaps completely gutted, leaving the top or gable storey so insecure that it had to be pulled down. After only a year's work the new building had reached the gable storey again, which suggests that it incorporated in part the walls of the old.

It was to work on the building of the third Longleat that Robert Smythson arrived in March 1568. But he is unlikely to have had anything to do with its design. For on 10 December 1567, three months before he arrived, Adrian Gaunt, the French joiner, received the first instalment of a total of £4 15s. for 'making ye modell for ye house of Longleate'.[11] This would have been a wooden model of the new design, the first recorded example of such a model being made in England, though in Italy and France they were common enough.

It used to be thought that the third, the post-fire, Longleat, was the same as the Longleat which we now see. But the manuscripts at Longleat, if carefully examined, prove conclusively that this was not so, at any rate as far as concerns its external appearance. The present façades of Longleat were not started until 1572. The third Longleat was a house of the same size and plan as the present one. But its top storey was gabled and there is no evidence to show that it had anything like the elaborate external detail of the present house. The third Longleat seems to have had two features that distinguished it from the second. First, its size and scale were greater: it covered more ground and the rooms were larger and higher, with three rows of lights instead of two, as in the earlier building. Secondly, there were eight little staircase turrets at the angles of the courtyards and these were carried up above the general roof-level in the form of domed turrets, or what the Elizabethans called 'types'. The specification for this stage of the building survives,[12] and describes them quite clearly: 'Item all the starres to Ryse above the howse and to be typed, and IIII to have lytle starres wonne fro the roofe so as they may serve as banketting howses.' Smythson was working on one of them in February 1569, when the steward, Richard Cavell, wrote to Thynne: 'Smithson willed me to shew you that oone tipe is in woorking and that he will make all the haste theirin as he can.'[13]

A good deal of the third Longleat still survives, half concealed behind the existing pilastered and parapeted façades, but easily visible from the roof. What is left all faces inwards on to the courtyards: here, confused and disguised by the alterations and additions of later centuries, are visible the gables, the plain rough-cut walls and above all the turrets of the earlier building (Plates 20 and 21.

46

20. On the roof at Longleat.

Col. Pl. II). There used to be eight of these turrets, four rectangular ones at the corner of the large west court, and four octagonal ones in the two small and irregular east courts. One of the latter vanished when Wyattville amalgamated the east courts in the early nineteenth century. The bigger rectangular turrets are the 'banketting houses', which were to (and one turret still does) have 'lytle starres wonne fro the roofe.'

The banquet was a great feature of social life in the sixteenth century. It was not a banquet in the modern sense of the word, but a dessert course of sweetmeats, fruit and wine, served either as a meal in itself or as a continuation of the principal meal; in the latter case (as in the case of coffee today) usually in a separate room. It was an intimate rather than a stately function; it acquired, in fact, a shady moral reputation. Increasingly throughout the century a special apartment was built

48

21. Another view on Longleat roof.

for it, usually in a position (either on the roof or in a tower in the garden) from which there was a pleasant view.

This was the *raison d'être* of the Longleat banqueting houses; and one can appreciate how charming a custom it must have been for Thynne's guests, well filled from a substantial meal, to wander in the cool of the evening up on to the roof, and, breaking up into intimate groups, to enjoy the view over the park and surrounding hills from these enchanting dolls-house pavilions. They, and the adjoining octagonal turrets, are the earliest known works executed by Robert Smythson. The conception of them dated from before his arrival, but the detailing may have been his own. Their fish-scale roofs and miniature classical lanterns make them works of considerable charm; in style, though not in position or function, they are markedly French. Although they may have been derived from contemporary houses which have since disappeared they resemble nothing else in England.

The exterior of the third Longleat was probably finished fairly early in 1570, but the interior remained to be fitted up. At the time of the fire Maynard had not been at Longleat, which he had left at the end of 1566; but he was back again by the March–May pay period of 1570. Thynne had now assembled the team of which the principal members were to stay with him till his death. The two principal masons were Smythson and Maynard, at 16d. and 14d. a day. The head carpenter was John Lewis at 12d. a day. Under him at 10d. a day was Richard Crispin or Chrispian, who had come to Longleat around March, 1568, and may have been a relation of Stephen Chrispian,[14] one of Henry VIII's carpenters at Nonsuch. The head joiner was Adrian Gaunt, at 12d. a day. Among the assistant masons John Hill or Hills, Edward and Valentine Merser, John King and John Hodgkyns had come with Smythson; in 1571 they were joined by Christopher Lovell, Humphrey's son. Hill came from near Maidstone (where the Kentish-rag quarries were); he was later to follow Smythson to the Midlands, work at Wollaton and Hardwick, and die at Worksop in 1592.[15] He was perhaps the same man as the John Hill who had worked for Somerset, and for Thynne at Brentford in 1550.[16] Altogether he and his companions were a capable group of men, probably unequalled at that time in England.

Apart from its increased scale and domed stair turrets, the third Longleat seems to have differed little in character from the second. But in 1572 Thynne started another complete reconstruction of his house; and over the next eight years the façades of the fourth and existing Longleat were wrapped, like an immense and highly decorated scarf, around the third house, itself a rebuilding only four years old. This final reconstruction involved building pilastered bay windows of three stages, Doric, Ionic and Corinthian, at regular intervals round the outside of the house; linking them by continuing their entablatures across the intervening spaces; remodelling the windows and probably refronting the façades.

The result of this final remodelling is shown in the invaluable sixteenth-century plans of the ground and first floors of Longleat which are now preserved at Hatfield. These give the original disposition of the rooms, which had been somewhat altered by the time the next surviving plan, that in *Vitruvius Britannicus*,[17] was made. On the other hand, the long gallery and the rooms below it shown in the Hatfield plan as on the north side seem never to have been built. They are not in *Vitruvius*, nor in a plan of 1800 in the library at Longleat. No long gallery of this importance appears in any of the surviving inventories of the late sixteenth or early seventeenth centuries; later on in the seventeenth century a smaller gallery was formed in another part of the house. The probability is that some time in the 1570s Burghley asked Thynne if he could see plans of the house and was sent ones showing the house as it was intended to be completed. But in fact the north wing remained unfinished until Wyatville filled the gap as part of his extensive work at Longleat in 1801–11.

During all the time that Smythson was working on the final remodelling he was living with his wife five miles away at the parsonage of Monkton Deverill; he rented it from Thynne in 1572, for an annual rent of £11 6s. 8d. to be paid half-yearly at Lady Day and Michaelmas.[18] Presumably he rode over to Longleat every day, on the 'nage kepte in your worshepes charges' for which Lovell had stipulated in his letter. Longleat at this time must have presented a scene of great activity. From all over the countryside the materials for the new work were converging on the building site. Wood was felled locally on Thynne's estates and cut up in a sawmill near the house; bricks for the inner walls were made in immense numbers at a local kiln; glass, brass, nails and panelling came down by water and land from London; slates were brought from Wales; iron was supplied by local smiths, but much of it was Spanish iron, carried by sea to Bristol.

Most important of all was the stone. For the three earlier Longleats Thynne had been content with stone quarried locally; but for the fourth Longleat nothing would do but the best Bath stone. For this purpose he acquired a quarry at Haselbury near Box, and supplemented the supplies from here with additional stone brought from the nearby quarries at Stoke. The transport of this Bath stone, on wheelless drags pulled by oxen for twenty-five miles up and down the steep Somerset combes, added considerably to the building costs of the house.

Neither at this nor at any other period at Longleat does there seem to have been any one whom the Elizabethan would have called the surveyor: that is to say someone who directed the whole building work and had overriding authority over the various craftsmen. Or perhaps it would be more accurate to say that Thynne acted as his own surveyor; there is little doubt that he interested himself in the minutest details of the building operations, and was constantly giving orders, or being consulted over the problems that arose. His various stewards acted as his deputies and his representatives when he was away; it was they, too, who would have been responsible for directing the complicated business of the supply and delivery of materials.

The actual craftsmen were organised on two different bases: they were paid either by the day, or for work supplied – for what was then called task-work or piece-work. Most of the more important jobs – the panelling of the rooms, for instance, or the masonry work of a new piece of building – were carried out on the latter system. In some cases the craftsmen actually signed a contract to supply a specified job of work for a specified sum; several of these survive at Longleat, notably Spicer's big contract for the new building of 1559, and there were probably others which have been lost.

In his first four years at Longleat Smythson was paid by the day at the rate of 1s. 4d. as laid down in Lovell's letter. But when the final reconstruction started in 1572, he (and Maynard with him) moved over to task-work. On this basis they supplied the greater part of the carved detail for the new façades. Their first payment was made at the end of 1572; that to Smythson runs as follows:

> To Robert Smythson for working XVIII chaptrells [capitals] alreadye sett at V^s le chaptrell IIII^{li}X^s and to him for CIIII^{xx}IX [189] fote cornishe frayse [frieze] and Arkytrave at II^s le fote XVIII^{li}XVIII^s for windo heddes CV fote and $\frac{1}{2}$ at XII^d le fote CV^s and VI^d for CXIII fote soylls [sills] at XII le fote CXIII^s for basse for the pyllesters XVIII at III^s le pece LIII^s for CCIIII^{xx}VII jawme [jamb] for windo at X^d le fote XI^{li}XIX^{s}II^d for CXXX fote basse for the petitstall [pedestal] at VI^d le fote LXV^s for XLIX fote and $\frac{1}{2}$ cornishe for the petitstall of Ionyk at VI^d le fote XXIII^{s}IX^d and for CCXI fot assheler at XPVI^d le C and abating for ye stoan out of ether C IIII^{s}VIII^d so remayneth XIII^{s}II^d in all
> 　　LIIII^{li}II^{s}VII^d

There are similar detailed payments to Smythson and Maynard in December 1573; these with the previous ones account for nine of the existing bay windows, up to the Ionic storey.[19]

There is no reason to suppose that Smythson and Maynard carved all the work for which they were paid; it is more likely that each had their own men under them, to whom much of the work was deputed and whom they paid themselves. On the whole the impression given by the documentary evidence is that Smythson's authority extended only over his own particular gang of masons; he and Maynard worked independently, each with their own teams. The problem of who supplied the plans to which they were working is, of course, a quite separate one, which will be discussed later on in this chapter.

In 1574 Smythson was not at Longleat, or at any rate is not mentioned in the accounts. He came back in 1575; but it is clear that some time during these two years his and Maynard's relations with Thynne became very uneasy. During his absence in 1574 one more of the great windows was built; but it was the work not of Maynard (though he was still at Longleat) but of three of the minor masons, King, Mercer and Vincent. A surviving document in Thynne's own hand headed 'The Price of all ye free masons worke 1574'[20] gives the prices that these three masons were paid, which are considerably lower than those which Smythson and Maynard had been getting. They had in fact been undercut. An undated letter[21] from them to Thynne, immense, rambling and vilely spelt, is clearly in reaction to this situation.

They say how sorry they are for 'youre disspessorre allrede consaved aganste us'. They and their men have been at Longleat since Easter, since which time they have not earned half enough money to pay for their food, and, moreover, have not received the wages owed to them, so that they are unable to pay their debts. But this is not the case with 'other men' who have got both employment and prompt payment, although they are far less capable of doing the work than Smythson and Maynard. They cannot understand why Thynne is so displeased with them, unless it is 'for takynge of youre worke' (by which they probably mean the change-over from day-work to task-work). But they do not want to leave Longleat 'exsept yt be youre plesoure' and will guarantee to do the work at a cheaper price than anyone else has offered to him.

Poor Smythson and Maynard were certainly in a predicament. Not only were they financially under pressure; they saw the magnificent new façades of Longleat (in which they must surely have taken some pride) slipping from their care when only half-completed and being handed over to a set of bunglers: King, Mercer and Vincent were never paid for the capitals of their bay window and were perhaps not able to complete the window to Thynne's satisfaction. Not unnaturally Maynard and Smythson gave in; they were back on the payroll in 1575, carving more great windows at the new reduced rates. The whole story gives an interesting (if not very endearing) glimpse of Thynne as a business man; it is not surprising that he got on in the world.

The 1575 payment to Smythson and Maynard marks the completion of the remodelling of the first two storeys of the house. The payments from 1572 to 1575 cover the erection of the Doric and Ionic stages of fourteen bay windows. This is certainly puzzling, for there are only thirteen windows of this type at Longleat, and one of them (that in the centre of the north front) dates from the nineteenth century. William Darrell, in this satire on Thynne (see p. 76), says that he 'beat downe windows for this or that fault, here or there'. It would seem that two of the bay windows must have been rebuilt; of these one suspects that the window started, but never completed, by King, Mercer and Vincent was one.

Another puzzle is provided by the elaborate two-storey porch which is shown in the Hatfield plan, but for which there are no detailed payments in the accounts for these years. It was perhaps a survival from the third Longleat, or a later afterthought; it must have marred the unity of the design and was in fact taken down in the seventeenth century.

At the end of 1575 bargains were made for over 800 feet of cresting. Cresting implies parapets, and this makes it almost certain that Thynne contemplated finishing his new façade at the second storey, leaving the old top storey with its gables sticking up rather incongruously behind. But there can be little doubt that in the next five years up till his death Thynne did add the third, Corinthian, storey, leaving the house externally much as it is today.

We know the total yearly expenditure for most of these years, which maintains a level not so much lower than that of the years before.[22]

	£
1568	1140
1569	800
1570	930
1571	627
1572	723
1573	879
1574	794
1575	730
1576	692
1577	731
1578 – October	Not known
October 1578 – December 1579	596
1580	491

(Thynne died in May, 1580)

Moreover, John Thynne, in a cancelled will dated 6 April 1579, includes a clause 'yf I happen to dye before I have fully fynisshed the buyldinges of my house at longeleat', his executors are to 'cause or pcure my sayed house at longeleat to be fully and pfectly finysshed and buylded in all thynges as well inwardly as outwardly accordynge as I have apoynted'. But in his second and last will made in April 1580, this clause has been dropped out.[23]

Finally in an MS account of the house written by the first Lord Weymouth, at the beginning of the eighteenth century, it is stated:

'The outside of ye house was finished in Old Sir John's life time and from ye hall to ye first side of ye Chappell Court was finished in ye inside by him. . . . The rails and ballisters were set up together wth many of ye tunnes of ye chimneys and some of ye towers were finished by ye 2nd Sir Jn. Thynne, by whom also ye Skreen in ye hall and much of ye wainscott was made.'[24]

Thynne probably intended from the start to carry up his new façade three full storeys, but had momentary second thoughts, perhaps because of the expense. A large and detailed design (Plate 22) for a portion of the south front survives, very much faded, in Longleat library, and shows it with the Corinthian order. It seems unlikely that the lower two-thirds of the façade would have been shown in such detail if the design had been for the addition of a top storey only. Moreover, the lower storeys are shown differing in a few details from the work as executed: the Ionic order has a convex frieze and consoles in its cornice; the sills, heads and transoms of the windows are continued as decorative strips in the spaces in between, whereas in the executed building only the sills were treated in this way.

53

In these obscure years one letter and a few scattered accounts survive,[25] which make it clear that Maynard and Smythson remained at Longleat. There is mention of Maynard in 1576 and 1579, of Smythson in 1576, 1577, 1579 and 1580. In 1576 Maynard is about to start on a chimney-piece for the great chamber. In January 1579, there is a joint payment of £37 12s. to Smythson and £53 10s. to Maynard, which looks very much as though it might be for work on the top storeys of the great windows. It is close in amount to the first of the payments, that of 1572, and would have been sufficient for adding the final stage to six windows.

The present outer fronts of Longleat were, as has been shown, wrapped around an older building. The efforts, or failure, to make them fit have resulted in various oddities and discrepancies. The façades are not as regular as at first sight they seem. Thus on the east front the south bay window is set 6 feet 8 inches from the corner of the house, but the north bay only 2 feet 1 inch. The middle bay is set not quite centrally between the two corner bays, with the result that one of the windows of the ranges in between the bays has had to be made narrower than its fellows. Every façade has a different proportion of window to wall. Over the parapet push up the turrets of the older building, which have no relation to the façade beneath them. The orders on these façades cannot be analysed according to any exact system of proportion.

Internally the extra height of the Ionic storey windows has been gained by pushing them right up to ceiling height, swallowing the 2 feet 7 inches of 'somme' and 'lengther' allowed in the 1567 specification of the window dimensions. This was later felt to be uncomfortable and, perhaps in the eighteenth century, the top row of lights was in many rooms blocked so that internally the windows are now only of two rows. On the storey above, the windows, to fit the external elevations, had to be set uncomfortably high, 4 feet 4 inches from the floor. The windows to the court, a few of which preserve the dimensions of the immediate post-fire work, are all set much lower, around three feet from the floor. Finally Bishop Ken's library, at the south-east corner of the upper floor, is still shaped inside by the lines of the original pointed roof; the external façade has been added as an unrelated screen and about half of the windows are false.

LONGLEAT: PLAN AND DECORATION

Smythson cannot have had much responsibility for the plan of Longleat, the final shape of which had been to a large extent settled in 1567, before his arrival; as has appeared, the Smythson–Maynard remodelling of the house in the 1570s was concerned only with the external façades. But certain elements in the plan undeniably influenced him and reappear prominently in his later buildings.

The most original features of the Longleat plan are its compactness and the various qualities which result in or from this: its height, its basement, its four-square exterior, and what might be called its outwardness. The internal court-

22. Alan Maynard's design for the façade at Longleat.

yards are for light, not for display; all the show is in the exterior façades, which are each of the same height and design, so that the house appears as a single compact block; the main entrance is on the outside of this block. This is a notable departure from the conventional large Tudor or medieval house, where a gate-house led into a great courtyard surrounded by ranges of buildings, with the hall range usually opposite the gatehouse and lodgings on either side. Even Somerset House had repeated this traditional formula.

It was probably the aesthetic, rather than the practical, advantages of the more compact plan which appealed to Thynne; the unified effect which it produced is impressive today, and must have been far more so in the mid-sixteenth century, when it was still something of a novelty. Longleat was not, however, a pioneer in being compact and outward-looking. In the later Middle Ages there is a long line of residential towers or tower-like buildings, clearly intended to make an architectural show but having no courtyards or only small ones; all have an element of fortification, but often the towers and battlements are there as much for show as for use. In the sixteenth century there are a few more purely domestic buildings which perhaps derive from the same strain. West Wickham Court in Kent, for instance, which was built by Sir Henry Heydon in about 1500, is a square building with a small internal courtyard and an octagonal tower at each corner.[26] At Mount Edgcumbe in Cornwall (1546) and, probably, at Michel-grove in Sussex (1536?) a new variety of plan appears, basically the same as that of West Wickham, but with the courtyard filled in with a clerestory-lit hall. The result is a house that is completely outward-looking.[27]

It is hard to see any close connection between buildings of this type and Longleat. There are two other late-Gothic buildings which superficially come closer to it. Herstmonceux Castle (c. 1430) is built round four small courtyards, and although access to the hall is through the largest of these, the show features of the house are its four external façades, symmetrically adorned with no less than seventeen regularly-spaced towers and turrets.[28] The Royal Lodgings at Richmond Palace (c. 1497–1501) were completely outward-looking, built round one small courtyard intended for light not display.[29] The three-storey block that resulted was diversified, rather less regularly than Herstmonceux, with fifteen or so turrets and bays, some of which were heavily windowed. Perhaps the thirteen great bays processing round the external façades of Longleat can be seen as classical versions of Herstmonceux and Richmond. But the Longleat bays derive, as will appear, from the Strand front of Somerset House, a totally unrelated source; and in any case Longleat was already compact, symmetrical and outward-looking before the bays were built. It is just possible that Thynne was influenced by Italian or the occasional French examples, such as the Château de Madrid, La Muette and Challuau; but the similarities are not very striking. It seems more likely that the initial impulse was an accidental one, the fact that Longleat grew around a cloister garth too small to be used as an internal courtyard

I. Longleat House, Wiltshire. Detail from a painting attributed to Jan Siberechts.

of the traditional kind. So it started of necessity outward-looking; and Thynne realised the possibilities of this and exploited them as the house developed.

One feature of Longleat, however, which came ultimately or immediately from the Continent is the high basement, containing the cellars, the offices and the lower part of the kitchen. This arrangement made for increased height and compactness, and was to have an important chain of successors in the course of the next fifty years. There was no English tradition of raising the house up on a podium in this way, except in a few examples where it was adopted for defensive reasons. But in France and Italy the basement was common enough (for instance, in the Château de Madrid) and Thynne would have known of it either through direct contact (he was in France in the 1540s) or by means of Serlio or du Cerceau. It is possible, however, that the idea had been introduced into England by the Protector Somerset, though the evidence for this is far from conclusive. His hall range at Somerset House seems always to have had basement offices and a basement kitchen rising through the ground floor, as at Longleat.[30] A similar arrangement may have existed at Syon House, but this has been so much altered in the course of the last four centuries that it is hard to be certain at what stage the existing basement appeared.

At the other end of the scale height and compactness were further achieved at Longleat by the employment of an upper storey, carried over the two-storey hall. This arrangement, besides making for compression, represents an early step in the dethronement of the hall from its position as the focal point of the house: a position it had already lost functionally and was soon to lose architecturally.

The plan of Longleat was an unusual one; but the accommodation fitted into this plan, though on a very lavish scale, was more conventional. By the mid-sixteenth century the suites of rooms considered necessary for a great house had already crystallised in a form that was to remain virtually unchanged for another seventy years.[31]

The state suite in all large houses almost inevitably consisted of a great chamber, a withdrawing-chamber, a bedchamber (usually with an inner chamber or closet leading off it) and a long gallery. The usual position for these was on the first floor, with a staircase of some pretension leading from a vestibule off the dais end of the hall up to a landing outside the great chamber. The family had by now given up the hall as an eating place, except on rare occasions; it remained the dining-hall and place of assembly for the servants, and in a great house the senior members of the household (which could number from fifty to a hundred or more) sat at the high table at the dais end. The family and their guests ate on formal occasions in the great chamber; the great chamber was also the room normally used for dancing and for the putting on of masques; in *A Midsummer Night's Dream* the drama of Pyramus and Thisbe was mounted after supper in the great chamber of the Duke of Athens. It, rather than the hall, was now the ceremonial centre of the house, and it was accordingly decorated with suitable splendour.

59

The withdrawing-room was the room to which the party withdrew after meals. The best bedchamber was used for important guests, from the Queen downwards, and usually led off either the withdrawing-chamber or the gallery. The long gallery had a number of functions; it was used as a picture gallery, often the only room in which any pictures (and those chiefly portraits) were hung; it was used for exercise in bad weather; it was sometimes used for music; perhaps as much as anything it was a prestige room, which caught on as a fashion, so that each family tried to outdo the other in the size and splendour of their galleries.

Quite distinct from this suite of grand rooms were the parlours, usually on the ground floor below the state suite. A parlour was roughly the equivalent of a common room in a college today; it was essentially an informal room, where the family, their gentlemen and gentlewomen (the hangers-on of good birth without whom no large household was complete) and officials such as the steward and the chaplain met, talked and relaxed. In some houses the parlour was also used for informal meals and it was then known as the dining parlour. A big house would have two or more parlours, sometimes with a more private withdrawing-room leading out of them.

The two-suite system was capable of considerable expansion and contraction; at its very lowest any house with pretension to gentility would have a great chamber upstairs, for state, and a parlour downstairs, for use.

At Longleat the arrangements were more lavish. The Hatfield plan (Plate 19) shows the sequence of the rooms, but has nothing to show their uses; some idea of these can, however, be gathered from a series of inventories,[32] of which the one made in 1639 appears to be the most complete. The state suite was in the usual position on the first floor, but was never completed. In 1639 it consisted of the 'great dining chamber' and 'withdrawing chamber'; these, there can be no doubt, were the great room at the south-east angle of the house (now the balcony room) and the room adjoining it on the east front. The two rooms to the north of this were bedrooms in 1639: the 'Redd bedchamber' and the 'upper corner chamber'. It is hard to believe that the Red bedchamber was not originally intended as a living rather than a sleeping room, for in the Hatfield plan it provides the only link between the great chamber and withdrawing-chamber, and the long gallery. But the suite failed to take on the form originally planned, for the long gallery seems never to have been built. The parlour suite was below the state suite, on the ground floor. In 1639 it consisted of the Parlour (Great Parlour in an inventory of 1594), outer Parlour (Little Parlour, 1594) and shovel-board Parlour ('Shoffellaberde chamber' 1594). The name of the shovel-board Parlour explains its use; it was the sixteenth-century equivalent of a billiard or ping-pong room.

The main staircase at Longleat (long since replaced by Wyatville's grand staircase further to the east) was approached off the dais end of the hall, rose in three flights round a square central pier, hollow and built of stone, and emerged

60

on to a very spacious landing outside the great chamber. A similar arrangement, though on a smaller scale, and in a more cramped space, survives at Wolfeton Manor in Dorset.[33] This almost certainly was a product of the Longleat craftsmen, for the magnificent stone doorcase (Plate 23) leading from the landing to the great chamber is unmistakably in their style, with a frieze that is a variant of the frieze of the hall fireplace at Longleat. The Wolfeton staircase is of stone with a handsome stone balustrade and a spacious upper landing (Plate 24); the same arrangement was probably used at Longleat, and was to reappear at Hardwick.

Not much remains to be said about the arrangement of the other rooms at Longleat, the position of many of which cannot be established for certain. The kitchen, as already stated, was in the basement, but rose up through the ground floor; it was buried in the centre of the house, between the three courts, and a flight of steps led up from it to the screens end of the hall.

It is difficult, on the basis of the plan and inventories, to work out where Thynne's own quarters were. The house did not acquire a chapel till the seventeenth century; but there is no doubt that at Thynne's death many of the rooms were still no more than shells. Minor staircases were scattered throughout the building; there was only a very rudimentary provision of corridors. On the other

23. (left) The doorway at the top of the staircase at Wolfeton Manor, Dorset.

24. (right) The stone staircase at Wolfeton.

hand, from a sanitary point of view the house seems to have been remarkably well equipped: the Hatfield plan shows at least twelve privies, opening into six vertical shafts pierced at strategic points through the house. Later alterations make it impossible to discover with what completeness this system was carried out; but the shaft in the south-east turret of the chapel court survives, together with the semicircular recess for the privy shown on the first floor plan. The shafts probably communicated with a comprehensive draining system; no one had yet been intrepid enough to explore what survives of this, but the gurgling of a big culvert flowing underneath the house can still be heard in certain parts of the basement.

Little remains of the original interior decoration at Longleat, and none of what does can be attributed with any confidence to Smythson. The three remarkable fireplaces (Plate 12), now in the hall, the old kitchen, and the new library (the two latter not in their original positions), were probably carved by Alan Maynard; there are references in the original documents to chimney-pieces being carved by him in 1563, 1565, 1566, and 1576, but Smythson is never mentioned in this capacity. The screen in the hall was the work of Adrian Gaunt (who was paid £13 6s. 8d. 'uppon ye workinge of ye Scrynes' as late as November, 1578) and the hall roof is undoubtedly due to John Lewis. The Hatfield plan shows semicircular alcoves hollowed out in the angles of nearly all the bay windows. One of these, in the west window of the south front on the first floor, has recently been uncovered: its head is filled with a delicately carved and very elegant shell. It is possible that more riches of this type may survive buried beneath later decoration. The group of five shell-headed niches still existing in the great chamber at South Wraxall Manor, and single shell alcoves at the Hall, Bradford-on-Avon, and Charlton Park no doubt derive from those at Longleat.

There is a small group of decorative sculpture, scattered over a considerable area around Longleat, which is almost certainly carved by one of the Longleat craftsmen.[34] All of it, like the surviving fragments at Longleat, is of a vigorous and capable French classicism, little affected by Low Country influence. Besides the work at Wolfeton already mentioned it includes two fireplaces at Woodlands Manor, Mere, and another at Upper Upham, both in Wiltshire, and tombs at Sherborne Abbey in Dorset and Nunney in Somerset. Maynard is more likely than Smythson to have been the craftsman concerned; the tomb at Sherborne, in fact, was probably carved after Smythson had left for the Midlands. Moreover, the work can be related to a small group of drawings at Longleat which can confidently be attributed to Maynard. One is for a little banqueting house or lodge, and is docketed 'Allan Maynard's draft for Rodminster Lodge'; it includes as œil-de-bœuf dormer in the roof which is similar to cresting on the tomb at Sherborne and the parapet at Longleat. In addition there are ornamental motifs for parapets, the large elevation of Longleat already referred to (Plate 22), and an exceedingly interesting elevation of an unidentified building (Plate 25).

62

If the provenance of the last drawing was not known, it would be assumed to be for a building in France rather than England. The comparatively small size of the windows suggests that it dates from Maynard's earlier years at Longleat. Although no such façade is known to have been executed, something not so very dissimilar was, and can confidently be attributed to Maynard. It survives as a fragment, much altered in the late eighteenth century, at Chalcot, a few miles from Longleat (Plate 26).[35] Three tiers of windows are joined horizontally by continuous entablatures and vertically by Ionic, Corinthian and (if anything) Composite pilasters, arranged so as to enclose the windows in aedicules surmounted alternately by straight and curved pediments.

A remarkably fine design for a classical chimney-piece in the Smythson collection (IV/10. PLate18) is both interesting and a little puzzling. One of the

63

25. Design for a classical façade, by Maynard.

South front of Corsham House before the addition

terms supporting its entablature derives from Agostino Veneziano's *Terms* of
1536; the frieze, on the other hand, comes from Vredeman de Vries. Its character
suggests Longleat, and if so it is perhaps the first evidence of the appearance of de
Vries in the Smythson orbit. But it is puzzling because the drawing of the figures
seems too good for Smythson or even (on the evidence of what little is known
of his draughtsmanship) for Maynard.[36]

CORSHAM COURT AND SHAW HOUSE

Two houses started in the mid-1570s show the influence, and perhaps more than
the influence, of Longleat, but suggest the hand of Smythson more than of
Maynard. They are Corsham Court in Wiltshire, and Shaw House, near Newbury in Berkshire.[37] They lack the delicacy and richness of Longleat, or the
drama of the later Smythson houses. But as a synthesis of comfortable Tudor
manor-house with a new classical sense of order they are remarkably handsome
and successful buildings.

At Corsham what seems to have been a decayed medieval manor-house was
bought in 1575 by Thomas Smythe (1522-91). Smythe[38] had been born in
Corsham, but spent his working life in London. From 1570 to 1588 he had the
farm of the London customs and administered them with considerable profi-
ciency and profit, both to himself and to the crown; in the late 1570s he also

65

26. (facing page) Chalcot House, Wiltshire.

27. (above) An early eighteenth-century drawing of the entrance front, Corsham Court,
Wiltshire.

acquired mining interests in the Lake District. He probably started to build a new house immediately after his purchase in 1575, and completed it by 1582, the date above the porch. The first surviving depiction of the house is an early-eighteenth-century drawing of the entrance front (Plate 24). It was subsequently much altered and enlarged in the eighteenth and nineteenth centuries, and only a few fragments survive of the original interiors; but the entrance front is more or less as it was built, apart from having been extended to either side in the style of the original during the eighteenth century.

Corsham was being built at the same time as Longleat was being embellished with its three tiers of classical orders. But Smythe lacked the resources and perhaps the desire to build anything as sumptuous. His house probably owes most to Longleat as it was before its final remodelling.

The house was a half-H in plan. As at Longleat, the main feature of the entrance front is a series of bay windows, articulated by entablatures over each floor, and linked to each other by the continuation of these entablatures all round the building. But the bay-windows are only two storeys high; they have no orders; they project much less boldly than the Longleat bays; originally they had glazing only on their front face (as at Somerset House); and they are capped by pediments, above which rise rows of gables, each surmounted by a lion carrying a shield. In general, the proportion of window to wall is much less than at Longleat. All this suggests what is known of Longleat before 1572; the pedimented bay-windows may have been versions of the windows with 'perymentes' dismantled there after the 1567 fire.

In addition to the lions on the gables, there are other details related to Longleat or Smythson. The transoms and mullions have similar sections. In each pediment is carved the projecting head and shoulders of a figure, similar to those on the parapets at Longleat. The most elaborate feature is the central porch (Plate 28). The entrance floor of this is treated with a Doric order, robust but not altogether scholarly. To either side of the door is a cluster of three Doric columns, oddly run together without any intervening pier, so that on plan they have a trefoil outline; the same device is to be found in two designs for screens (one for Worksop Manor) by Robert Smythson. Above the Doric entablature is a panel ornamented with the motif of a rectangle within a rectangle; a similar motif is used in the gable of Smythson's design for a bay window, related to the bay windows at Longleat. The porch is surmounted by a circular pediment remarkably like one shown in J. A. du Cerceau's third *Livre d'Architecture*, which was first published in 1572.

It is likely that Robert Smythson was directly concerned with the design[39], and possibly even the building, of Corsham. Shaw House is more marginal: further from Longleat geographically, less closely connected with it architecturally. Yet houses of its style and quality were still a comparative rarity in the 1570s, and there are enough resemblances to suggest at least the hand of someone in the same circle as Smythson: perhaps the shadowy Humphrey Lovell, the Queen's Master Mason, who had considerably property in Berkshire.[40]

66

28. The porch at Corsham.

It was a remarkable house to be built by a rich Newbury clothier, with no known London or court connections (Plate 29). According to tradition it was begun by the elder Thomas Dolman, and its building was certainly celebrated by a couplet which entered local folk-lore:

Lord have mercy on us miserable sinners
Thomas Dolman has built a new house, and turned away his spinners.

This Thomas Dolman died in 1575; the house was completed, and possibly even started by his son, Thomas Dolman the younger. The rain-water heads and porch are dated 1581.

The porch is carved with inscriptions in both Greek and Latin. The explanation of this show of erudition probably lies in John Dolman, the younger son of Thomas Dolman senior, who graduated at Oxford in 1557, and whose translation of Cicero's *Tusculanarum Questionum Libri Quinque* was published in 1561. An interest in the classics appears in the architecture as well as in the inscriptions. The house is built of a mixture of brick and finely wrought ashlar. The porch is decorated by a very creditable Ionic order and it and the projecting bay above are crowned by amateurish pediments, the latter handsomely embellished with a lion's mask. Apart from this central projection, there are no bay windows but, as at Corsham, classical entablatures run round the building above the ground and first floors, beneath a gabled attic. All four façades are symmetrical.

The interior was largely remodelled in the eighteenth century and later, but at least one original chimneypiece survives, details of which derive from Serlio. Best of all is the garden door on the east front. It has a pediment and Corinthian pilasters, of as good quality as anything being produced in England at the time.[41]

LONGLEAT: THE DESIGN

As soon as one begins to ask who actually designed Longleat, an embarrassing number of candidates appear, even discounting John Thorpe and John of Padua, to whom, on no possible grounds, the design was confidently attributed in the eighteenth and nineteenth centuries. John Chapman and William Spicer, who have also been suggested, had left Longleat long before the fourth house was started, and so can reasonably be disallowed. More likely candidates are Humphrey Lovell, the Queen's Master Mason, John Lewis, the head carpenter, Adrian Gaunt, the head joiner, and Sir John Thynne himself. In 1569 Humphrey Lovell, the man who sent Smythson to Longleat, had provided, jointly with Thynne, a design for a house for Lord Hertford, the Duke of Somerset's son.[42] In the same year Hertford asked for the advice of Thynne and John Lewis on the design of a 'garden house'.[43] Adrian Gaunt had made the model of the third Longleat in 1567. Thynne, together with William Spicer, 'made and signed' the design for part of the second Longleat in 1559,[44] and in his will he ordered his tomb to be built 'accordynge to a plott thereof made and signed wth my own hande'.[45]

68

29. Shaw House, Berkshire.

There is one considerable objection to crediting any of these with a major share in the final design for Longleat. They had all been present or available in its earlier stages and yet between them had been unable, even as late as 1567, to work out anything approaching the boldness and coherence of the fourth Longleat. The remaining two candidates, Smythson and Maynard, are not in this position. Maynard arrived after the conception of the second Longleat, and was away (from 1566–70) during the conception of the third. Smythson only came to Longleat after the model for the third house had been made. It is at least a possible inference that the design of a Longleat so much in advance of anything that had been built before was in some way connected with the arrival of these two men.

A letter and a group of drawings support this inference. In their long, undated and not over-coherent letter to Thynne, Smythson and Maynard, in the course of complaining that work has been taken from them and given to others, make one very interesting statement: 'Bout for youer works wye thynk our selfes better abele to doue yt then thaye be *for the ordenanse therof cam frome us* as yore worshipe douthe knawe they ware nevere able to dowe it.'

'Ordenanse' can mean 'drawing' or 'design' in the sense that Baret, in his *Alvearie* of 1580, talks of 'the first ordinaunce or first draught, which is done with a cole', meaning the first charcoal sketch for a painting. Or it can mean 'composition' or 'arrangement': Evelyn, in 1683, says 'Verrio's invention is admirable, his ordinance full and flowing'; Caxton in 1485 says 'to devyde the mater by chaptyres is the best ordynaunce that I shall conne'; and Lord Berners in his 1523 translation of Froissart, 'I have enterprysed this hystory on ye forsaid ordynaunce and true fundaison'.[46] But whatever the exact sense in which Smythson and Maynard were using the word, they seem to be making something very like a claim that they were responsible for the design of Longleat.

Responsibility for the design presumes the making of drawings, and fortunately a few drawings survive to bear out their claim. The drawings by Maynard at Longleat have already been described. In the Smythson collection is a design for a bay window (Col. Plate III), which, though not identical with the bay windows at Longleat, has every appearance of being a variant design for them. The style of draughtsmanship links up with other drawings in the collection and the design is almost certainly Smythson's.

So not only do Smythson and Maynard, besides erecting the façades of Longleat, appear to claim to have designed them, but also their designs for or related to them survive. In the light of this it is hard to deny them the principal credit for the house as we now see it. But a careful analysis of Longleat, from the design point of view, may help to suggest which member of the partnership was responsible for what, and how much they owed to the work of their predecessors.

The most prominent features of the exterior of Longleat are the bay windows (Plate 31). There is no doubt that the design of these derives ultimately from the two windows on the Strand façade of Somerset House (Plate 30). As has already

70

appeared, the window which Spicer covenanted to build at Longleat in 1559 may have been another version of these Somerset House windows. The design (Col. Plate III) in the Smythson collection (which, incidentally, is probably the earliest surviving drawing by Smythson) may reasonably be assumed to have been made some time between his arrival at Longleat in 1568, and the commencement of the existing windows in 1572. It is very close to the Somerset House windows, being, like them, composed of two stages of paired windows, the lower framed by a Doric and the upper by an Ionic order. But it is finished off at the top in a different manner, and is for something on a much larger scale, each window being of twelve, instead of four, lights. The design is a competent one except for the entablature of the Doric order, which is totally incorrect.

The latter solecism is put right in Maynard's elevation (Plate 22), which also introduces the refinement of moulded frames and elegantly designed aprons for the windows. The design, for three storeys not two, is much closer to the work as executed than Smythson's; the parapet is different, but there is little doubt that the existing parapet was designed by Maynard, for its motifs derive from French *œil-de-bœuf* dormer windows, and a similar motif appears in the design for Rodminster Lodge, which is certainly by Maynard.

The evidence of the drawings suggests, in short, that the detailing of Longleat owes more to Maynard than Smythson. This conclusion is borne out by the fact that, as far as can be gathered from the accounts, Maynard, not Smythson, carved the chimney-pieces at Longleat. Smythson's banqueting-houses show that, even when he first arrived at Longleat, his knowledge of classical ornament was at least competent; but Thynne obviously considered Maynard the expert. There

30. The Strand façade of Old Somerset House, London (1547–52).

is plenty to show that he was justified in this: Maynard's own work at Longleat, the work in the Longleat area that can reasonably be attributed to him, and his few surviving drawings.

The Somerset House façade, taken as a whole, is not a very impressive design. It does not hang together: the bay windows, the intermediate windows and the gatehouse are related to each other only in the loosest way. Longleat improves on this. The intermediate windows are of the same height, and have the same frames and aprons as those in the bays. Moreover, each bay window is joined to its neighbours by the continuation of its entablatures (the pilasters being omitted) across the intermediate façades. So the three entablatures extend the whole way round the outside façades of the house, the proportions of which are dictated by the proportions of the orders. This kind of treatment was a commonplace in France by the mid-sixteenth century and Maynard perhaps suggested its use at Longleat; although in England too at this time it had already begun to appear, as for instance in the courtyard at Burghley in the 1560s.

There were two bay windows at Somerset House; there are thirteen at Longleat. The Somerset House windows were 14 feet wide, $3\frac{1}{2}$ feet deep, and 35 feet high. Those at Longleat are 25 feet wide, 10 feet deep, and 65 feet high, excluding the cresting. The Somerset House windows were strictly speaking not bay windows at all, their projection being very shallow with glass along one side only. The Longleat bays have glass on three sides and project much further. They are not incidents in the design, as at Somerset House; by their scale, boldness, number and regular rhythm they dominate it.

This repetition of a projection unit to give cohesion to a design has parallels in France (in Lescot's Louvre) and in Italy (in Bramante's Belvedere court at the Vatican). Thynne and his team may have known of these examples. But the bay window is an exclusively English feature, and the idea of using it as the dominating and unifying motif of a building appears for the first time at Longleat.

Its use in this way leads to results which cannot be paralleled on the Continent. The bay window is invariably found built away from the corners of a house, unlike towers, or the pavilions of the Continent, which normally mark the angles. At Longleat, accordingly, the right-angle of the corner of the house juts out between the right-angles of the bay windows to either side – leading to a three-dimensional effect of stepping, or receding right-angles, which is exceedingly effective. Moreover, the glorification of the bay window in this way encouraged the Elizabethan tendency to make the house a glass-house. This, as has been discussed in the Introduction, had its roots in Perpendicular Gothic; and it was already under way by the time the new façades at Longleat were being created. The great glass wall of the hall façade at Kirby had been started in 1570. But the comprehensiveness, scale and glitter of the fenestration at Longleat were something new: it is the first of Elizabethan lantern-houses.[47]

In France at this time windows were tending to get smaller rather than larger as the influence of Italy (wall- rather than window-architecture) increased.

72

31. One of the bay windows at Longleat.

Maynard's design for a portion of an unidentified façade has relatively small windows, in complete contrast to Longleat. But Smythson's variant design for Longleat is remarkable for the scale of its windows: that is how it develops on its Somerset House original.

There is a certain dichotomy of character in the outside of Longleat. In some lights and at some angles it is the mass and weight of the bay windows that predominates, the crisp contrast of light and shade, the play of right-angles, the gleam of glass, the grid of mullion and transom (Plate 32). At other times, especially from a frontal view, it is the detail that wins, and the impression of boldness and simplicity is replaced by one of an overall curl and ripple of delicate small-scale ornament (Col. Plate I).

These two aspects probably reflect the personalities of Maynard and Smythson. The delicacy and correctness of the detail come from Maynard; the simplicity and drama of the design from Smythson. His later work suggests that the division is a correct one. With the one exception of Wollaton, it is not because of their ornament that Smythson houses are interesting, and even Wollaton lacks the delicate distinction of Longleat. But the dramatic possibilities of Longleat were developed by Smythson to the full.

At Longleat he inherited a house already compact and outward looking, and at any rate the memory of the Somerset House windows. He developed the window theme so as to emphasise the compactness and expand the outwardness. His later houses are even more compact and more of a unity. The turrets that form the main feature of the skyline at Longleat are relics of an earlier scheme and bear no relation to the bay windows. At Worksop and Hardwick turrets and bay windows are elided and their scale increased. At the same time ornament is reduced to a minimum. The result is a gigantic cage of glass; but it is also a composition in right-angles, bold in its modelling and bold in its skyline. In so far as Longleat anticipates these houses it seems reasonable to give the honour to Smythson.

But it would be grudging not to add the name of Thynne to the Smythson-Maynard partnership. Thynne, like so many of the self-made men of the Renaissance, is not an accessible or attractive character. The stilted phraseology of his letters gives nothing intimate away; even to his family he never shows the faintest sign of any tenderness, nothing more personal than a certain limited humour: 'I trust to be at home before her comyng, for womens mynde doe often change' – or an irascibility expressed in an occasional rocket to his son: 'I have received your letters ... so scribled as I can hardly rede them wherefor seek to mend yor hande in some reasonable sort as men may rede it besides you have the worst frase of speche in your letters as ever I red in any mans res though he had never gon to scole.'

The books which he bought show that he was not an uneducated man: the works of Chaucer, Froissart's *Chronicles*, Fox's sermons, 'a boke of Morall philosophie', 'Plutarches Moralls in French', Erasmus's *Colloquia*, the *School of*

74

32. Looking along the south front at Longleat.

Merie conceytes, 'one volume of Luther'. But in his letters he never strays for more than a second from practical matters, from lawsuits, the getting of jobs, and the arrangement of marriages. There is little to show that he was interested in anything except gaining and keeping money and power.

It was no doubt as an expression of money and power that he began on the building of Longleat; but he kept at it for so long that it seems ultimately to have become an end in itself and one in the pursuit of which he becomes for the first time attractive. He cannot have been an easy man to work for. He was, as his surviving letters to his stewards show (and they arrived sometimes three or four times a week), overbearing, nagging, demanding, and liable to continuous changes of mind that must have been the despair of his employees. It is not surprising that Spicer, Maynard and Smythson all, at one time or another, fell out with him. But he had a restless enthusiasm that must have been infectious: he was chasing the phantom of the perfect house, which continually eluded him, and yet he kept on, rebuilding, altering, starting again, never deterred by his continuous set-backs and disappointments, and never satisfied with what he knew was not the best.

His neighbour, William Darrell of Littlecote, wrote a satire on Thynne, in which the house of Longleat complains in person of its restless life: 'But now see him that by these thirtie yeares almost with such turmoyle of mynd hath byn thinking of me, framing and erecting me, musing many a tyme with great care and now and then pulling downe this or that parte of me to enlardge sometyme a foote, or some few inches, uppon a conceyt, or this or that man's speech, and by and by beat down windows for this or that fault here or there.'[48]

This is not written in a friendly spirit, and yet it shows Thynne in a more sympathetic light than his own arid and ambitious letters, or the record of his selfish and successful career.

When the perfectionism of Thynne found at its service the talents of Smythson and Maynard the result was explosive. Thynne, who had only just finished rebuilding his house for the third time, started again on an even more ambitious scale. But this time he had at last got what he wanted, and there were to be no more alterations. Maynard had the knowledge; Smythson had the genius; but Longleat would never have taken the form it now has if Thynne had not supplied the driving power and the ideal. The result was a sudden efflorescence of splendour that ushered in the great age of Elizabethan architecture.

76

33. Design by Robert Smythson, possibly for the gatehouse at Wollaton (II/12).

2 Wardour & Wollaton

Some time before 1576, while he was still working at Longleat, Smythson took on another piece of work, at Wardour Castle, also in Wiltshire, for Sir Matthew Arundell. The evidence for this consists of a casual reference in a letter from Arundell to Thynne, dated June 1576, about the sale of some beds.[1] Arundell had asked £100 for them, but Thynne had only offered £90: 'syns wch tyme', Arundell wrote, 'I herd agayn by Smythson you wold willingly have them, and before his coming I had undowtydly graunted them to Sir William Courtney, who at this present is not here but will be this week, if he may be perswaded to let them go I will consent to do my endever, but as he seayd before Smythson, he wold not forgo them.'

78

34. Wardour Old Castle, Wiltshire, remodelled 1576–8. The entrance front.

35. (facing page) Doorway and staircase in the inner court, Wardour.

Wardour Castle[2] was half demolished during the Civil War; but the ruins still survive and show clearly enough that Smythson was there as a mason, and not only to bargain over beds. Sir Matthew's work at Wardour consisted of fitting up the remarkable late fourteenth-century hexagonal castle as a modern residence. This involved piercing both the exterior and the inside courtyard walls with larger windows; adding a classical gateway and alcoves to the entrance front (Plate 34), and a classical doorcase (Plate 35) to the entry of the stairs which led up from the courtyard to the hall; inserting new chimney-pieces and one or more doorcases in the interior; and forming a great outer courtyard with a boundary wall exactly echoing the hexagonal plan of the castle which it enclosed. The work was completed in 1578, as an inscription over the entrance gate records.

Stylistically the connection with Longleat is revealed by Sir Matthew Arundell's coat of arms over the gateway, decorated with one of the 'wave' scrolls which were a favourite motif of the Longleat craftsmen; and by the door added to the hall staircase, a vigorous example of the Longleat classical style. But in other parts of Wardour new influences appear. The remains of an elaborate black marble fireplace, dug up from the castle well, include two Longleat-style terms

80

36. Wardour Old Castle from the south.

and also a great deal of strap-work, more Flemish than French, that is, more angular and rigid than such strap-work as there is at Longleat. A Smythson drawing at the R.I.B.A. (II/37) for a fireplace is very similar to these Wardour remains, and may be a design for one of the Wardour fireplaces that have been destroyed. It seems likely enough that Smythson carved the marble fragments as well. If so, they are no great addition to his reputation, but probably a fair enough indication of his limited capacities as a sculptor.

In the entrance gateway and the alcoves on the main front another new element appears: rustication. The gateway itself, with its three square blocks to each pilaster, could easily have been derived from Serlio. But in the little pilasters to the alcoves on either side the number of blocks has been reduced to one, an oddity probably of Smythson's own invention, which he was to repeat, as we shall see, at Wollaton.

Finally, the new windows draw on another and quite different source, the Tudor Gothic window with its square head, but four-centred arch to each light. Such windows were still being set up in traditional and provincial buildings throughout England. But it is a quite different matter, and extremely surprising, that they should have been introduced by Longleat craftsmen, who for the past few years had been cutting the great Longleat twelve-light grids. The explanation must be that their use was a deliberate anachronism, and that they were intended to harmonise with the Gothic castle into which they were inserted: an early and interesting example of Elizabethan appreciation of the Middle Ages. Even so, these windows were not exact copies of Gothic prototypes. The bigger ones (Plate 36) have exaggerated long thin lights, without the transoms which would have divided them in early Tudor times. And they have all been inserted with a regard for symmetry that involves several false windows; these can never have been anything but false, for they have chimney-flues behind them. With a similar orderliness, several of the original fourteenth-century archways in the central courtyard have been re-set, slightly shifted to left or right in order to obtain a more complete symmetry.

But Wardour is important in Smythson's career more because of what he found than what he added. He must have been working there, on and off, for at least three years. Of necessity he acquired first-hand and detailed knowledge of one of the most remarkable of medieval buildings. Wardour is compact and very high. It has two great towers, plain and rectangular. The stone staircase rises romantically on a curve from the courtyard, up and out of sight. The main rooms are on the first or second floors, with vaulted rooms down below. The great traceried windows of the hall are high up at the top of the building. All these features were to reappear in Smythson's later work.

WOLLATON AND ITS BUILDER

In 1580 (as an inscription over the door records) Arundell's cousin and brother-

in-law, Sir Francis Willoughby, began a new house, at Wollaton near Nottingham. The house still exists externally almost untouched, but inside it has been almost entirely redecorated, so that the hall is the only important Elizabethan survival.

Building accounts for the house remain, though the series is incomplete.[3] The first book starts in March 1582, and there are others running, with gaps, up till 1588. Robert Smythson is first mentioned in March 1583, in connection with work let out in the previous four months; but it is probable that he was involved from the start, and he certainly remained till the end. His going to Wollaton was no doubt due to Arundell; once there, he stayed until his death in 1614. His position was more responsible than that which he had occupied at Longleat. He was paid in the accounts not as a freemason (with one possible exception) but as Mr Smythson, letting tasks to the craftsmen and riding to the quarries to pay the quarrymen. He was, in fact, what the Elizabethans called the Surveyor, a post which he never held at Longleat. Among the Smythson collection in the R.I.B.A. are drawings by him for the plan (Plate 38), the elevation (Plate 55), and the hall screen (Plate 46) at Wollaton.[4] On his monument in the church he is described

82

37. Wollaton Hall, Nottinghamshire. The entrance front.

as 'Architecter and Surveyor unto the most worthy house of Wollaton with divers others of great account'. Wollaton is not only one of the most important of Elizabethan houses; it is the only one of its class for which so much responsibility can be given on secure evidence to one man.

There is, however, always the patron to be considered. Sir Francis Willoughby[4] was one of those curious people who, though endowed with talents and resources well above the ordinary, somehow fail, in the adding up, to be satisfactory or even impressive characters. His family (originally and less romantically called Bugge) had risen to the level of gentry in the thirteenth century and since then, by a series of fortunate marriages, had acquired large estates in the Midlands and the West Country. Francis was the nephew and, for a time, the ward[5] of the Duke of Suffolk, first cousin of Lady Jane Grey, and connected with both the Seymours and the Dudleys. The origin of his wealth stretched well back beyond the Reformation; his links with the Middle Ages were strong and the character of his household, with its hospitality, its waste, its swarms of scheming and gently-born retainers, was far more medieval than were, for instance, the calculated and organised splendours of Sir John Thynne or Lady Shrewsbury. He was no *nouveau riche*; if anything he was overbred. He was exceedingly proud of his own ancestry, but very far from stupid. At Cambridge in the 1560s he had had the best classical education available in England. He was an avid reader and book-collector all through his life; he was far and away the most cultured of Smythson's patrons. At the same time he had the intelligence and energy to exploit the new opportunities of his age. He was one of the first of the great industrialists. Wollaton was in the middle of a coal field as rich as any in England and he developed coal to the full, both on his own estates and elsewhere.[6] He had at various times interests in mines in Nottinghamshire, Derbyshire, Warwickshire and Leicestershire; at least a third of the cost of his new house was paid for out of their profits. In addition he mined and forged iron in south Derbyshire; he may have blown glass; he cultivated woad, to establish a dye industry; he planned to weave arras.

This almost feverish industry he applied, too, to his personal life, drawing up elaborate regulations for his servants, collecting a library 'of the most valuable books of his time', writing himself about theological subjects, composing sermons for his own chaplain to preach to him. Yet there must have been some flaw, some basic insecurity, in the character of this pin-headed little man, with his plucked and nervous face (as he appears in George Gower's portrait): for his life was a dismal series of suspicions, jealousies, favourites, rows, and real or imagined plots, so that all his organisation ended only in muddle and disaster. He failed miserably in his relations with his wife, by nature a somewhat hysterical woman; his sister and servants trickled scandal and hatred on his mind; little by little he believed them and, after ten years of steadily more miserable co-existence, she left him. He spent the rest of his life suspicious of his family, who seem to have been genuinely fond of him, and credulous of and dominated by his servants, who cheated and lied to him; convinced that his son-in-law was slandering him, scheming for his inheritance, and planning to murder him; that his daughters were against him, and his agent swindling him; quarrelling with them all, quarrelling with his neighbours; and yet, in the midst and perhaps because of this hate and distrust, he entertained with extravagance and built fantastically, paying the men who brought him stone from Ancaster with baskets of coal.

In spite of his great inheritance and his industrial adventures, he out-built, out-entertained and out-organised himself, and left a confused and impoverished estate; after a life-time of quarrelling with his family he died lonely and miserable, though not yet an old man, sucked dry by a dominating second wife: 'the whore and her minions have stripped him both of goods and lands and left him nothing where he lies but what hangs upon his back';[7] and notwithstanding his erudition and his ancestry, he is generally written off today as an ostentatious *nouveau riche*. The house which he built reflects something of his character: it is methodical and yet crazy; in the newest fashion yet looking back to the Middle Ages; original, extravagant, uncomfortable and restless, to the fringe of lunacy.

The house is basically a rectangle, with square towers at the corners. Wrapped up in the middle is a rectangular hall, lit only from its top storey, where it rises above the main roof. On top of the hall is another room, known as the prospect room, of the same length and breadth as the hall and externally dominating the house. A plan by Robert among the Smythson drawings (Plate 38) shows the house as the centre of a scheme of gardens, courtyards and outbuildings. Eight square or rectangular courts form together with the house an enormous square, on the periphery of which four minor buildings, gatehouse, stable, dairy with laundry, and bake with brewhouse, gaze across at the four façades of the house. Certainly some and perhaps all, of this layout was carried out; remains of it are clearly visible in the bird's-eye view painted by Siberechts in 1697 (Col. Plate V).[8]

The house was set deliberately on the top of a considerable hill, well above the old home of the Willoughbys, which was on low ground by the church; as Camden said when the house was fresh built, 'standing bleakly but offering a very goodly prospect to the beholders far and near'. It was one of the first examples of a major building so situated for aesthetic rather than military reasons. The possible excitements of this site, both in the way of views of and views from the house, were fully exploited by Smythson. The traveller coming from any direction sees from long away that amazing silhouette brooding on the horizon. On coming nearer, supposing the original plans were fully carried out, he would gradually have seen the house in detail, rising dramatically above the long courtyard walls. When he reached the entrance, on one one side would have been the gatehouse,with its four turrets echoing in little the four towers of the house behind, and on the other an extensive and heaving view. Up and away from this a long and somewhat narrow tunnel of steps led into a shut-in

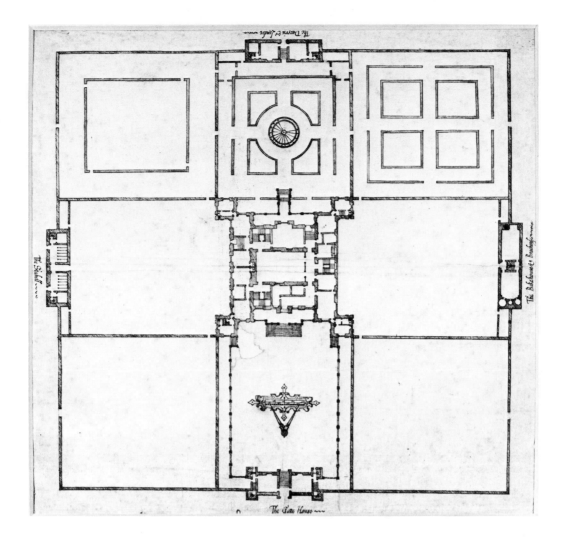

courtyard, with, on three sides, walls and raised terraces; no means of escape from the great decorated front of the house which would have borne down on the spectator in two overbearing steps of windowed and pilastered masonry; above which floated, enormous and improbable, the prospect room, with its buttresses, its turrets, and its gigantic frog's-eyed windows.

At the head of the courtyard another broader and three-sided flight of steps led to a terrace, before the porch steps and between the horns of the house, from the elevation of which, over the walls of the courtyards, the view would once more have opened out. From the porch an L-shaped corridor went into the hall (Plate 50), of the traditional form, with screens, dais, and open timber roof; but being three storeys high and lit only from the top storey, somewhat claustrophobically high and narrow. Those differences in level, which, together with changes in planc, Smythson had exploited to such effect in the exterior, reappeared inside in the form of a profusion of staircases. There were three great staircases round open wells, two off the dais and one off the screens; separate flights of steps running down into the basement or the courtyards; and subsidiary

38. Robert Smythson's original design for Wollaton and its outbuildings (I/25(1)).

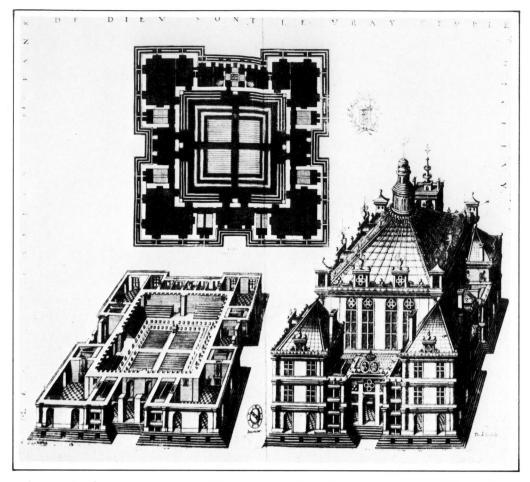

staircases in the corner towers. Up one or other of these access could have been gained, past the state rooms of the first floor, on to the vistas and open platform of the roof, and off this again a cramped and dark little newel led and still leads to the great prospect room. Its traceried windows surveyed a generous slice of the Midlands, including the occasional smoke of the ironworks, the buildings of the coal mines, which financed the house with their profits and the swollen successors of which have since oozed over so much of the landscape.

So prominent a house was bound to be talked about. Wollaton was certainly well-known to Willoughby's contemporaries: Camden described it in his *Britannia;* Robert Burton commended its situation in his *Anatomy of Melancholy;*[9] John Thorpe drew its plan (with, as was his practice, modifications of his own) and it was the inspiration of at least one of the other designs in his book.[10] More unexpectedly, it was without any doubt the model for one of the curious and fascinating buildings engraved in Jacques Perret's *Du Fortifications et Artifices . . . Architecture et Perspective* (1601). The design in question is for a Huguenot temple; perhaps Perret, who was himself a Huguenot, visited England during the religious persecution in France.

The interior of Wollaton was badly damaged by fire in the early seventeenth century, and was substantially redecorated in the late seventeenth and again in

86

39. A design from Jacques Perret's *De Fortifications et Artifices . . . Architecture et Perspective* (1601).

the early nineteenth centuries, the latter time to the designs of Wyatville.[11] Wyatville knocked smaller rooms together on the ground floor to make a big library, saloon and dining-room, but otherwise the plan remains much as shown in Robert Smythson's drawing, complete with the three great staircases. The only original detail to survive inside, however, is in the entrance hall (Plate 48), and in some vaulted rooms in the basement. The superb condition of the external stonework may reflect some re-facing by Wyatville, but much of it is original.

In the first surviving account-book, for March 1582-3, the windows, parapet and external orders on all three storeys were being carved by three men, Christopher Lovell, John Rodes (known as Rodes Senior) and Christopher Rodes (Rodes Junior). Christopher Lovell, son of the Queen's Master Mason, we have already met at Longleat. The Rodes were almost certainly local men and were to reappear at Hardwick. These three were not paid a regular weekly wage, as were the other masons, but received lump sums, as Smythson and Maynard had done at Longleat, for task-work. A typical entry (for the Rodeses) ran as follows; 'Strayght basse and cornisc double and single heds and soylles monioll and transom pilasters architrave frize and cornisse wth flat bands in the pilasters to be all paneled(?) to the wall for all stories as the cam to work at vii[th] the foote one with the other'; and again, 'Taske letten to Lovell the vi of Nov 1582 as followes the pedstalle upon the leades and toure in number 33 letten in greate with hallfe ballisters where occation shall serve.'

Lovell disappears after October 1585. The Rodes stay on till 1587, but in the last three years are paid only a weekly wage, 14d. per day, along with the other masons. The payments for task-work in 1586 and 1587, £175 in all, are made to Robert Smythson himself; but as they are sometimes 'for taske worke' and sometimes 'to pay owte for task worke' it is impossible to be certain whether he was actually carving stone himself.

In 1588, the last year of the accounts, all task-work payments are made to a William Styles for work 'done by him and others'. From 30 March in this year a Smythson is paid as a mason at 10d. a day. This is almost certainly the first recorded appearance of Robert's son, John.

Other craftsmen besides Lovell had come with Smythson from Longleat. Among the masons was John Hills; he had arrived at Longleat with Smythson in 1568 and stayed with him ever since. The head carpenter at Wollaton throughout was Crispin, probably the Richard Crispin or Chrispian who had been the second carpenter at Longleat. He had working under him till September 1582, one Lewis; he was probably the younger John Lewis, son of Thynne's head carpenter, who had been working at Longleat since 1573.

Another craftsman working at Wollaton was Thomas Accres, who in 1584 was being paid a quarterly wage of £7 10s. He was a carver in stone and marble who is first heard of in 1576, carving for Lady Shrewsbury at Chatsworth,[12] and who was to reappear, as a figure of some importance, at Hardwick in 1594.

There is never any specific mention in the accounts either of the hall screen or of the portrait heads with their cartouche surrounds, though these are the most elaborate pieces of carving at Wollaton. If Lovell or the Rodes had been responsible for them, one would have expected to find them mentioned in the specifications of 1582-3. They may have been covered by the money Smythson 'paid out for task work' in 1586 and 1587, but who carved them remains a problem. It could have been Thomas Accres, who worked in stone as well as marble; or the mysterious William Styles, who appeared for the one year of 1588; or possibly Smythson himself, who certainly, as his drawings show, took a lot of trouble over the design of the screen.

WOLLATON: ITS DESIGN, SOURCES AND PLAN

The sources of the design and plan of Wollaton include Longleat itself, Serlio's *Architecture*, the works of Jacques Androuet du Cerceau, the Flemish publications of Vredeman de Vries and various strands of English Gothic architecture, military, domestic and ecclesiastical. It is in fact an extraordinarily eclectic building, and one not unentertaining to analyse.

Its monstrous flamboyance may seem a long way removed from the restrained richness of Longleat, but the influence is there nonetheless. The high basement comes straight from Longleat, though at Wollaton it is higher still, high enough to contain the whole height of the kitchen. From Longleat also comes the division of the façades by three storeys of pilasters carried consistently round the four sides of the house. As at Longleat the first-floor windows are higher than those on the ground floor, showing the whereabouts of the main rooms. The column-chimneys, the roundels of emperors, the lions' masks, the great size of the windows and their frames and aprons are also unmistakably derived from Longleat.

But various pattern-books exerted an even more important influence on the detail and, to a lesser extent, the plan of Wollaton. There is little doubt that Willoughby's library of 'the best books of his time', referred to in the early eighteenth century by his descendant Cassandra, Duchess of Chandos, included one of the best collection of architectural and related books then in existence in England. Such books, published in the sixteenth and early seventeenth centuries, are richly represented in a late seventeenth century catalogue of the library;[13] it is likely that most or all of these were acquired by Francis Willoughby and his son-in-law and heir, Percival Willoughby, in whose service Robert Smythson continued after Francis's death. The list includes Daniel Barbaro's 1567 edition of Vitruvius; Serlio's *Architecture*, including his Seventh Book; Palladio's and Vignola's great treatises, the latter in an edition of 1596; Philibert de l'Orme's *Nouvelles Inventions pour bien bastir* (1561 ed.) and his *L'Architecture*; J. A. du Cerceau's *Plus Excellents Bastiments de France* and two, and possibly three, of his three *Livres d'Architecture*; and Bluom's *Quinque Columnarum ...* (1550 ed.).

40. (top left) Smythson's adaptation (I/25(4)) of de Vries, for the panels of Wollaton screen.
41. (top right) Base of a Doric column, from de Vries's *Das Erst Buch* (1565).
42. (centre left), 43. (bottom left) de Vries metopes copied for use at Wollaton.
44. (centre right), 45. (bottom right) Doric entablatures, from de Vries.

Oddly enough, there is no clear mention in the catalogue of any of the publications of Vredeman de Vries, although their influence is more obvious at Wollaton than that of any other pattern-book. Among the Smythson drawings are straight copies[14] from three of his books, which Smythson must therefore have seen, and which probably belonged to Willoughby: the *Das Erst Buch* of 1565, the *Pictores, Statuarii, Architecti* of 1563, and the undated *Caryatidum*. For his own designs Smythson drew on these and at least two other de Vries publications, although he usually adapted rather than copying exactly. At Wollaton, the gables probably derive from *Das Erst Buch*; the alcoves between the pilasters from his *Architectura*, of 1577; and various details in the screen from *Das Erst Buch, Pictores, Statuarii, Architecti*, and the *Deorum Dearum Capita* of 1573. Some of the cartouches derive from engravings after Cock; a book of engravings after Cock, Floris, and others, was in the sale of the Wollaton library in 1925. But all this Flemish decoration is wrapped round a building of a shape and plan far more exciting than any in the Low Countries, and is interpenetrated with elements from Longleat. The one-block rustication of the pilasters comes neither from de Vries, nor Longleat, but from Wardour.

The screen in the hall (Plate 46 and 47), for which there are several drawings in the Smythson collection, is also eclectic. Its metopes are copies, and its strapwork panels adaptations, from de Vries (Plates 42–5). But its shape as a whole, and the figures in its arch spandrels, are not from de Vries and derive perhaps ultimately from French choir screens, by way of English screens such as the one in the Middle Temple Hall. The hall fireplace draws on yet another source, being taken from one of the Doric fireplaces in the third book of Serlio's *Architecture* (Plates 49 and 50). Another interesting derivation from Serlio is the ceiling of the great hall. The hammer-beam roof (modelled on that at Longleat) is a fake: it does no useful work but is in fact slung from the ceiling which it appears to support. But there can have been no single timbers available wide enough to span the 32 feet width of the hall, and instead the system illustrated by Serlio, of morticing together shorter timbers in a kind of grid or Chinese pattern, has been adopted.[15]

The great central feature at Wollaton seems, at first sight, externally somewhat French in its detail, a transplantation from the valley of the Loire. Smythson may have got ideas for its turrets and windows, Gothic in inspiration but not in detail, from the turrets of Anet and Chenonceau and window tracery at Chenonceau and Challuau, as depicted in du Cerceau; windows of similar tracery are also found in Vredeman de Vries. But these features of Wollaton probably also owed something to buildings less far afield. At Repton in south Derbyshire Prior Overton's Tower (*c.*1440), now part of the buildings of Repton School, has exactly the Wollaton combination of corbelled out corner turrets with buttresses (Plate 51); and four such turrets reappeared nearby at Mackworth (*c.* 1495), at the corners of a rectangular tower lit by large square-headed traceried windows.

III. (facing page) Design by Robert Smythson for a bay window, probably for Longleat House, Wiltshire.
IV. (following page) Wardour Old Castle, Wiltshire, from the north.
V. (subsequent page) Wollaton Hall, Nottinghamshire. A detail from the painting by Jan Siberechts, 1697.

46. (top) The hall screen, Wollaton.
47. (bottom) Smythson's design for the screen (I/25 (7)).
VI. (facing page) Wollaton Hall, Nottinghamshire. Looking from the roof to one of the towers.

There is no other design of this date in England in which (at least in the original plan) so thorough an effort was made to stamp the intellect not only on the house but also on the ground around it, so that house, gardens, courtyard and outbuildings were combined in one scheme of complete four way symmetry: an orderliness that must have delighted Sir Francis Willoughby. The lay-outs of Holdenby and Theobalds were tentative in comparison to this, though arranged in some kind of relationship to the house and on a scale far more ambitious than that of Wollaton. In France the *châteaux* of, for instance, Anet, Maune or Charleval had settings of elaborate symmetry, views and plans of which Smythson had probably seen in du Cerceau's *Plus Excellents Bastiments*; but their complex formalities have been distilled at Wollaton into a much simpler lay-out. In much the same way Smythson may have realised through du Cerceau the dramatic use which could be made of flights of steps. But if he took over the drama, he never emulated the complications, of staircases such as that in the Cour Ovale at Fountainebleau.

There can be little doubt that the plan of Wollaton (Fig. 1), though it resembles that of Longleat to a certain extent in being compact and outward-looking, derives more closely from Mount Edgcumbe in Cornwall (Fig. 2), that is to say from the line of medieval houses already referred to in Chapter 1 (p. 56).[16]

97

48. (facing page) Wollaton: the hall.
49. (top left) Doric chimney-piece, from Serlio's *Architecture*.
50. (top right) The hall chimney-piece, Wollaton.

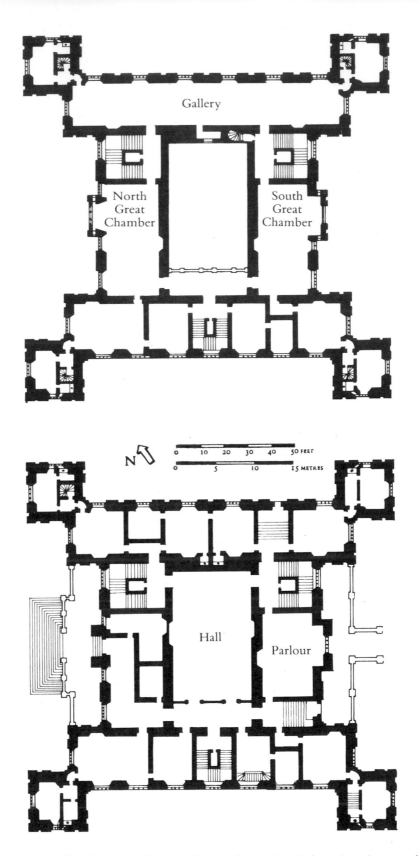

Fig. 1. Wollaton Hall. The ground-floor plan as shown by Robert Smythson and (top) a reconstruction of the original arrangement of the first floor.

"RICK TOWER at REPTON"

51. Prior Overton's tower, Repton, Derbyshire (c. 1440).

52. (bottom) Mt Edgcumbe, Cornwall (1546), as drawn c. 1735 by Edmund Prideaux.

Mount Edgcumbe was begun by Sir Richard Edgcumbe in 1546, so that Smythson could have had nothing to do with it. It was later much altered, was gutted in the last war, and has been restored; but we can be certain about its main original elements. The plan (Fig. 2) was rectangular, with small round turrets at the four corners, later enlarged to octagonal towers. Its most remarkable feature was the position of the hall. This was enclosed in the centre of the house, where one would have expected a courtyard, and was lit by clerestory windows (Plate 52). There were cellars, but no high basement as at Longleat and Wollaton; the kitchen was on the same level as the hall. What original detail survives is Tudor Gothic, with no admixture of Renaissance elements.[17]

ELEVATION of the SOUTH FRONT in the PRESENT STATE

There seems to have been a house of similar plan and earlier date at Michel-grove in Sussex (Plate 53), built by Sir William Shelley and apparently dated 1536.[18] Both Edgcumbes and Shelleys had Court connections, and the compact and unconventional plan of their houses was perhaps evolved by an official of Henry VIII's works; however, no royal building of this date is known to have had this type of enclosed hall. The plan seems to be a product of the native tradition, and to owe nothing to continental influence.

Mount Edgcumbe was a house well known throughout England, for it had a position more sheltered, but even more public and spectacular, than Wollaton's. It was built up above Plymouth Sound, a landmark to all the ships which came into Plymouth harbour (Plate 52). But there was a more personal reason why it was almost certainly known to Smythson: the Arundells of Wardour were by origin a Cornish family and its builder, Sir Richard Edgcumbe, had married Matthew Arundell's aunt.

Two of the most important features of Wollaton, the clerestory-lit hall and the corner towers, almost certainly derive from Mount Edgcumbe. But the Mount Edgcumbe theme has been much developed and elaborated, quite apart from the lavish use of ornament already discussed. At Mount Edgcumbe the main entrance was probably (it has been altered since) on the line of the screens of the hall, and so destroyed the symmetry of the entrance façade. At Wollaton the porch is central, and was linked to the screens by an L-shaped passage; the space between this passage and the hall was filled with a closet and a porter's lodge. This arrangement was subsequently destroyed, and a vestibule now leads straight from the porch to the middle of one side of the hall.

Above all Wollaton is more dramatic than Mount Edgcumbe. The relatively inert mass of the former house has been squeezed upwards to a far greater height;

100

53. Michelgrove, Sussex (1536), as drawn shortly before demolition in the early nineteenth century.

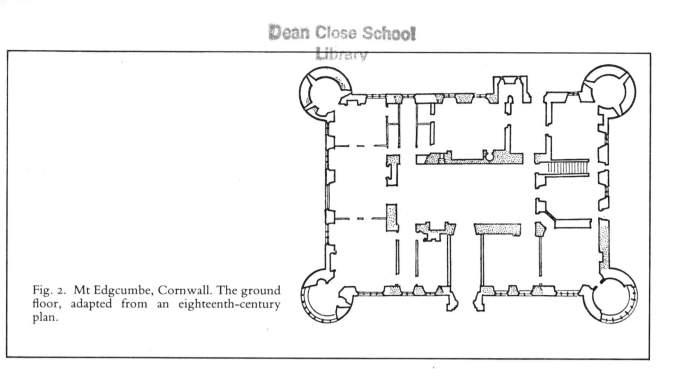

Fig. 2. Mt Edgcumbe, Cornwall. The ground floor, adapted from an eighteenth-century plan.

the main façades are recessed in two bold steps back from the towers to the porch (Plate 54); the position is even more spectacular. Unlike Mount Edgcumbe, Wollaton is full of movement. As one walks round, towards or away from it, it expands, unfolds, contracts; the great central mass lifts up its glittering horns and then sinks down again. The recession of the façades, the spread-out corner towers, the complex skyline, all contribute to this effect. In its use of bay windows Longleat had anticipated the movement of Wollaton, but in a much less dramatic way. In his later houses Smythson continued to experiment in this as yet unexplored country, with equally exciting results.

Finally, the small windows of Mount Edgcumbe have become huge grids of glass; Wollaton is one of the most sensational of Elizabethan lantern-houses. The whole upper portion, being only one room thick, is transparent, and, in the evening sunshine, the combination of this transparency with the spread of window down below makes the house, rearing its extraordinary skyline on the hilltop, an unbelievably fantastic sight.

There had been a foretaste of the bold stepping of Wollaton in the treatment of the external corners at Longleat; but Wollaton carries it much further. Smythson clearly appreciated the visual effect of Wollaton's massing, for he drew a corner of the house in perspective (Plate 55). The result is probably the earliest surviving perspective drawing made by an English architect.[19] It seems to reflect the influence of du Cerceau's many perspective engravings of houses. These include examples of vigorous three-dimensional modelling in, for instance, du Cerceau's designs for Verneuil, in the *Plus Excellents Bastiments* and in many of the house designs in the first *Livre d'Architecture*.

Intriguing evidence of awareness of du Cerceau at Wollaton survives in the form of an undated plan among Francis Willoughby's papers.[20] With minor

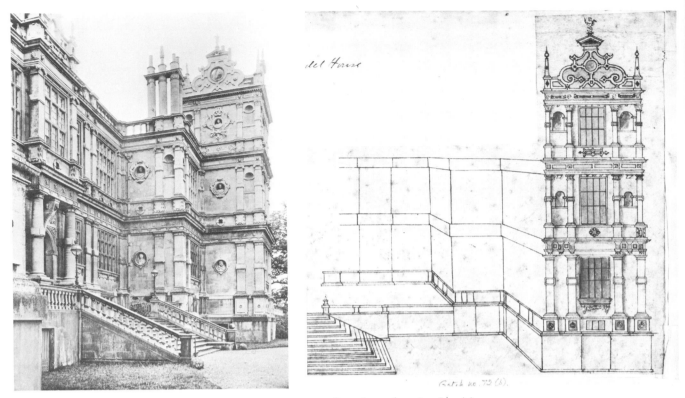

54. One of the corner towers at Wollaton. 55. Smythson drawing I/25(2).

modifications, this is a copy of a plan engraved in du Cerceau's *Petits Habitations* of *c.* 1560. The plan (Plate 56) is of a house with a central hall running through the house from west to east, and lit at either end. There are round towers at the four corners, each of them subdivided into smaller rooms, matching staircases to either side of the hall, and a corridor running along its south side. The middle of the two main fronts is recessed in front of the hall.

Although there are many differences, this plan seems to relate to the one finally adopted at Wollaton, especially in the recession of the centre and the subdivision of the towers; that of the two southern towers, each containing an inner chamber, a closet, and a garderobe, is especially close to Wollaton. It suggests the ambience out of which the plan of Wollaton grew: a conflation of du Cerceau with an enclosed hall derived from Mount Edgcumbe. But the plan is in many ways puzzling. The hall is a French or Italian salle or sala, and no attempt has been made to arrange it in the English manner, with a screens passage. The draughtmanship does not suggest Robert Smythson, although the differences from his usual conventions of drawing may be due to a close copying of those of du Cerceau. Another possibility is that it was an early, abortive scheme for a new house, and was provided by a mysterious 'platt-maker' who 'came from London' in May 1573;[21] but the wording of the payment to him in the accounts suggests that he came to survey land rather than to provide architectural 'platts', although he may have combined the two functions.

102

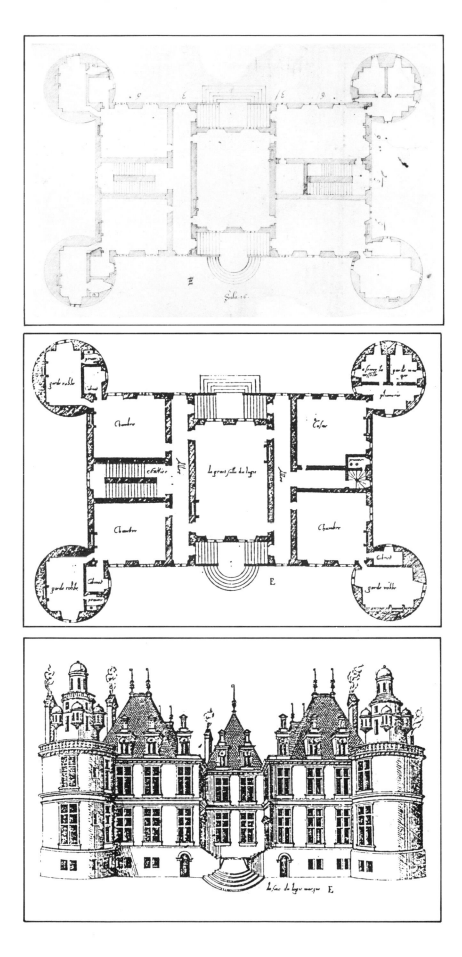

56. A plan in the Willoughby papers.

57 (a, b). Plan and elevation from J. A. du Cerceau's *Petites Habitations* (c. 1560).

The planning of Wollaton has three peculiarities: the enclosed hall, the provision of matching great chambers to either side of the hall on the first floor, and the size and position of the prospect room above it.

The hall itself has already been discussed. North and south great chambers[22] are listed in inventories of 1596 and 1598, and still exist on the first floor of Wollaton, though all their sixteenth-century decoration has long since disappeared. Each were (and still are) approached by matching great staircases, and if, as seems likely, the planning of the first floor today is basically the same as in the sixteenth century, they led to similar sets of rooms in the south-west and north-west corners of the house. The east side of the house was filled by a long gallery; the plan of the first floor was, in fact, almost completely symmetrical.

This symmetrical plan is exceedingly interesting. It was clearly inspired by plans in du Cerceau, and possibly also in Palladio, but adapted to English usage. The provision of two great chambers is not uncommon in grand houses from the Middle Ages onward. It allowed for the arrival and putting up in style of a royal visitor or other great person and their retinue, which would take over one great chamber and its ancillaries, while the owner and his household occupied the other. In royal houses it reflected the division of any such house into two parts, a King's side and a Queen's side, each with their own great Presence Chamber.

But to arrange the two sets with complete symmetry was something quite different. An unexecuted design of about 1540 for a royal house in Waltham Forest comes close to a symmetrical division between King's and Queen's sides, but, as far as is known, such an arrangement was never actually carried out in any of the palaces of Henry VII or Henry VIII, except possibly at Nonsuch.[23] In the 1570s Sir Christopher Hatton's huge house at Holdenby seems to have been planned with a grand set of rooms along the garden, intended for Queen Elizabeth but never occupied by her, and another set on the other side of the house for Hatton himself.[24] But there was no balance between them; Hatton's set, suitably enough, was considerably less grand than the Queen's. Total symmetry, or something near to it, appeared in unexecuted designs of 1605 for a royal house at Ampthill, and in the executed designs for Audley End, of c. 1605, and Hatfield, of 1608.[25] The last two houses were both designed by great people in anticipation of royal visits; as by then there were a King and Queen to accommodate, complete balance was appropriate.

Wollaton anticipates all these by twenty-five years and more. Its plan suggests that Willoughby expected, and possibly hoped, that the Queen would be attracted to visit his grand new house; in fact she never came. But the combination of symmetry in the plan of the house with the surrounding symmetry of the six courts makes one wonder if the planning was dictated by aesthetic as much as, and possibly more than, by practical reasons.

Certainly, practical reasons played little if any part in the conception of the enormous room over the hall. It is one of the great follies of English architecture.

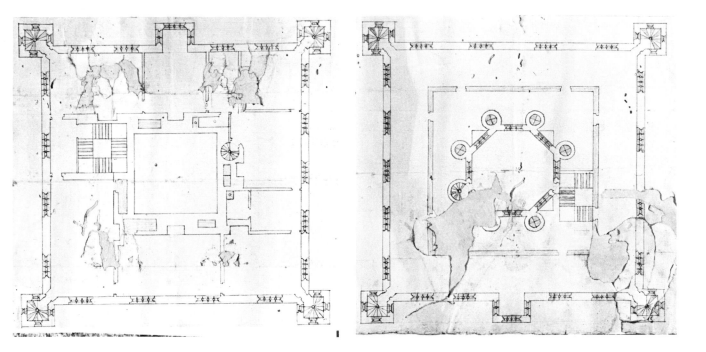

Halls and long galleries apart, it is the biggest surviving room in any Elizabethan or Jacobean house. But it has no fireplace and can never have had one; it can only be approached by a mean newel staircase off the leads of the roof; it does not feature in any of the early inventories, and probably remained unfurnished. It floats improbably above the house, looking more like a halting-place for passing djinns than a room for ordinary human beings.

What seems to be the embryo of the Wollaton prospect-room appears in a curious design (Plate 58), which is now preserved in the library at Longleat. It consists of two plans, apparently for the two top storeys of a house; the elevations no longer survive (if they ever existed) and the plans have no signature or inscriptions. Because of their resemblance to Wollaton, and presence at Longleat, they can reasonably be attributed to Smythson. The first floor plan shows a square house with turrets at the corners and the top half of a big room in the centre; similar, in fact, to Mount Edgcumbe, with the difference that the central room and the house as a whole are square, not rectangular, and the turrets are square, not circular. On the second floor, above the central room, is a large octagonal belvedere. Up the corners of the octagon run big round buttresses, one of which is enlarged to turret size to contain a newel staircase; the others are in reality chimney-stacks carrying up the flues from the fireplaces, which are all concentrated in the immensely thick walls around the central room. A continuous gallery runs along the four sides of the house at top storey level, opening internally on to a roof-level courtyard, from the middle of which bursts the top and windowed portion of the central room, with the octagon above it. The central room could not, in view of its shape, ever have been a hall; it is hard to see what its purpose was, except to support the octagon. This octagon appears to derive from Melbury House[26] in Dorset, built by Sir Giles Strangways before

105

58. Two anonymous plans in the library at Longleat.

1540 in the late Gothic style and crowned by a six-sided prospect room (Plate 59) rising from a windowed square, with pinnacles, of a form derived from chimney-stacks, at its angles.

Melbury provides one of the most important of a group of look-out towers,[27] the first of which seem to have appeared in the early sixteenth century. Stowe, in describing the house, near St Margaret Pattens in the City of London, of Angell Dunne (d. 1509), a rich London alderman and grocer, says that 'he builded in this house an high Tower of Bricke, the first that ever I heard of in any private man's house, to overlooke his neighbours in this Citie'. This building has long ago disappeared, but what must be a near contemporary look-out tower survives in the form of the Spye tower at Warwick Castle. It is five storeys high, of a rather complex plan; and in the top storey is a prospect room, one side of which is almost continuous window.[28]

The Melbury hexagon may owe something to the Spye tower, but its immediate inspiration was more probably the great octagonal look-out tower which

106

59. The hexagonal prospect room at Melbury House, Dorset (c. 1530).

rose prominently above the roofs of Oatlands Palace.[29] This was being finished in 1538 and was almost certainly built of timber. By the mid-sixteenth century look-out towers seem to have become very much the fashion: apart from the view which could be enjoyed from them they were no doubt popular because of the distinction which they gave to the outside of the house. Sharington's tower at Lacock Abbey, Wiltshire, is well known, and other good examples (both of c. 1550–60) survive at St Osyth's, Essex, and Bisham Abbey, Berkshire. A tower of some sort was built at Longleat at the same period; and the roof-top turrets (the banqueting-houses) that still survive there are variants on the same tradition. So the Wollaton prospect-room takes its place as the member of a family, though admittedly both an outsize and off-beat one. Prospect-rooms, hill-top houses, banqueting-houses, hunting-towers, belvederes, gazebos, and roof-top walks are all related expressions of a growing sixteenth-century appreciation of nature. The enclosed medieval garden was too confined for the Elizabethans; they wanted, on occasions at any rate, to command a gigantic prospect.

Mount Edgcumbe, it is worth remarking, was built as a hunting-lodge, even if a hunting-lodge on the grand scale. It was an appendage to the family's main seat at Cotehele, some miles up the River Tamar. These lodges form one of the most interesting types among sixteenth and seventeenth-century buildings. Apart from their purely sporting functions they served a distinct purpose as a retreat from the formality and pomp of the great house, a place to which the owner could retire with a few friends and a reduced staff, when he kept what was known as 'secret house'. They were a natural vehicle for architectural experiment – rather like the Whig landowner's 'villa' in the eighteenth century. By their nature they were well suited to a compact plan, as opposed to the traditional courtyard plan of the great house; and their use as belvederes, from which to watch the hunt and the movement of the deer, made a lofty site, height, and the provision of towers and flat roof-top walks desirable. The lodge type plays an important part in the development of the country house, and influenced the design of houses that – like Wollaton – were not lodges at all. Their influence strengthened the general trend towards height, compactness, and the choice of a site isolated in a park, rather than attached to the town or village; at Wollaton, for instance, the house was moved from its old position down by the church to a new one up on top of the hill. Very often a house originally built as a hunting-lodge became so attractive to the family that built it that in the end they made it their main residence, enlarging it if necessary. This happened, for instance, at Mount Edgcumbe itself; at Westwood in Worcestershire; at Wootton Lodge in Staffordshire (see p. 199), and in numerous other cases.

WOLLATON: THE SUMMING UP

As one analyses Wollaton and realises, bit by bit, what an extraordinarily eclectic building it is, one's admiration for Smythson grows. He was no more than an ignorant local mason, with no intellectual training; yet how far he was from being swamped, as many local masons were, by influences he could not control and did not understand. Instead, from the late Gothic of the Midlands and West Country, from his own Longleat, from the great lay-outs of France, from du Cerceau, from Serlio, from the extravagance of the Low Countries, he selected, adapted and integrated until in the end he produced what his client required: a building that was at once a magnifico, every bit as resplendent and ornamented as the most expensive Elizabethan courtier; an original, one of those 'ingeniose devices' which the age pursued with such enthusiasm, in literature and the arts; and a fantasy, an early expression of a new romantic urge, which was to show itself in many ways, from Philip Sidney throwing off his cuisses at the battle of Zutphen to Lord Pembroke and his friends dining at Ludlow in the dress and with the names of the knights of the Round Table.[30]

Yet although in the abstract Wollaton can heat and excite both intellect and imagination, as carried out it is undoubtedly something of a monster. There is too much going on. On top of new and startling arrangements of mass comes the heavy overlay of the decoration. Pilasters jostle against windows; niches are squeezed between pilasters; gables crowd around chimneys. Flemish strapwork and cartouches are piled on with remorseless over-abundance. The central feature bears no relation, in form or treatment, to the rest of the house.

These weaknesses are perhaps partly due to Smythson's own inexperience; his position was more independent than it had been at Longleat, and the excitement may have gone to his head. But they are probably more the result of the character of Francis Willoughby. He had greater intellectual pretensions than any of Smythson's other patrons, and there is certainly something pretentious about Wollaton's display of the latest ornamental fashions. More than that, he must surely have had a streak of megalomania. Lust for power and an admiration of ruthlessness were undoubted strands in the Elizabethan character. The examples range from Marlowe, with his glorification of Tamburlane, 'the scourge of God', to Spenser's friend, Gabriel Harvey, that pathetically crabbed and ineffective don, sitting in his study dreaming of himself as Alexander, Caesar Borgia, or Machiavelli. There is a good deal of Harvey about Francis Willoughby. But unlike Harvey, he had money: even if his personal life was a fiasco he could afford to build a house that would stare down the county. There, up in the clouds in his great desolate prospect-room, he could think that he was the superman or even God himself.

Among Willoughby's books[31] was a religious tract which has been carefully gone through, page by page, and the name of the pope scratched out wherever it occurred. He was not a balanced man, nor did he build a balanced house. Wollaton has something of the quality of nightmare. For many it must have been an experience unforgettable but awful to climb the long avenue up the hill, to round the corner, and to stagger back – amazed and excited, yes, but also appalled, by the basilisk glare, the crash and glitter, of that fantastic façade.

108

60. A design by Robert Smythson, probably for the hall screen at Worksop.

3
Worksop & Related Houses

SOME time in the 1580s, while Wollaton was still in building, the Earl of Shrewsbury started to remodel and enlarge a hunting lodge at Worksop, at the other end of Nottinghamshire. The result, although much less elaborate than Wollaton, was even bigger, just as extraordinary, and in some ways perhaps more successful.

The house descended to the Dukes of Norfolk and was burnt down in 1761; it survives for us only in a plan of the ground floor among the Smythson drawings (III/17 and Plate 63), one or two inadequate eighteenth-century descriptions, and in the views of Hall (Plate 62), Buck (Plate 61) and Couse, none of them entirely satisfactory.[1] It filled a ground space not so very large: basically an attenuated rectangle 180 feet by 40 feet. The accommodation necessary for a great nobleman and his household was obtained by building up from this narrow base to an extravagant height. The main parapet must have been some 80 or 90 feet above the ground, rising, that is, not only far higher than the main block at Wollaton but almost as high as the prospect-room; and above the parapet domed lanterns rose higher still. The main body of the house was only three storeys high, but at the sides it was, in places, of six storeys, for there were a number of mezzanine floors. This great block, lit by huge areas of windows of many lights, was absolutely unadorned; but it was transformed from a barracks to a building of surprising groupings and silhouettes by the addition of square projecting bays, four in the centres of the long and short elevations (two crowned with round domed turrets of continuous glass), and four set off from the four corners of the main block. The effect of this lantern and skyscraper of a house, with the rise and fall, the advance and recess of its towers and bays, set as it was at the top of a considerable slope, must have been overwhelmingly dramatic.

Inside, the ground floor contained the hall, kitchen and offices. The hall was 24 feet high, and there was a mezzanine floor over the rooms to the west of it. The main staircase was off the hall-dais, and led up to the great chamber on the first floor, immediately above the hall and of the same dimensions. The second floor, higher than the other two, was almost entirely filled by the long gallery: 212 feet long and at its narrowest 33 feet wide, enlarged and variegated by a succession of projecting bays, and encircled on three sides by a continuous range of enormous windows. The illustrations of the exterior suggest that the main part of the gallery had an arched plaster ceiling, but that over the bays the ceiling was flat, to allow for a storey of low attic rooms. These probably consisted of lodgings, and more and better lodgings must have been fitted in on the first floor, and in the lower mezzanines. The two round rooms in the roof-top lanterns were presumably used as prospect-rooms, as their walls were entirely of glass.[2]

George Talbot, sixth Earl of Shrewsbury, the builder of Worksop, was head of an old and illustrious family and perhaps both the richest and the most powerful man in the northern half of England.[3] He held the great office of Earl Marshal of England; his family were renowned for their loyalty to the Crown

61. (top) Worksop Manor, Nottinghamshire (completed 1586). The south front, from an early eighteenth-century drawing by Samuel Buck.
62. (centre) Worksop Manor, from a drawing by Robert Hall engraved in Thoroton's Nottinghamshire (1677).
63. (bottom) A survey plan of Worksop by John Smythson (III/17).

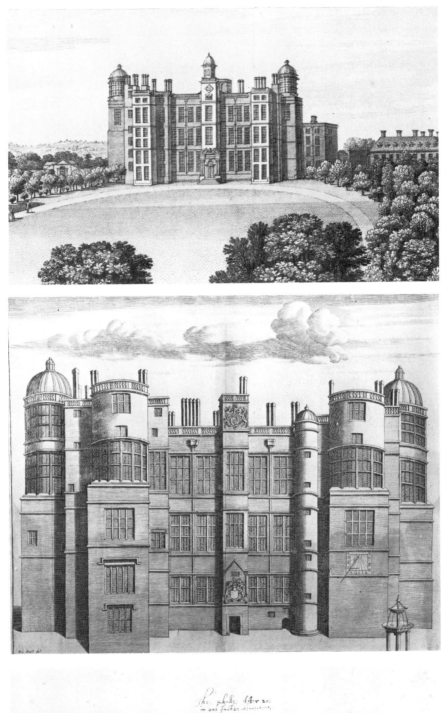

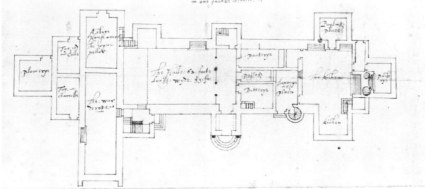

and from 1569 to 1584 he was in the honourable but burdensome position of host and gaoler to Mary, Queen of Scots. He was an honest, industrious and conscientious man, but by nature a pessimist and a worrier. A much more formidable figure was his wife, the famous Bess of Hardwick,[4] one of the most remarkable of Elizabethan women, but far from comfortable to live with. Lodge's description of her has not been bettered: 'A woman of masculine understanding and conduct, proud, furious, selfish, and unfeeling, she was a builder, a buyer and seller of estates, a moneylender, a farmer, and a merchant of lead, coals, and timber; when disengaged from these employments she intrigued alternately with Elizabeth and Mary, always to the prejudice and terror of her husband.'[5]

Bess's passion for building has become a legend. Worksop had such striking resemblances to her other houses, both earlier and later, that it is hard to believe she did not provide the initial impulse to remodel it. But her relations with her husband had been showing signs of strain since the late 1570s, and in 1583 he excluded her from his houses and did his best to cut off her income. Although she may have been concerned in the original plans for the house, she can have had nothing to do with any but the early stages of the actual building operations. In the inscription on her tomb she is described as 'aedificatrix' of Chatsworth, Hardwick and Owlcotes, but no such claim is made for Worksop.

Why Worksop was built at all presents something of a problem. In 1580 Shrewsbury had complained bitterly, in letters to Burghley, of the expense he was put to in maintaining the Queen of Scots and her household. Early in 1581 Queen Elizabeth reduced the allowance allowed him for her upkeep, and his personal expenses must have increased proportionately. His financial groans were probably louder than they need have been; but he undoubtedly left a very embarrassed estate when he died. Yet at the same time as his letters suggested imminent financial ruin, he started to build a house on the scale of a palace.

It was not as though he were short of living accommodation. The castles of Tutbury, Pontefract and Sheffield; the manor-house of Sheffield, with, across the park, a more intimate and newly-built lodge at Handsworth; the great Derbyshire manor at South Wingfield, still surviving today as a magnificent ruin; the converted monastery buildings at Rufford Abbey; the house by the baths at Buxton, built by Shrewsbury partly for himself, partly as a hostel for visitors who came to take the waters; commodious hunting lodges at Tutbury and Worksop itself; these were the more important, but not the only, Talbot residences. In addition, Shrewsbury had a life interest in his wife's great house at Chatsworth, which had come to her through her second marriage, to Sir William Cavendish, and where they frequently resided.

But the Elizabethan age was above all competitive. Shrewsbury was the greatest man in the North Midlands; and Sheffield Manor. Wingfield and Chatsworth gave him architectural as well as social supremacy. But in the early 1580s Wollaton started to rise on a site that was visible for miles around; though not as big as Shrewsbury's bigger houses, it was far more up-to-date, striking and original. At the same time Chatsworth, owing to increasing difficulties with his wife, became a source of resentment rather than pride. The most convincing explanation for Worksop is that it was remodelled as an answer to Wollaton, and an alternative to Chatsworth.

Sheer bulk and height made Chatsworth impressive, but in most respects it was not a very original or imaginative building, and by the 1580s it was already a little old-fashioned. Wollaton must have immediately taken its place as the most talked-of house in that part of England. Flashing and glittering on its bare hill-top, it dramatically introduced the concept of the lantern-house to the north Midlands. But Worksop was even more dazzling, more enormous, and more exciting than Wollaton. The prospect-room at Wollaton was a novel and daring conceit, but as a room it was impractical and inaccessible; the long gallery at Worksop was slung up as high, and at the same time had adequate access and a recognisable use. It soon became, in fact, famous all over England. In 1590 Robert Cecil wrote to Lord Talbot, in his smoothly jocular way: 'It were a much more ease for a man's Coach or horses to visitt you at Chelsea with a fayre payre of oares from London than to come through yor craggy stoney lanes where in seeking for ye fayrest gallery in England a man shall meet never a cupp of good drink.'[6] And in 1607 George Chaworth, in a description to the then Earl of Shrewsbury of the enormous house which Lord Dunbar was building near Berwick, ended: 'Only, therefore, I will say what in pticular I heard (to use their own phrase) one of them creak, that Worsopp gallerye was but a garrat in respect of the gallerye that woold there be.'[7]

No building accounts survive for Worksop and only a very few letters. Of the four relevant ones three are from one Richard Torre to the Earl of Shrewsbury. Beside naming some of the craftsmen employed on the house they give interesting details of the garden and waterworks.

The first is dated 19 April 1585: 'All your lords thyngs at worsoppe and yor lo: lodgyng at Worsop lodge are well . . . for I do applye those workemen there as well as I can and so by gods grace I wyll do untyll [I see] yor honour home the wch I hope in god wylbe [soon] for I never longed so sore to see yor Lo: as I do now . . . I did recyve from London ye vith of apryll last past xxx orange branches wch where sent in a shippe of hull called emanuell one george baldwyn did write unto me and I went presentlye for them and they where all dead sawing II yet I have put them all in ye garden at Worsoppe. . . . Your lords plumers done make pipes for ye water worcks I praye god y^t ye same worckes do come to good effect in ye ende for I do lyke yll of ye [expense?] . . .'[8]

On 28 May he wrote: 'Ye waterman wch he shypped ys come home alredy this daye for your Lo: waterworks but I can gett no leade yet to make ye pypes of untyll the next week. I would have your lo: to appoynte Robynson to bye xii cradels of glass for else yor lo: must wante glasse at lodge gylles greves hath almost sett uppe yor honors chmy pase in ye gallerye but I myslike of ye storye so y^t I wylnot paye hym all hys mony untyll hyt be hamended burgow and hys folckes are workyng abowte ye wat^{r}works.'[9]

And on 17 June: 'All yr ho: thyngs at Worsoppe are well. John Longly wyll finysse the tarres upon ye tipes of the howse ye next weeke the plasterers are in fynyshyng of ye chymny with lyme and heare I think y^t Robert Stotte and hyss folke wyll finysse the sealyng in ye gallery this saturday.'[10]

Finally in a letter from William Deckenson, bailiff, to the Earl of Shrewsbury, dated 29 September 1586, one entry in a list of expenses probably refers to Worksop: 'Ye chardge at ye new buyldinges at yr manor ... Carpenters and Laborers xiii$_{li}$ ... and to Langley y^r·mason xx$_{li}$ and to deckenson the slater iii$_{li}$ v$_s$ iiii$_d$.'[11]

Giles Greves's chimney-piece in the gallery was seen by Vertue when he visited the house with Lord Oxford in 1727. It was dated 'Fr XXVII. Ano. Dni 1585' and decorated with a bas-relief – no doubt the 'storye' which Torre misliked – of 'a Man with a Sword and a woman giving a child to drink with Verses underneath'.[12]

If the gallery was being fitted up and the parapet built in the summer of 1585, building work must have been started some years before. But the speed of the operation would undoubtedly have been increased by the fact that the new house incorporated an older building, described by Leland in his *Itinerary* of 1547 as 'the fair lodge in Wyrksoppe Park, not yet finished. This Erle of Shrewsbury's father was about to have finished hit, as apperith by much hewyd stone lying there.'[13] This explains the minor oddities and irregularities of Worksop: the immensely thick walls of the hall and its assymetric oriel, the round staircase turret and the projecting wing on the main front. In Hall's view of Worksop (Plate 62) the first two floors of this wing are shown lit by little hood-moulded windows, a clear relic of Leland's Lodge.

Another complication is that Mary, Queen of Scots, was at Worksop in June and September 1583.[14] For reasons both of security and convenience it seems unlikely that she would have been allowed to go there while building work on as grand a scale was in progress; on the other hand it is also unlikely (although not impossible) that a remodelling on the scale of the house that finally emerged could have taken place within two or three years. The explanation may be that the completion of Leland's unfinished lodge was carried out in two stages: the first, involving the ground and first floor only before 1583; the second between late 1583 and 1586, involving the gallery floor and the addition of the projecting bays. The second stage would have turned a relatively unassuming house into a very grand one, and need not necessarily have been envisaged at the time of the first; the first need not necessarily have involved Smythson.

Hall's engraving suggests that the final result, however splendidly dramatic in its general effect, had a somewhat makeshift element, the result of the incorporation of the older building, and possibly the different stages in which it was

114

remodelled. Money had been saved and speed gained at the expense of consistency; but both speed and saving would have appealed to Shrewsbury in his circumstances at the time.

There was probably no one in the Midlands capable of producing a design which would outshine Wollaton except its creator, Robert Smythson, and there is little doubt that Shrewsbury got the design of Worksop from him. The plan of the house among the Smythson drawings (Plate 63) is not Robert's: it is a survey plan by his son John. But Robert certainly made the design for a hall-screen for Worksop (1/26 and Col. Plate X), also at the R.I.B.A. This can never have been executed, for it is both wider and higher than the hall as described in the eighteenth century and shown on John Smythson's plan (37 by 28½ feet, as opposed to 33 by 24 feet). But a similar design for a section of a screen (II/14 and Plate 60) which shows a height of 22 feet and, if extended in the logical way, a width of not more than 34 feet, is very probably the design for the Worksop screen as executed. This suggests that Shrewsbury considered rebuilding the house entirely on a wider ground plan, but gave the project up, no doubt because of the expense. Both designs are impressively competent for their date; they resemble the screen at Wollaton, but consist of two tiers of arches instead of one, and lack (not to their disadvantage) Wollaton's elaborate de Vriesian embellishments.

The fact that Robert Smythson designed a screen for Lord Shrewsbury at Worksop makes it probable that the design for remodelling the house also came from him. In view of the plan and appearance of Worksop, the probability becomes something near a certainty. For it is an unmistakable development of the theme of Longleat. 'Roughly', as Sir John Summerson says, 'it was as if Longleat had been compressed into one of its shorter sides and then built upwards half as high again.'[15] Rectangular bay windows projected at regular intervals from the long thin block of Worksop, just as they project from the bigger, courtyarded block of Longleat. But the Worksop bay windows were bolder, bigger and plainer than those at Longleat, and four of them were carried up above parapet level in the form of turrets and lanterns. This roof-top furniture probably derived from the banqueting-houses on the roof at Longleat. But while at Longleat the house and its skyline, partly owing to the complication of its building history, bear little relation to each other, at Worksop the two were fused into a single dramatic whole.

THE HIGH HOUSE IN THE MIDLANDS

Longleat and Wollaton were not the only prototypes for Worksop. Houses of considerable height, compact plan, and turreted outline were no novelty in the Midlands, and had in fact probably been introduced into those parts by the Shrewsburys. Elizabethan Chatsworth (Plate 64), unlike Wollaton and Worksop,

was built round a courtyard; but this was a relatively small one, and the ranges around it were of consistent and considerable height so that the dominant impression must have been of a high and compact mass. The main façade had four towers, one at either end and two in the centre, the latter forming a gatehouse.

> *The noble front of the whole edifice*
> *In a surprising height is seen to rise*

wrote Charles Cotton in his *Wonders of the Peak* of 1681. Knyff's drawing of 1699 shows the Elizabethan west or entrance front still existing alongside Talman's new south front, with the corner turret of the former reaching as high as the balustrade of the latter, that is nearly 74 feet from the ground; the central gatehouse seems to have been a little higher, the intervening portions a little lower. Old Chatsworth was, in fact, the first expression of a passion for high buildings that stayed with Bess of Hardwick throughout her life.[16]

The dimensions of the great seventeenth-century block at Chatsworth are conditioned by that of Bess's building; as a result it is considerably higher than other great houses of its date, and a great deal higher than the average Palladian mansion of the eighteenth century. Not only its general mass, but the arrangement of its rooms, followed remarkably closely what existed before; so that the ghost of the Elizabethan house is still there, even if no visible details meet the eye. One of the most curious features, seen in a late seventeenth century context, of

116

64. A needle-work view of old Chatsworth (*c.* 1551–75).

the new Chatsworth is its great range of state rooms skied up on the second floor along the south front. These in fact replace an equivalent suite of Elizabethan rooms approached, in the usual Elizabethan way (as the present state rooms still are), by a staircase off the end of the great hall. The present State Dining Room occupies the position of the Elizabethan great chamber; the latter opened into 'the high gallery', running along the south front where the remaining sequence of seventeenth-century state rooms now is. Unfortunately no picture of the Elizabethan south and east fronts at Chatsworth survive. But in the needlework view of the west, entrance, front (now at Hardwick) the end of the gallery can be seen pushing into the entrance front in the form of a large ten-light window, equivalent to two storeys of smaller windows in the centre (Plate 64).

In the seventeenth-century house the use of a giant order cannot altogether conceal the oddity of a classical house that has its largest windows on the top floor. Even in an Elizabethan context skied state rooms are out of the ordinary; the conventional position would have been on the first floor. Second-floor state rooms clearly appealed to Bess, for the same type of plan reappears on level sites at her later buildings at Worksop (if indeed she was concerned with it) and Hardwick Old and New Halls.

There is no sure precedent for this individual, and very important, feature of Chatsworth, although there may have been a similar arrangement at Richmond Palace.[17] Certainly, the high, compact towered mass of Chatsworth clearly derives, in its general format, from great late Gothic buildings of the Richmond Palace type. The exact dating of Bess's work can only be surmised. A 'platt' had been made for her and her first husband, Sir William Cavendish, by a certain Roger Worthe in 1551. It is likely, however, that as in the case of Burghley, Theobalds and Longleat, what had been begun on a relatively modest scale in the 1550s was steadily enlarged and remodelled as the owners grew in prosperity during Elizabeth's reign. The Chatsworth accounts are missing between 1560 and 1576; when they start up again, in 1576, elaborate interior decoration is being carried out, suggesting the last stage of a grand-scale remodelling of the house, undertaken as a result of Bess's marriage to the Earl of Shrewsbury in 1568. It is possible that this involved adding an extra floor or floors to an existing house, as at Worksop. In any case the final form of the house had certainly been evolved well before Robert Smythson appeared in the Midlands in 1580.

Of Lord Shrewsbury's house at Buxton, which was rebuilt in the seventeenth century, no adequate illustrations are known to survive; this is a pity, for it seems to have been an interesting building, a smaller and more compact Chatsworth. Cotton describes it, in perhaps over-eulogistic terms, as a 'Pallace' and

> *A mansion proud enough for Saxon Kings*
> *But by a lady built, who Rich and Wise*
> *Not only Houses rais'd but Families*

though he goes on to say:

> *But, either through the fault of th' Architect*
> *The Workman's ignorance, knavery or neglect*
> *Or through the searching nature of the air*

it had become unsafe and ruinous, and had recently had to be rebuilt. A seventeenth-century survey of Buxton shows, on a tiny scale, a high and symmetrical façade with three towers, but apparently no courtyard.[18] Dr Jones, in his treatise on Buxton Waters (1572), described it as 'a very goodly house, four square, four stories hye, so well compacte with houses of office beneath and above and round about, with a great chambre and other goodly lodgings to the number of 30; that it is and will be a bewty to behold'.[19]

118

65. Queen Mary's Tower, Sheffield Manor (1572).

66. Thorpe Salvin, Yorkshire (before 1582).

Two smaller buildings are also evidence of a Shrewsbury fondness for towers. One is in the building now known as Queen Mary's Tower, adjoining the scanty remains of Sheffield Manor (Plate 65). Traditionally this was built for the safe-keeping of Mary, Queen of Scots, and there is good evidence for dating it to 1574.[20] It has three storeys, each containing two rooms; a stairs at one corner rises above the rest of the building in the form of a turret opening on to the leads, from which a superb view can be enjoyed. A similar but rather more decorative building is the Hunting Tower at Chatsworth (Col. Pl. VII), on the crest of the hill above the house. In Elizabethan days it was known as the Stand and was used to watch hunting from, and possibly also as a base from which to shoot at the deer. It is a square tower, four storeys high, with circular turrets at each corner: these rise above the parapet level to provide access on to the roof, and three minute but delightful circular rooms, two of which retain very decorative plasterwork. The Hunting Tower cannot be dated exactly, but it is most likely to date from the early 1580s, in which case Smythson may have been involved with it.[21] The detailing of the turrets, with their gazebo upper storeys, is reminiscent in miniature of the gazebo towers at Worksop.

A house, or rather the ruin of a house, at Thorpe Salvin, near Sheffield, probably gives as good an idea as can be gained today of the effect of Buxton and (on a much larger scale) old Chatsworth, for its design was almost certainly influenced by theirs. The gatehouse and entrance façade are all that survive today, and the latter is gradually crumbling: but even so, as seen from the middle of the little village, it remains an impressive silhouette (Plate 66). Its design is simple and effective: three storeys high, round towers at the corners, a central rectangular

119

porch and, between the porch and each tower, three pairs of windows divided by a massive and prominent chimney-stack, which rises higher than the porch and towers. Enough of the foundations of the remaining outer walls survive to show that the house was in plan a rectangle, with a round tower at each angle: the dimensions suggest there was a small internal courtyard. The porch led into a screens passage with kitchen to the left and a one-storey hall to the right; the dais end of the hall opened into a newel staircase in one of the towers. The largest windows are on the top floor, suggesting that there may have been a skied gallery and great chamber, as at Chatsworth. Thorpe Salvin is said to have been built by Hercy Sandford ('whose ancestors', according to his epitaph in the church, 'came from Westmorland in 1420'); he died in 1582, and the house probably dates from the 1570s.[22]

In contrast to Wollaton, the exterior detail of Chatsworth, Thorpe Salvin, and probably of Buxton, was very plain. There was a certain amount of Renaissance detail, especially on the gatehouse at Chatsworth; but on the whole the houses obtained their effect by means of their height, symmetry, towers and skyline. Worksop was equally plain, and in this respect marks a turning-point in Smythson's work: he never again used the elaborate classical ordinance of Wollaton and Longleat.

In many ways, in fact, Worksop only accentuated an existing North Midland tradition. But what distinguished it from Chatsworth and Thorpe Salvin was its great expanse of window and the fact that its dominant features were towers or bay windows set away from the corners of the main building. The latter difference was by no means negligible, for the combination of two projecting bays with the corner angle jutting out between them resulted (as at Longleat, but on a bolder scale) in a drama of movement of planes of masonry advancing and falling back, lacking in Chatsworth and Thorpe Salvin. And the very prominent (and successful) use of chimney-stacks at Thorpe Salvin is something seldom, if ever, found in a Smythson building; his tendency was always to put the chimney-places and flues in the internal partition walls, leaving the outer walls free for a maximum display of glass. Thorpe Salvin and Chatsworth were not glass-houses, at any rate to anything like the same extent as Wollaton and Worksop.

HOUSES IN THE WORKSOP CIRCLE

Concurrently with Worksop and Wollaton two other houses were being built, one in Derbyshire and one in Yorkshire, which were clearly related to them, though considerably smaller in size. These houses are twins, a unique case in Elizabethan architecture. Barlborough Hall, in Derbyshire (Plates 67 and 69), is dated 1583 on the porch and 1584 on a fireplace; at Heath Old Hall (Plate 68) the fireplace in the great chamber is said to have been dated 1585. Barlborough survives, but Heath Old Hall was largely demolished in 1961 after fifteen years

120

67. (top) Barlborough Hall, Derbyshire (1583–4). A detail of the entrance front.

68. (bottom) Heath Old Hall, Yorkshire (c. 1585). The entrance front.

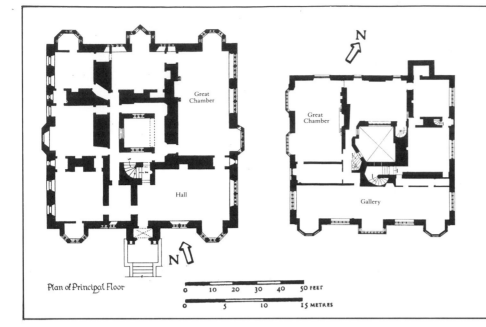

Figs. 3, 4. Ground-floor plan of Barlborough Hall and (right) first-floor plan Heath Old Hall.

Plan of Principal Floor

of neglect. Both houses are (Figs. 3 and 4) basically square in plan, built up on high basements around very small courtyards; both are enlivened, first by projecting porches with long flights of steps, and second by bold five-sided bay windows, set just off the corners of the main fronts (and at Barlborough, the rear façade as well), and rising above the roof-line in the form of turrets. Barlborough has in addition a newel staircase lit by an octagonal lantern which added a fifth tower to its skyline.

There is nothing among the Smythson drawings which can be directly connected with either of these houses, nor is there any other documentary evidence that Smythson had a hand in them. But in the case, at any rate, of Barlborough, there can be little doubt that he supplied plans. For Francis Rodes, who built the house, was a successful lawyer who probably owed his success to the patronage of the Shrewsbury family.[23] In recognition of this he displayed the Shrewsbury arms on the main front at Barlborough, above his own shield and below the arms of the Queen.

The imposing pedigree of the Rodes family printed in genealogies and county histories tends to obscure the fact that Francis Rodes was a largely self-made man, sprung from a line of, at best, very small gentry living at Staveley Woodthorpe in Derbyshire. But his career in the law, ending in a Judgeship of the Common Pleas in 1585, made him a large fortune, and he used it to buy land on a considerable scale, in Derbyshire, Nottinghamshire and South Yorkshire. His mother was a Hewett of Wales, the Lord Mayor was his uncle, and the Hewetts of Shireoaks were his cousins. The Hewetts and Rodeses were both, in fact, ambitious new local families whom Lord Shrewsbury had the good sense to assist and keep on good terms with, no doubt to their mutual advantage.[24]

Francis Rodes married Elizabeth Sandford, the sister of Hercy Sandford of Thorpe Salvin, and in their compactness, height and towered silhouette there is

122

a certain similarity between the two houses. But Barlborough has other features of an undeniably Smythsonian origin. The very high basement, containing the kitchen and offices, is clearly related to the similar basement at Wollaton. The chimney-stacks, unlike Thorpe Salvin, are all in the internal walls, leaving the outer façades free for an imposing display of windows. The four turrets are set away from the corners of the house like the towers at Hardwick and Worksop; like them, they are a development of the bay windows at Longleat.

Barlborough has the remarkable feature of a corridor running, on each storey, round the four sides of the internal courtyard. In this it was well in advance of almost all Elizabethan houses. One of the exceptions was Chatsworth, which had corridors running along the north and south sides of its courtyard, at ground and first floor level.[25] But an arrangement even closer to that at Barlborough had been devised half a century or so earlier, at Hengrave Hall. It was built about 1525-38, and had corridors round three sides of a courtyard considerably larger than that at Barlborough.[26] In 1582 Charles Cavendish, Bess of Hardwick's second son, married Margaret, the elder daughter and heiress of Sir Thomas Kytson of Hengrave.[27] According to the marriage settlement Hengrave and most of the Kytson property was ultimately to come to them and their issue. In fact it never did, because Margaret Kytson died in childbirth the year after the marriage. But the years in which Barlborough must have been started were also the years of the short connection between the Kytsons of Hengrave and the Shrewsbury-Cavendish circle in which Francis Rodes moved. It is perhaps not coincidence that the house which Robert Smythson designed for Charles Cavendish himself at Slingsby, probably in the 1590s (see page 179) had a corridor system reminiscent of that at Barlborough and Hengrave, though less complete.

In other respects, the plan of Barlborough is also an unusual one.[28] While the outside walls are of normal thickness and the courtyard walls relatively thin, the

123

69. A drawing by S. H. Grimm of the north front at Barlborough.

interior walls are immensely massive, though very badly built, of every kind of rubble and rubbish. In addition to the central circulation provided by the corridors, a series of doors just within the outside walls provide nearly complete perimeter circulation round the house. Owing to the thickness of the cross walls these doors are double with a little lobby or closet between them, hollowed out of the thickness of the wall and each lit by a small single-light window. There is nothing similar to this arrangement in other Elizabethan houses or in any of the Smythson plans.

The only original staircase to survive is at what would have been (before seventeenth-century alterations) the screens end of the hall, and is a spacious newel staircase (altered in its lower flights), rising from the basement to the first floor and lit, elegantly and conveniently, by the central lantern. Barlborough is unusual in having its great chamber on the same floor as the hall, across a lobby from the dais end of the hall. The original function of this room (now a chapel) is shown by an inventory of 1639,[29] and by its surviving decoration: stone Doric

124

70. The Jezebel chimney-piece, formerly in the great chamber at Heath Old Hall.

pilasters on the walls and a splendid two-tier chimney-piece. The inventory shows that the house had no long gallery and only one living-room beside the hall and great chamber: the 'small dining chamber' off the great chamber on the north front. A final feature worth remarking on at Barlborough is the bay window in the centre of the north front. In plan this is a combination of a triangle and a rectangle, a device clearly inspired by complex early Tudor windows such as appear in Henry VII's Tower at Windsor, at Thornbury Castle and at Hengrave.[30]

Heath Old Hall was further from Smythson's headquarters at Wollaton and no link is traceable between its builder, John Kaye, and Lord Shrewsbury or Sir Francis Willoughby. So it seems likely that Barlborough was the original and Heath the copy, though the difference in time between them appears to have been exceedingly small. The planning of Heath was more conventional: there was a great chamber and long gallery on the floor above the hall, and no corridor or closet system comparable to Barlborough's, though, as at Barlborough, there was a newel staircase leading off the screens passage of the hall.[31]

At Heath and Barlborough, as is usually the case with Smythson and indeed with every other Elizabethan surveyor, it is dangerous to be dogmatic in allotting responsibility for the detail. There is nothing reminiscent of Smythson's known work in the curious parapets to be found at both houses. The portrait medallions on the façades at Barlborough (of unusually good quality) are a common enough Elizabethan feature, which had appeared on the great gatehouse at Chatsworth well before Smythson used them at Wollaton. On the other hand the entrance portal at Barlborough and the superb Jezebel fireplace at Heath (Plate 70) have a straightforward and competent classical character, scarcely touched with Flemish influence, which is certainly reminiscent of the portal at Wardour and the screen design for Worksop. But the archway inside the Barlborough portal has a Tudor Gothic profile and mouldings quite out of keeping with its surroundings, though similar to other internal doorways throughout the house. This suggests that Smythson may have supplied a drawing for the surround, and a few other features, but that most of the details were left to the executive mason.

Barlborough is in some ways a disappointing house, a near miss, exciting, odd and romantic when one first sees its turreted façade high and grey at the end of the avenue, but failing to live up to expectations as one comes to know it better. Later alterations have impaired rather than enriched its character, and unlike most Smythson houses, its situation is not an especially good one. Heath Old Hall was more dramatic and more haunting, on a wooded hill above a sweep of the river; in its last years the decay and ruination of the house, the industrial landscape, the huge cooling-towers next door, gave it a tremendous poignancy.

A small but unusual and romantic house which may owe something to Smythson is North Lees Hall, near Hathersage, a few miles from Chatsworth (Plate 71).[32] This stands in a beautiful and secluded position, on the edge of the moors and at the top of a little valley. It is in the form of a simple rectangular

tower, with a staircase turret very slightly projecting at one angle. The front half of the house contains three large rooms, one above the other; in the rear are the stairs, and four storeys of lower rooms, one room and one closet to each floor. The stairs rise in a turret above the rest of the house, and open on to the leads. There is a basement which perhaps only contained cellars, though if so it is hard to say where the kitchen was, unless the lower and later wing now adjoining the tower is a replacement of something older. The plasterwork in the big ground-floor room is dated 1594.

If the fabric of the house was of the same date, its builder would have been William Jessop, who owned and occupied North Lees in the 1590s. Jessop's father had lived at Worksop; Richard Cotes, the keeper of Worksop Park, was a trustee of his will, and was probably the father of an earlier husband of William's wife. This Worksop connection suggests Smythson; the North Lees arrangement of three high and four lower storeys under the same roof is certainly reminiscent of, and the plan is worth comparing to, a somewhat similar Smythson plan for a

126

71. North Lees Hall, Derbyshire (1596).
VII. (facing page) The Hunting Tower, Chatsworth, Derbyshire.
VIII. (following page) Barlborough Hall, Derbyshire. The entrance front.

A Platte
at :

For A Screene
worsope :

To bee Builte
manner :

A Screen at Worsop Manner by Smithson

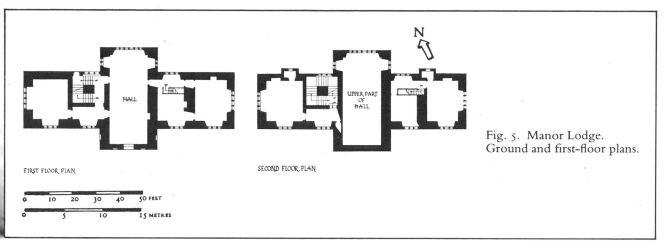

FIRST FLOOR PLAN

SECOND FLOOR PLAN

N

0 10 20 30 40 50 FEET
0 5 10 15 METRES

HALL

UPPER PART OF HALL

Fig. 5. Manor Lodge.
Ground and first-floor plans.

small tower-house of three storeys and a basement (II/22). If by Smythson, this little building would be an interesting link between earlier Midland buildings of the type of Queen Mary's Tower at Sheffield and the far more ambitious but in some respects similar Keep or Little Castle at Bolsover.

All traces of the great house at Worksop have long ago disappeared, but half a mile or so away from its site a smaller Shrewsbury building of considerable interest survives. This is the house called, in the seventeenth and eighteenth centuries, Worksop Lodge, and known today as Manor Lodge (Plates 72, 73, and Col. Plate IX): a strange lost house, in one of those pockets of Nottinghamshire farm-land that seem all the remoter for the collieries and industrial housing that now hem them in.

The plan of Manor Lodge (Fig. 5) is an unusual one. It is shaped like a cross, with a short but wide cross-bar and long and rather thin wings to either side. The wings contain five storeys of fairly low rooms, and attics in the gables. The cross-bar was once largely filled with two enormous rooms, running right across the house, the lower corresponding to the first and second floors in the wings, the upper to the third and fourth. Half of the lower room has been partitioned off; the upper room is still undivided, but has lost nearly all its original decoration. The enormous windows that lit either end of these rooms can be clearly seen from the outside, although many of the lights have been blocked. There can be little doubt that the lower room was the hall, and the room above the great chamber; and that the main entrance originally led by way of a flight of steps into the hall on the first floor, the ground floor containing the kitchen, cellar and offices. But in the eighteenth century the main entrance was transferred to ground level, and the old hall door replaced by a round-headed eighteenth-century window. The original position of the hall is a remarkable and unusual one, and undeniably reminiscent of, though slightly different from, that of the halls at Old and New Hardwick, which will be discussed in Chapter IV.

There is a main staircase in the west wing, and a subsidiary staircase in the east wing; the latter is a later replacement, but the main staircase is the original one, with flights of wooden steps rising round a rectangular central newel of beautifully dressed ashlar. This newel has been broken off at the top, and the existing

131

IX. (preceding page) Manor Lodge, Worksop, Derbyshire. A view of the rear façade.

X. (facing page) Design by Robert Smythson for (top) the façade of an unidentified house and the hall screen at Worksop Manor, Nottinghamshire.

gabled roof has every appearance of being later than the main structure. According to J. Holland's *History of Worksop* (1826) the lodge was 'said to be curtailed of two stories of its original elevation'. This may be an exaggeration, but the evidence suggests that the lodge had at any rate one extra storey, perhaps containing a gallery: it is very possible that it originally ended in a balustrade and a flat roof, as at Worksop Manor. A curious feature are two what appear to be chimney-stacks on the rear elevation: these are corbelled out at first-floor level and in fact contain a series of small closets, each lit by a single-light window: the flues run up the walls to either side and only come into the stacks at the fourth floor. The detail of windows, doors and fireplaces throughout is nearly all of the plainest, with simple unmoulded chamfers: but the house is admirably built. Its plan, though unusual, is a logical one, a simple and straightforward way of combining two very large and a number of smaller rooms beneath one roof. Its analogies with Worksop Manor and other Smythson buildings, and the fact that it was built by the Shrewsbury family, suggest that Robert Smythson provided the plans, though it is admittedly unlike his documented works in its complete absence of both towers and bay windows.

The first certain mention of it that has come to light is in the survey of Worksop made by John Harrison in 1636. After describing the Manor he continues: 'about halfe a mile from the said Mansion house is another house fairely built of stone and well contrived called the new Lodge, besides the old Lodge wherin the Keeper dwelleth'.[33]

72, 73. (right) Rear and front views of Manor Lodge, Worksop (*c.* 1594–5).

It can probably be identified with 'Mr Portyngton's newe lodge in worsopp' which Richard Torre described as nearing completion in August 1595.[34] This was clearly a substantial building, since thirty tons of plaster and half a ton of iron 'for wyndoe barres' was needed to complete it. It was almost certainly the same as an unlocated 'lodge' where Richard Mason, apparently a stone-mason, was in charge and asking the Earl for money in March of the same year.[35] Mr Portyngton must have been Roger Portington, of Barnby-on-the-Don, near Doncaster, who makes occasional appearances in Talbot and related papers of the time.[36] What exactly his role was at this Lodge remains obscure, as it was clearly being built on the land and at the expense of Gilbert Talbot, seventh Earl of Shrewsbury. It is possible that Robert Smythson's old associate, the mason John Hills, was connected with its early stages, for he died at Worksop in October 1592, leaving Robert Smythson as his executor.[37]

In its original state, with an extra storey or two storeys, it must have been an impressive building; it is high enough, and impressive enough, today: the plain detailing and rows of little windows give it a not unattractive gauntness, curiously prognostic of the multi-storey mills that were to be built in the same area in the late eighteenth and nineteenth centuries. Typologically it is an interesting and typical example of the lodge, to which some reference has already been made in Chapter II. In its relationship to the nearby big house it should be compared to Wothorpe Lodge, which Lord Exeter built a mile or two away from Burleigh to go to 'when his house of Burleigh was sweeping';[38] to the two lodges in the

park of Lord Salisbury's great house at Hatfield; and to the lodge at Handsworth[39] which Lord Shrewsbury himself built (probably in 1577) on the edge of the park of Sheffield Manor, and to which he ultimately retired to die. A literary equivalent is provided by the *Arcadia*. In this one finds King Basilius building himself a star-shaped lodge as a retreat from the cares of government; and at the end of a vista was the smaller lodge where his daughter lived 'so that the Lodge seemeth not unlike a fair Comete whose taile stretcheth itselfe to a starre of lesse greatnes'.[40] Both these houses, big and small, were called lodges. In a sense the big house at Worksop was also a lodge, even if an immensely inflated one; it was built around an older hunting-lodge, and its particular value, in the great conglomeration of Shrewsbury houses, was its position on the edge of Sherwood Forest. These considerations may have weighed in the choice of a compact non-courtyard plan, in spite of the grandeur of its scale.

A mile and a half from Manor Lodge, on a tree-surrounded rise in a loop of the River Ryton, is the mutilated fragment of a house rather larger than Manor Lodge, but similar in many respects. This is at Shireoaks (Plate 74), a village

134

74, 75. (right) Front and rear views of Shireoaks Hall, Nottinghamshire.

better known today for its colliery. It is a moving experience, in the lonely fields, under the shadow of the slag-heap and lifting-tower of the colliery and on the edge of the suburbs of Worksop, to go along a rutted country lane from one to other, and see Manor Lodge rising tall and ghostly above the trees or come across the shattered but noble façades of Shireoaks, hidden away among ponds and canals. The two form an irresistible pair; but Shireoaks, although the influence of Manor Lodge is evident in it, probably dates from twenty years or so later.

The history of the house is a little obscure. The land originally belonged to the Thornhill family; then, according to Thoroton's *History of Nottinghamshire*, 'It came from Thornehill to Hewitt, a citizen of London: Sir Thomas Hewitt had it'[41] The 'citizen of London' was probably Thomas Hewett, who died in 1575 and left Shireoaks to his son Henry in his will.[42] Thomas was the younger brother of the famous Sir William Hewett. This Elizabethan tycoon was born in the village of Wales, next door to Shireoaks, went to London, made one of the biggest fortunes of the century as a cloth merchant, became Lord Mayor, and died in 1567. It was his daughter and only child who was rescued by her father's

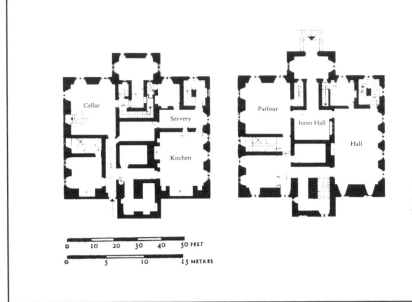

Fig. 6. Shireoaks Hall. A reconstruction of the ground and first-floor plans.

apprentice, Edward Osborne, when she fell off London Bridge into the Thames, married him, brought him her father's fortune, and became the ancestress of the Dukes of Leeds. Sir William was a good friend of the sixth Earl of Shrewsbury (who is said to have tried to arrange a marriage between Sir William's daughter and one of his sons) and left him a gold ring with his initials and the inscription 'Forget not me' in his will. One of his apprentices, incidentally, was Henry Bosvile, whose elder brother Geoffrey married Bess of Hardwick's sister, Jane.[43]

Many of his connections seem to have done well in the city, no doubt under his aegis. His brother Thomas was one of these; another was his namesake, Sir William Hewett of Killamarsh, a Derbyshire village a few miles away from Wales and Shireoaks. This Sir William made money in London, died in 1599, and was buried in St Paul's (Dugdale gives an engraving of his monument[44]). His exact relationship to the other Hewetts is obscure, but the links were tightened by the marriage between his daughter and Thomas's son Henry. It must have been Henry Hewett or his son Thomas who built the existing house at Shireoaks. There is no documentary evidence for its date; the proportions of the windows suggest that it was built a little later than Manor Lodge, perhaps after 1610. At the beginning of the 18th century Henry's grandson Sir Thomas Hewett, of Shireoaks, became Surveyor-General of the Woods under Queen Anne, and Surveyor-General of the Works under George I. He was a notable eccentric, of whom a great many curious stories are told.[45]

At some period, probably when the house belonged to the Surveyor-General, sash windows were inserted, the floor levels altered, and the interior remodelled. Later on a large portion of the house was taken down, it is said on the aftermath of a fire. The entire basement survives, however, and enough traces of the

136

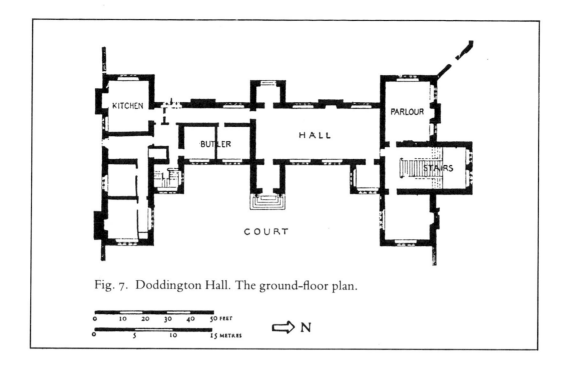

Fig. 7. Doddington Hall. The ground-floor plan.

KITCHEN
BUTLER
HALL
PARLOUR
STAIRS
COURT

| 0 | 10 | 20 | 30 | 40 | 50 FEET |
| 0 | | 5 | | 10 | 15 METRES |

N

original arrangement on ground and first floor to enable their arrangement to be established with reasonable accuracy.[46] A second floor must have existed, but has completely disappeared. The ground falls away to the north-east, so that at the back the basement becomes a full floor. Even today, with the top floor gone, the house rises dramatically high on this side (Plate 75), especially as it is now enclosed by a courtyard and two later pavilions, probably built by the Surveyor.

The plan resembles that of Manor Lodge in that it is cruciform, has no embellishments in the way of towers or bay-windows, and varies the floor levels in order to combine high and low rooms. But there the resemblance ends. At Shireoaks the proportions of the cross are different, and its short arm, instead of containing hall and great chamber, as at Manor Lodge, contained the main staircase at the back, a small entrance hall or vestibule and other rooms at the front, and lobbies or closets in the centre; the last can never have been adequately lighted except on the top floor, where there was probably a lantern. The main hall was to the right of this central spine, and the great chamber on the first floor to the left. The ceiling-level of the hall was higher than that of the other ground-floor rooms, and the great-chamber floor lower than that of the other first floor rooms; this arrangement allowed for a combination of high and low rooms on both floors. The main staircase has gone, except for a few traces, but a subsidiary staircase, of stone round a rectangular stone pier, survives on the high-chamber side of the house.

In its plan and section Shireoaks relates closely to the Little Castle at Bolsover, where building work started in 1612. The proportions of the windows at Shireoaks is also similar to that of the Little Castle windows; there are no many-lighted grids, as at Manor Lodge. It would be interesting to know which

137

came first, Shireoaks or Bolsover; in the lack of evidence all that one can say is that Shireoaks was probably built some time between about 1610 and 1620, and may have been designed by John Smythson rather than Robert.

Another house which it is most convenient to treat of here, though chronologically it perhaps should come in a later chapter, is Doddington Hall in Lincolnshire (Plate 77).[47] This was built between 1593, when the property was bought by Thomas Tailor, Registrar of Lincoln, and 1600, which was the date discovered marked on the lead of one of the cupolas. Tailor was a typical Elizabethan figure, a self-made man who, as a result of his administration of the huge estates of the Bishopric of Lincoln, amassed enough money to buy nearly 9,000 acres in various parts of the county. The house he built is clearly related to Worksop. The plan (Fig. 7) is a similar one; the house has no courtyard, there is a hall on the ground floor, a great chamber on the floor above it, and a long gallery filling almost the whole of the top floor above that. The house has a flat roof and a parapet, with no gables; three of the rectangular projections that give diversity to the façades are continued above parapet level in the form of little octagonal cupolas that derive from the roof-top gazebos at Worksop. The parapet was originally decorated with semi-circular lunettes, similar to those on the parapet of Elizabethan Chatsworth. Apart from the cupolas and the handsome porch the house has no external classical detail.

Doddington is not as large as Worksop was, nor as high; the hall, for instance, is 13 as opposed to 24 feet, high. On the other hand the house has a basement, though admittedly a very low one, containing only cellars. The height to the top of the parapet is 52 feet, high enough but not nearly as high as Worksop. Inside,

138

76. Doddington Hall, Lincolnshire (*c.* 1593–1600).

all Elizabethan detail was swept away when the house was redecorated in the 1760s, but the plan has been little altered. The porch leads into the relatively low great hall, with the kitchen and offices to the south. To the north, on the same level as the hall, were two parlours, with the main staircase between them. The Elizabethan staircase has been replaced by an eighteenth-century one, and the original arrangement can only be guessed at.

There is no documentary evidence to connect Smythson with Doddington, but the stylistic connections are strong enough to make it probable that he supplied the design. In the absence of Worksop it gives us some idea of the effect of that house; and it is, in any case, an admirable design in its own right. Much of its great romantic appeal comes from its setting and the mellow red of its

77. A detail of the entrance front, Doddington.

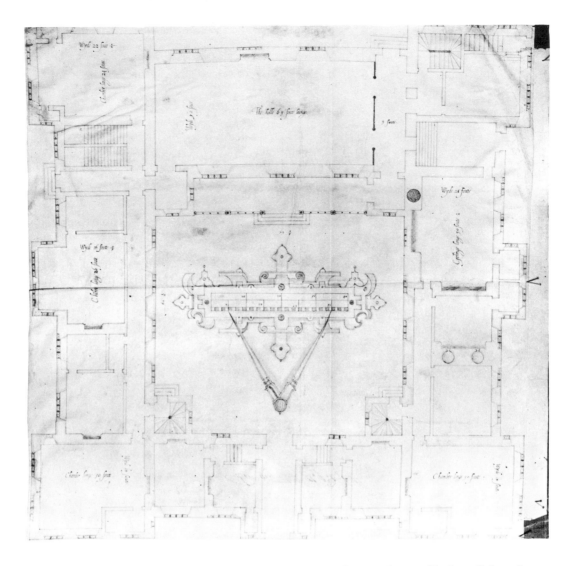

brickwork. But the recession of the entrance front, the enfilade of the three cupolas, and the simple geometry of angles and curves have always been there; and the resulting effect of movement and bold simplicity is typical of Smythson.

Robert Smythson probably designed one other house in Lincolnshire, for Edward, the second Lord Sheffield, ultimately (in 1626) created Earl of Mulgrave. Among the Smythson drawings (I/18.1–2) are the plans (on vellum) for the ground and first floors of a house annotated as 'for my Lord Sheffield' (Plate 78). Another very similar groundfloor plan (I/18.3) also on vellum, is clearly a variant design for the same house. The plans keep much closer than was normal for Smythson to the conventional early Elizabethan type. Both designs are for a courtyard house, entered through a gatehouse, with the hall in the opposite range. There is no basement, and the state rooms are in the normal position on the first floor: a grand staircase off the dais end of the hall leads up to the great chamber, beyond which is a long gallery filling the whole length of the gatehouse range. There is a small staircase turret in each corner of the court, as in the chapel

140

78. Robert Smythson's design for a house for Lord Sheffield (I/18(3)).

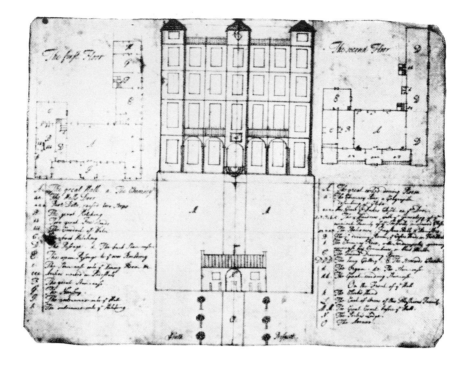

court at Longleat. At each outer angle of the house is a large rectangular tower or pavilion, and between these, in the middle of three of the ranges, a smaller projecting bay, similar to the ones at Longleat. The simplicity and symmetry of the treatment is typical of Smythson; but the angle-pavilion type of plan was no creation of his. It probably derived from semi-fortified medieval buildings of the type of Lumley and Bolton Castles; it had been used in the early sixteenth century in the great house built by William and Anthony Cope at Hanwell, in Oxfordshire; it was used, on a very grand scale at Burghley, Theobalds, Holdenby and ultimately Audley End. In the north it appears at the long-vanished Howley Hall, near Leeds, built by Sir John Savile in the 1580s (Plate 80),[48] and at Stonyhurst in Lancashire,[49] where the scheme was never completed. Smythson may have been connected with the two latter houses, though there is no evidence; if he was, he would have been working, as at Lord Sheffield's house, to a well-established pattern at the wish of his employers.

It is unlikely that any of these plans were ever carried out. The Sheffields were originally seated at Butterwick in Lincolnshire, and acquired two additional properties in the sixteenth century: Normanby, also in Lincolnshire, which was bought by the second Lord Sheffield, probably in 1589, and stayed in the possession of his descendants until a few years ago; and Mulgrave in Yorkshire, a property given to him by the Queen in 1591 and from which he ultimately took the title of his earldom. He also inherited considerable property in the neighbourhood of Nottingham, including manors at Chilwell, Ruddington and Beeston; this may have provided the link with Robert Smythson.[50] There is no record of any large Elizabethan house being built at Butterwick, Mulgrave, or on the Nottinghamshire manors. But at Normanby Lord Sheffield built a house of which plans and an elevation are given in a survey drawing of about 1700 (Plate

141

79. Lord Sheffield's house at Normanby, Lincolnshire, from a survey drawing of c. 1700.

80. Howley Hall, Yorkshire (c. 1585).

79), while a later eighteenth-century engraving shows it when only a fragment of the ground floor remained.[51] It had a hall and kitchen on the ground floor, a great chamber over the hall on the first floor, and two further floors above that. Three turrets on the entrance front, one above the hall porch in the centre and one at each corner, rose a storey higher than the rest of the house. A long gallery stretched out at the back into what is marked on the plan as the 'new building'; perhaps there was originally a gallery on one of the two upper floors.

As the later engraving shows, the survey plan and elevation considerably compress the house, making it look thinner and higher than it actually was. Nonetheless, with its turrets and four rows of many-lighted windows, Elizabethan Normanby must have been impressively high and compact. It was, in fact, more Smythsonian in character than the Sheffield plans among the Smythson drawings. Perhaps Robert Smythson provided Lord Sheffield with a number of different designs, of which the house built at Normanby represents the one chosen – one suspects, his favourite one. Its plan has a curious resemblance to the hall range of the two courtyard plans, with the accommodation in the other three ranges piled up on top of it. There is no precise evidence as to when it was built; it was probably started fairly soon after Lord Sheffield acquired the property in 1589, and in 1598 his friend, Sir John Holles, was writing to him 'I know yr hart is still ye same, as great at Normanby as ever it was at Court'.[52]

142

81. (right) Design by Robert Smythson for Bess of Hardwick's monument in All Saints' Church, Derby (I/6).

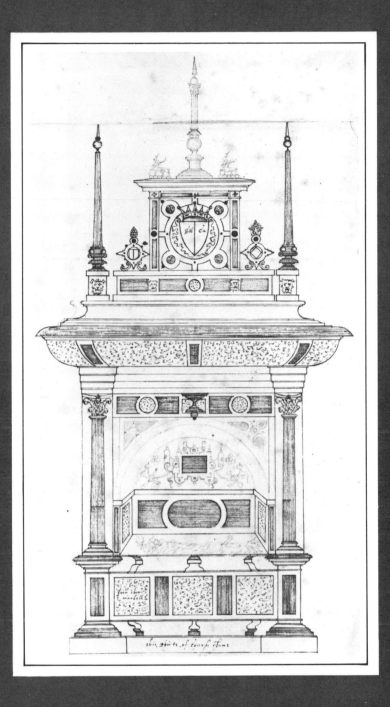

4
Hardwick

FTER Bess of Hardwick had separated from her husband, she retired for a short time to Chatsworth and had protracted rows with him as to whether, by the terms of their marriage settlement, she still had the right to live there. In 1584 she dismantled the house, garrisoned it against her husband with her Cavendish sons, William and Charles, and moved off to the little manor house where she had been born, on top of the hill at Hardwick. In 1586 her husband complained that she had 'called him knave, fool and beast to his face, and mocked and mowed at him'. They were never reconciled, more through his obduracy than hers, for she soon grew tired of the loss of income and standing which her estrangement involved, and tried to make up their quarrel.

For a few years he managed to keep her very short of money; but a legal ruling in April 1587, settled the dispute in her favour rather than his, established her right to Chatsworth, and gave her an assured and substantial income. But Chatsworth was entailed on Henry Cavendish, her eldest son by her second husband; she hated him because he had taken Lord Shrewsbury's side and moreover he had no legitimate children. So she turned her immense energy and ambition to Hardwick, and set about making it the dynastic seat of the Cavendish family, in favour of her second son, William.[1]

Building accounts survive from July 1587, by when work was well under way.[2] By 1591 a modest and probably decayed house had been transformed into a very large one (Plate 82); its battered and blackened shell still stands beside the second and even more magnificent house which she started at the end of 1590, before she had finished the first. The end result at the Old Hall was curiously disorganised, as though Bess had been uncertain of her aims in the troubled years when she started, but had got increasingly grand ideas as the work proceeded, and once the settlement of 1587 gave her the means.

The centre portion is irregular and gabled. The wings to either side have more pretensions, and are clearly related to Worksop. They have (or had) level balustraded parapets; and at the top of each of them, above three storeys of

144

82. Hardwick Old Hall, Derbyshire (mostly 1587–90), from a drawing by S. H. Grimm.

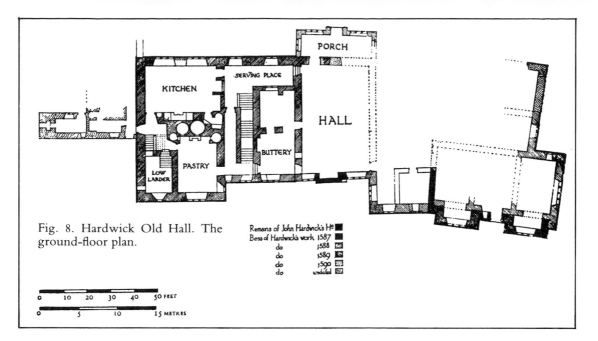

Fig. 8. Hardwick Old Hall. The ground-floor plan.

Remans of John Hardwick's H?
Bess of Hardwick's work 1587
do 1588
do 1589
do 1590
do undated

0 10 20 30 40 50 FEET

0 5 10 15 METRES

comparatively low rooms, were a series of immense and lofty state rooms, lit by towering windows. One wing has a tower six storeys high, the other has shallow projecting bays running all the way up. Like Wollaton, the house had two full-scale great chambers, the Hill Great Chamber and the Forest Great Chamber, at the west and east ends of the house. Much of the rest of the planning cannot be accurately ascertained, owing to partial demolition. But about the most revolutionary feature there can be no doubt; the great hall, two storeys high, went across the centre of the house, in a position radically different from the conventional medieval one.

The influence of Worksop at Old Hardwick is unmistakable and yet it gives the impression that Lady Shrewsbury acted as her own architect, for it has little of the drama or bold groupings of Worksop: the north façade, some 180 feet long, was almost completely flat. Externally it is absolutely without ornament. It must always have been somewhat forbidding and now, gutted and dirty, it is very grim.

The death of Lord Shrewsbury on 18 November 1590 increased Bess's income by over a third, for by the terms of their marriage settlement she inherited a life interest in a substantial portion of the Shrewsbury estates. Perhaps she was dissatisfied with what she had done at the Old Hall; at any rate, immediately after her husband's death and possibly even a week or two before,[3] she laid out the foundations of a new, more magnificent and more regular house a hundred yards from the old. The shell had been finished by the end of 1593, but she did not actually move in until 4 October 1597. She moved to the sound of music, as the accounts show, 'Geven at your Ladyships removeing into the new Buyldinges three poundes. Geven to Mr Starkye Mr Parker Rich Abrahall and John Good when they played XXs.'[4]

Bess was in her early sixties when she started the new Hardwick, and after a lifetime's experience of building she clearly set out to create the perfect house.

She knew what she wanted and she got it: Hardwick remains the supreme triumph of Elizabethan architecture.

Any correspondence connected with the building of New Hardwick has disappeared, but building accounts from 1590 to 1599 survive. In November 1591 John Rodes, who had carried out much of the exterior work at Wollaton, contracted for the whole of the masonry at Hardwick, and from then on there are payments to him in detail, at the rates of ashlar 1½d. a foot, windows 4d. a foot, architrave 1½d. a foot and cornice 6d. a foot. In all this he was helped by his brother, Christopher, who had also been at Wollaton. Some of the exterior trimmings were left to other masons: balusters, chimney-shafts and pedestals to Henry Nayll and Richard Mallery, the columns in the colonnades to William Gryffyn and James Adams. Inside Gryffyn carved the hall screen, for which he was paid £6, the stone doors in the High and Low great chambers, and, jointly

146

83. (top and bottom left) Two chimney-pieces from Book VII of Serlio's *Architecture*.

84. (top right) One of the long-gallery chimney-pieces, Hardwick Hall.

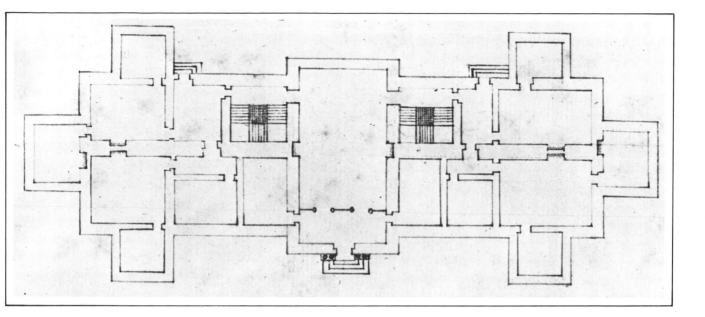

with Adams, a door on the chapel landing.[5] The marble chimney-piece and marble pedimented doorway in the best bedroom were the work of Thomas Accres, a marble carver who had been both at Chatsworth and Wollaton. He was probably responsible for much of the remaining marble work in the house, including the chimney-pieces in the Long Gallery; but no specific payments survive. In stone he carved the coat of arms on the parapet over the hall door; that on the other side of the house was carved by Abraham Smith, mainly a worker in plaster, who had also been at Chatsworth and who modelled many elaborate overmantels in the new and the old house.

This detail at Hardwick probably owes most, ultimately or immediately, to Flemish pattern-books. But there are also borrowings from Serlio: the pilasters of the chimney-piece in the lower withdrawing chamber, for instance, are taken from one of his composite fireplaces, and the gallery chimney-pieces seem to derive from another design in his seventh book (Plates 83 and 84).[6] In quality the Hardwick detail varies a good deal. At its worst, particularly in some of the plasterwork, it is, as Sir Nikolaus Pevsner describes it, 'coarse but jolly work'. At its best it admirably suits the mood of the house, at once sober, splendid, and fantastic.

There is no evidence, in the accounts or among his drawings, for connecting any of this detail with Robert Smythson.[7] But there are powerful reasons for thinking that he gave the general design for Hardwick.

First, there is the previous and subsequent connection between the two families. Robert had already worked at Worksop; either Robert or his son drew the design for Bess's tomb, some years before she died; and both John and Huntingdon spent most of their lives working for her children and grandchildren. More important still is the evidence of three of the Smythson drawings. One is a plan (I/8) for a house very close indeed to Hardwick, differing only in being somewhat

85. Robert Smythson's variant plan for Hardwick (I/8).

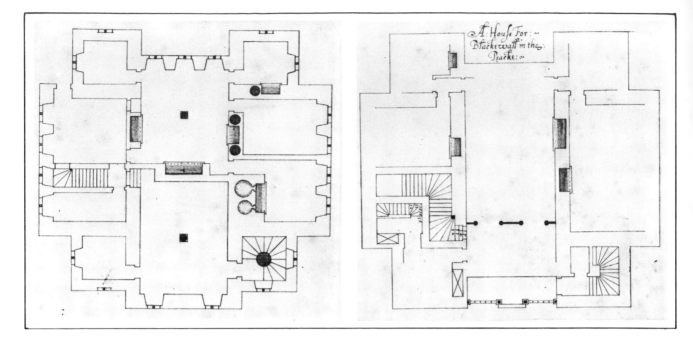

86. Designs for Blackwell-in-the-Peak, Derbyshire (I/1).

larger and thinner, with no colonnade, towers a little smaller, and staircases differently planned (Plate 85). Another plan (I/1) is for a house, probably never built, at a Cavendish property, Blackwell in the Peak (Plate 86). It may have been designed for Bess's youngest son, Sir Charles Cavendish, for the manor of Blackwell descended to his branch of the family. It is Hardwick in miniature, with the hall placed in the same way, a tiny colonnade, and four instead of six towers.[8]

Finally there is the elevation (II/11) of a strange and intriguing house, in the style of Hardwick with reminiscences of Wollaton (Col. Plate IX). It has the sobriety, entablatures, balustrades and towers of Hardwick. It has the stepping of Hardwick carried to its furthest limits; the house falls back from the central tower in four planes of increasing and then lessening width. But the gable of the central tower is a simplified version of those at Wollaton and behind it rises a mysterious mass which could be the clerestory of an enclosed hall. The top storey of the towers is considerably lower than at Hardwick; but the accounts show that the Hardwick towers were designed to be lower and only heightened, by an extra light, in the course of execution.[9]

The building accounts have no mention of any payment for a design, nor would one necessarily expect to find one there, for like many Elizabethan account books they cover only the actual operations of building. But in the general account book for November 1591–7, there is one significant entry[10] for the week ending 27 March 1597:

'Geven to Mr Smythson the surveyour   XXs
    and to his Sonne   Xs'

148

In the Hardwick general accounts any payment made direct for some service rendered always details the service: 'Paid unto one of Mr Maynard's men that brought the picture of the King of France, 6s 8d.', and so on. So it seems probable that these payments to the Smythsons are presents. It is certainly tempting to suppose that Bess made such a present because she was pleased with the house that Smythson had designed for her and which was then at last nearing completion. The general account book for 1590 and the main part of 1591, which may well have contained more specific payments to Smythson, have unfortunately disappeared.

'Surveyour' is interesting but ambiguous. As its best it could mean 'The Surveyor of the Work at Hardwick'; but as there is only the one mention of Smythson in the accounts from 1591-7, it seems unlikely that he had any such close supervision of the buildings. Or it might be used in a more general and less tied sense as an equivalent to 'Architect', though this would certainly be a very early example of a use of the word in a way which became a commonplace in the seventeenth and eighteenth centuries. Finally, it could mean that Smythson combined designing buildings with land and property surveying as did John Thorpe and his own grandson Huntingdon. A survey (I/21) of the medieval castle of Warwick survives in the Smythson collection and may have been made by Robert.

Three of Smythson's principal workmen at Wollaton reappear at Hardwick: Accres, the marble carver, and the two Rodes, masons. This is another pointer towards Smythson as its designer. But the most powerful argument is Hardwick itself. It is Worksop perfected and simplified, with the polish though not the exuberance of Wollaton. Not only has it the right-angles and great windows of Worksop, the height, the huge rooms at the top of the house, but a plan which in outline is strikingly similar: a basic rectangle with additional rectangular projections, three at either end and one on each side of the centre. But at Worksop these projections were of different sizes and treatments, some rising above the roof-line, some not; at Hardwick all ambiguities have been cleaned away, the centre projections reduced to slight breaks forward, the end ones increased to six towers of identical height and design, all rising well and clear above the main block; with no round cupolas, but square all the way, and the whole house square in feel, and this squareness emphasised by the great mullioned windows, more vigorous and less variegated than at Worksop, by the cut-stone, the entablatures, the long level lines of the balustrades. But the edge of what could be a too ruthless angularity is tempered (some would say not sufficiently) by the hall butting slightly forward in the centre, with its cut-away edges, by the light and shade of the colonnades and the arabesques of the tower parapets.

The result is something that, in a wonderful way, gets the best of both worlds, so that it can with perfect truth be called a house of great and romantic beauty, or a ruthless, admirable and uncompromising design: a perpetual delight, so simple is it, so ingenious, so obvious, so effective, as one walks round and watches

149

87–90. Four views of Hardwick Hall, Derbyshire (1590–7).

the masses group and regroup, contract and spread out, advance and fall away (Plates 87–90), shifting from the full weight and splendour of the main elevations to the view from the side, when the house shuts up narrow and bears down with the race and speed of a ship in full sail.

The setting of Hardwick, which greatly adds to the general effect of the house, derives, in a less ambitious and comprehensive form, from the lay-out that was planned for Wollaton. The house and the two square courts on its long façades make up a long thin rectangle, on either side of which are two further courts, the whole forming together a huge walled rectangle, irregular owing to the fall of the ground. The corners of the east side are marked by pavilions; in addition, at the corners of the entrance court are two more pavilions, with a gatehouse between them.

Externally, the house is as rigorously symmetrical as Wollaton. The west front exactly matches the east, and the north the south; moreover, unlike Wollaton, the architectural treatment is the same all the way round. It falls happily between the over-abundance of Wollaton and the severity of Worksop. Classical detail is of the simplest, and is confined to the colonnades, the entablatures which divide the storeys, the console brackets under the windows, and the balustrade. Flemish ornament is only in evidence in the cresting of the towers; this is reticent in everything except its glorification of Bess, whose initials are repeated three times on every tower. Obelisks and strapwork process in unforgettable silhouette along the courtyard walls and on the gatehouse and turrets.

The colonnades or loggias at Hardwick are a somewhat unusual feature. Not that loggias were new in England. A stock feature of the courtyard houses of the mid-sixteenth century was an arcaded loggia in the courtyard, usually along the side opposite the hall. Such loggias are, or were, found at Burghley, Copped and Gidea Halls, Theobalds, Slaugham, Kirby and Holdenby. Burghley, Gidea Hall and Slaugham also had loggias on the external façade facing on to the garden. These loggias were one of the main vehicles for displays of the classical ornament so fashionable in the 1560s and 1570s. But Hardwick is the first surviving example of loggias in a house without an internal courtyard. Moreover, as the stonework shows, they were originally planned to run right round the house between the towers, making its plan at ground level a simple rectangle. The side loggias were never built, no doubt because it was felt they would take too much light from the ground-floor rooms. The two loggias that were completed, on the east and west fronts, are unlike most Elizabethan examples in that their openings are not arched: massive cylindrical columns, of simple but effective design, support a horizontal entablature.

Structurally Hardwick is not without interest. At roof-level the inside walls of at least five of the six towers do not rest on load-bearing walls carried down to the ground; instead, to allow for the great window-bays in the gallery and in the two great chambers, they have to be supported on arches. The corner angles where the main block of the house is seen through the towers are more than just visually effective; they are also acting as buttresses, taking the thrust of the arches which support the tower walls.

Hardwick remains the best house in which to study Smythson as a planner, for unlike most of the buildings with which he was concerned, it has scarcely been altered since it was built: even up to the outbreak of the war in 1939, when the house was last fully lived in, the use to which the rooms were put varied remarkably little from Bess of Hardwick's time.

The Hardwick-type plan in the Smythson drawings, which can reasonably be assumed to be the first design for the house, is almost completely symmetrical inside as well as out; it suggests, supposing the missing upper-floor plans followed the treatment of the ground floor, a house with a plan as balanced as that of Wollaton. But as built the plan was only symmetrical in parts, so that a certain amount of improvisation was needed to make it fit the rigid symmetry of the exterior. Several of the great windows are false, or light two floors of low-ceilinged rooms instead of a single lofty one; the High Great Chamber is over to one side instead of above the central hall, as the outside elevations might suggest. It seems likely that considerable alterations were made to the original plan, possibly even in the course of building.[11] No doubt Bess exerted a powerful influence; on the other hand many of Smythson's later designs show a similar ingenuity in fitting complex asymmetrical plans into a symmetrical exterior.

The most conspicuous and commented-on feature of the plan is the cross-hall. This is two storeys high and runs right through the centre of the house, with its long axis at right-angles to the long axis of the house as a whole. As already remarked, this unconventional arrangement had been anticipated at the Old Hall. Halls of this type were to reappear in some Elizabethan and many Jacobean houses. They had two obvious advantages. What, as used in medieval times, was essentially an asymmetrical feature could now be neatly incorporated into a symmetrical plan. And the cross-hall was a useful means towards achieving a compact building, for the rest of the house could be built two rooms or more thick with no internal courtyard. If the hall was two storeys high the screen gallery provided a useful first-floor link between the two wings of the house; and no limit was put on the height of the house as a whole, as it was in the case of a clerestory-lit hall such as that at Wollaton.

The fact that such halls featured prominently in the publications of du Cerceau, Serlio and Palladio meant that they were almost bound to be adapted for use in England in the end. The earliest known example to be built was in what was known as the Banqueting-House at Holdenby (Plate 91).[12] This was in fact more of a lodge than a banqueting-house; it was situated on the edge of the gardens of Sir Christopher Hatton's great house, and was built some time between 1580 and 1587. The cross-hall in Hardwick Old Hall must have followed it very closely.[13] The hall at Manor Lodge, Worksop, clearly relates to those at Hardwick, but

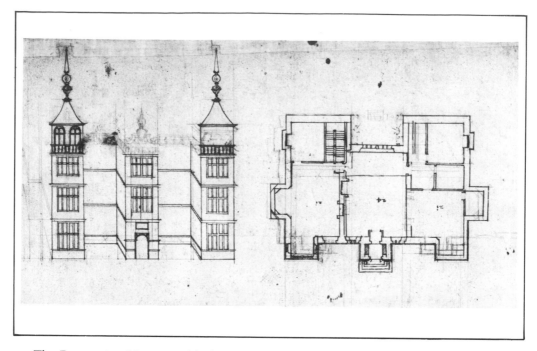

91. The Banqueting House, Holdenby, Northamptonshire (before 1587), as drawn by John Thorpe.

may be a few years later. It is possible that Bess or Smythson knew of the Holdenby example, but the immediate inspiration for cross-halls in the Midlands was just as likely to have come direct from du Cerceau, Serlio, or Palladio. Smythson almost certainly had access to all of these; he must also have known (and may even have been responsible for) the unexecuted design now in the Willoughby papers, with its cross-hall inspired by du Cerceau. As discussed in the chapter on Wollaton, this may date from 1580 or even earlier.

Hardwick has the usual Elizabethan two-tier system of living rooms, but is unusual in that these are skied, each tier being a storey higher than was conventional in an Elizabethan house. As has already been discussed, these skied rooms may have been inspired by Richmond Palace, and had already appeared at Worksop Manor, at Hardwick Old Hall, at Chatsworth and possibly at Buxton and Thorpe Salvin. But at Hardwick, unlike the other examples, the arrangement survives intact. It is similar to that which already existed at Chatsworth, but much more compact.

As Hardwick, unlike Worksop, is two rooms thick, the gallery does not have to be on a separate floor of its own, but lies on the second floor with the other state rooms; as a result Hardwick is a storey lower than Worksop, though still a storey higher than the main bulk of Wollaton. The suite of rooms so formed consists, on one side of the house, of the High Great Chamber, leading into the Withdrawing Chamber, leading into the Bed-Chamber, the last with its own servant's and inner room; and running along all these on the other side of the house, the Gallery.[14]

On the floor beneath this – that is, on the first floor of the house – was contrived the lower but still very splendid range of Bess's own lodgings. The

154

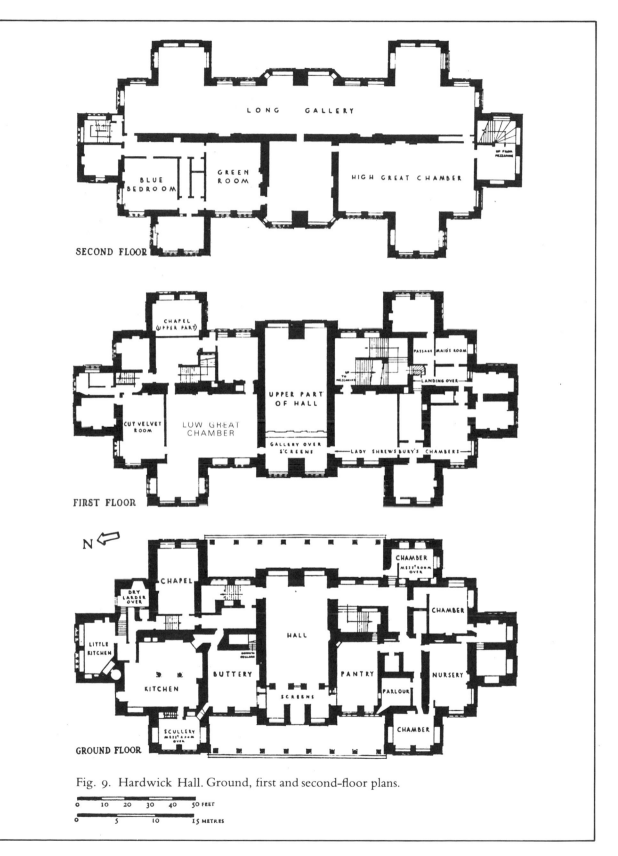

LONG GALLERY

BLUE BEDROOM

GREEN ROOM

HIGH GREAT CHAMBER

UP FROM MEZZANINE

SECOND FLOOR

CHAPEL (UPPER PART)

CUT VELVET ROOM

LOW GREAT CHAMBER

UPPER PART OF HALL

GALLERY OVER SCREENS

LADY SHREWSBURY'S CHAMBERS

UP TO MEZZANINE

PASSAGE MAID'S ROOM

LANDING OVER

FIRST FLOOR

N

CHAPEL

DRY LARDER OVER

LITTLE KITCHEN

KITCHEN

BUTTERY

SCREENS

HALL

PANTRY

PARLOUR

NURSERY

CHAMBER

MEZZ^d ROOM OVER

CHAMBER

CHAMBER

SCULLERY
MEZZ's ROOM OVER

GROUND FLOOR

Fig. 9. Hardwick Hall. Ground, first and second-floor plans.

0 10 20 30 40 50 FEET

0   5   10   15 METRES

entrance to these passed by the gallery of the chapel and went through the little dining chamber (which may originally have been only an ante-room) to what was called the low great chamber, though in the south it would probably have been known as a dining-parlour; from this the hall gallery led across to Bess's withdrawing-room, off which was her own bedchamber, maid's room and inner room, and the rooms of her granddaughter and ward, Arabella Stuart. At the other end of the house on this floor were further bedrooms for guests.

These two independent suites, on their different floors, each have their own approach by separate staircases on different sides of the hall. One of the advantages of putting the state rooms up on the top floor was that their approach could be made very long and magnificent, with plenty of room for incident and drama. Another was the splendid views from their windows. A third was that in quiet seasons they could easily be sealed off and forgotten. The disadvantage, of course, was their remoteness, the great number of steps that had to be climbed to get to them. The route from the kitchen to the High Great Chamber is an immensely long one, but this was not a factor that seems to have bothered the Elizabethans; indeed it provided a ceremonial route for what was an essential feature of any grand Elizabethan entertainment, the formal procession of ushers and waiters carrying up each course of a meal.[15] The little dining-room and low great chamber were conveniently placed, on the other hand, immediately above the kitchen, with access by a staircase straight to it.

The ground floor was filled, on one side of the hall, by nurseries and lodgings, on the other by the kitchen and offices, and the servants' part of the chapel. The house was built up on a basement, like Longleat and Wollaton, but a basement that is less of a feature, being lower, and containing only cellars, store rooms, and the lower part of the kitchen.

The division into storeys at Hardwick was not completely rigid, but broken through here and there to allow the main rooms to be sufficiently high, and to prevent the small rooms from being uncomfortably so. On the ground floor the important rooms were given the height they needed in two different ways: the hall and chapel[16] were carried up through the floor above, the kitchen sunk to include the basement.[17] Conversely, the top floor was cut horizontally into two in the north-east corner, where the best bedrooms were. This stopped them from being over high and allowed the insertion of a mezzanine floor of four further bedrooms, somewhat low, but very commodious. The two floors do not appear separate outside, for they are concealed behind one range of windows.

To describe the bones of Hardwick's internal planning may give some idea of its ingenuity, but reveals little of its excitement. For just as a walk round the outside of the house provides a continual drama of changing arrangements of mass, so, inside, to move from room to room or climb from floor to floor is equally full of spatial adventures.

The unusual shape of the house, with its six great towers, is exploited internally by many permutations and combinations. The towers in their different stages

156

sometimes contain one or two self-contained and comparatively small rooms; sometimes portions of the staircases; sometimes are opened up into the great rooms and enliven their shape. On the first floor they make the Low Great Chamber L-shaped; on the second floor the High Great Chamber T-shaped, and the long gallery a double T with a wider block between the two cross-bars.

The house makes the most, as does Wollaton, of its magnificent views. On the first floor, four doors let on to walks on the top of the colonnades; four further doors survive blocked up, which were to have led on to the unbuilt colonnades at the corners. The main roof itself is an enormous level platform, easily reached by a spacious stair in the north turret; and the top room in the south turret is carefully fitted out (a descendant of Longleat through Worksop) as a prospect-room or banqueting-house, with elaborate plaster decoration. Then there are or were the views inside the house: the great vistas of the staircases and the gallery; the view down into the hall from the gallery that links the Low Great Chamber to Bess's withdrawing chamber; the view down through the chapel from the first-floor landing.

The contrast in height between the various floors of the house gives to a tour of its rooms an exhilarating effect of culmination and expansion. The ground-floor rooms are low and dark, some made darker still by the colonnades. The rooms above are higher, lighter, and more spacious. But the great rooms on the top floor are of heroic size, and, when the sun is in them, ablaze and soaked with light. And if one climbs higher still one gets on to the even vaster and windy spaces of the roof.

The two staircases, which link these levels and are threaded elaborately and ingeniously through the house, are perhaps the most unique and daring feature of Hardwick's interior.[18] Both start just off the hall, both end some 80 feet away from their beginning, in the north and south turrets respectively. They reach their ends only after many windings, doublings back, long runs and spacious landings (Plates 92–4). They are at their most mysterious and romantic in the long tunnel of steps that rises up and up from the landing outside Bess's withdrawing chamber, finally curling out of sight around the corner; but, if followed, leading to a second landing which is the vestibule, tall and cool, of the High Great Chamber.

Less spectacular but even more original is the way these stairs play with right-angles, providing the internal equivalent of the criss-cross, and the advance and retreat, of the exterior. Of this the most powerful example is the first-floor landing of the second staircase. Its elements are the grid of the chapel screen, the L-shaped grid of two internal windows, now blocked, a projecting corner that contains a splendid decorated door, the elbow of the staircase balustrade, and the staircase itself, dropping down to the floor below. The composition that results (Plate 95), with its angles and patterns, its light and shade, its shifting levels and planes, the way that its spaces are linked and yet divided, is, as Sacheverell Sitwell says, 'the lesson and precursor of much modern architecture'.[19]

92. (facing page) Hardwick Hall. The first flight of the great staircase.

93. (left) The last stage, and the door to the High Great Chamber.

94. (bottom) From the first to the second floor.

The germ of this long staircase can be found a hundred yards away, across the road in the old house. Here the staircase to the Hill Great Chamber was a dog-leg of two narrow but very long flights of steps. Smythson, who had had an eye for steps, from Wardour onwards, developed these into something far more spacious and effective: reminiscent of the great Gothic staircase at Wells, which, indeed, he may well have seen.

No discussion of Hardwick can discount the influence of its builder; Bess was not the sort of person to leave the details of her house to others. Many of the idiosyncrasies of its planning are probably due to her; it was probably she who increased the height of the towers in the middle of building, and who ordered the corner colonnades to be abandoned. It is clear that she had a passion for height, light, squareness, and symmetry. But one only has to compare the old with the new Hardwick to see how Smythson transformed her overbearing and somewhat crude preferences into a work of art.

Squareness of plan and outline, square towers, great windows with grids of transoms and mullions, all the elements which emerge in their most forthright and developed form at Hardwick, stripped of most classical detail and accentuated

95. Hardwick Hall. The chapel landing.
96. (facing page left) Late medieval design for a tower, from the Smythson collection (IV/3).
97. (facing page top right) A Smythson design for vaulting (II/25).
98. (facing page bottom right) Robert Smythson's drawings of Westminster Abbey, 1609 (I/15).

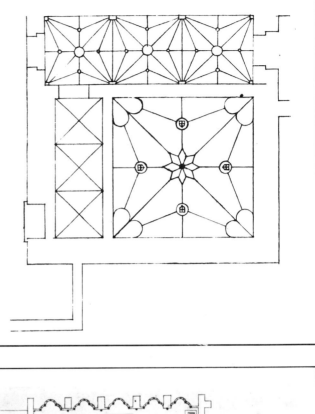

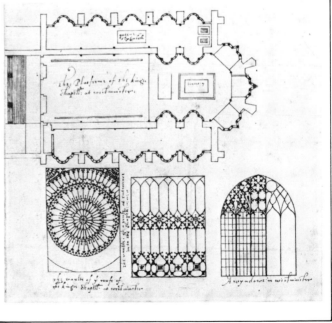

The Smythsons and Gothic

by what little remains, are to be found as well at Longleat, Wollaton and Worksop. Among the Smythson drawings is a late medieval design (IV/3) for a square tower with square turrets and great square-headed windows, very suggestive when compared with these houses, particularly Hardwick. There can be no doubt that the Smythsons appreciated Gothic, especially Perpendicular, architecture and used its forms though very seldom its detail (Plates 96–9). The lantern in the Longleat library plan, the prospect-room and clerestory at Wollaton were based on Gothic precedents. In 1599 Robert or his son designed classical versions of rose-windows (IV/33–4), and in 1608–9 he made careful plans and sketches of Henry VII's and King's College Chapels (I/4 and 15). Gothic was in Robert Smythson's blood, the style, in all probability, in which his father and grandfather had worked, a style still hot and in use all over England. The more splendid of medieval, especially Perpendicular, buildings were still universally admired.[20] Gothic was not to be treated as a barbarous style until well on in the seventeenth century.

But it is worth distinguishing two unclassical strains, allied but separate, in this period of English architecture. First, the deliberate medieval make-believe that emanated from the court and was part of a general romantic movement covering many fields; and second, the less obvious and perhaps less conscious medievalism that appears in houses such as Wimbledon. Both strains are to be found in the works of the Smythsons: on the one hand, Bolsover and perhaps Lulworth, on the other Hardwick and Worksop, with Wollaton in the centre, combining the two and adding other elements as well. The court romanticism, that curious, flaunting, and indeed un-Gothic chivalry, exudes a peculiar fascination. But it is perhaps too artificial, too posturing, trembling always on the edge of absurdity. The other style is deeper, more epic and more inventive: possibly a style that owed more to the artisans than their patrons, and one in which Smythson, when left to himself, was most happy to work.

This Gothic element in Elizabethan architecture has always been recognised. But to say 'design remained Gothic and ornament classic', to talk of 'that bastard style which intervened between Gothic and Grecian ornament'[21] is an absurd and an unfair simplification, true only of the earlier or more provincial buildings. No style can be a virgin birth, unfertilised by what has happened before or what is happening all round. But Elizabethan architecture at its best is not an undigested mixture, but a true synthesis, a style in its own right. It could not last; too many external influences were hammering at the door. But for twenty supreme years houses were being built all over England of which we can justly be proud, for not only were they of the greatest daring and beauty, but they were unique to England. Of these houses none is more daring or more beautiful than Hardwick, preserved by some miracle with so much of its tapestry, plasterwork, paintings and fittings intact, dominating the landscape from the crest of its hill, its drama only intensified by the slag-heaps, the chimneys, the scarred and ravaged landscape around.

162

XI. (facing page) A distant view of Hardwick Hall, Derbyshire.
XII. (following page) Burton Agnes Hall, N. Yorkshire. Looking along the entrance front.
99. (subsequent page) Robert Smythson's design for a round window, 1599.

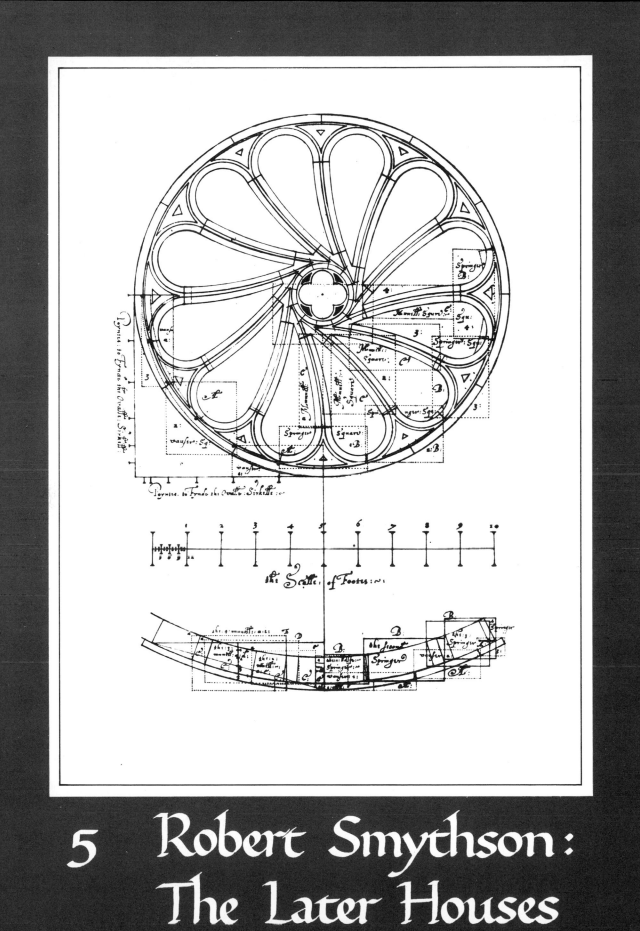

5 Robert Smythson: The Later Houses

HARDWICK is the centre-piece of Smythson's work. Up till 1590 he had been simplifying, consolidating, clarifying, leaving out, until at Hardwick he produced, with inspired economy, a logical and clear-cut combination of the plainest rectangular forms. But immediately he began to move towards a style more complex, more full of contrast, towards houses where the arrangement is no longer transparent, the elements are grouped with the eye of a painter rather than a geometrician. Hardwick is made up of six towers, of the same size and treatment, placed symmetrically around an oblong block. But in the later houses towers are combined, and at times crowded together, with bay windows of different shapes and sizes, with round staircase turrets, sometimes with gables. These new elements, all Gothic by origin, greatly increase the vertical stress, with results that can be both compressed and soaring. In all this Smythson was taking part in, perhaps even leading, the general movement of English architecture, which everywhere was exploiting the shifting, the variegated, the complex and the picturesque, up till the inevitable reaction and the uncompromising blocks of Inigo Jones and Pratt.

ROBERT AND JOHN SMYTHSON, 1590–1614

A certain amount of documentary evidence has come to light for this period of Smythson's life. Throughout it he stayed in the service of the Willoughbys, first of Sir Francis and then, after the latter's death in 1596, of his son-in-law Sir Percival. He is known to have been employed in a number of capacities which had nothing to do with building. It is likely that work of this kind, and a regular salary from the Willoughbys, provided his staple income and that the drawing of 'platts' at a pound or two a time was only a side-line, however important in terms of English architecture.

He collected rents for Francis Willoughby, apparently as early as 1588.[1] In 1596 he made and signed an inventory of bedding at Wollaton.[2] In a law-case referring to events taking place about 1600 he is called 'Robert Smythson, bailiff to Mr. Percival Willoughby'.[3] In 1602 Henry Willoughby, Percival's cousin and also the steward of his household, empowered 'my very loving friend Robert Smythson of Wollaton' to act for him in transactions involving William Cavendish and his mother, the Countess of Shrewsbury.[4] He was, almost certainly, the 'Mr. Smythson' who was doing business for Percival Willoughby in London and at the Nottinghamshire coal pits in and around 1602.

This business was connected with Huntingdon Beaumont, the younger brother of Sir Henry Beaumont, of Coleorton in Leicestershire.[5] The Beaumonts owned coal pits at Coleorton (hence its name) and at Bedworth in Warwickshire; in the 1570s both these mines were being worked by them in partnership with Francis Willoughby. Huntingdon and his brother Francis were in charge of operations at the Bedworth pits in the 1590s. But as a youngest son Huntingdon obviously thought there was more future for him if he employed his coal-mining experience outside the family circle, and, accordingly, early in the seventeenth century he started to exploit his family connection with the Willoughbys. It was a good moment to do this because Sir Percival Willoughby was desperately trying to work off the huge load of debts and law-suits bequeathed to him by his father-in-law, Sir Francis, and was receptive to any scheme that held out hopes of quick profit. Huntingdon leased the Wollaton coal pits from Sir Percival in October, 1601, and shortly afterwards acquired an interest in the adjacent Strelley pits, then leased by the Byron family from the Strelleys. The Strelley dealings culminated in a comprehensive twenty-one-year lease granted to Huntingdon by the Byrons in October 1603, for £4,000.

Wollaton and Strelley were the principal coal pits in the Nottingham area, and by controlling the two of them Huntingdon hoped to get a monopoly of the local market. Sir Percival was in effect working in partnership with him, bearing a share of the costs and collecting a share of the profits. The scheme ended, for a number of reasons, in total failure. A parallel venture into the Newcastle coal-fields was equally disastrous. Huntingdon Beaumont was imprisoned in Nottingham gaol for debt in October 1618, probably at the instigation of the disappointed Sir Percival, and he died in gaol in March 1624. But in the early years of the century, with which we are concerned at the moment, the two were friends and full of hopes. Sir Percival was then spending much of the time in London, on law business; and an interesting correspondence between him and 'your verie lovinge tenante and ever assured frende' Huntingdon Beaumont survives.

In a letter dated 20 April, and probably written in 1602, Huntingdon writes: 'Good Sir, though it may seeme a thinge needeles to write by Mr Smythson who can very well make knowne unto you the state of your affaires here, yet surely I best contente my self when I take all occasions any waies offred unto me to signifie unto you how the worlde goeth with you.'[6] Then follows a report on colliery business, and a request for a specific lease of the Bretland area of the Wollaton coal pit, which for some reason had not been fully covered by the lease of October 1601. 'I pray you', the letter continues, 'let Mr Smythson at his retorne bringe doune a sufficient writing with him' to deal with the Bretland affair.

In another letter dated 13 June, but again no year, Huntingdon reports bad sales and that consequently 'I have bin compelled to call upon Johnson and have received fivetie poundes from him of that which I paied you, Mr Smythson hath made it out a hundred poundes and about seaven and twentie poundes more which I have had from him to pay the colliers.'[7]

These are the only three references to 'Mr Smythson' in the surviving correspondence. It is almost certainly Robert or John who is referred to, and Robert, as the senior of the two and a trusted servant of the Willoughbys over the last twenty-two years, is much the more likely candidate. But there can be little doubt that John's son Huntingdon, who must have been born at this period, had Huntingdon Beaumont as his godfather, and was christened accordingly. The

Wollaton-Strelley operations included the laying-down of a wooden railway for colliery wagons in 1605. This is the first recorded railway in the British Isles, and it is certainly intriguing to think that one, or both, of the Smythsons may have been connected with its construction.

In these years John Smythson first begins to emerge from the shadows, and it is worth putting together what little is known of his early career. He had made his first recorded appearance working as a freemason at 10d. a day, at Wollaton in March 1588. He reappeared in March 1597, when he visited Hardwick with his father, and was given ten shillings by Lady Shrewsbury. Three years later at St Peter's, Nottingham, in December 1600, 'John Smythson gen. of Wollaton' married 'Margaret Newton, spinster, of Kirkby-in-Ashfield'.[8] His eldest son Huntingdon must have been born within a few years of the marriage.

These facts give some information and allow of a few fairly plausible deductions. John Smythson was trained as a mason, as his father had been. He was travelling with his father in 1597 and still living in Wollaton in 1600. This, combined with the connection with Huntingdon Beaumont, suggests that he was working as his father's assistant in the 1590s, and perhaps on into the 1600s. Perhaps one of the houses where he worked was at Kirkby-in-Ashfield, where Sir Charles Cavendish had started building in 1597; and there he may have met Margaret Newton, whom three years later he married. In 1599 building work at Kirkby was suddenly and finally interrupted by the attack of the Stanhopes (see p. 175). One wonders whether John Smythson was among or led the 'workmen' whose arrival caused the Stanhopes to flee, and probably saved Sir Charles's life.

The Newtons were Sir Charles's principal tenants at Kirkby, and may have had freehold land of their own as well.[9] They were prosperous farmers who before long were to start calling themselves gentlemen. The little manor house which they built opposite the church at Kirkby still survives. Under the Commonwealth the Cavendish property in Kirkby was forfeited for treason, and William and Christopher Newton, 'gents', bought it up. But at the time of John Smythson's marriage the Newtons are still described as 'yeomen' in their leases.[10] His marriage into such a family, about to cross the border line between yeomen and small gentry is probably an accurate indication of the Smythsons' own social position.

Apart from the one entry of 1597 in the Hardwick accounts, none of the relevant deeds, letters or other documents which have come to light give any information about Robert or John Smythson's actual architectural activities between 1590 and Robert's death in 1614.[11] The latter's monument in the church at Wollaton refers to him as 'architector and survayor unto the most worthy house of Wollaton and diverse others of great account'. The main evidence for the 'diverse others' of the last decades, and for any other designs of this period, is supplied by the drawings. Even here only two are dated: a design for 'a rounde windowe standinge in a rounde walle' of 1599 (Plate 99), and a survey plan of Wimbledon House, near London, of 1609. But there is a large group of his own

168

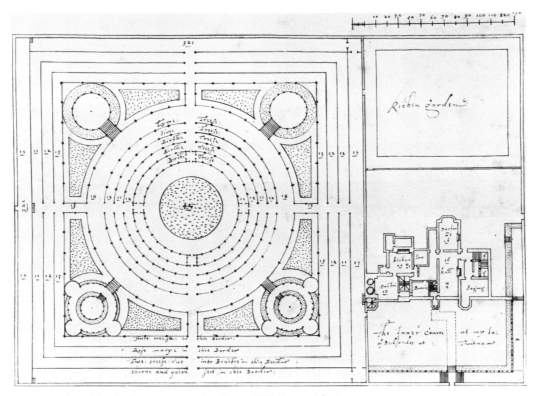

100. Lord Bedford's house at Twickenham, Middlesex (I/20).

designs which are not dated, but can be assigned, with reasonable certainty, to the 1590–1614 period. One is for Bess of Hardwick's monument in All Hallows, Derby (Plate 81); in her will, dated 27 April 1601, this is described as finished, but not yet set up. One is for Burton Agnes, in Yorkshire, built between 1601 and 1610. One is for a rebuilding, only partly carried out, of Welbeck Abbey in Nottinghamshire. One is an unexecuted design for a new house on the site of Slingsby Castle in Yorkshire. The others have remained so far anonymous, but on stylistic grounds clearly belong to the same group. These plans, together with the houses already discussed, give a clear enough idea of Smythson's range and development to make it possible to classify a number of other houses, in the Midlands and North of England, as by or, at any rate, after Smythson.

None of the drawings, dated or undated, is signed by Robert Smythson. But the 1609 plan of Wimbledon House is one of a group of drawings made on a southern journey which are almost certainly by Robert, for they are inscribed in a different handwriting to that on a second group, recording a similar journey in 1618–19, one of which is signed by John. The design for the window is inscribed in the same hand. Most of the other designs have no inscriptions, or inscriptions in an impersonal script, and on grounds of draughtmanship it is hard to make a firm attribution; but they develop logically from earlier works which can certainly or convincingly be attributed to Robert. It seems probable that Robert remained active and industrious into his old age, although John may have made drawings and directed buildings under his supervision.

169

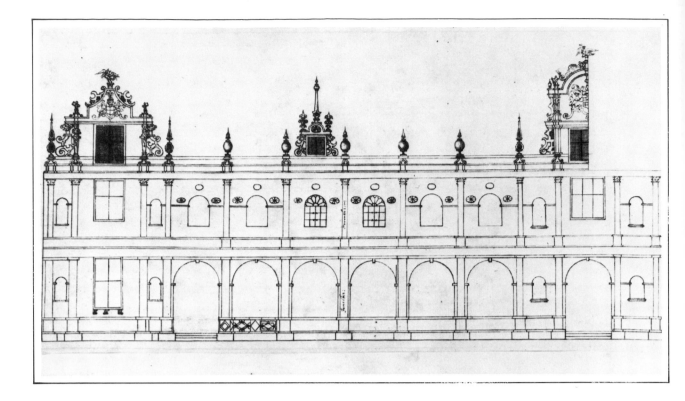

John Smythson's southern visit of 1618–19 had an important influence on his own designs, but there is no evidence that this was the case with Robert in 1609. He was an old man when he went there, with only five years to live, and moreover London was not then full of new architectural ideas, as it was to be ten years later. But it is interesting to see what caught his eye. The principal houses of which he drew plans were Wimbledon, Ham, Somerset House and Northampton House in the Strand, and Lord Worcester's house at Nonsuch. These were all fine houses, but they had little to teach him. At Worcester Lodge he must have been interested and perhaps flattered to find a cross-hall, of the Hardwick type but rather less advanced. Wimbledon, Ham and Northampton House were impressive essays in the dramatic and picturesque Elizabethan tradition, but no more dramatic or picturesque than many of his own houses. Indeed he seems, to judge from his drawings, to have been more interested by gardens than by houses; it is possible that he was collecting ideas for the new garden which Sir Charles Cavendish was in course of laying out at Welbeck.[12] He drew the plans of a number of elaborate formal gardens (Plate 100), probably much more ambitious than anything then existing in the Midlands: in their symmetrical complexity they were exactly the kind of 'ingeniose device' that would have appealed to him. No doubt for the same reason he took the plans of Henry VII's and King's College chapels, and drew a selection of the tracery at Westminster Abbey (Plate 97). It was the pattern- and form-making aspect of Gothic architecture which intrigued him rather than the structural problems involved.

170

101. The New Exchange, the Strand, London (I/11).

Robert also made plans of the first banqueting-house at Whitehall, the riding-school at St James's Palace, and James I's huge stables at Theobalds, probably because they were buildings of a type that he had not met with before. Finally he drew both plan and elevation of the New Exchange in the Strand (Plate 101), which was opened in April of the year of his visit, and must have been the most talked-of building in London at the time.[13] The New Exchange, on which Inigo Jones may have collaborated, represented an early and immature stage in the movement back to Italian Renaissance models: a movement analogous to that in existence when Smythson was a young man, and which, to judge from the way he drew the Exchange, had become very remote to him. For his drawing is inaccurate and shows none of his old feeling for the orders; the elaborate Jacobean flourishes on the skyline are probably his own invention, and the building's real significance had clearly eluded him.

LATER HOUSES: THE INNER RING

These London drawings are interesting, but, from the point of view of Robert Smythson's style and development, unimportant. Far more relevant are his own later plans which must now be considered, beginning with those that can be connected with identified buildings or projects.

The 1599 design for a round window (Plate 99) is probably connected with a round window of different design at Heath Grammar School, Halifax, which was built between 1597 and 1600 on land given by Gilbert Earl of Shrewsbury, Edward Savile and Sir George Savile.[14] The executive masons were John, Abraham and Martin Akroyd, who later moved to Oxford. The school has been rebuilt, but the window was reset in the new building; it appears to be the ancestor of a group of traceried round windows scattered over Yorkshire. The design for Bess's tomb must date from about 1600. Other Cavendish or Talbot projects of the same period are likely to have involved Robert Smythson. In the 1590s the Talbots and Cavendishes started on at least three houses, Owlcotes in Derbyshire, Kirkby-in-Ashfield in Nottinghamshire, and the house known impartially as Pontefract Old or New Hall in Yorkshire. The two Midland houses have long ago disappeared; Pontefract survived until the 1960s, though only as a most shattered ruin (Plates 102 and 103). Its builder was Edward Talbot, Bess's younger stepson, best known today for his involvement in one of the most lurid of the rows and feuds that periodically split the Talbot-Cavendish clan. In 1594 he was accused by his brother Gilbert, Earl of Shrewsbury, of plotting to murder him; the agent, it was alleged, was to be Gilbert's physician, a certain Wood, and the means a pair of poisoned gloves. Wood was condemned to imprisonment and loss of cars as 'a most palpable Machivilian'; Edward escaped without punishment, but the two brothers remained unrelenting enemies, and when Edward inherited the earldom in 1616 it was found that Gilbert had left all the Talbot property he could away from him.[15]

102. New Hall, Pontefract, Yorkshire. The main front in 1885.

Pontefract was dated 1591[16] over the porch, that is, it was approximately contemporary with Hardwick. Like Hardwick its erection was probably made financially possible by the death of Bess's husband in 1590. It has much in common with Hardwick, though on a considerably smaller scale: height, towers, level parapets, great windows, symmetry, and squareness. Yet in many ways it is very different, and just as Hardwick is the culmination of one type of design so Pontefract is the starting-point of another. Its front is recessed with extruded corners, as is the front of Wollaton. But at Pontefract the emphasis is placed differently, with the sides relatively wider, the centre far narrower and crowded out by a great five-sided bay, three tiers of twenty-six light windows going right up the middle of the house: a smaller but more abrupt and powerful version of the gentle five-sided bays in a similar position at Hardwick. Moreover, set a little back from the outside corners of the front are two towers, rising well above the general parapet level. These not only frame and tie the front together but also link it to the sides, where they are paired to form compositions of two towers, set just off the corners of a flat façade. The result is something more complex than any house described so far, a house that advances and retreats, on five

172

103. The side façade of New Hall.

different vertical planes, with effective contrast between the crowded mass of
windows in the centre and the plain and restful expanses of wall at the sides, and
a further violent contrast between the main front, with its delicately shifting
levels, and the bleak and castle plainness of the subsidiary façades. It is very
different from the simple groupings and unvarying fenestration of Hardwick, far
closer in feel to Jacobean houses such as the Greenwich Charlton, Holland House,
or Hatfield, all of which it anticipates by fifteen to twenty years.

One of the R.I.B.A. plans (II/5) has certain similarities with Pontefract, though
it is for a house built on a much larger scale (Plate 104). If it were telescoped in

173

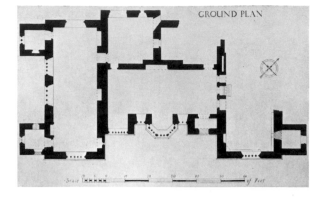

GROUND PLAN

Scale ⊢⊢⊢⊢⊢⊢   of Feet

Fig. 10. New Hall, Pontefract. The ground-floor plan.

104. A Smythson plan related to New Hall (II/5).

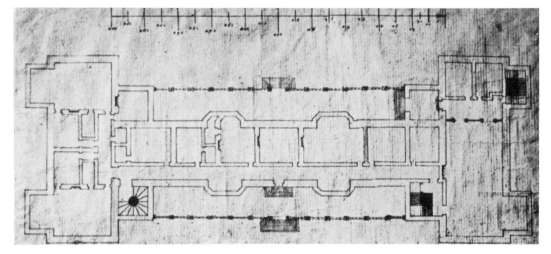

the middle, so as to have one bay window instead of two, the main and side façades would externally be of the same plan as Pontefract, with extruded corners and two rectangular projections on either flank. But outside it differs from Pontefract in having the back symmetrical to the front, and inside the arrangement is completely different, with the hall unusually placed in one of the side wings. Pontefract as built had a more conventional hall, filling the middle of the house, with its porch and dais oriel in the two extruded corners. As a whole the plan was not of the Hardwick type. The hall was only one storey high with a great chamber above it on the first floor. On the top floor there is said to have been a gallery, 90 feet long. A staircase at the back of the house led up from the dais end of the hall to the great chamber and on to the gallery; this staircase may possibly have been enlarged after the house was built, for the projection that contains it must have destroyed the symmetry of the rear façade. The detail throughout is relatively homely, and off the main front the fenestration is somewhat casual. Smythson probably supplied only a plan and perhaps a single elevation, leaving the execution to local men, who may have followed neither exactly.

James I stopped a night at New Hall on his way to Scotland in 1617, but by the eighteenth century, when Carter sketched it, the house was already abandoned. In its last years, at best a dirty shell, one corner quite vanished and many portions crumbling away, stuck between a coal mine and a railway embankment, with pigs nosing in the ruins and a hen-run across the entrance court, it had passed beyond the limits even of romantic decay.

Owlcotes in Derbyshire, a couple of miles from Hardwick, is mentioned on her monument as one of the houses built by Elizabeth Shrewsbury. But though the property belonged to her, and though she clearly took a great interest in the erection of the house, the Hardwick MSS make it clear that it was built for, and for the most part at the expense of, her favourite son William. Her own account books mention the house four times. On 28 March 1593, 'Delivered unto Mr Wm Cavendishe uppon a reckoning, towardes the buildings at Oule Coattes two hundred poundes'. On 4 May, 'Delivered to my La: at her goinge to Oule Coattes three poundes. del. there unto her more xls' – perhaps tips for the workmen. And there are further gifts to William of £100 for Owlcotes on 29 May 1593, and 7 April 1599.[17] His own personal account books do not start until 1597, in which year there are payments for £190 for building and repairs at Owlcotes,[18] which make it clear that the main work had already been done.

Meanwhile in 1597 Bess's other son, Charles, started a house at Kirkby-in-Ashfield in Nottinghamshire, also only a few miles from Hardwick. He received in that year £300 towards it from his indulgent mother, and another £100 in March 1599.[19] But in November of the same year:

> Sir Charles Candish being at his new building, which is some quarter of a mile from his little house where he and his lady do lie, and going from thence to a brick kill, as far distant from that building as that is from his house, being attended by these three persons only, Henry Ogle, Launcelot Ogle, his page, and one horse-keeper, he discerned to the number of about 20 horse on the side of a hill, which he thought to be Sir John Biron with companie hunting, but sodainly they all gallopping apace towards him, he perceved he was betrayed; whereupon, being upon a little nagge, he put spurres to him, thincking to recover the new building, but the titt fell with him, and before he could recover out of the stirrop he was overtaken and before he could drawe his sworde, two pistolls were discharged upon him.[20]

The attackers were the Stanhopes, bitter enemies of Bess's stepson, Gilbert Talbot, and hence of Sir Charles, who was his brother-in-law and greatest friend. In the middle of an heroic and unequal fight – Sir Charles and his three men had rapiers and daggers only and some at any rate of their twenty opponents were armed with pistols – a party of workmen arrived from the new buildings and the Stanhopes made off, leaving two of their party behind them. But Sir Charles is said[21] not to have wanted to go on with a house in a neighbourhood which had been polluted by violence and death. At any rate, whatever had been built was in 1612 being used as a quarry for his new house in Bolsover;[22] and by now all traces have disappeared. Owlcotes survived longer, going by marriage to the Pierrepont family; but it too was demolished in the late seventeenth or early eighteenth century.[23]

175

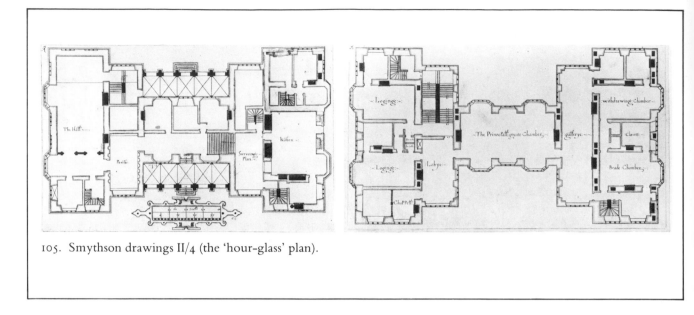

105. Smythson drawings II/4 (the 'hour-glass' plan).

No identifiable drawings or plans of the two houses, both of which may have been examples of Smythson's work, have come to light. But a contract for the stonework at Owlcotes survives, dated 8 March 1592(3).[24] The contract is between Bess and William Cavendish on the one hand, and Godfrey, Reynold, George and Ralph Plumtree, Robert Ashmore and John Warde (all described as wallers) on the other. All six men had worked at Hardwick. The new building seems to have been added on to an existing old one, and have been two rooms thick; it had two turrets; the hall was 20 feet high; no ashlar was involved and the work was to be finished in eight months. The last two provisos suggest a house considerably smaller and simpler than Hardwick, as might have been expected.

Among the anonymous Smythson plans at the R.I.B.A. is a group the planning of which is so clearly modelled on that of Hardwick that one can surmise Cavendish or Talbot patrons. They all have in common the specifically Shrewsbury peculiarity of a great chamber and long gallery at the top of the house above a two-storey hall. But within this basic resemblance they have considerable variations. The different situations of the hall, the different relationships between the main staircase, the great chamber and the long gallery, the different combinations on the exterior of bay windows and turrets of different shapes, are all worth studying and are powerful evidence of Smythson's experimental mind.

One of these houses (II/4 and Plate 105) has considerable resemblance in its general outline to Pontefract. But its internal planning is much less conventional. The house is shaped roughly like an hour-glass, with the hall at one end and the kitchen at the other. The two ends are joined by a broad gallery into which the main entrance of the house opens, running along the centre of the house. This centre and the hall end are built up on cellars: but at the kitchen end there are no cellars, the extra space being used to provide a high kitchen and two storeys of low rooms, to one side of it. The shifting of the levels so as to fit in together rooms of different heights is a very Smythsonian feature.

176

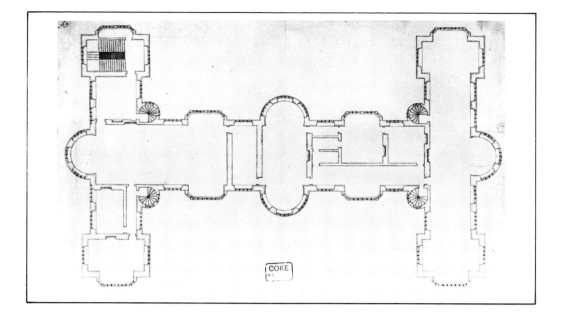

Analysis of the plans makes it reasonably certain that they are for the ground and second floors of a house, and that the first-floor plan is missing: otherwise the house would be without parlour accommodation, and there would be far more flues on the upper floor than fireplaces on the floor below. The top floor has approximately the same accommodation as at Hardwick, but differently arranged; the relatively small gallery, for instance, runs across the house between the great chamber and the withdrawing chamber, a position without parallel in any other plans of the period. The placing of the hall to one side (with its main axis at right-angles to the entrance front) occurs in this plan and several other of Smythson's designs. It is one way of incorporating a medieval-type hall conveniently into a symmetrical house. But the arrangement is only rarely found in executed buildings. It probably occurred at Lulworth (see p. 224) and is certainly found at Gawthorpe in Lancashire (see p. 192). It was, however, clearly much less popular than the central cross-hall, of the Hardwick type.

Another design (II/1 and Plate 106) seems to belong to this Hardwick-type group, though only the plan for the great chamber floor survives. It has an outline of remarkable intricacy, with a lavish use of curved projections: four semi-circular bow windows and four small circular staircase turrets. The charm of the design lies in the way the façades agree with the internal planning – as is by no means always the case in a Smythson plan. The impression is, not that an amusing outline has been drawn and the rooms fitted in it as well as they would go, but that the house has been built up out of blocks of space, as if from a box of ingeniously cut bricks.

The rooms are all well lighted and are of every kind of shape, some of them both novel and delightful. The long gallery which fills one upright of the II, has a rounded bay in the centre, and flowers out at either end with two half-rectangles and a half-octagon. The great chamber runs along one extremity of the cross-bar, and so has its semi-circular window at one end; at the other end two half-

177

106. Smythson drawing II/1.

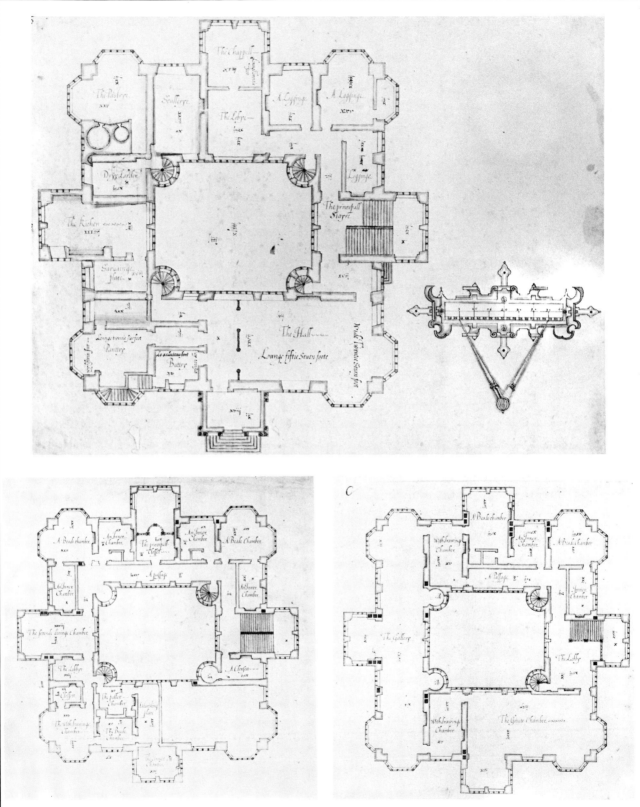

107. Smythson drawings II/2. a (top) ground floor, b (bottom left), c (bottom right) first and second floors.

octagons make the cross-bar to a T. And in the centre of the house is a drawn-out oval (probably the withdrawing room), lit at either end by two semi-circles of glass, as near as the Elizabethans ever came to the oval rooms of the eighteenth century.

The two other designs in the group (II/2–3) share the same outline plan, each being for a square house built round a small internal courtyard, with four identical external façades, consisting of a rectangular central projection (one of which contains the main staircase) with a three-sided bay window to either side. A roof plan exists for one of these houses, showing the rectangular bays rising up above the top storey in the form of towers. The same house (Plate 107) provides a nicely graded series of lodgings: three single-room lodgings on the ground floor, two two-room lodgings on the the second floor, and two three-room lodgings on the first floor. This is more carefully thought-out than at Hardwick, on which, otherwise, the planning is closely modelled.

Another feature in which this house improves on Hardwick is in the provision of corridors: there are well-lit eight-foot-wide passages running round approximately two sides of the courtyard. Similar passages are shown in the other design. The relationship with Barlborough is obvious, though there the corridor system is even more comprehensive.

A third design (I/19 and Plates, 109 and 110) has the same outline and, unlike the other two, is not anonymous. It is annotated 'for Slingsby', a property near Malton in Yorkshire which was acquired by Sir Charles Cavendish in 1595. The plan was perhaps made around 1599, when the half-built house at Kirkby was abandoned. It can never have been carried out: for when Dodsworth the antiquary, visited Slingsby in 1619 it is clear that no such house existed; and some time in the 1620s Sir Charles Cavendish's younger son built a house of quite different size and design on the same site.[25]

At Slingsby the remains of a considerable castle survived into the seventeenth century. As Dodsworth describes them, they included a chapel and a gatehouse. In the plan most at any rate of these remains have been destroyed. But the island site with its moat is retained, joined to the mainland by four bridges, and ringed round with pavilions or towers and walls that rise straight from the water and enclose the garden and courts, in the middle of which is placed the house itself. The main entrance leads across the moat up a combined bridge and flight of steps to a terrace before the porch. This terrace is raised above the general level of the island, as high as the top of the outer wall, and is surrounded by an open balustrade, so that from it there would have been a view both of the moat and of the country around.

The Slingsby plan is the only one of the three in which the internal court is made an architectural feature. A passage leads into it from the porch, on the right is the hall and at the end a colonnade is set in front of a passage leading to the screens end of the hall. On the other side of the court to the hall another passage

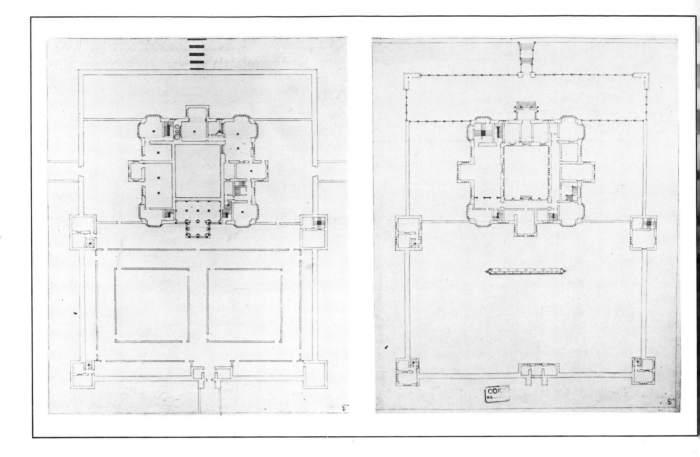

gives access to a staircase, and small rooms, probably lodgings. The plans for the floors above have not survived but judging from the hall floor plan they too must have been well equipped with passages and in this respect as advanced as the plans just discussed.

Owing to the front terrace being considerably higher than the courts and the garden, what appears a basement on the entrance façade becomes a full storey on the other three sides. There would have been no route from the hall floor into the garden, except by going down to the lower floor by the flight of stairs letting off the passage to the screens. This lower floor is shown filled mostly with kitchen, cellars, store rooms, bakehouse, and so on, with all the bigger rooms vaulted. But the room in the centre of the garden front is given a different treatment, vaulted more elaborately, with no access to the other rooms on its floor but with a square projecting bay open all round to the garden. It would in fact have been a vaulted garden room or grotto, decorative rather than useful, and one of the earliest of its type in England. The garden itself is shown quite shut in, with no view except of its walls and of the house. But from the four pavilions at its corners, intended perhaps either as lodgings or gazebos, it would have been possible to look outwards, on to the water and the countryside around.

Smythson may have got the idea for this Slingsby plan from du Cerceau's *Plus Excellents Bastiments*, where there are several designs for houses set symmetrically

180

108. (top left) Robert Smythson's unexecuted plan for Slingsby Castle, Yorkshire. The basement plan (I/19).

109. (top right) Slingsby Castle. The ground-floor plan.

TAB XXXVII

in the middle of moated islands. But he must, too, have been very conscious of its castle allusions, for its walls, towers and vaults are a clear forecast of Bolsover Castle, designed for the same patron (though perhaps by Robert's son) a decade or so later. The gatehouse, which is shown set asymmetrically just off the centre of the garden wall, may be the original medieval gatehouse deliberately retained as a feature in the new design. All this must express Charles Cavendish's personal taste, and other aspects of the design probably owed much to his directions. The corridors are reminiscent of those at his father-in-law's house at Hengrave; and when he sent a design for Hatfield to Robert Cecil in 1607, it included something like the Slingsby garden room. 'Upon the garden side below', he wrote, 'I have likewise given fair vaults for without such singularities I think a house greatly defective.'[26]

This Slingsby is one of the saddest of Smythson's might-have-beens, for it would have been a house of the greatest mystery and romance, rising high and solitary behind its moated walls, resembling, with its vaulted rooms, its terrace above the water and its enclosed and secret garden, the home of some sleeping beauty or enchanted princess. But its effect has not been entirely lost, for a miniature version of it, which still survives, was built at Caverswell Castle in Staffordshire (Plate 110). As at Slingsby there had been a medieval castle there, the outline and some portions of which were used as a setting for the new house.

181

110. Caverswell Castle, Staffordshire (c. 1611), from an engraving in Plot's *Natural History of Staffordshire* (1686).

This has many of the elements of Slingsby: the moated walls and towers enclosing a garden, the toy gatehouse, the bridge across the water, and the house, with a porch between two bays, rising tall and thin from the garden. But although the general idea of a mimic castle with its keep is unmistakable, there is no show of medieval detail. The chimney-shafts and porch are of classical design, the towers and house are (or were) capped with classical balustrading, of the same form as that at Hardwick, and a similar balustrade opens out, as at Slingsby, one side of the enclosure to the moat.[27]

Like Slingsby, the house has a basement kitchen; but apart from the entrance front there is none of the four-way symmetry of a full-blown Smythson plan, and one of its principal features is the big staircase tower placed asymmetrically on one side. The windows too are lower and less dominant than in a typical Smythson house. Nonetheless, its relation to the Slingsby plan, and a number of Smythsonian features (such as the basement kitchen), make it tempting to surmise some connection between Robert Smythson and Caverswell. But what little evidence there is suggest that it was built, possibly after his death or at best at the very end of his life. Its builder, Mathew Cradock, was Mayor of Stafford in 1614, Member of Parliament for Stafford for the first time in 1620, and died in 1641. His father, who lived in Stafford, died in 1611, and this may have given him the means to build himself a house.[28] It cannot be altogether ruled out, but seems unlikely, that he started building earlier, and of course, it is perfectly possible that he did not build till some years later. Even in 1611 Robert Smythson though still alive, was an old man of seventy-six. So the possibility must always remain that Caverswell, if due at all to a Smythson, was due more directly to John, who may have adapted and scaled down the Slingsby plan which he had inherited from his father.

Mathew Cradock was a new man, though one generation off a self-made one. As Sir Simon Degges pointed out in 1669: 'Yet by country trades, in this late age, many are crept into handsome estates, as Mr Mathew Cradock's father, a wool-buyer of Stafford.'[29] His moat and towers may have been designed to give him the illusion of antiquity and an ancient name, in much the same way as, in the early nineteenth century the new rich built themselves sham abbeys and castles.[30]

Charles Cavendish, after he had abandoned his building operation at Kirkby and given up the idea of building at Slingsby, finally settled at Welbeck Abbey in Nottinghamshire, which he leased from his brother-in-law, Gilbert Talbot, in 1597 and bought outright ten years later.[31] It remained the principal residence of him and his descendants. Welbeck had been a house of the Premonstratensians, and there were considerable remains of the monastic buildings. Robert Smythson got out a plan (I/23 and Plate 112) for rebuilding it on an enormous scale, incorporating in the plan some of the medieval remains, including the great vaulted undercroft which still survives at Welbeck. Only a tiny part of this plan,

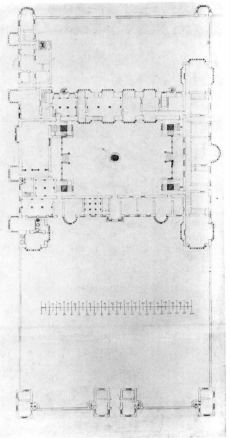

111. (top) The south front of Welbeck Abbey, Nottinghamshire, in the early eighteenth century.

112. (right) Robert Smythson's plan for rebuilding Welbeck. Only the top left-hand corner was carried out.

comprising the wing extending from the dais end of the hall, was ever carried out; basically it still exists as what is known as the 'Oxford' wing, owing to its remodelling by Lady Oxford in the eighteenth century.[32]

This abortive scheme incorporated several features found in other Smythson designs: the use of a wide variety of bay windows, for instance, and (as illustrations of the completed portion shows) of towers, cupolas, and balustrading. But there the resemblance ends. The typical Smythson high, compact and unified house has been abandoned for something lower, more variegated, and spread over an immense area. In this the plan seems to be imitating great southern houses such as Theobalds, Holdenby or Burghley, and as a result is one of Smythson's least typical creations.

But at Welbeck, as already at Slingsby and later at Bolsover, Charles Cavendish's own tastes and skills have to be taken into account. His son, William, wrote from exile to his own son in 1659: 'If ever I see you I will make Welbeck a very fine place for you. I am not in despair of it, though I believe you and I are not such good architects as your worthy grandfather.'[33] That Charles Cavendish was consulted by his contemporaries is shown by two remarkable letters[34] which he

wrote to his sister and brother-in-law, Lord and Lady Shrewsbury, in May 1607. They accompanied the 'plat' of a house; the date, the presence of the letters today at Hatfield, and the fact that one ends 'Present my service to that noble Earl' make it clear that the plat was for Hatfield, where the Earl of Salisbury had chosen the site for his new house in April.

In the letters Charles Cavendish refers to and criticises a 'model' by an un-named 'inventor' which he had seen at Lord Lumley's. Next March Salisbury asked Shrewsbury for, and was sent, a 'plot' of Hardwick. At this period he was collecting ideas and plans[35] from all over the place. There is no reason to suppose that the Cavendish plan was adopted although elements of it may have been.[36] The letters are significant because they show Charles Cavendish describing plans (but not elevations or ornament) with considerable expertise and as his own invention; but also because they make it clear that he had not drawn them up himself. He apologises for 'something mistaken by the drawer in my absence'.

The 'drawer' was almost certainly a Smythson, at this date most probably Robert. One may wonder how much he had helped to give shape to Sir Charles's ideas. But clearly the latter knew what he was talking about and had opinions of his own. The letters show that he liked a 'fair lobby' before the great chamber,

184

113. Burton Agnes Hall, Yorkshire (1601–10).

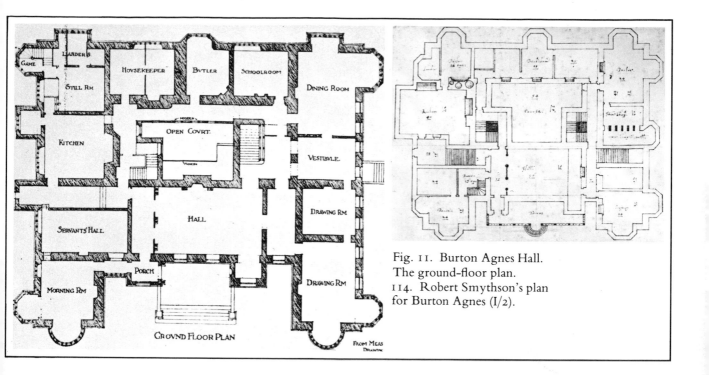

Fig. 11. Burton Agnes Hall.
The ground-floor plan.
114. Robert Smythson's plan
for Burton Agnes (I/2).

to break the noise from the hall, as was later to be provided at Bolsover;[37] he liked 'fair vaults'; he liked a house orientated at 45 degrees to the compass points. They also show something of particular relevance to Robert Smythson. A plan drawn up, probably, by him was being despatched as far afield from Nottinghamshire as Hatfield. Could something similar have happened at, for instance, Lulworth?

Although Burton Agnes,[38] in North Yorkshire, is closer to Wollaton, it is still well out of the Smythson country. But it is certainly based on designs by Robert. It is the only one of the later houses where both a plan by him (I/2 and Plate 114) and the house itself survives. It is dated 1601 above the porch, and other dates up to 1610 appear on other parts of the building. Its builder, Sir Henry Griffiths, had spent his earlier days in Staffordshire,[39] but finally settled on family property in Yorkshire, perhaps on becoming a member of the Council of the North in 1599.

It is quite different in plan from Worksop, Hardwick or Pontefract, but is not unlike Slingsby in that it is a square block with bay windows and a small internal courtyard. At Burton Agnes, as at Pontefract, all the display has been concentrated on the entrance façade (Plate 113), which is indeed a splendid and glittering composition, boldly recessed in the centre, but getting its main swagger from its great many-windowed and many-shaped projecting bays, two square in the centre, two semicircular at the sides, and two five-sided around the corners. The variety of these projections is echoed in the variety of the skyline, which alternates between gables, level parapets, and a combination of the two.

This main façade is built a storey higher than the rest of the house, in order to contain a long gallery running its full length along the second floor. As a result

the side façades are asymmetric, being higher at one end than the other – a lop-sided but not unattractive arrangement. All the subsidiary fronts are much quieter than the main façade, and on the west or kitchen side any pretence of symmetry is abandoned.

The two square projecting bays in the centre of the front contain the porch and the bay window at the screens end of the hall. This was a traditional arrangement, but given a new twist, for the two projections appear, from a frontal view, exactly the same size and treatment, with the doorway to the porch placed where it does not show, not in the front but in the side of its projection; in this way symmetry is ingeniously preserved.

Inside, the main rooms are all varied by the deep and generous recessions of the bay windows; but the glory of the house is its long gallery (Plate 115), running the length of the main front and covered by a splendid wagon-roofed and richly plastered ceiling. This second-floor gallery is clearly modelled on the one at Worksop; but the great chamber (now divided into two) was placed conveniently on the first floor, above the parlour. The house has suffered from the substitution in many cases of sash or Venetian windows for the original mullions. But it still retains a great deal of seventeenth-century fittings: carved woodwork, plaster and alabaster, of lavish though not always sophisticated design, for which Smythson is unlikely to have been responsible.

It is interesting to compare the Smythson plan with the house as built (Plate 113), for they differ in several particulars. Externally, in the plan all four of the great bay windows at the corners of the main front are five-sided; but in the building two are semicircular. The central bay of the east front has dropped

186

out,[40] the corner bays of the north front have become square, and the whole of the west front has been much altered. Finally, the door of the porch is shown in the plan frontal instead of at the side.[41]

These variations make it impossible that the plan could be only a survey of the house. It must be at any rate the first version of an original plan produced by Smythson for Sir Henry Griffiths. It is difficult to say how far the variations in the existing house are due to second thoughts on the part of Smythson himself, how far to alterations made by Griffiths or the masons and carpenters who actually built the house. The semicircular windows were very probably Smythson's own contribution, for such windows appear prominently in two of his other house plans. But it is possible that he planned a house with a level parapet, and of the same height throughout, and that these features were altered or omitted by a conservative or economising patron.

THE MARKS OF A SMYTHSON HOUSE

The hard core of Smythson houses, those that can be connected with him either on conclusive or very powerful evidence, have now been dealt with. The houses concerned are Longleat, Wollaton, Worksop, Hardwick, and Burton Agnes; unfinished, unbuilt, or vanished houses at Blackwell-in-the-Peak, Normanby, Slingsby and Welbeck; and several anonymous houses for which only plans survive.

The group is large enough for generalisations to be made about it. Smythson houses tend to be high and compact, with no courtyards or only small ones. They owe their height to three different (though sometimes combined) causes: high basements, containing the kitchens, cellars, and offices, as at Longleat, Slingsby, Wollaton and Blackwell; long galleries, great chambers, or other large rooms upon the second or third floors, as at Wollaton, Worksop, Hardwick, Burton Agnes and at least four of the anonymous houses; and towers or lanterns, as most notably at Wollaton, Worksop and Hardwick.

Ingenuity of planning is another Smythson attribute. The examples include unconventionally treated halls, at Wollaton, Hardwick, Burton Agnes, Slingsby, and many of the anonymous houses; use of passages at Slingsby and elsewhere; the Hardwick staircases; and the use of different floor and ceiling levels in one house, as at Worksop and Hardwick. All these features build up the impression of someone who was not prepared to take the traditional Elizabethan plan for granted. Combined with this experimental approach to the arrangement of rooms is an obvious delight in the formal aspect of the house plan; by this is meant the combination in different ways of towers and bay windows, often of different shapes, in order to produce plans of striking and ingenious outline. Most of the anonymous plans are of this kind; Hardwick is perhaps the most impressive executed example to survive.

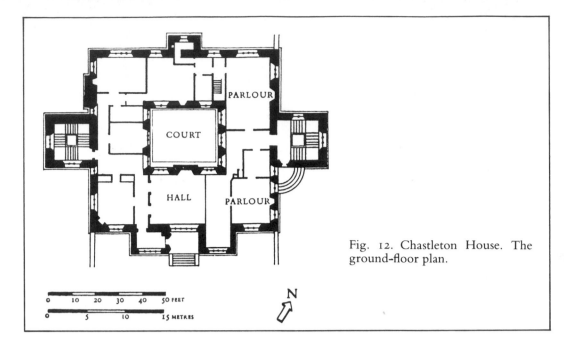

PARLOUR

COURT

HALL

PARLOUR

Fig. 12. Chastleton House. The ground-floor plan.

0 10 20 30 40 50 FEET

0 5 10 15 METRES

N

There remains something more impalpable but all-pervading, the sense of drama. A Smythson house seems to call out for a hill-top. Who could ever forget the first distant view of Hardwick, with its six towers flashing in the evening sun? Or of Wollaton, looking across the city murk of Nottingham from its eyrie, like some immense and unlikely heraldic bird? Bold grouping, deep recession, soaring height, evocative silhouette: among the glittering and amazing group of Smythson houses there is none that is without one or other of these attributes.

If one were able to circle a thousand feet or so above the Midlands and North of England, one would see the few survivors among these houses rising at long intervals out of the landscape with dramatic suddenness. But one would see occasional other houses, equally dramatic, equally strange fowl among the manor houses of the Elizabethan vernacular, which it would be irresistible to connect with Smythson, in spite of the lack of any kind of documentary evidence. Of these houses Doddington, Heath, Barlborough, Manor Lodge, Shireoaks and Caverswell have already been described; but there are others of equal importance.

LATER HOUSES: ATTRIBUTIONS AND SUGGESTIONS

Chastleton[42] in North Oxfordshire is a house which it is tempting to connect with Burton Agnes, for it follows hard on it, started in 1602 or soon after by Walter Jones, a prosperous wool merchant from Worcester. Its hall has exactly the same arrangement as Burton Agnes, of twin projecting bays for porch and oriel, and there is a sideways entrance to the porch. Moreover, it is planned, as is Burton Agnes, round a small internal court, the long gallery has the same kind of wagon-roof (Plate 116), much of the woodwork is very similar in detail, and the staircases are (or were) of the same type, built of wood around an open wooden cage. But it is (in effect, at any rate) a higher house than Burton Agnes,

188

for the plan (Fig. 12) is more compact, and not only is there a second-floor gallery, but also a high kitchen basement. The kitchen is at the back of the house, and owing to the slope of the ground from south to north is in fact at ground level; on the entrance front this floor becomes a true basement, and a vaulted and columned cellar runs right the way across the front beneath the hall.[43]

The main front (Plate 117) is, in a curious and illuminating way, a derivation from that of Hardwick, with every accent altered so as to produce a totally different effect. Like Hardwick, it consists of a main block, with two subsidiary blocks projecting from its front and two set back at either side. But at Chastleton the two front blocks are quite different in size and treatment to those at the side, and are crowded very close together at the centre. The effect of the first step is to contrast, instead of link, the centre to the sides, and of the second to intensify the vertical stress of the design, and this is emphasised still more by the five gables on top of the central block, and by the way that the central windows and strings are lifted considerably higher than those on either side.

The result is most startling, like a row of jets of water shot up suddenly and poised for the split second before they collapse; yet the whole composition is to some extent balanced and made solid, in a way reminiscent of Pontefract, by the

189

116. Chastleton House, Oxfordshire. The long gallery.

117. Chastleton House. The main façade (*c.* 1602).

great width and level battlements of the towers at either side. These towers contain the two staircases of the house, as do the upper stages of the side towers at Hardwick; and again reminiscent of Hardwick is the way the composition dissolves as one moves off the frontal axis, and regroups in dramatic steppings and sharp stripes of light and shade (Plate 118). Chastleton could be a classic example of how Smythson took one of his earlier houses and transformed it to suit his new preference for more varied design. If so he can have done no more than provide plans, with perhaps an elevation that was altered in execution, for the handling of the details is typical of the Cotswold vernacular style. And it has to be remembered that there is no documentary evidence at all to connect him with Chastleton (though equally there is none to connect it with anybody else); that it is in Oxfordshire, well out of his known orbit; and that its builder, Walter Jones, had no obvious connection with any of Smythson's known patrons.[32]

A possible link, however, exists in the person of Ralph Sheldon, the tapestry manufacturer, who was the uncle by marriage of Sir Henry Griffiths of Burton Agnes and also a friend and possibly business associate of Walter Jones. Jones bought Chastleton through Sheldon; he acquired an important set of Sheldon tapestries; and a chimney-piece at Chastleton carries the Sheldon arms. Sheldon's

118. Chastleton from the east.

own house, a few miles from Chastleton at Weston, seems to have had the same arrangement of matching hall porch and oriel as is to be found at Chastleton and Burton Agnes.[44]

It may or may not have been coincidence that it was from Whichford, the next door village to Weston (and one about to be bought by the Sheldons), that the village rector set out to build a house in the Smythson manner in Lancashire. The clergyman in question was Laurence Shuttleworth, who inherited his elder brother's property in 1599, and built a new house at Gawthorpe, near Burnley, between 1600 and 1605. These dates are firm, for it is the only house of those discussed in this chapter where the building accounts survive.[45] The chief mason was called Anthony Whitehead; there is no mention of any payment for drawings or a plan. The house survives intact, apart from having been extensively touched up by Sir Charles Barry in 1849-52.[46]

A number of unusual features make it tempting to surmise that Smythson provided plans, which may have been only partially carried out. There are no chimney stacks on the external walls; the flues were concentrated in the walls of a staircase tower, and emerged like pinnacles, spaced around its parapet. This tower rose prominently above the main roof and may have ended in a prospect

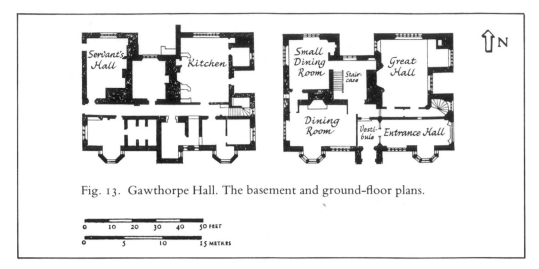

Fig. 13. Gawthorpe Hall. The basement and ground-floor plans.

room. All this is very reminiscent of the plan in Longleat Library. The hall lies along the side of the house instead of on the front; variations of this unusual arrangement are found in several Smythson plans. The kitchen and offices are in the basement, but owing to the fall of the ground the basement became a full storey on the kitchen side, as at Chastleton. The entrance and west fronts are symmetrical, the former (Plate 119) very handsomely so; on the east front irregular but very effective fenestration (altered by Barry) resulted from the insertion of a newel staircase and five storeys of little rooms in the south-east corner, corresponding to the four storeys of the rest of the house (Plate 120).

Smythsonian parallels are even more in evidence at Fountains Hall in York-shire, a building which has been compared to Chastleton.[47] It is a wonderfully dramatic house built deliberately (for there was no earlier building) at the side of a narrow, steep-sided valley, shooting up and out of it in a high and sudden cluster of verticals, with a great semicircular window set back, like a jewel or a lantern in its centre (Plates 121 and 122).

Just as Chastleton is a variation on Hardwick, so is Fountains on Wollaton. It has the two-step recession and corner towers of Wollaton, but its centre is narrower and more crowded and as a whole it is complicated by its three bay windows, and by the forebuilding built out in front of the lower half of its centre. This centre is filled, on the top storey by the great chamber, lit and its shape enlivened by its semicircular window; below it and behind the forebuilding is the hall, running lengthways across the house and with the kitchen beneath it in a basement. The forebuilding itself contains a long flight of steps, running diagonally up and across it and linking the screens end of the hall to the kitchen below. Half-way up this flight of steps, and in the centre both of the forebuilding and the whole façade, is the main entrance doorway; on entering which one can turn either right up to the hall screens or left down to the kitchen. Thus a central entrance to the house is combined, as at Wollaton, with a traditionally placed and asymmetrical screens passage.

The top right and bottom left-hand windows of the forebuilding light the staircase, and the top left and bottom right the outer face of concealed bay

192

119. (top right) Gawthorpe Hall, Lancashire. The entrance front before Barry's alterations.

120. (bottom right) Gawthorpe Hall. The east front.

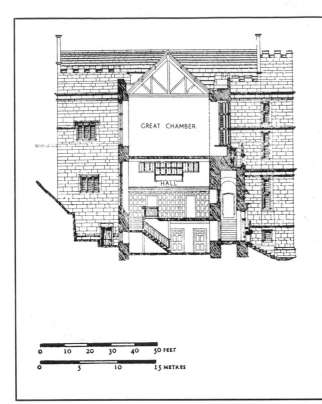

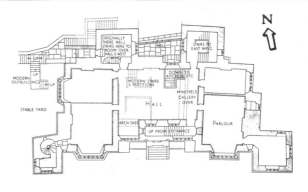

Figs. 14, 15. Fountains Hall. The section and ground-floor plan.

windows for the hall and kitchen respectively. Yet more light is provided by internal windows on the inside of the forebuilding staircase, in a manner directly reminiscent of Hardwick. But as a whole the scheme is an amalgamation, carried out on two floors, of the passage entrance to the hall at Wollaton and the passage joining hall to kitchen in the 'hour-glass' plan. As a new solution to an old difficulty it has all the charm and tidiness of a problem in geometry.

As at Worksop there are fewer storeys in the centre than at the sides. Externally the relationship appears very simple: kitchen and hall in the centre equivalent to basement and first storey at the sides; great chamber to second and third storeys; the top storey at the sides rising above the parapet level at the centre; and all the storeys clearly divided by level and continuous entablatures. But internally it is more complicated than that (Fig. 14). The central cornice outside expresses only the height of the forebuilding. In fact the main body of the hall rises well above the ceiling level of the rooms to either side, roughly as high as the top of the forebuilding balustrade. The great chamber as a result is on a different level to both of the two subsidiary floors that flank it, access to the lower of which is gained off a half-landing on the stairs leading from the great chamber to the hall. In this way a hall and great chamber of appropriate height are fitted in conveniently with smaller rooms of quite different heights.

Something of the same scheme in the top storey seems to occur in the 'hour-glass' plan (page 176 and Plate 106), though in a plan it is impossible to be sure of the exact arrangement of the ceiling levels. Its centre on the top floor is filled with a great chamber, and the two sides with lodgings, which, if of the same

121. Fountains Hall, Yorkshire (c. 1611).

height as a decent great chamber, would have been uncomfortably high. But the plan suggests that they were in fact considerably lower, with a mezzanine floor of more lodgings above, as at Fountains; for it shows at either end of the house two subsidiary but capacious flights of stairs, one starting only on the great chamber floor and both continuing upwards.

Moreover, as variously at Pontefract, Chastleton and in the 'hour-glass' plan, the corner towers buttress and frame the façade and the weight of window is concentrated towards the centre. The shape of the bay windows themselves, five-sided, rectangular, and semicircular, were favourites of Smythson in his later

period. The entablatures and window mouldings are similar to those at Hardwick
and the balustraded walk above the forebuilding is a miniature of the terraces
above the Hardwick colonnades. As at Hardwick and Chastleton the staircases
are in towers, though these project from the rear, not the side, of the house. Such
stylistic links and the whole feel of the house, with its height, tightness and
audacity, make it very probable indeed that Smythson provided designs for
Fountains. But there are certain oddities and discrepancies which suggest that he
did not supervise its erection, but only sent platts from Nottinghamshire. Of
these the most glaring is the way the windows of the two subsidiary floors to
either side of the great chamber do not synchronise with the rooms behind them
but are pushed uncomfortably up, with their tops higher than the floor levels of
the storey above them. A little further ingenuity could have prevented that.
Moreover, the whole plan is a little askew, the left tower is narrower than the

196

122. Fountains Hall. The main front.

right, the left bay window does not exactly match the right, and the window to the right of the central bow is slightly but asymmetrically projecting.[48]

The house was built by Sir Stephen Proctor and is dated, but only traditionally, 1611.[49] If this date is correct, it would, if by Smythson, be a work of the very end of his career. Proctor was an interesting man.[50] His fortune was made or at any rate founded by his father, an iron magnate who received the first Elizabethan patent for smelting iron with coal instead of wood, sold his product to, among others, the Emperor of Russia, and left his son enough money to buy the great estates of Fountains Abbey in 1597.

Stephen continued his father's industrial interests, and owned his own coal and lead mines. In addition he was an extreme Protestant, a friend of Sir Timothy Whittingham (the son of the Calvinist Dean of Durham), and a relentless hunter-down of recusants; on the strength of this he got himself made, around 1606, collector and receiver of fines on penal statutes. He was thoroughly hated by his Yorkshire neighbours; they complained that he was so inflated with pride because of his wealth that he forgot his humble origins; they twice tried to assassinate him, wrecked his lead-works and destroyed his coal mine. He was a figure very typical of his age: the new man, the hard-headed business tycoon, the industrialist, the red-hot Calvinist, fighting his way to wealth and position, chipping down the most splendid abbey in Yorkshire to build a house itself as remarkable and up to date as any then building in England, filling it not only with Protestant theology but with music, for he had married the daughter of Ralph Green, one of the Queen's musicians; while outside behind the bushes the assassin was hiding, and all round his neighbours, at once jealous and contemptuous, waited for the first chance to do him down.

In all this he had aspects in common both with Sir Francis Willoughby, with Lady Shrewsbury and the Cavendishes. With the latter he probably had dealings as well, for he owned land bordering on that of William Cavendish, in the manor of Baldersby just south of Thirsk.[51] But unlike the Cavendishes he failed to found a family; he was one of the victims of the Elizabethan jungle, no one knows where or when he died, no one knows whether he went mad or bankrupt or both, but by 1620 he was dead, his name forgotten, his house and estates sold.

What is one to think of the Hall at Bradford-on-Avon? This was built by the Hall family, rich Wiltshire gentry from whose quarries a certain amount of the Longleat stone had come in the 1570s. In all likelihood Smythson had had dealings with them then. But the Hall was probably built well after he had gone up to the Midlands: the evidence is far from conclusive, but it seems likely that it was started by John Hall the younger, soon after he inherited the property from his father in 1597.[52] No accounts have survived. As a compact gabled rectangular block the house can be grouped with a series of manor houses of this type in Wiltshire and adjacent areas, such as Boyton Manor, Stockton and Lake House. The detail, inside and out, can confidently be attributed to William Arnold, on the analogy of work known to have been done by him. But the

famous show front (Plate 123), with its huge acreage of glass and two compass windows, is more overbearing and heavily windowed than any other known building by Arnold, and is like nothing else to be found locally. The design may have come from another source – perhaps from London, or just possibly from Smythson.

The front has an aggressive and confident swagger which is undeniably reminiscent of Wollaton. The great height of the two main floors, and the

198

123. The Hall, Bradford-on-Avon.

continuous expanse of window, are certainly Smythsonian: the two bay windows (deriving from perpendicular windows such as are found at Thornbury Castle, Gloucestershire) are worth comparing with the bay window on the north front at Barlborough (Plate 69), and over the porch at Fountains (Plate 121). It is just possible that John Hall applied to Smythson, who may have kept up his Wiltshire connections: and that Smythson sent down a platt for the main front (one suspects, without the gables) but left the execution to Arnold.

The four-way symmetrical plan of Slingsby and its two fellow R.I.B.A. designs does not appear in any Elizabethan or Jacobean house either surviving or known to us through engravings or drawings. But the scheme was used constantly in the early seventeenth century just for the main façade of houses of square or rectangular plan. It appears at Caverswell, though with the porch projection not carried up the whole height of the façade. It appears at Gawthorpe, with the porch bay complete. There are other examples of the same scheme at Howsham Hall, only a few miles from Slingsby, and, further from Smythson's usual beat, at Chipchase Castle in Northumberland and at Felbrigg in Norfolk. These houses lack the proportionate height of Caverswell and Gawthorpe, and are more likely to have been, if anything, influenced by Smythson than designed by him: though admittedly Howsham's amazing spread of glass is very much in the Smythson manner.

The surviving example that comes nearest to the complete four-way scheme is at Wootton Lodge in Staffordshire.[53] The situation of this house (Plate 124) is a perpetual delight and surprise; one comes on it suddenly, on looking down over a gate at the end of an avenue, withdrawn and secluded towards the end of a little peninsula that sticks out into a deep and precipitous valley. From here, it has a quality both enchanted and toy-like, a true 'sugared conceit', with its two little pavilions framing the exquisite symmetry, the long-drawn-out verticals of its façade. This façade (Plate 125) is of three storeys on a high basement, with a level balustrade on top. It has not only the porch and the two three-sided bay windows of Gawthorpe, but also two further bays, semicircular this time, just round the two corners of the front. Such a corner combination of round and angular bays occurs elsewhere only at Burton Agnes. Further, unlike Gawthorpe and Caverswell, the second and third storeys are higher by some 4 feet than the first, which itself is a good deal higher than the basement, so that the house lengthens its pace as it rises, in the way of Hardwick and Fountains.

Moreover, the situation is such as Smythson would have delighted in. There is a wonderfully vivid transformation from the broad level space of the forecourt by the narrow and overhanging terraces at the sides to, at the rear, a little triangular court and a garden house, at the apex of the peninsula and perched above a precipitous descent to the lakes below.

Backward from the semicircular windows symmetry, bay windows and balustrade vanish; and the rear of the house is an extraordinary and forbidding blank wall. It is difficult to work out its building history with exactitude or confidence.

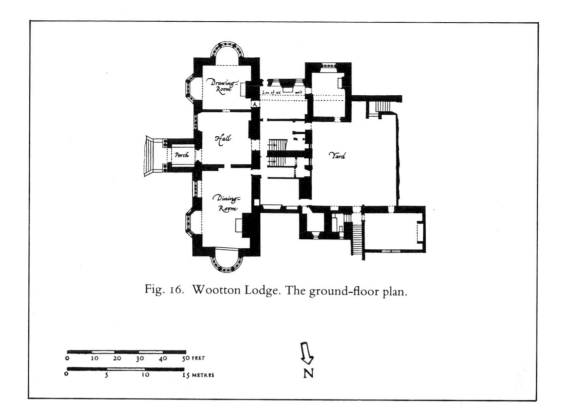

Fig. 16. Wootton Lodge. The ground-floor plan.

0 10 20 30 40 50 FEET
0   5   10   15 METRES

N

There had been a deer park at Wootton since the thirteenth century and the rear portions of the house may incorporate the walls of an earlier hunting-lodge. It is possible that this rear portion was remodelled a few years before the show front was added, which would explain why it is so much less ambitious, though similar in detail. The house was bombarded and perhaps sacked in the Civil War; it is described in a document dating from the Restoration as 'demolished in the late wars', and though 'demolished' is used in its old-fashioned and less extreme sense it was undoubtedly left derelict and perhaps gutted.

When John Wheeler, a Stourbridge ironmaster, bought it at the end of the eighteenth century, he probably pulled down a wing at the rear, before which it may have been a courtyard house. He also completely refitted the interior, and built the present entrance steps, balustraded parapet, pavilions and garden house. On the analogy of Barlborough, Hardwick and similar buildings it seems likely, however, that the house had a balustraded parapet of some kind from the start, though some of the projecting bays may originally have been carried above parapet level in the form of turrets. Accounts of the Civil War siege mention a porter's lodge – probably in the form of a gatehouse at the entrance to the forecourt.

The exact original arrangement of the rooms can only be conjectured at: but one would suspect that the front range contained kitchens in the basement, hall and parlour on the entrance floor, great chamber above the hall, and a long

201

124. (left) Wootton Lodge, Staffordshire. The distant view.

125. (following page) Wootton Lodge. The main façade.

gallery filling the whole length of the top floor. The chimney-stacks are at present very curious: they seems to be column-chimneys of the same type through different detail to those at Wollaton and Caverswell, but with their drums truncated at some later date.

The Elizabethans and Jacobeans never did better than in the entrance front of Wootton. It is as though, after a long and painful struggle between the various elements in its inheritance, English architecture had for a short period reached a quiet haven. There is an atmosphere about Wootton of peace after a battle – the peace of achievement. Much has been assimilated, more has been discarded. Apart from the balustrade and the handsome but discreet classical surround of the porch there is no ornament; only proportion, symmetry, and the interplay of cubic forms. The building seems to float or balance on a single pin-point of creative intensity – incredibly simple, effortlessly beautiful.

There is no documentation for the entrance front of Wootton, but stylistically it is perhaps the most Smythsonian of all the buildings in this chapter. Its builder, Sir Richard Fleetwood, was, incidentally, a cousin of Sir Henry Griffiths of Burton Agnes. But there is no especial need to look for such ties, for Wootton is well in the Smythson country. On the other hand, if by Smythson it probably dates from the very end of his career. It was built by Fleetwood as a hunting lodge or alternative residence to his seat at Calwich Abbey, a mile or two away. His arms are over the doorway; on them is the bloody hand of Ulster, which limits the arms at any rate to 1611, the year in which he was given a baronetcy. Supposing the arms are contemporary with the house, even if they were put up in the final rather than in the first stages of building, the house is unlikely to have been started before about 1607 or 1608. In this case it would be a work, like Fountains, of the last years of Smythson's life, when he was an old man in his seventies. Certainly one could ask for no swan-song more moving or more serene.

126. (preceding page) Wootton Lodge. The view from the terraces.

127. (right) A design for a fountain by John Smythson (III/25(3)).

6 Bolsover Castle & the Revival of Chivalry

A FEW miles north along the ridge on which Hardwick stands a little promontory pushes out from the rest of the ridge, rises like a wave with a long slow raking line, and then breaks abruptly and precipitously 150 feet into the valley. On this promontory stands Bolsover Castle. The keep or Little Castle built by Sir Charles Cavendish is on the crest, with a sheer drop to the northwest; leading up to it is the longer and lower line of the buildings of his son, ultimately the Duke of Newcastle.

All around the promontory is coal-mining country. Bolsover is a colliery town, and there is a colliery and slag-heap immediately below the castle, and more works farther along the valley. From the hills on either side of the valley there are huge undulating views, in which farmland and collieries are curiously mixed together. It is hard to express the peculiar quality of this remote and spacious landscape. In spite (or perhaps because) of the slag-heaps and the little, ugly, red-brick terraces, the valley below Bolsover is a magic valley out of which rise, each on their own hill-top, enchanted castles or palaces. At one end is Hardwick, the six towers of which, endlessly changing in their arrangement, seem to haunt the countryside for they are always appearing unexpectedly, as one lifts one's eyes to the skyline. Further on is the hill-top on which Owlcotes was built: it is all gone now, and only a strange isolated eighteenth-century

206

128. Bolsover Castle, Derbyshire, seen from the valley.

129, 130. (facing page top and bottom) The south-west and north-west façades of the Little Castle, Bolsover, from drawings probably made in the 1630s.

The North Side taken
below the Hill

The front of the howse
being west taken w.th in
the courte standing att
the Gate of the Courte

3

manor house on an adjacent summit remains to give some idea of how it must once have stood. A mile or so beyond Owlcotes is the great eighteenth-century mansion of Sutton Scarsdale, black, opulent and gutted, with the corn fields coming right up to its walls.

From Bolsover one can look across the valley to Sutton Scarsdale, or along it to the distant towers of Hardwick. From Sutton Scarsdale one can survey the whole length of Bolsover and see it, perhaps, on a summer evening, with the little upright block of the keep and the long range of the terrace buildings glistening whitely in the sun against a stormy sky (Plate 128). Even from here it is both unmistakably a castle and yet like no castle that ever was. As one crosses the valley and comes closer it appears still more extraordinary and improbable, The road climbs steeply up the hill, beneath the high turreted mass of the keep, which rises sheer above cliff and battlemented walls; this is its most fortified and formidable aspect, yet one could still never suppose that it was meant for serious battles. Then comes the little town, and a side road, and the long-tree-lined approach to an entrance gate, flanked by rusticated pillars of heroic scale.

Inside is a huge court lined with gutted or empty buildings. As one crosses the court to the keep, climbs a flight of steps to a massive creaking wooden gate between battlemented and arrow-slitted turrets, and crosses a secret inner court-yard into the keep itself, the special atmosphere of Bolsover grows more and more overpowering. Inside the keep it conquers and one is in a dream-world with its own reality. There are cavernous vaulted cellars and kitchens, and a vaulted Gothic hall with a strange hooded fireplace. There are mysterious stone staircases and little hidden rooms with painted ceilings and intricate chimney-pieces of alabaster and marble. In the Pillar Parlour the bosses of the vaulting are each carved in the shape of four horses' heads, and the stone-flagged floor is patterned like a honeycomb. The rooms have a curious living stillness, as though the music from the bundles of instruments carved on the chimney-pieces had only just died away. One wanders through them entranced but also puzzled, for Bolsover is like nothing else in England. It is completely convincing expression of something but of what?

By an unlikely miracle the keep at Bolsover has survived into this century as an almost untouched expression in stone of the lost world of Elizabethan chivalry and romances – romances which young girls once read enthralled through the dark hours of the night, but which have been abandoned long ago to the cold embraces of scholars. It is a castle, not from the Middle Ages, but from the *Faerie Queene* or *Orlando Furioso*. It was built, not for genuine barons of the Middle Ages, not even for the Sir Lancelots, Gawains and Tristrams of the *Morte d'Arthur*, but for the half-allegorical knights and ladies of Spenser, Sidney and Ariosto, with names such as Florimel, Britomart, Calepine and Triamond. A great tournament of knights in armour should be taking place in its courtyard – not a medieval tournament, however, but one such as those held before Elizabeth and James I, in elaborate fancy dress to the accompaniment of masque and allegory.

209

131, 132. (top and bottom) The Little Castle, Bolsover. The hall (above) and pillar parlour.

To obtain any kind of understanding of Bolsover, it is necessary to make a short expedition into this forgotten world.

ELIZABETHAN AND JACOBEAN CHIVALRY

In 1606, six years or so before Sir Charles Cavendish began the keep at Bolsover, the Duke of Lennox and the Earls of Southampton, Pembroke and Montgomery issued this challenge for a joust – a challenge which could almost have emanated from Bolsover, for the mood of the two is identical:

> To all honourable Men at Arms and Knight Adventurers of hereditary note and exemplary nobleness, that for most maintainable actions do weild either sword or lances in quest of glory:
>
> Right, brave and chevalrous; wheresover through the world we Four Knights Errant denominated of the *Fortunate Island*, servants of the Destinies, awaken your sleeping courages with Mavortial greetings:
>
> Know ye that our Sovereign Lady and Mistriss, Mother of the Fates and Empress of high achievements, revolving of late the Adamantine leafs of her eternal volumes, and finding in them that the triumphal times were now at hand, wherein the marvellous adventures of the *Lucent Pillar* should be revealed to the wonder of times and men (As *Merlin*, Secretary to the most inward designs, did long since prophecy) hath therefore (most deeply weighing with herself how necessary it is that sound opinions should prepare the way to so unheard of a marvel) been pleased to command us, her voluntary but ever most humble votaries, solemnly to publish and maintain by all the allowed ways of knightly arguing these four undisputable propositions following:
>
> 1. That in service of Ladies no knight have free will.
> 2. That it is Beauty maintains the world in Valour.
> 3. That no fair Lady was ever false.
> 4. That none can be perfectly wise but Lovers.
>
> Against which, or any of which, if any of you shall dare to argue at point of launce and sword in honorable lists before rarest beauty and best judgements; then again know you, that we the said Four Champions shall, by the high sufferance of Heaven and virtue of our knightly valour, be ready at the valley of Mirefleure . . .[1]

The tournament which this challenge announced was nothing out of the ordinary; such tournaments were held several times a year under both Elizabeth and James, and were among the most colourful and widely publicised features of their reigns.[2] For tilting was still a living sport, though one largely confined, like polo today, to the very rich. It was a sport that called for toughness, and was not without danger. Henry II of France was killed fighting in a tournament at Paris in 1559, and although after this the rules tended to be modified for safety's sake, a man still had to be young and in good training to indulge in it.

210

133. The Little Castle, Bolsover. A pendant in the pillar parlour.

Nonetheless, apart from the purely athletic side, tilting could be used as a vehicle both for romantic spectacle and for propaganda, and this happened increasingly in the reign of Elizabeth. The individual largely responsible was Sir Henry Lee of Ditchley. It was he who inaugurated the series of Accession Day Tilts, in which the Queen's loyal knights jousted before her on each 17th of November, the anniversary of her accession. Lee himself as self-appointed 'Knight of the Crown' was the Queen's chief champion, and the Accession Day and other tilts became a more and more elaborate expression of loyalty in which jousting was combined with allegory and ornament of the most extravagant description.[3] The Accession Day Tilts may have started early in the reign, but do not seem to have reached their fullest development until the 1580s. As early as 1565, however, a romantic element can be discovered in tilting, with challenges appearing under the Arthurian pseudonyms of Sir Segremore, Sir Guy and Sir Lancelot. Such pseudonyms became a commonplace later on, the Red, Green and Black Knights, the Knight of the Tree of the Sun, the Frozen Knight and the Forsaken Knight being among those employed.

Another feature which was the subject of endless thought and interest was the device or *impresa* which each knight had emblazoned on his shield, and which was carefully chosen to be relevant to his situation. On a May Day tournament in 1571, for instance, Thomas Coningsby, who was hopelessly in love with Frances Howard, sported the device of a white lion (the Howard crest) devouring a coney, with the motto 'Call you this Love'.

In a tilt of 1565 the four challengers rode into the tiltyard each accompanied by 'an Amazon apparelled in a long gown, with long sleeves of crimson satin'. In April 1581, Lords Arundel and Windsor, Sir Philip Sidney and Fulke Greville, calling themselves 'the Four Foster Children of Desire', formed part of an elaborate mock-attack on the Queen, who was ensconced in 'the Castle of Perfect Beauty', where she remained, of course, inviolate.[4] In the Accession Day tournament of 1584 there were retinues of attendants disguised as savages or wild Irishmen, and knights with horses caparisoned like elephants. The most famous and perhaps the most elaborate of Accession Day tournaments was that of 1590, in which year Sir Henry Lee, 'being by age overtaken', resigned his post as Knight of the Crown to the Earl of Cumberland.[5] It was at this tournament that the Earl of Essex appeared in black armour wearing a black plume, in a chariot drawn by black horses and with a retinue all in black, in mourning for Sir Philip Sidney. This and other features are described in George Peele's *Polyhymnia*, which was written to celebrate the tilt. A passage from the opening stanzas gives a good idea of the atmosphere of Elizabethan chivalry:

> *Wherefore it fares as whilom and of yore,*
> *In armour bright and sheen fair England's knights,*
> *In honour of their peerless sovereign,*
> *High mistress of their service, thoughts, and lives,*

212

Make to the tilt amain; and trumpets sound,
And princely coursers neigh and champ the bit:
When all, addressed for deeds of high devoir,
Press to the sacred presence of their prince.

The tilt concluded with the singing of Peele's beautiful song *My golden locks time hath to silver turned.* Five years later Peele wrote another poem, *Anglorum Feriae,* inspired by the Accession Day Tilt of 1595. Henry Lee himself was probably responsible for the elaborate speeches – a considerable number of which survive – made both at the tilts and at his two entertainments presented before the Queen, the first at Woodstock in 1575 and the second at Ditchley in 1592. The Woodstock entertainment started with two knights (one of them Lee himself, under the pseudonym of Loricus) tilting before Elizabeth, and an important figure in the festivities was the Fairy Queen, who there made what was probably her first Elizabethan appearance.

Spenser's *Faerie Queene* was published in 1590: its theme of devotion to a virgin ruler, its elaborate apparatus of chivalry thickly charged with allegory, philosophy, and poetic sentiment, its mixture of classical and Gothic elements, is exactly in the mood of Lee's tilts, a mood it evokes immediately with the opening couplet of the first canto:

A Gentle Knight was pricking on the plaine
Y cladd in mightie armes and silver shield...

Tilting plays an important part in Sir Philip Sidney's *Arcadia,* culminating in the tournament between the Knights of Iberia and the Knights of Corinth, in which Elizabeth, Lee and Sidney appear thinly disguised as Helen, Queen of Corinth, Lelius, and Philisides.[6] The Arcadian tilters are clearly inspired by the knights of the Accession Day celebrations, in which Sidney himself played a prominent part, and their equipment is equally, and at times even more, fantastic: a Frozen Knight wears armour representing ice, a Shepherd Knight is covered in wool and has a shepherd retinue carrying lances disguised as sheep-hooks, a Phoenix Knight bursts into flames from which he and his horse emerge unharmed, and so on. But none of these tilting episodes appears in the first version of the *Arcadia* of 1580; they were inserted for the enlarged edition of 1590, and this probably reflects the extent to which the Accession Day and other tilts had increased in significance and reputation in the previous decade. By now the language and attitudes of chivalry had become part of the poetic imagination of the Elizabethans, so that Campion, for instance, was thinking as much of the present as the past when he wrote:

Then wilt thou speake of banqueting delights,
Of masks and revels which sweete youth did make
Of Turnies and great challenges of knights,
And all these triumphs for thy beauties sake.[7]

213

The World of the Tournament

This efflorescence of chivalric pageantry was by no means confined to England: every aspect of it described in this chapter could be equalled and probably surpassed across the channel,[8] just as the works of Spenser, Sidney and their circle were matched, and in part inspired, by the Spanish and Portuguese romances, and the two great Italian epics, Ariosto's *Orlando Furioso* (1516) and Tasso's *Gerusalemme Liberata* (1575). Moreover, the great tournaments and pageants of the Continent have been visually preserved for us, most notably in the series of Valois tapestries, now in the Uffizi Gallery in Florence. No representation of an Elizabethan or Jacobean tournament is known to survive. There are, however, a fair number of portraits or miniatures of Elizabethans in tilting dress (Plates 135 and 136); and much of the armour worn by the knights of the tournaments is still preserved, some in the original in the Tower of London or Windsor Castle armouries, more in the collection of exquisitely coloured drawings (Plate 134) made at the time by a German armourer at work in London, and now in the Victoria and Albert Museum.[9]

Tournaments went on right through the reign of James I and into that of Charles, who as a young man was a skilful tilter. The equivalent of the Accession Day Tilts were those held annually on what was known as the King's Day, the anniversary of James's coronation on 24 March. Tournaments were also held to celebrate special occasions: that of June 1606, for instance, for which the challenge quoted earlier was written, was held in honour of the visit of the King of Denmark. The years 1610 and 1613 – between which Bolsover was conceived and started – were bumper ones for tilts. On the King's Day tournament of 1610. 'The Duke of Lennox exceeded all in Feathers; the Lord Walden in Followers; and Sir Richard Preston in a Pageant, which was an Elephant with a castle on the back.'[10] Later on in the year, in June, there were magnificent celebrations in honour of Prince Henry's installation as Prince of Wales. 'Upon Wednesday in the afternoone, in the Tilt-yeard, there were divers Earles, Barons, and others, being in rich and glorious armoure, and having costly caparisons, wondrous curiously imbroydered with pearls, gould, and silver, the like rich habiliaments for horses were never seene before. They presented their severall ingenious devices and trophies before the King and Prince, and then ran at Tilt, where there was a world of people to behould them.'[11]

Of the King's Day Tilting of 1613 it was written at the time 'there was more gallantry both for number and bravery than hath been since the King came in'.[12] But perhaps the most elaborate chivalric pageantry of the reign was that connected with the marriage, on 26 December of the same year, between the King's favourite, the Earl of Somerset, and the Countess of Essex (who had poisoned her first husband to make the marriage possible). The marriage was followed by a masque, written by Thomas Campion and acted in the old Banqueting House in Whitehall.[13] Six knights, turned into pillars of gold through the enchantments of a sorceress, were rescued by the act of the Queen, while the chorus sang:

134. (top left) Tilting armour worn by Sir Henry Lee of Ditchley.
135. (top right) Prince Henry exercising with the lance.
136. (bottom) Lord Herbert of Cherbury, from the miniature by Isaac Oliver.

Since knightly valour rescues Dames distressed
By vertuous Dames let charm'd Knights be released.

For the following day Ben Jonson provided an entertainment in which two cupids announced a tournament to be held on New Year's Day. The cupids were depicted as quarrelling, and challenged each other in terms that were simplified from those used by the Knights Errant in 1606: 'I challenge thee of falsehood; and will bring, upon the first Day of the New Year, in to the lists before this Palace, ten Knights armed, who shall undertake against all assertion, that only I am the child of Mars and Venus', and so on.

The history of chivalry runs continuously from the early Middle Ages to the Jacobean age and beyond, but it has its peaks and its troughs. The decades between 1490 and 1520, and between 1580 and 1610, represent peaks, with the lowest point of the trough between them coming in the reign of Edward VI. It is possible to correlate the trough with the influence of the Renaissance, and the Elizabethan revival with subsequent anti-classical reaction. There may be a certain amount of truth in this, but it is an over-simplification. Other factors were also at work.

The Elizabethan government was run by a comparatively small élite of nobility and gentry, whose position was by no means a secure one. The country at the start of the reign was bankrupt and divided. The Protestantism which they all supported was regarded with apathy by the great proportion of the population and with hatred by a minority. A country with a Protestant government was one of a small and relatively weak group of nations in constant danger of invasion, and this danger increased with the advance of the Counter-Reformation. The Queen, whose death would undoubtedly mean the immediate overthrow of the government and the governing class, was in equally increasing danger of assassination.

The Accession Day Tilts and related pageantry were useful vehicles for propaganda. They helped to foster loyalty to the Queen and to build her up as a national figure. They gave her romance and mystery. To some extent they satisfied the appetite for colour and ceremony which had formerly been satisfied by the Catholic religion. They linked the existing régime to the past, but an aspect of the past which could be freed from religious associations. And in them the Protestant point of view could be subtly put across by means of allegory, a tool particularly suited to the temper of the times.

It is hard to know to what extent Lee and his circle were deliberately trying to bring all this about. Perhaps, in satisfying their own emotional needs, they unintentionally answered a need in others. In any case, the Accession Day Tilts were a success, just as the whole Elizabethan adventure was a success. Protestantism and nationalism fused together. The war with Spain was fought and won. Elizabeth became a national hero and symbol. It was not coincidence that the decade of the great blossoming of the tilts was the decade of the Armada.

The efflorescence of national pride and consciousness resulted naturally enough in an increasing interest in national history. The great Elizabethan series of history plays starts in the 1580s and gets fully under way in the 1590s. Shakespeare's *Henry V*, with all its romance of nationalism, was probably written in 1599. In 1595 Thomas Daniel published the first five books of his historical epic, *The Civile Wars*; in the following year Michael Drayton published a similar work *Mortimeriados*, which he revised and issued as *The Barons Warres* in 1603. This was the most ambitious of a series of historical poems by Drayton, of which the best known (and the shortest) is perhaps the Ballad of Agincourt, first printed in 1606:

> *Upon Saint Crispin's day*
> *Fought was this noble fray*
> *Which fame did not delay*
>   *To England to carry;*
> *O, when shall English men*
> *With such acts fill a pen,*
> *Or England breede againe,*
>   *Such a King Harry.*

Historical poetry of this kind is distinct from the literature of chivalry, but both helped to create a picture of the Middle Ages as a period of heroic deeds, thrilling stories, and national glory rather than one of ignorance and superstition.

Influences of this kind, combined with the increasing conservatism of a government of ageing revolutionaries, helped to bring about a return to, or strengthening of, tradition. In a more general architectural context something was said about this in the introductory chapter. The influence on the great Elizabethan house of late Gothic Court architecture was commented on there. It is perhaps worth remarking that this Court architecture was conterminous with the peak of chivalry that preceded the Elizabethan; and that just as Burghley and Worksop drew inspiration from Richmond Palace, so much of the procedure and imagery of Elizabethan chivalric pageantry was inspired by the pageantry of Henry VII and the young Henry VIII.

MOCK CASTLES IN PAGEANTRY AND ARCHITECTURE

The display side of the Elizabethan and Jacobean tournament is only a section of the field of pageantry, to which a very great amount of time and trouble was devoted throughout the period. Before discussing Elizabethan castles of stone, something ought to be said about Elizabethan castles of cardboard or canvas, for the latter is the larger group, and perhaps helped to inspire the former. The castle had been a feature of masques and pageants since medieval times, and it continued through the sixteenth into the seventeenth century. Mimic castles were (to quote a few of many examples) features of the pageantry accompanying Henry V's return to London from Agincourt in 1415; Henry VII's entry into York in 1486; Charles V's reception at London in 1522; the coronation of Anne Boleyn in 1533; Elizabeth's coronation procession in 1558; her entry into Warwick in 1572; and the Lord Mayor's show of 1612, 1613 and 1635.[14]

A favourite feature of pageants was the assault of a castle – usually, for symbolic reasons, garrisoned by ladies. At the wedding masque of Arthur and the Princess of Spain in 1501, for instance, a castle on wheels 'right cunningly devised' was drawn into the hall by 'fower great beasts with chaines of gold.... There were within the same Castle disguised VIII goodlye and fresh ladyes, looking out of the windowes of the same, and in the foure corners of this Castle were IIII turrets ... in the which ... was a little child apparelled like a maiden.' The children sang as the pageant moved up the hall, and the castle was later assaulted by 'VIII goodly knights naming themselves Knights of the Mount of Love' who captured the ladies.[15]

In 1511 a castle containing 'a maiden with a garland' was drawn by a lion and an antelope into Westminster Hall where it was 'by the king's gard and other gentyllmen rent, brokyn, and by fors karryed away'.[16]

In 1581, as already described, the Castle of Perfect Beauty was occupied by the Queen herself, and was unsuccessfully assaulted by the Four Foster Children of Desire. Twenty-five years earlier, when she was a Princess at Hatfield, a masque with a 'devise of a castell of clothe of golde' drew from her the comment that she 'mysliked these folliries'.[17] But there is no doubt that she took the greatest pleasure in the 1581 and similar entertainments, for in the course of her reign she moved a long way from the humanist purism of her early womanhood.

In Paris in 1572 a sham-castle nearly played a sinister part in the festivities at the wedding of Marguerite de Valois and Henri de Navarre, that culminated in the Massacre of St Bartholomew's Day. A friendly battle was to have taken place, with the King and the Catholics defending the castle against the assaults of Coligny and the Huguenots. But (according, at any rate, to the Protestants) the real intention was to make the entertainment a trap, in which the Catholics, seriously armed, would massacre the unsuspecting Protestants. However, owing to the sickness of Coligny, the fight was cancelled.[18]

A castle or fort on an island in a lake was a feature of the elaborate entertainment which Lord Hertford mounted for the Queen at Elvetham in Hampshire in 1591 (Plate 137). The castle – 'twenty foot square every way and evergreen with willows' – is described as 'environed with armed men' and the Spirit of the Lake appeared on the water to tell Elizabeth (among a great deal else) that 'That Fort did Neptune raise for your defence.' A display of fireworks from the fort followed; perhaps more was intended, but a good portion of the programme seems to have been abandoned owing to the usual bugbear of English pageants, continual drenching rain. The entertainment is the only Elizabethan one of which an engraving survives: the castle appears prominently in it, an absurd little toy fort with three round towers, battlements, and flags flying bravely.[19]

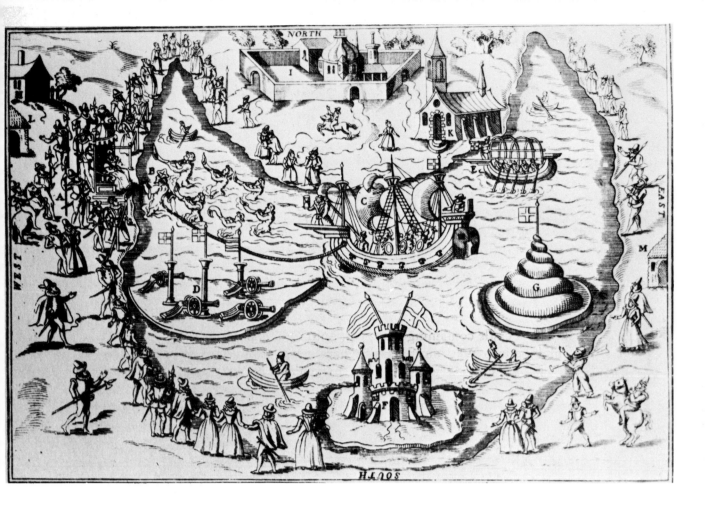

A pageant castle with a certain family likeness to the Elvetham one is illustrated in an engraving of the 'carrousel' held on the Place Royale in Paris to celebrate Louis XIII's marriage with Anne of Austria. This took place in 1612, the year of the probable commencement of Bolsover. The castle was called '*le palais de la Felicité*' and was defended against all comers by five Chevaliers de la Gloire, Almidor, Léontide, Alphée, Lysandre and Argante.[20]

An account of sham-castles could go on interminably. To end with two in the Bolsover era, the Prince of Wales's entertainments of 1610 included (besides the tournament which has already been referred to) a great water-fight of ships-of-war and galleys 'against a great castle builded upon the water', followed by 'many strange and variable fierworkes in the castle';[21] and a similar castle, of which an illustration survives (Plate 138), played its part in the fireworks display given to celebrate the marriage of Princess Elizabeth to the Elector Palatine early in 1613.[22]

The motives for having sham-castles in pageants and tournaments were reasonably obvious. Sham-castles in architecture are more complex. In most buildings of the time it is easy enough to find Gothic echoes and roots. But there are a few where the evocations of the Middle Ages, chivalric pageantry, or the world of

219

137. The pageant castle erected for the Queen's entertainment at Elvetham, Hampshire, in 1591.

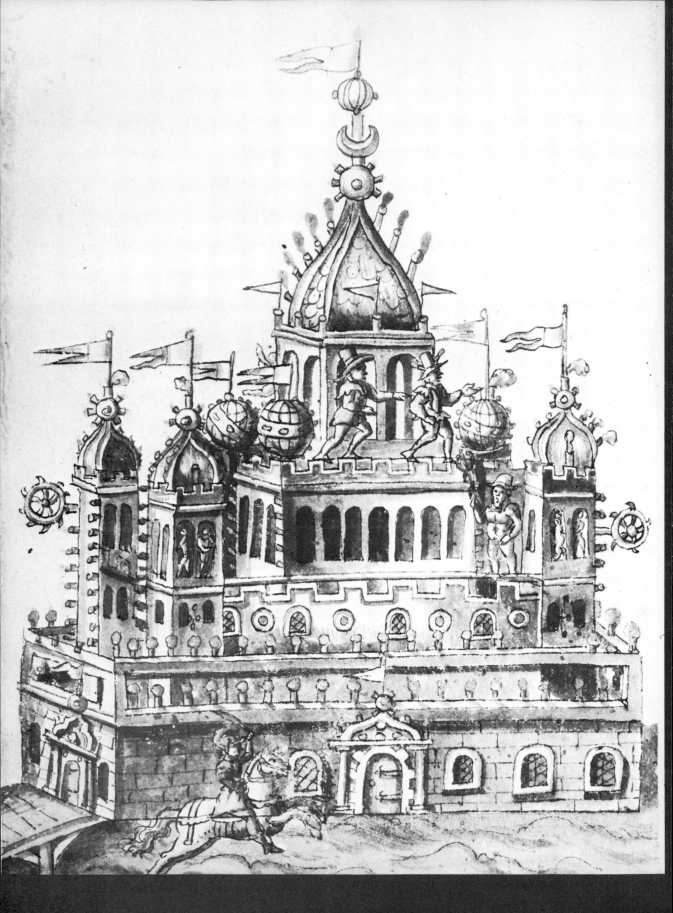

the romances is so strong as to set them in a class by themselves. These are the Elizabethan and Jacobean castles. They are a somewhat variegated group, because of the differences of their starting-points. In some the intention is clearly to evoke a medieval castle – usually because there was a medieval castle on the site before. Some seem to be inspired more by contemporary chivalry and romances. The two moods were closely related and are often hard to disentangle. Even in the former group the point of view is never more than marginally an archaeological one. For their builders were not producing copies, they were creating devices – evolving something novel and clever out of an allusion to the past.

By this period chivalry and Gothicism were related but by no means conterminous. Both the tournaments and the romances were heavily loaded with post-medieval content. Symbolism, allegory, fancy dress and philosophic notions from the Renaissance were combined with much else that derived from the Middle Ages. In the great festival held at Fontainebleau in 1564, there was a tourney in which the opposing sides fought in the dress of Greeks and Trojans.[23] In the tournaments of the Arcadia, knights in armour charge down the lists against a background that, nebulous though it is, appears to be that of classical Greece. Mixtures of this kind were not considered illogical or bizarre at the time; for, with the exception of a few humanists, mostly at the beginning of the reign, the Elizabethans do not appear to have thought of Gothic and Classic as necessarily hostile elements. In their literature, their buildings and their entertainments they poured everything in happily together; equally, in their sham-castles the mixture is seldom a pure one.

There are one or two buildings which are not sham-castles at all, or only very remotely so, but which have a certain deliberately fantastic or Gothic element in them which sets them apart from other houses of the period. Of these none is more evocative or successful than Cranborne Manor in Dorset (Plate 139). Basically this is a thirteenth-century hunting-lodge built for King John, but it was completely remodelled by William Arnold around 1608, as a hunting-lodge for the Earl of Salisbury. The remodelling was carried out in a spirit of delicate fantasy; Gothic elements and classical detail of, one suspects, an intentionally playful nature were subtly combined to create a holiday atmosphere for what was essentially a holiday house. The buttresses, tower, and arcaded Gothic cornice of the old building were not removed: instead new buttresses and a new tower were added to make the arrangement symmetrical, the Gothic cornice was duplicated where necessary, but the buttresses were clothed with a delicate embroidery of pilasters and arcaded loggias were introduced in the centre of the two principal façades.[24]

There is a sophistication about Cranborne which is absent at Wollaton, perhaps because twenty-eight years of development separate the two. Yet the mixture in the two houses is not so very different: there is the same mingling of Gothic and Classic, the same element of fantasy. But the castle elements at Wollaton are stronger; the situation is more commanding, the silhouette more overpowering.

221

138. The Magician's Castle, erected as a centre-piece for the fireworks display held to celebrate the marriage of Princess Elizabeth to the Elector Palatine in 1613.

The reminiscence of a keep, rising amid the lower towers of its curtain wall, must have been present in the minds of Willoughby and Smythson. Yet Wollaton is not a sham-castle in the same way as Lulworth or Bolsover: too great a diversity of elements have gone to compose it. The same could be said about Longford Castle, which like Wollaton is a kind of pocket encyclopedia of Elizabethan ideas. It became a 'Castle' only in comparatively recent years, but the change of name reflects something in its nature: combined with the symbolic plan, the great classical frontispiece, are the squat round towers, unmistakably castellar in silhouette if not in detail, and, inside, the extraordinary hanging rib-vault (Plate

139. (facing page) Arcadian architecture: Cranborne Manor, Dorset (*c.* 1608).

140. (top) A Spenserian interior: the great chamber at Longford Castle, Wiltshire.

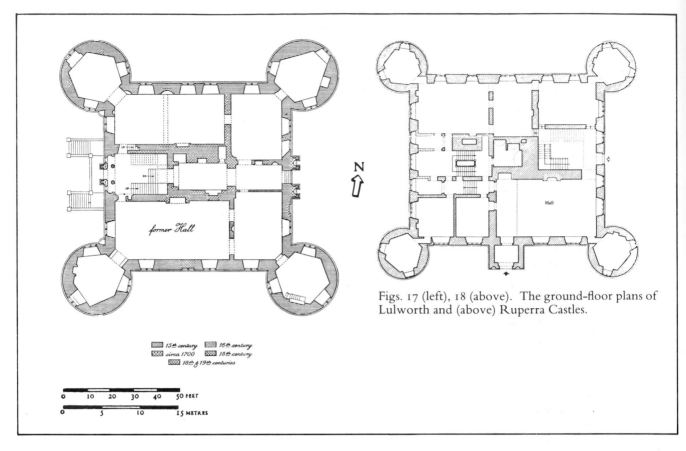

former Hall

Hall

N

Figs. 17 (left), 18 (above). The ground-floor plans of Lulworth and (above) Ruperra Castles.

15ᵗʰ century   16ᵗʰ century
circa 1700   18ᵗʰ century
18ᵗʰ & 19ᵗʰ centuries

0 10 20 30 40 50 FEET
0   5   10   15 METRES

140) of the Marble Room – resting, typically enough, on Corinthian columns.[25] In the diversity and richness of their background, and a kind of self-consciously romantic quality, Longford and Wollaton are perhaps the nearest architectural equivalents to the *Faerie Queene*. Longford was actually built by patrons of Spenser, and it is even possible that he had it in mind when he described the Castle of Temperance:[26]

> *The Frame thereof was partly circular*
> *And part triangular – O work divine . . .*

In a separate class to these Spenserian buildings are the cases of the Elizabethans adding to or altering medieval castles in a sympathetic spirit. The gatehouse at Kenilworth Castle, which probably dates from the 1570s, has, with its four octagonal corner towers, clearly been built as a paraphrase of a medieval gate-house, just as Leicester's new wing of the same date is intended to be in keeping with the medieval castle. But this is a matter of height, outline and grouping rather than detail; in fact the most prominent decorative feature of the gatehouse is a portal of elaborate and advanced classical design. Similar portals form a prominent feature of the alterations to Wardour Castle, carried out at much the same time as the additions to Kenilworth. But, as has been described, these were combined with new windows of a deliberately Gothic type. The result was eminently successful, because Wardour Castle was the product of an earlier age of chivalry – its fortifications perhaps half-serious, half-romantic – and was built to an ingenious geometric plan, both qualities which made it sympathetic to the Elizabethans. What was done was to make sufficient alterations to convey it smoothly from the world of Malorie into the world of Spenser.

Carew Castle in Pembrokeshire is another example of a medieval castle altered under Elizabeth. In this case an entire range was added, with huge windows looking over the moat and projections in the form of towers, but with their character changed from defensive bastions to circular lanterns of glass. This is an obvious and deliberate conceit, and should perhaps be compared to the forecourt architecture of Montacute where, as it has been sensitively interpreted, 'the gatehouse has become a gateway, the curtain walls open balustrading, the bastions toy temples, the corner towers bower-like pavilions'.[27]

Forty miles or so from Montacute, however, the garden at Hazelbury Manor was surrounded, probably in the early seventeenth century, with walls which imitate rather than etherealise medieval fortifications, with battlemented circular bastions at the angles of the enclosure.[28]

Similar fortified gardens existed at Ware Park and Audley End, and survive at Lismore Castle in Ireland.[29] The Ware Park garden took the form of a mock-fortified enclosure in the middle of the main garden. A similar conceit was used in a park rather than a garden to produce Walton Castle, on a hill-top above the Bristol Channel near Walton-in-Gordano.[30] Considerable ruins of this interesting and little-known building survive; it is a perfect example of a structure of pageant-fort type made permanent in stone. Within an octagonal and embattled curtain-wall with round towers at the angles is an octagonal central building decorated with cross-shaped arrow slits. It was built by the first Lord Poulett in about 1615–20, probably as a stand or banqueting house.

Walton can serve as an introduction to four full-scale Jacobean castles: Lulworth in Dorset, Ruperra in Glamorganshire, Caverswell in Staffordshire and Bolsover in Derbyshire. The border-line between these and the houses already discussed is not a hard-and-fast one; they employ a language in which the castle elements predominate, but it is still a mixed one. At Lulworth, for instance, there are towers, battlements, Gothic windows and a rose window reminiscent of the hall windows at Wollaton; but there is also a classical porch, balustrading and alcoves, and a vaulted room supported on Tuscan columns, as in the kitchen at Wollaton. Moreover, the attenuated Gothic windows resemble no genuine medieval windows; nor does the rose window; nor is the castle as a whole anything but a fantasy on a medieval castle. Lulworth is in the mysterious Spenserian world, neither Gothic nor classic, bathed in an unreal light; that is its attraction.

Ruperra and Lulworth (Plates 141–3) form a pair, like Barlborough and Heath; either they had a common original, or one inspired the other. Both are compact square houses, with battlements and round towers at the corners. Both are three storeys high, and have arched window-lights of Tudor-Gothic type. Both, by Jacobean standards, have a low ratio of glazing to wall. The two houses

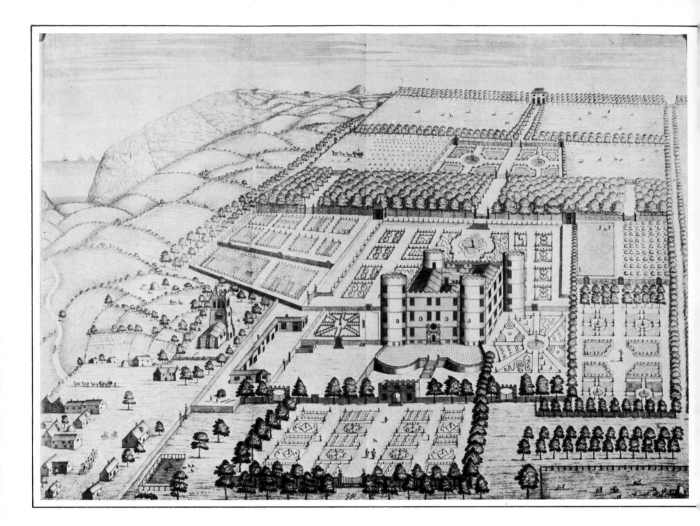

are almost identical in size and have remarkably similar plans, in which the same number of rooms are grouped in the same way round a square central core; at Lulworth this core rose above the roof in the form of a little tower, and in both houses the main chimney-flues seem to have been carried up in it. Both houses have become ruins; Lulworth, high up on the downs above the sea, is an especially evocative one.

Lulworth is the earlier of the two houses.[31] It was built as a very grand hunting-lodge, an appendage to the main family house at Bindon a few miles away. It was approaching completion in 1607 when its owner, Thomas Howard, third Viscount Howard of Bindon, wrote as follows to the Earl of Salisbury: –

Yf the lyttyll pyle yn Lullwourth parke shall prove pretty or wourthe the labor Bestowed yn the erectyng of yt, I wyll acknowlege as the truth ys, that your Lo: powrefull speche to me at byndon to have layde the fyrst foundatyon of the pyle yn my mynd, wch ever synce hath labored for a spedy fynysshyng for the contentment of thos, for whos farder likyng of that place the care ys taken. Thankyng your Lo: from my harte for the fyrst good motyon . . .[32]

141. (top) Lulworth Castle, Dorset, from an eighteenth-century engraving showing the central tower.
142. (facing page top) Lulworth from the south-east.
143. (facing page bottom) Ruperra Castle, Glamorgan.

In spite of this letter, there is some possibility that the house had been started in 1588 by Thomas's elder brother Henry, had been discontinued and was started again some time after Thomas inherited the property in 1601.[33] The two brothers belonged to the inner ring of Elizabethan society, but they were not an attractive couple. Henry, in particular, was quarrelsome, extravagant, lecherous, brutal and a drunk. Thomas was not much better; he did his best to prove that his niece was illegitimate, in order to disinherit her in his favour; according to Ralegh (who cordially disliked him, and perhaps is not a reliable witness) he poisoned his wife.

Ruperra is said to have been dated 1626 on the porch.[34] It was built by Sir Thomas Morgan (1564–1632), the seventh son of a Welsh squire who made a fortune as steward to the Earls of Pembroke and was knighted in Wilton in 1623. When the seventh Earl of Shrewsbury's daughter (and Sir Charles Cavendish's niece) Mary Talbot married the Earl of Pembroke in 1604, Thomas Morgan was one of the trustees of the marriage settlement.[35]

There is a possible basis for a Smythson connection here, and the nature of the two houses makes one take it seriously. Their four round towers are suggestive of the mysterious plan at Wollaton. The enclosed core containing the main flues and rising above the roofs as a tower seems to relate to the plan in the library at Longleat, and to Bolsover and Shireoaks. The windows are suggestive of Smythson's windows at Wardour (Sir Matthew Arundell of Wardour had for a time been closely connected with Henry Howard, the second Lord Howard of Bindon[36]). At Lulworth (but not Ruperra) the hall ran along one side of the house, with its main axis at right angles to the axis of the entrance porch. This position is an unusual one for a hall, but similar to that found in several Smythson drawings, and at Gawthorpe, Shireoaks and Bolsover. But the detail at Lulworth is probably by William Arnold;[37] if Robert Smythson made any contribution (perhaps through the medium of Charles Cavendish) it must have been limited to plan and elevations.

Caverswell Castle has already been discussed and illustrated; it is an interesting example of how unmistakable and deliberate castle outlines and layout (inspired by its castle site) could be combined with an almost complete lack of castle detail. As has been suggested, it was probably inspired by the first project for Slingsby Castle in Yorkshire. And with Slingsby one comes securely to Charles Cavendish and the Smythsons.

The houses built or planned by Charles Cavendish and his sons form the most important group of castle architecture of the period. Blackwell-in-the-Peak with its vaulted kitchen and cellar, compact plan and four towers, would, if built, have had something of a castle air. The first Slingsby (Plates 108 and 109), with its completely vaulted basement, its moat, towers and gatehouse, would have carried the illusion further still, yet basically the plan of the house was a typically Elizabethan one. In the plan for Welbeck (Plate 112) the castle allusions are less strong, but there are a series of vaulted rooms and an approach consisting of a

228

XIII. Bolsover Castle, Derbyshire. The chimney-piece in the Star Chamber of the Little Castle.

turreted gatehouse between turreted pavilions. The Little Castle at Bolsover (Plate 145) is the culmination, carrying the castle masquerade further than any other house of the period.

SIR CHARLES CAVENDISH

Sir Charles Cavendish, Bess's third and youngest son, was born in 1552, travelled abroad as a young man with his step-brother and brother-in-law, Gilbert Talbot (later the seventh Earl of Shrewsbury), commanded troops in the Dutch wars in 1578, and was knighted in 1582. He was famous for his skill as a horseman and a swordsman. He was a patron of the great madrigalist, John Wilbye, who dedicated a book of airs to him in 1598.[38] His friendship with Gilbert Talbot lasted all his life; he was 'always at his elbow, politic, and having great sway with him'. Gilbert Talbot was a difficult man, and through this friendship Sir Charles was involved in violent quarrels with his mother and his neighbours, the Stanhopes, who made the attack on him in 1599, which he repulsed so bravely. On the other hand, it was from Gilbert Talbot (who was extravagant and always short of money) that he acquired both Bolsover and Welbeck, at very reasonable prices. He died in 1617 and Ben Jonson wrote his epitaph.[39]

His surviving letters suggest that he was lively and fond of gossip. But he remains a shadowy figure, a little man (as his portrait shows) but brave as a lion. One would like to know more of him for, to judge from his buildings, he must have been an unusual person. He clearly inherited something of his mother's passion for building, and was thought by his contemporaries to be skilled in architecture. The houses which he built or planned to build were all curious and full of character. Moreover, they all had something of a castle or Gothic air. Just as Sir Thomas Tresham had a passion for religious symbolism, Sir Charles Cavendish had a passion for castles. Tresham's predilection can be explained in terms of his religious background: Sir Charles Cavendish's is more mysterious.

It would certainly be satisfying if any of the Elizabethan castles could be proved to have been built by someone closely involved in the tournament world, but this cannot be done, though the Arundells, Howards, Gorges and Pouletts all had Court connections and the world of Elizabethan chivalry would not have been strange to them. In the light of the circumstances of the time and his own reputation as a horseman, Sir Charles Cavendish is unlikely to have been entirely ignorant of tilting. But there is no evidence that he was an enthusiast, or ever took part in the Accession Day or other court tournaments.

On the other hand, at the time that Bolsover was built (when he was aged sixty and past tilting) he was doubly connected with the Jacobean tournament world through his nieces, the daughters of his friend and brother-in-law, Gilbert, Earl of Shrewsbury. In 1604 Mary Talbot married William Herbert, Earl of Pembroke; in 1606 her sister Alethea married Thomas Howard, Earl of Arundel.

XIV. Bolsover Castle. The Venus Fountain.

Arundel, Pembroke and Pembroke's brother Montgomery were among the most conspicuous of the little band of enthusiasts whose names occur regularly in the lists of tilters during James I's reign. In 1606 Pembroke and Montgomery were among the four deliverers of the challenge quoted at the beginning of this chapter. Pembroke's wedding in November 1604, was celebrated by a great tournament at Wilton at which (one may surmise) Sir Charles Cavendish was very probably present (and Thomas Morgan of Ruperra certainly was). According to John Aubrey, some of the shields used in this tournament, 'of pasteboard painted with their devices and emblemes, which were very pretty and ingenious', were still hanging at Wilton in his own day.[40]

Sir Charles's son William was certainly a tilter. On Good Friday, 1624, when practising running at the tilt, he had a bad fall, which Laud noted in his diary with the comment, 'Should not this day have other imployments?'[41] In a list made in 1618 containing 'Names of those Lords and others' who had not so far taken part in the King's Day tournaments, 'Sir William Cavendish, Sir Charles's son' is among those especially starred and directed to appear 'without faile' at the tournament that year.[42] Although he did not in fact do so, his presence on the short-list suggests that he had some kind of reputation as a tilter. This prompts one to wonder how much tilting went on outside the immediate Court orbit. Is it possible that tournaments similar to that held at Wilton took place elsewhere in the provinces, and that Sir Charles was the presiding spirit of tilting in the Midlands? It is a tempting idea, but no evidence to support it has come to light.

Or could the secret of Sir Charles's castle-mania lie in his wife? The building of castles as a romantic offering to the woman one loved would be in keeping with the age; and it would have been particularly appropriate in Sir Charles's case, for his wife was the heiress of an ancient Border family, the Ogles, of Bothel and Ogle Castles in Northumberland. Romanticism and snobbery tend to go together. The Cavendishes, though with a respectable pedigree, had only been rich for two generations. But Sir Charles's choice of an Abbey and two historic castle sites for his own seats of residence seems to show a desire to link himself with tradition. The union of new money with ancient lineage could have set up the kind of psychological situation of which sham-castles were the result.

All this is too much in the region of surmise and it is perhaps time to describe the buildings themselves.

144. Design by John Smythson for the gallery doorway in the terrace wing, Bolsover Castle (III/1(5)).

7 The Buildings of John Smythson

THERE had been a twelfth-century castle at Bolsover,[1] the keep of which was probably on the site of the forecourt of Sir Charles Cavendish's keep, where foundations have been found. The walls of the original inner bailey may form the core of the massive walls surrounding the existing fountain garden, which adjoins the seventeenth-century keep on the east. There is no means of saying how ruinous all this was by the time Sir Charles acquired Bolsover. The surviving accounts contain many payments for demolition. This probably involved the destruction of whatever remained of the old keep and as much of the bailey wall as was necessary in order to clear a space for the new buildings.

BOLSOVER: THE LITTLE CASTLE

The accounts[2] run from 2 November 1612, when work started, to 12 March 1613-14. They are only a fragment of the original set, and stop before the completion of the ground floor. They include periodic payments for 'Smithson's charges', 'Smithson' clearly being in charge of the building operations. These entries almost certainly refer to John rather than Robert, for by 1612 Robert was an old man of seventy-seven and he died in October 1614. His simple but effective monument, no doubt designed by John, is inside the church at Wollaton

234

145. The Little Castle, Bolsover. The forecourt and entrance front.

(Plate 171). If he was connected with the design of Bolsover he can only have been so in the early stages.

The building work started by Sir Charles Cavendish at Bolsover in 1612 consisted of the keep itself (usually called the 'Little Castle') and, possibly, its small forecourt (Plate 145). In them a deliberate effort was made to produce buildings reminiscent of a medieval keep – far more so than would have been the case at Slingsby. The Little Castle has turrets at three corners and a big staircase tower at the fourth; unlike Slingsby it has no bay windows. It is battlemented throughout, as are the four turrets and the arrow-slitted curtain walls of the forecourt. On the other hand, in the interests of convenience, a considerable number of square-headed mullioned-and-transomed windows, with no Gothic overtones, have been introduced. Even so the proportion of window to wall is lower than was usual at the period: in particular the garden front (Plate 146) is almost windowless, clearly in order to increase the castle effect. An octagonal cupola rises from the centre of the roof, and this has pointed windows with vaguely Gothic tracery.

The basic format of a high block with three turrets and a staircase tower is undeniably reminiscent of a number of Norman keeps, notably that of Castle Rising in Norfolk. If this resemblance is intentional, it is a unique example of

235

146. The Little Castle, Bolsover. The south-east front, facing the Fountain Garden.

what might be called an archaeologically slanted Jacobean plan. A point in favour of it being so is that the corner tower forcibly disrupts the symmetry of plan and elevation. For a quality house of the period this was an extraordinary departure.

The entire basement and ground floor are stone-vaulted, and there is a marble vault in the Marble Closet (Plate 147) on the first floor. The basement vaults are of a simple cross type, without ribs; but the upper rooms have elaborately detailed rib-vaults. In the basement are the kitchen and offices (Plate 148) and a large cellar.[3] On the ground floor are the hall (Plate 131) and parlour (Plate 132), the latter known today as the Pillar Parlour and approached by an ante-room. On the first floor are the great chamber (known as the Star Chamber, Col. Plate XIII), off which is a little withdrawing room (the Marble Closet); and what was probably the best bedchamber with two inner chambers off it (the Heaven room and the Elysium room). On the top floor there are a series of chambers grouped round an octagonal lobby under the cupola. The main staircase, which is of stone and built round a stone central pier, rises beyond the upper floor to the top of the tower, where a door opens out on to the leads.

The floor levels are managed with some ingenuity (Fig. 19). The house can be divided into three sections, as one looks at it from the north-east, the left, the right, and the spine running through the centre back from the porch. In the basement the rooms are of the same height throughout. On the ground floor the

236

147. The Little Castle. The Marble Closet.

floor levels are the same, but the ceiling level of the left, that is the hall, is some 4 feet higher than the right, that is, the Pillar Parlour and its vestibule. On the floor above exactly the opposite is the case: the floor level of the right, that is the Star Chamber, is lower than the left; a flight of steps joins them, running up across the spine from the Star Chamber and, in the rest of the spine, the marble closet is on the same level as the right, and the Heaven room as the left. But the ceiling level is the same throughout, making the left-hand rooms considerably lower than those on the right, and allowing the rooms on the floor above to be all of the same height and on the same level. It is a neat way of fitting one big high room and several lower rooms on each of the two main floors.

In the plan there seems at first an extravagant number of staircases, but they all have their functions. There is a front door and a back door, the front door leading into the ground floor and the back door into the basement. The basement is divided into two halves, the right belonging to the kitchen and the left to the cellar; the back door leads into a lobby in the spine between them. The cellar and kitchen have their separate staircases up to the hall, where the servants ate, from which there is easy access to the Pillar Parlour, where the gentry ate. A third staircase runs from the vestibule up the spine, and could either have served as a way straight from the back door to the ground floor, or as a separate access from the cellar and kitchen to the Pillar Parlour, or as a way of exit for food and drink

237

148. (upper left) The Little Castle. The Scullery.

Fig. 19 (upper right). The Little Castle, Bolsover. The section.

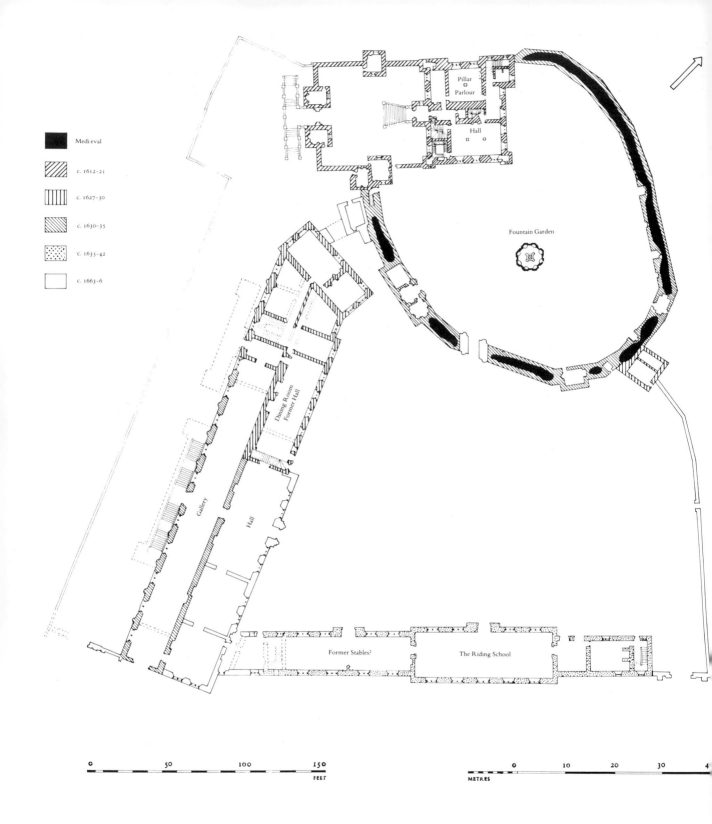

Medieval

c. 1612–21

c. 1627–30

c. 1630–35

c. 1635–42

c. 1663–6

Pillar
Parlour

Hall

Fountain Garden

Dining Room
Former Hall

Gallery

Hall

Former Stables?

The Riding School

0   50   100   150
                          FEET

0   10   20   30   4
METRES

Fig. 20. Bolsover Castle. The ground floor.

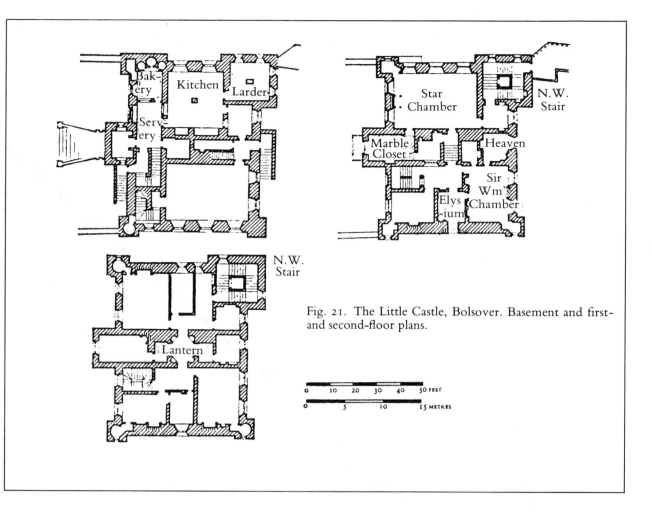

Fig. 21. The Little Castle, Bolsover. Basement and first- and second-floor plans.

from both hall and parlour, so as to allow for unimpeded one way traffic. In the upper floor of the house there are two staircases, the main one in the corner tower in the right, and a subsidiary and smaller one running up from the hall on the left.

The main weakness of this plan is a certain amount of waste space and darkness in the spine, the latter not entirely got round by the use of internal windows; though on the top floor light is very adequately provided from the lantern. Even so the plan remains a neat thing, and provokes one strong reflection. How reminiscent it is of Robert Smythson, who had still two years to live when building started. It is hard to resist the conclusion that, even if Robert did not draw the plan, his son consulted him about it; and that the planning and possibly the main lines of the façades but not the ornament of Bolsover are one of the last products of his ingenious and experimental mind.

Little of the interior detail of the Little Castle was executed in Sir Charles's time. The hall fireplace is dated 1616, which suggests that by that year the fabric was finished and the decoration of the interior had progressed as far as the basement and hall. In April of the next year Sir Charles died, leaving his son

William to complete the work. But William Cavendish, as we know, considered his father a 'good architect'. He introduced one or two novelties derived from London, which will be discussed in a later section; but on the whole he finished the building with remarkable sympathy, in a spirit close to that in which his father had started it.

This spirit is that discussed in the last chapter, the spirit of Jacobean chivalry and the Jacobean romances. It is a fascinating study, as one wanders round the keep, to try to disentangle its mixture of Gothic and classical sources. The vaulted rooms of basement and ground floor, for instance, are medieval in ultimate inspiration, but little if any of their detailing is in the least Gothic, though the vault of the hall has arches of Gothic section. These rooms are the most remarkable surviving example of Sir Charles's self-confessed taste for 'fair vaults'.[3] The hooded chimney-pieces (Plates 149-56), which occur in almost every room, are also Gothic in general form and far from Gothic in detailing. In fact, their immediate inspiration seems to have been a familiar and quite un-Gothic source – Serlio's book of architecture. The final result is neither Gothic nor classic, but a series of completely original little masterpieces in the true spirit of the romances. All except the hall chimney-piece, which is of stone and the plainest of the series, date from William Cavendish's time. But a variant design (Plate 159) for the hall chimney-piece has panelling of coloured marbles, as in the rest of the series, and shows that the basic type had been evolved before Sir Charles died.

In his fourth book Serlio gives nine fireplaces, one for the Tuscan order and two for each of the other orders; five of these fireplaces are hooded. There are more hooded fireplaces given in Book VII. These fireplaces (Plate 157) follow the medieval tradition in having their openings bridged by horizontal architraves. One of the distinctive features of the Bolsover fireplaces is that all their openings are arched, with their arches pointed and often made up of complex combinations of curves. It has been suggested that this was a deliberate Gothicism. But although the Gothic associations of these arches may have been recognised and welcomed, once again they derive more immediately from Serlio. His two Ionic, and one of his composite, fireplaces have subsidiary openings under the main lintels decorated by arches very similar to the more complex of the arches at Bolsover. What has been done at Bolsover is to move these arches up, and combine them with the main lintel.

This in itself shows a talent for adaptation; and such a talent appears throughout these fireplaces. They use Serlio only as a basis on which they improvise and expand. Perhaps they started intentionally on the Serlian scheme: Tuscan in the hall, Doric in the Pillar Parlour, Ionic in the Star Chamber; but after that they break loose. They take the plain panelling of Serlio's fireplace hoods and complicate and enrich it. They take occasional motifs – the console pilasters of the hooded Doric, the extended volute and shell ornament of the unhooded Ionic – but alter and adapt them. The strapwork cresting that crowns the Pillar Parlour hood is elaborated from a hint in one of the fireplaces (M) in Book VII. The

242

149-56. (previous page) Eight chimney-pieces in the Little Castle.

157. (top left, top right) Ionic chimney-pieces, from Book IV of Serlio's *Architecture*; (bottom left, bottom right) Two chimney-pieces from Serlio's Book VII.

mouldings are enriched with delicate and original patterns, and the spandrels with bundles of musical instruments or military arms. Finally there is added what Serlio could not show, colour: the conjunction and contrast of delicate pink alabaster, marbles of various colours, and yellow stone, beautifully and smoothly cut.[4]

The interior of the Little Castle was most carefully and thoroughly detailed throughout: enough remains, apart from the chimney-pieces, to make this clear, though the rooms were largely dismantled in the eighteenth and nineteenth centuries. With the exception of some of the paintings the impression – rare enough for the period – is of one controlling mind at work. The vaults and columns of the hall, Pillar Parlour, and Marble Closet are well worth study: the detailing of ribs, capitals, and pendants is different in each room, and sensitively designed to give each room a different character. The Pillar Parlour pendants, each with four brackets in the form of a horse's head, are particularly delightful creations (Plate 133], no doubt referring to William Cavendish's passion for horsemanship; the inspiration may be a variant composite capital in Serlio, which has winged horses' heads instead of volutes.[5] The basement rooms are, naturally enough, less carefully finished than the others, but even here the capitals of the columns, in their own simple and massive style, could scarcely be improved on (Plate 48). Other features worth noticing are the grate in the hall, which has a medievalist quality exactly in keeping with the rest of the room; the splendidly studded entrance door; and the enchanting octagonal lobby beneath the cupola on the top floor, with its alternation of alcoves and arches.

The rib vaults in the keep are an interesting example of the survival or revival of this method of roofing, worthy of comparison with the hanging vault (Plate 140) at Longford (c. 1590) and the great fan-vault of the staircase at Christ Church, Oxford. One of the Smythson drawings (II/25 and Plate 97) is for a sequence of vaulting schemes still more elaborate than those at Bolsover; in view of Charles Cavendish's known penchant for vaulted rooms, the drawing is probably connected with work for him. One would like to know whether John Smythson acquired his skill in vaulting from his father, or by careful observation of Gothic vaults: these he would have known of, for instance, from the surviving medieval undercrofts at Welbeck and at Rufford Abbey, another of the Shrewsburys' many houses.

William Cavendish called his father a 'good architect', and there can be no doubt that the Little Castle embodies many of his ideas and that he kept a tight control over the work. But it is highly unlikely that he was responsible for the creative brilliance of the detailing. Bolsover Little Castle is a fortunate example of a building where the patron's concept has been given convincing expression by the architect and craftsmen. The fireplaces in particular are such unique and accomplished creations that it has been suggested, not implausibly, that they were the product of foreign craftsmen, rather than of John Smythson. There is certainly no evidence to show that John was capable of executing such delicate

244

work, or indeed that he ever carved stone or marble at all except in his early days at Wollaton. But what evidence there is suggests that the actual design of the chimney-pieces and all the interior detail in his responsibility. Although his surviving drawings for the Little Castle are few they cover a wide range, including chimney-pieces. Among them are the plan for the basement, designs for the kitchen fireplace and internal windows on the staircase, variant designs for the hall chimney-piece (Plate 159), cupola and possibly the balustrading of the steps, a sketch for the black-and-white marble room with its corner chimney-piece (Plate 158), and the drawings of the southern details from which he derived the balcony windows and the panelling of the Pillar Parlour. Moreover, enough of his other works, both drawings and executed buildings, survive to show his qualities as a designer: sometimes eccentric, sometimes naïve, but with undeniable creative originality.

JOHN SMYTHSON AND THE CAVENDISHES

Although John Smythson did a certain amount of outside work after 1612, the Cavendishes had become his principal patrons, and by at any rate 1615 he had become a permanent Cavendish employee. He maintained a link with the

158. A design by John Smythson related to the Marble Closet (III/1(2)).

159. Variant design by John Smythson for the hall chimney-piece in the Little Castle (III/1(3)).

Willoughbys, designing a glass-house[6] for Sir Percival in 1615, and a formal lay-out (III/16) for an orchard at Wollaton three years later; the latter was immediately to the south of the garden and was arranged round the central feature of a raised mount, the plan of which echoed the plan of the house. He may have started to move from the Willoughby into the Cavendish orbit in the early years of the century, to judge, at any rate, from his choice of god-parents. Huntingdon Beaumont, the probable godfather of John's first son, Huntingdon, was, as has appeared, a Willoughby protégé. But for his second son, John, he acquired as godparent no less a patron than Sir Charles Cavendish's wife,[7] Baroness Ogle in her own right, who brought the great Ogle estates in Northumberland into the Cavendish family.

As has been seen, he may have worked for Sir Charles at Kirkby-in-Ashfield in 1597-9. According to Vertue, who visited Welbeck early in the eighteenth century, two arcades at either end of the canal there were inscribed with the date 1604, and had been built by John Smythson.[8] But Vertue is not altogether to be relied on when he attributes them to John. He was probably incapable of distinguishing between John and Robert, and may anyway have based his attribution on John's definite connection with the Welbeck riding-house, which was not built until 1623. As in so many cases, however, the likelihood remains that father and son were working here together.

On 4 October 1615, Sir Charles granted John Smythson the lease for life, at a nominal rent, of a farm and ninety acres of land at Kirkby-in-Ashfield 'for and in consideration of the just and faithful service to him heretofore done and hereafter to be done'. The grant is made out to 'John Smithson gen. – servant unto the said Sᵣ Charles' and the farm is described as being 'now in the tenure or occupacon of the said John Smithson'.[9] He had perhaps been living there since work started at Bolsover, for, as the accounts show, the house which Sir Charles had begun to build at Kirkby was used as a quarry for the new castle. By at any rate the time of Sir Charles's son, William, he was serving the Cavendish family in capacities other than architectural. In a valuation of his estates in the latter's handwriting, his property in Kirkby, Hardwick, Fulwood and Annesley Woodhouse is annotated 'Smithson the elder Balife'.[10]

John Smythson was to remain a servant of the Cavendish family until his death. Work was going on at Bolsover throughout this period, and Bolsover remains the most important monument of his career. But before discussing these later Cavendish buildings something must be said about his new Cavendish employer. With William Cavendish,[11] subsequently Viscount Mansfield, and Earl, Marquess and Duke of Newcastle, one suddenly comes out of the Elizabethan world into a mellower and more spacious age. The Elizabethans are brilliant, glittering and romantic figures; but how remote they are and how uncomfortable. William, with two generations of wealth behind him, could afford to relax. He is a man of whom it is impossible not to be fond, so gentle was he, so generous, so brave, so tolerant, so easy. He had a genius for getting on with people. In exile in Antwerp he charmed his creditors to such an extent that they 'swore he should not want if they could help it' and kept him in comfort till the Restoration. Even his horses used to whinney in greeting whenever he came into the stables.

He had many interests. As a young man he had travelled with Sir Henry Wotton to the court of the Duke of Savoy. He was extravagantly fond of music, patronised Van Dyck and Ben Jonson, and himself wrote poems and plays. He was a friend of Hobbes and Descartes, and dabbled in experimental philosophy. Like all his family he was a great builder, adding to both Bolsover and Welbeck, building a house at Ogle in Northumberland and, after the Restoration, the great castle on the cliff at Nottingham. But the main passion of his life was horses and the *Haute Ecole*, a passion to which his book *La Méthode Nouvelle* of 1657, decorated with engravings after Abraham Diepenbeke, many containing views of his own houses in the background, is a curious and charming memorial (Plates 167, 172, 176).

He had his weaknesses. He suffered from a certain flabbiness; he was perhaps a little absurd. His writings have no shape and his scientific dabblings were very superficial. He was, in fact, a hopeless and incurable dilettante. Moreover, he hated bother, and if life grew too uncomfortable he ran away from it. His position and popularity made him the unquestioned leader of the Royalists in the North, but it was not a position to which he was well adapted. Charm and great personal bravery could not make up for lack of drive or organising capacity. He was always 'retiring to his delightful company, music, or his softer pleasures, to all of which he was so indulgent and to his ease, that he would not be interrupted upon what occasion so ever'. After the disaster of Marston Moor, where he was forced to watch the massacre of the Whitecoats, the troops raised from his own northern estates, he gave up the struggle, sailed away to the Continent, and spent the years till the Restoration in the more sympathetic company of his horses.

There could be no greater contrast than between the splendid and sprawling Duke and his grandmother, the formidable Bess, tough, concentrated and on the make. Their houses stand within sight of each other; and it is a curious experience to go from one to the other and sense the family likeness, and yet the enormous difference, between them; from the strength and directness and pride of Hardwick, to Bolsover where there is nothing arrogant or heroic, but much that is odd, and individual, and delightful.

THE 1618-19 JOURNEY TO LONDON

William Cavendish seems to have done little at Bolsover in the year in which his father died, but in 1618 he married, and probably as a result of this started to fit out the rooms in the Little Castle which his father had left undecorated. The fireplace in the Pillar Parlour can, from the heraldry, be dated 1619 or 1620; a painted panel in the Star Chamber above is inscribed 1621. At about the same time he also made two important external insertions, in the form of the balcony windows on the entrance and garden façades. These introduced a new element at Bolsover, for they were in the pure Italian style which had only just become fashionable in Court circles in London. They were the first spoils of a journey to London on which he had sent John Smythson in 1618.

A confused memory of this journey may have given rise to the story Vertue heard, when he visited Welbeck, that 'this Smithson was sent into Italy to take the Model of a Castle'.[12] In fact he went no further than London, as the sketches which he had made on that journey, many of which have survived, make clear (Plates 160-3, Col. Plate XV). One signed drawing (III/13 and Plate 160) proves beyond dispute that the whole group are by him. For on the way down he stopped at Theobalds, by then a royal palace, and drew the panelling in the great chamber, endorsing it: 'The Platte of the Seelinge of the greate chamber at Thyballes taken the 8th November, 1618: by Jo : S.'

He came to London fresh from the provinces with a naked and untrained eye, and found three new arrivals on the building scene which particularly attracted him. First was a new form of gable, derived from the Low Countries, with a pedimented top and scrolled sides. He drew two of these, on Lady Cooke's and Fulke Greville's houses in Holborn; both houses were almost certainly designed by Inigo Jones, before he had developed the pure Palladianism of his later years.[13] Second were windows opening on to balconies, of which he drew examples at Arundel House, Fulke Greville's house and the house of Colonel Cecil in the Strand. These balcony windows were probably also of Low Country origin: certainly Colonel Cecil's balcony was directly copied (again, by Inigo Jones) from Plate XVIII in the Fleming Jean Francquart's *Premier Livre d'Architecture* (Brussels, 1616). Thirdly, he drew rustication in all its varieties: Inigo Jones's new gateway at Arundel House, with its rusticated arch surround and blocked pilasters; another plainer rusticated gate at Arundel House; and the basement storey of the Inigo Jones Banqueting House, probably the only part of the building that had been completed at the time of his visit. All these three were of Italian inspiration, and the two former were in fact described by Smythson, as 'Italyan' on his drawings.[14]

Jones's own design for the big Arundel House gateway survives, though the gateway itself has gone; and, of course, the Banqueting House is still there. Comparison of the Smythson drawings with these immediately makes it clear how very inaccurate the drawings are. It is hard to believe that John Smythson did anything more than make his drawings from memory, or at most based them on rough preliminary sketches made on the spot. He was doing something very different from Inigo Jones, when the latter carefully measured and drew Roman remains in Italy. The whole classical discipline, with its scholarship and respect

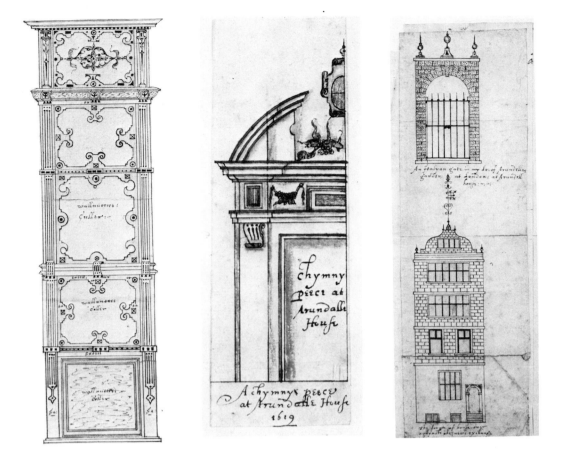

for authority, was alien to him; he was still in the Elizabethan tradition, and regarded the repertory of classical architecture as something to be plundered, rather than revered and imitated.

One chimney-piece he apparently both drew himself and made enquiries about having copied, presumably for Bolsover or Welbeck. The evidence for this comes from a drawing of a chimney-piece in the Smythson collection (IV/ 11) drawn in a freer style than the rigid draughtsmanship of the Smythsons themselves, on which is scribbled the following note:

> Mr Smithsonn this is the direct plot of the chimney in Arundel howse in every poynt wch is all of whit marble but only the herth and iii peeces of towch. . . . and the lowest prize wch I will take to paterne it in every poynt is 100 pounds,
>
> Your loving ffrend
Tho: Ashby.

This was 'Thomas Ashby of St Martin's in the Fields, Carver, and Tombe maker', who signed an agreement on 3 October 1618 to make a tomb for Sir Fulke Greville, for £280.[15] The resulting canopy tomb of noble Roman architecture is in the old chapter house at St Mary's, Warwick. Ashby may well have carved the Arundel House chimney-piece himself; both it and the tomb were

249

160. (top left) Panelling at Theobalds, Hertfordshire.
161. (centre) Chimney-piece at Arundel House, London.
162. (top right) Gate at Arundel House and house by New Exchange. Drawings made by John Smythson on his southern visit in 1618-19.

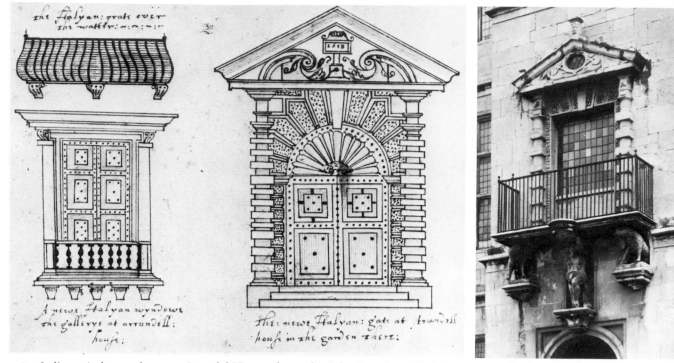

The Italyan: grate over the watter:o:o:o:o:

A newe Italyan wyndowe the gallerye at arrundell: house:

The: newe Italyan: gate at arundell hous in the garden theire:

163. Italian window and gate at Arundel House, drawn by John Smythson (III/7(1)). 164. The balcony over the entrance to the Little Castle.

possibly designed by Inigo Jones. But this friendship, which John Smythson struck up with a craftsman probably connected with Jones and his style, does not seem to have led to anything. The copy of the chimney-piece does not survive and may never have been made; certainly its style had little perceptible influence on John Smythson's later work

When he got back to Bolsover he immediately started putting into practice the new fashions which he had seen in London. The result is most obvious on the exterior. The fabric of the Little Castle must already have been finished; but into it he inserted two of the external balconies or 'pergulas' which he had so much admired. The pedimented frame of one of the balcony windows (Plate 164) is based on the Arundel House gateway, but with much coarser mouldings, as he had drawn it (Plate 163); the other (Plate 146) is decorated in a chaster and perhaps rather more Jonesian style. These two balconies were sensitively placed, particularly that on the garden side, which is set in and set off by the otherwise almost windowless wall.

Inside, the influence of the London visit is less obvious. The panelling of the Pillar Parlour is a direct copy of the Theobalds 'seelinge', adapted to fit the arches of the vault (Plate 132). But there is nothing Jonesian or 'Italyan' about this panelling. Nor is there anything Jonesian about the most notable feature of William Cavendish's interior decorations, the series of chimney-pieces; for these, as has already been pointed out, are variations on the type established in Sir Charles's time. Two other internal features, however, are possible results of the London visit. The first is the use in the smaller rooms of corner hooded

250

chimney-pieces, the earliest known examples of this type in England. The second is the black-and-white scheme of the Marble Closet adjoining the Star Chamber, with a black-and-white marble chimney-piece, a white marble vault with black ribs, and alternate black and white marble tiles on the floor (Plate 147). This is a very early example of the change-over, most obvious in the tombs of the period, from the coloured marble decorations inherited from the sixteenth century to a more sober and classical black-and-white. John Smythson had seen such a colour scheme in the Arundel House fireplace and perhaps elsewhere in London.

Lord Arundel was William Cavendish's first cousin: this was no doubt the reason why much of John Smythson's time in London was spent at Arundel House or with the craftsmen connected with it. But one gets the impression that William Cavendish did not much appreciate the architecture of Arundel's protégé, Inigo Jones. The balcony windows obviously attracted him, but the Palladian doorcases used on the balconies had few offspring in later Cavendish buildings. The Arundel House fireplace was perhaps never copied. Even the Holborn gables do not seem to have been used at Bolsover or Welbeck until fifteen years or more after John Smythson drew them in London – by which time they had become almost a cliché in England though Inigo Jones himself had abandoned them for more correct Italian detail. The truth seems to have been that William Cavendish preferred something a little more bizarre. Although the castle tradition inherited from Sir Charles grows fainter and fainter in John Smythson's work in the 1620s and 1630s, the element of fantasy remains, while Jonesian or Palladian echoes are few and far between.

CAVENDISH BUILDINGS AT WELBECK, OGLE AND SLINGSBY

Three years after his London visit John Smythson was planning a Riding School for William Cavendish at Welbeck. His plan and elevation for it survive at the R.I.B.A., dated 1622 (III/15, 3-4 and Plate 165). According to Vertue, over the door was inscribed 'Jo. Smithson Curatore fabriciencis 1623' and an internal doorcase dated 1623 is shown in one of the eighteenth-century drawings by Samuel Hieronymus Grimm.[16] So its date and authorship are well attested. But it was not aesthetically a very ambitious work, indeed it was clearly not intended to be, but was designed primarily as an utilitarian structure. It was most impressive inside (Plate 166), from its size and bareness, and its splendid though relatively plain hammer beam roof, an interesting example of John Smythson using a traditional medieval feature.

The internal doorcase shown by Grimm is very similar to the balcony window on the garden side of the Little Castle at Bolsover. Outside there are, or were, a few pieces of detail on which John Smythson left his mark. Curious little open-work finials, like lanterns, are perched on the base and peak of the two gables. These lantern finials are different from the more conventional ones shown in the

165. (top) John Smythson's design for the Riding School, Welbeck Abbey, Nottinghamshire (III/15(3)).

original design and were to reappear in later buildings by John Smythson. The door derives from a feature popularised in England by the London artisans, a broken pediment with a pedimented tablet inserted between its two segments. But with John Smythson derivation was often a long way from imitation. In his Welbeck version the mouldings of the lower pediment are amalgamated with those that run round the sides and top of the tablet, to form a continuous moulding that resembles – with very odd effect – the neck and shoulders of a bottle.

The Riding School was remodelled in 1889 to contain a library and chapel. Outside, its shape and some detail remains: inside all has vanished,[17] though its original appearance survives in the eighteenth-century drawing by Grimm.

Two years later William Cavendish's horses received further new quarters at Welbeck, in the form of a range of stables built, according to Vertue, in 1625. There is an undated plan and elevation for these at the R.I.B.A. (III/15, 5–6 and Plate 168) and they are shown in one of the series of engravings by Diepenbeke illustrating Newcastle's book on horsemanship (Plate 167). If Diepenbeke's view is reliable, the building as executed was a little different from the Smythson elevation. These stables (which were demolished in the eighteenth century) were more decorated than the Riding School. For the first time in a Cavendish building, classical detail was applied lavishly to the exterior. Not only was the central door elaborately cased, but all the windows were pedimented, with one long range of pediments alternately triangular and segmental: this was perhaps a remote Midland echo of the Whitehall Banqueting House. But the stables had other and less classical elements: lantern pinnacles, like those of the Riding School; little ogee domed pavilions (shown round in the engraving, square in the drawing) at either end of the façade; and cross arrow-slits, as at Bolsover, to light the upstairs lofts. Inside they were stone vaulted, and the vault was secured externally by thin rusticated buttresses. The resulting mixture must have been individual and not unattractive.

The stables are shown as part of a long irregular range, including granaries and perhaps grooms' quarters. Towards their right hand is a gatehouse surmounted

165. (top) John Smythson's design for the Riding School, Welbeck Abbey, Nottinghamshire (III/15(3)).
166. (facing page top) The interior of the Riding School, from the drawing by S. H. Grimm.
167. (facing page bottom) The stables at Welbeck, from the view by Abraham Diepenbeke.

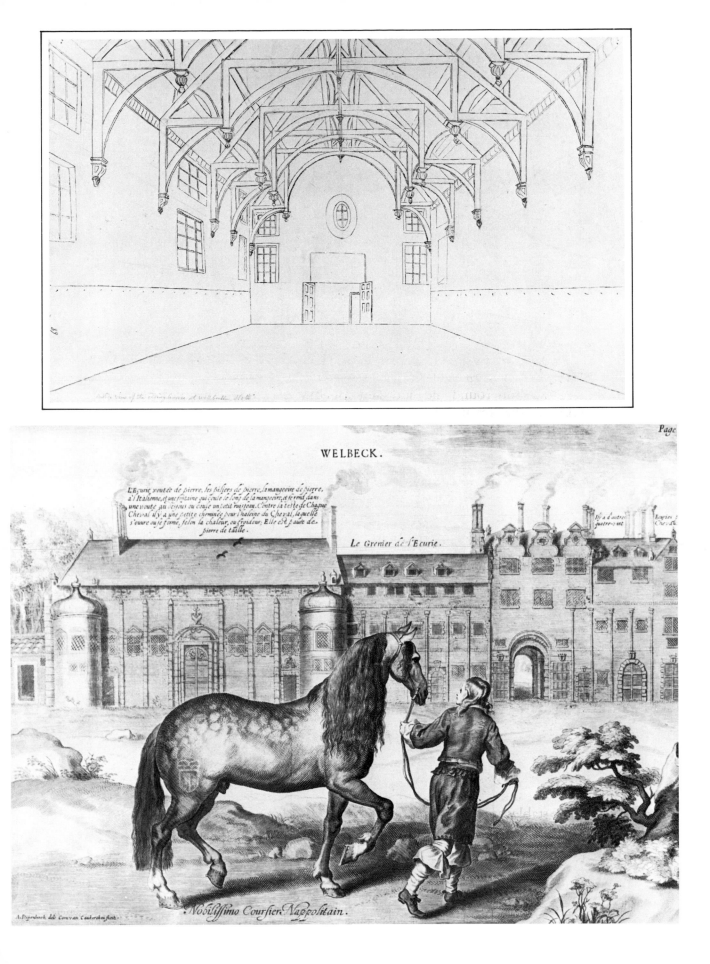

A little view of the riding house at Welbeck Hall

WELBECK.

L'Ecurie voutée de pierre, les pilliers de pierre, la mangeoire de pierre,
à l'Italienne, et une fontaine qui coule le long de la mangeoire, et se rend dans
une voute au desious ou coule un petit ruisseau. Contre la teste de Chaque
Cheval il y a une petite cheminée pour l'haleine du Cheval, laquelle
s'ouvre ou se ferme, selon la chaleur, ou froideur, Elle est faite de
pierre de taille.

Le Grenier de l'Ecurie.

Il y a d'autres
quatre-vint

Ecuries
Che.d.

Page

Nobilissimo Coursier Nappolitain.

A.Diepenbeeck, del. Cor.van Cauberchen fecit.

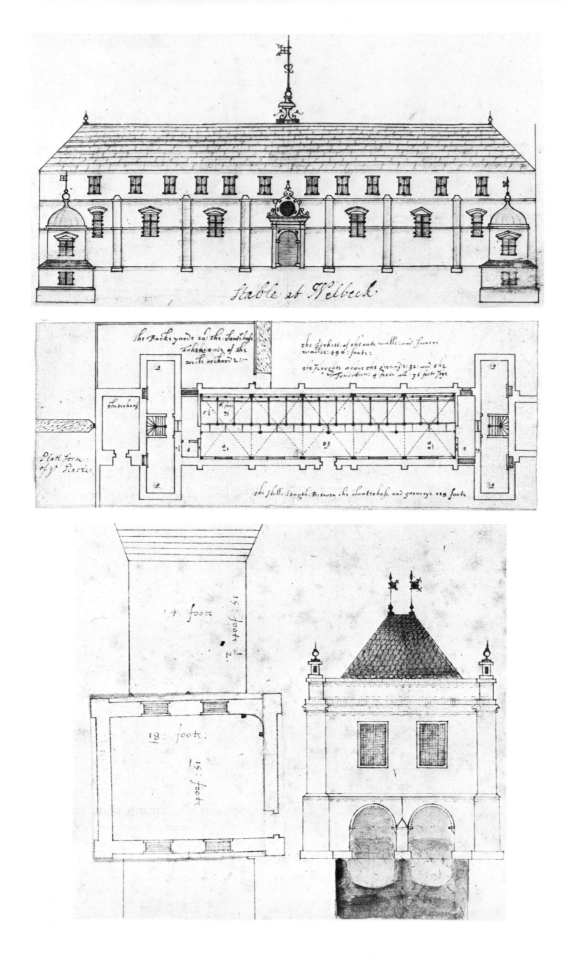

Stable at Welbeck

170. A chimney-piece designed by John Smythson at Welbeck.

171. The monument to Robert Smythson (d. 1614) in the church at Wollaton.

by three small pedimented gables. This gatehouse was probably built in the same years as the Riding School and stables; but curiously enough the gables are not of the scrolled type which John Smythson had sketched in London, but slightly chastened versions of the Elizabethan and Vredeman de Vries type which Robert had used at Wollaton.

A survey of Welbeck and its surroundings, made by William Senior in 1629, shows elaborate water gardens to the south and east of the house.[18] What appear to be the arcades of 1604, described by Vertue, are shown to either end of a long canal to the east; to the south another canal flows under two taller buildings, approached by steps. John Smythson's designs for one of these survives, a charming little pavilion built on two arches to bridge the water and decorated with his distinctive vanes and finials (Plate 169). The resulting gardens, and the buildings that went with them, belonged to an interesting group of early-seventeenth-century water gardens, the first examples of this type in England, all of which have disappeared.[19]

A certain amount of John Smythson's work survives inside Welbeck, marooned amid the remodellings and additions of later centuries. What is left is all in the north-west corner of the house, which Diepenbeke and Grimm show (it has been remodelled since) as an irregular gabled range probably dating from the days of the Talbot ownership. The Smythson work is as follows. There are remains of vaulting, with detail akin to Bolsover, in the basement. On the entrance floor is an elaborately decorated little room containing panelling,[20] a ribbed sexpartite vault carved with Cavendish and other crests, and a stone tablet

168. (a, b, facing page top and centre) John Smythson's plan and elevation for the Welbeck stables.

169. (facing page bottom) Design for one of the water pavilions in the garden at Welbeck (III/24).

of the Cavendish stags set into one wall. In a room on the floor above is a massive, clumsy, but impressive stone chimney-piece (Plate 170) set in a stone panel with a moulded surround which resembles those of the chimney-pieces at Bolsover, and of Robert's monument at Wollaton, presumably designed by John (Plate 171). But the Welbeck chimney-piece is unlike them in that it is not hooded; although with John Smythson's inevitable variations, it unmistakably derives from Serlio's Doric chimney-piece, already used by Robert for the hall at Wollaton. These fragments appear to be the remains of embellishments carried out in the 1620s.

Another Smythson relic from Welbeck is now attached to the manor house at Whitwell, three miles away. It is the porch for which the design survives among the Smythson drawings (III/15, 1–2), inscribed in a late seventeenth- or early eighteenth-century hand, 'Porch at Welbeck'. This may have been the original front porch which was added on to the medieval hall; it is certainly similar to the porch shown by Diepenbeke and Grimm, and the differences can perhaps be put down to their inaccurate draughtmanship. In the nineteenth century Whitwell formed part of the Welbeck estate, and the porch was no doubt moved when the house was being altered.

It is a fairly unambitious little structure; its most unusual feature is a parapet pierced with Gothic quatrefoils, an interesting example of Cavendish-Smythson medievalism. But a more curious example of tournament fantasy is an anonymous design for a fountain (III/25 and Plate 127), which, on stylistic ground, has all the appearance of having been made for Sir Charles Cavendish, possibly for

256

172. Ogle Castle, Northumberland. From the view by Diepenbeke.

Welbeck; above a conventional base arises an extraordinary superstructure of pinnacles and flying buttresses, surmounted by mimic arrow-slitted turrets from which fly little flags.

In the background of his engraving of Newcastle out hawking, Diepenbeke depicts a house at Ogle in Northumberland on the property which Newcastle inherited from his mother in 1629 (Plate 172). This house has disappeared without trace, nor is there any Smythson drawing which can be connected with it.[21] Its design was clearly due to John, for in style it is very close to the Welbeck stables. In plan it is a rectangular courtyard house, with a round turret at each corner. As in the stables, the windows are pedimented alternately segmental and triangular, the turrets have little ogee caps, and the walls are buttressed, suggesting the presence of a vaulted room or rooms. The roofs have dormers of exactly the shape of those in the wings adjoining the Welbeck stables. The house, as shown in the engraving, has all the odd attractiveness of the Welbeck stables, increased by the charm of its position, for it rises straight out of a moat, and is approached by a long timber causeway and a drawbridge. But in spite of its situation, and unlike other Cavendish buildings, it is almost totally free of sham-castle elements.

The long pedimented ranges of windows which John Smythson used at the Ogle and Welbeck stables appear most impressively in a house built, perhaps about 1630, not for William but for his brother, the younger Sir Charles Cavendish. It is at Slingsby (Plate 173), in Yorkshire, where the first Sir Charles had planned but never built a house.[21] There is an elevation and some detail

257

173. Slingsby Castle, N. Yorkshire.

designs for it at the R.I.B.A. (III/12 and Plate 174) and an elevation and plan (Plate 175) of *c.* 1700, now at Hovingham Hall nearby, show it as it was actually built, with minor variations on the Smythson elevation. Unlike Ogle and the Welbeck stables, a good deal of it survives, including much of the fabric of basement and turrets, but very little of the main façades.

The younger Sir Charles is movingly described by Clarendon, who made friends with him as an exile in Antwerp after the Civil War:

The conversation the Chancellor took most delight in was that of Sir Charles Cavendish, brother to the Marquis; who was one of the most extraordinary persons of that age, in all the noble endowments of the mind. He had all the disadvantages imaginable in his person; which was not only of so small a size that it drew the eyes of men upon him, but with such deformity in his little person, and an aspect in his countenance, that was apter to raise contempt than application; but in this unhandsome or homely habitation, there was a mind and soul lodged that was very lovely and beautiful; cultivated and polished by all the knowledge and wisdom that arts and sciences could supply it with. He was a great philosopher, in the extent of it; and a excellent mathematician; whose correspondence was very dear to Gassendus and Descartes, the last of which dedicated some of his works to him. He had very notable courage; and the vigour of his mind so adorned his body, that being with his brother the marquis in all the war, he usually went out in all parties, and was present, and charged the enemy, in all battles, with as keen a courage as could dwell in the heart of man. But then the gentleness of his disposition, the humility and meekness of his nature, and the vivacity of his wit was admirable. He was so

258

174. John Smythson's elevation for Slingsby Castle, N. Yorkshire, *c.* 1630 (III/12(1)).

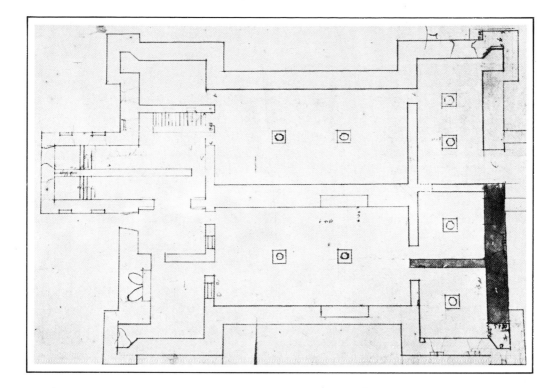

modest, that he could hardly be prevailed with to enlarge himself on subjects he understood better than other men, except he were pressed by his very familiar friends; as if he thought it presumptious to know more than handsomer men used to do. Above all, his virtue and piety was such, that no temptation could work upon him to consent to anything that swerved in the least degree from the precise rules of honour, or the most severe rules of conscience.[22]

This gentle and intelligent dwarf has a particular claim to our affection, because he managed to buy up Bolsover under the Commonwealth and so prevent it from being destroyed. Both in intellect and character he was clearly more serious and developed than his brother; which is perhaps why Slingsby has none of the more obvious oddities of some of John Smythson's other buildings.

Its plan derived originally from Wollaton: that is, the two main fronts were built up on a high basement and recessed in two steps, with square towers at their outside corners. But the drama of Wollaton has been melted down to the very gentlest recession, with towers that have shrunk to little turrets, just sufficient, along with the battlemented parapet, to give the house a faintly castle air. This would have been supported by the staircase towers, one on the centre of each side elevation, which had hood-moulded windows. These castle and Elizabethan reminiscences are used as a setting for a full-spread of classical motifs, not only a pedimented and rusticated door, and a Bolsover balcony, but two rows of pedimented windows.

The detail of these windows is curious. The lower cornices of the pediment have dwindled to flat strips, nearly flush to the wall, so that the raking cornices

259

175. The basement plan of Slingsby, from a drawing of *c.* 1700 at Hovingham Hall, Yorkshire.

above appear like a series of pointed eyebrows. The raking cornices themselves are oddly made up of a vast cima recta moulding sandwiched between two insignificant fillets. There seem to have been pediments of similar form on the Welbeck stables, and they were to reappear in even odder form, later on at Bolsover.

Slingsby shows a feeling for texture which was perhaps new to John. A thin ribbon of rustication, of a curious and individual knobbliness (which had first appeared in embryo on the balcony windows at Bolsover) goes right round the house between the two storeys; there is a similar rustication beneath the pediments of the windows. The little openings of the turrets and the basement windows have surrounds of an unusual shape, such as are to be found at Bolsover set flush to the wall, but at Slingsby project crisply from it; and the strong quoins at the corners are similarly projecting. These surrounds, the quoins, the window cases, the rustication, are all of a different and lighter stone from the rest of the house.[23] Inside, all but the basement has largely vanished, but here there are vaulted and pillared rooms, some of which have capitals of the same form as those in the hall of the keep at Bolsover.[24] The arrangement of the basement is similar to that at Bolsover: there are spacious and completely separate kitchen and cellar ranges, each with its own staircase to the upper floors. These basement rooms are admirably built, as indeed is whatever survives of the rest of the house. This, combined with the delicate balance between old and new motifs and the sharp contrast in colour between the two stones, must have made Slingsby an attractive building; it is sad that ruin has reduced so much of it to irretrievable shapelessness.

THE TERRACE RANGE AT BOLSOVER

Detail reminiscent of Slingsby, though far more extraordinary, appears on the new gallery (Plate 179) which William Cavendish added to Bolsover, and the history and antecedents of which must now be discussed.

It seems unlikely that Sir Charles Cavendish thought of the Little Castle at Bolsover as more than an amusement, or at best an occasional residence, for it contains relatively little accommodation and Welbeck is only a few miles away. It was in the lodge tradition. But his son clearly grew fond of it; moreover, his appointment as Lord Lieutenant of Derbyshire in 1628 may have made him feel that he should have a major residence in Derbyshire as well as Nottinghamshire.[25] At any rate, in about 1629 he began to expand. The Little Castle itself could not be added to without spoiling it, and instead he built a new free-standing wing, on one side of the outer castle courtyard, following the line of the hill to the south (Plate 176). Today it is known as the Terrace Range, after the terrace built in front of it above the valley, probably in the mid-1630s. The new range may have been intended for servants and guests (including very grand ones), leaving the Little Castle for family and intimates. It was gutted in the eighteenth century but the shell survives.

This new range seems to have been built in two sections, but the whole was probably envisaged from the start, though perhaps not in the form which it finally took. The first section was later somewhat altered, but its original appearance is clearly shown in the relevant Diepenbeke engraving; this, like the other engravings of Newcastle's houses in *La Methode Nouvelle*, was made in Antwerp in the 1650s, on the basis of drawing made in England, probably in the mid-1630s (Plate 176). The drawings of Bolsover survive, and are now at Renishaw in Derbyshire (Plates 129 and 130).[26]

The first section of the new terrace range was somewhat eccentrically shaped, as its northern end was skewed, probably to follow the line of the medieval bailey wall. The main portion had straight-sided gables (since removed or altered) four facing the valley, and two the court, Each gable was surmounted by a chimney-stack and decorated at its base by little lantern finials, like those on the Welbeck Riding School and stables. The skewed end is more elaborately treated, with curved and pedimented gables of the Wollaton type, as on the stable wing at Welbeck. The whole section has hood-moulded windows similar to those in the staircase tower at Slingsby. The masonry is curiously decorated with square studs projecting slightly from the face of the wall at regular intervals. In the

261

176. The Little Castle and terrace range at Bolsover, from the view by Abraham Diepenbeke.

177. John Smythson's plan for the terrace range, *c.* 1630 (III/1/4).

skewed block by the keep some of the studs are carved with the following dates and initials: M.C. 1629, M.W. 1630, E.L. 1630, G.D. 1629, and H.S. 1629. The date of the wing as a whole may be assumed to be 1629–30; H.S. has always been interpreted, reasonably enough, as the initials of John's son, Huntingdon.

The second section is shown in a plan by John Smythson, probably made in or about 1630. It provided a great hall, a 'best lodgings' of great chamber, withdrawing chamber, bedchamber, and closet, a chapel and a gallery, opening at either end into withdrawing chambers. There was a basement kitchen and other offices beneath the north end of the gallery. The hall and perhaps the gallery were designed to be two storeys high, but there was a second floor above the lodgings. All this was on a much grander scale than anything previously built at Bolsover. The plan was altered after work on the basement and hall had started, probably in order to improve the view from the gallery; the level of gallery and lodgings was raised some three or four feet higher than that of the hall and ground floor of the 1629–30 work, and the height of the kitchen increased accordingly. The shell of the hall and gallery survive; the chapel was probably never built; the site of the other rooms (which may have been demolished or partly demolished in the Civil War) is now occupied by a very grand and somewhat deeper new range, built to the design of Samuel Marsh in 1663–6.

The kitchen was vaulted, and has a central column identical to those in the Little Castle. Externally, the hall has similar detailing to that in the 1629–30 work. It was clearly never meant to be showy, but the same could not be said of the gallery front, overlooking the valley. Its architecture is the maddest and most extravagant at Bolsover (Plate 179). The basement kitchen is at one end, but otherwise it is of one storey only, with a central doorway and eight windows. These windows have mouldings almost identical to those at Slingsby: but it is as though someone has taken a hammer to the Slingsby pediments and smashed them into three separate fragments. In a similar spirit a lost chunk of curved moulding is tethered like a balloon above the broken pediment of the central doorway. Between the windows are what for convenience can be called buttresses, but they support nothing and resemble paraphrases in stone of cannon, half submerged in the wall. All these features are rusticated in the knobbly style

262

XV. Drawings of houses in Holborn and the Strand made on John Smythson's London visit, 1618–19.

My Ladye: Cookes: house: in Houlborn
at London: 1619:~

The Pergula: House in ... at Coronall: Sisfell
the Strande

the Fronte of Bathe House: Sʳ foulke Gryvslles: in houlborn
1619

of Slingsby. Similar rustication decorates the pedestals, which stick out on ogee shaped corbels at intervals along the battlemented parapet: below them great stone water spouts jut out like the mouths of cannon; and from the middle of the parapet rises a balconied window, leading nowhere, the pediment of which was once as curious as that of the pediment below.

There is another of these shattered pediments on a doorway leading out from the staircase tower of the Little Castle (Plate 181). It opens on to an elevated walk, known at the time as the Stone Walk, that goes along the top of the wall round the fountain garden and over an archway into the 1629-30 building. The door leading from the archway bridge into the latter is dated 1633. The central fountain, round which the garden is planned, is carved with an earl's coronet and must date from 1628 or later. In the absence of any conclusive documentary evidence it seems reasonable to assign to the hall, the gallery, the walk, and the doorway at the end of the walk to the same few years.

In May 1633, Charles I stopped at Welbeck on his way up to Scotland, and there, on 21 May, Newcastle presented before him a masque by Ben Jonson, *The King's Entertainment at Welbeck*. The King returned to Welbeck with Henrietta Maria in July 1634, and from there went over for the day to Bolsover, where he was lavishly entertained. Newcastle would undoubtedly have known at the end

265

178. Bolsover Castle. The terrace range from the courtyard.

XVI. The Stand, Swarkeston, Derbyshire.

of this first visit that the King was planning a second one. That gave him fourteen months for preparation. It is possible that the form finally taken by the gallery was inspired by the foreknowledge of the King's return. Newcastle may have hoped to complete the new range and accommodate the king in it, but if so his hopes were almost certainly disappointed. The main feature of the masque was a 'dance of mechanics', in which a surveyor, carver, free-mason, carpenter, and so on took part. The dance was probably inspired by the fact that the new range was unfinished and building work still in progress. Certainly Charles and Henrietta Maria lodged at Welbeck, not Bolsover, and the refreshment offered to them at Bolsover was confined to a banquet, in the Jacobean sense of the word. But the fountain garden must have been completed, or complete enough, since the king and queen 'retired into a garden' to watch the dance of mechanics. The central figure of the fountain (Col. Plate XIV) is of Venus, a deity appropriate to the title of the masque, *Love's Welcome at Bolsover*.[27] In the surrounding wall, under the Stone Walk, little secret rooms and alcoves are hollowed out; two rooms have hooded corner chimney-pieces, as in the Little Castle.

The eyebrow and shattered pediments on the gallery at Bolsover reflect the addition of a new pattern-book to John Smythson's repertory, one which provided new and exciting alternatives to Serlio and de Vries. This was Wendel Dietterlin's *Architectura*, first published at Nuremberg in 1593, and one of the

266

179. (top) Looking along the terrace at Bolsover.

180. The entrance to the long gallery in the terrace range.

most remarkable and disturbing books on architecture ever produced in Europe. Dietterlin, perhaps inspired by Michelangelo, had taken the conventional elements of classic architecture and distorted them into an intensely personal style of an extraordinary fantasy, vigour, ingenuity and unpleasantness. His *Architectura* was famous all over northern Europe. The pediment was one of the classical features with which he had most fun, twisting, breaking and interweaving it into an infinite number of patterns and shapes (Plates 183, 184). For a searcher after precedents for Smythson there is no shortage of eyebrow and fragmented pediments.

At Bolsover much of Dietterlin's content has been drained away; the crowding, the twining, the grotesque figures, the contorted columns and all the unpleasantness have gone. But this kind of transformation was typical of John Smythson. That Dietterlin was his source for these Bolsover details is made clear by a couple of other designs by him, dating from about the same time. One of his drawings is without any doubt based on a plate in Dietterlin (Plates 188 and 190), but has been much simplified so as to have exactly the same kind of resemblance to Dietterlin as the Bolsover windows and doorways.[28] The drawing in its turn was modified to produce an extremely handsome chimney-piece (Plate 189) in the great chamber at Clifton, near Nottingham, where John Smythson also designed stables in 1632.

The truth seems to be that he had a very surprising mind. Something could be pushed in at one end and heaven only knew what was likely to come out at the other. Cornices, rustications, the Serlian chimney-piece, the broken pediment all underwent a strange sea-change, not because he was trying to copy and failing, but because he was pursuing his own individual and eccentric way.

John Smythson's distinctive pediment mouldings, which make their last and most exaggerated appearance at the Bolsover gallery (Plate 180), present rather a puzzle. Michelangelo, in the upper storeys of the Farnese Palace of Rome, had introduced pediments of bold and simplified mouldings, a crowning cima recta and a broad moulding of rectangular section below. This combination was much imitated; it appears frequently in Dietterlin and, for instance, in Rubens's house at Antwerp. But in the Smythson pediments the lower moulding has almost completely dwindled away, leaving the cima recta all but in a vacuum. There are precedents for this in his own drawings of the Arundel House gateway (III/7 (1) and Plate 163) and a new building at St James's Palace (III/8, 1). But there exists what seems to be Inigo Jones's own design for this gateway showing the pediment with far more conventional mouldings. Yet John Smythson's version cannot be put down to incompetence, for his drawing of the chimney-piece at Arundel House (Plate 162) has none of the oddity of his gateway drawing.

JOHN SMYTHSON: A MISCELLANY

As a servant first of Sir Charles Cavendish and then of his son, it is not surprising that the most important group of buildings by John Smythson were for the

181. (top left), 182. (top right) Designs by John Smythson for the door from the Little Castle to the Stone Walk, and the balcony over the gallery door (III/1(7–8)).
183. (bottom left), 184. (bottom right) Two designs for windows, from Dietterlin's *Architectura* (1598).

younger branch of the Cavendish family. But, like his father, he also provided designs for a wide group of other clients, on projects scattered over the Midlands.

He was involved on at least three occasions with Sir Charles Cavendish's elder brother William, later the first Earl of Devonshire. 'Sir Wm Cavendishes Surveyor' to whom William Cavendish the elder gave twenty-two shillings at Hardwick on 27 August 1619, was undoubtedly John Smythson.[29] The gift was probably in connection with designs or advice concerning work at the east end of Hardwick Old Hall, on which nearly £650 was spent between 1619 and 1622. In August 1621, £13 6s. 8d. was 'given Mr Smithson' at Leicester.[30] Here Smythson was probably involved in alterations to Leicester Abbey, which William Cavendish bought in 1613.

The work at Hardwick Old Hall has disappeared, and only a few unimportant fragments remain at Leicester Abbey. The third of these Cavendish projects survives. It is the tomb of the first Countess of Devonshire, dated 1627, in the little church of Ault Hucknall, on the edge of the park at Hardwick. It seems to be an adaptation of a Smythson drawing (III/27), which is itself a copy of a design by Vredeman de Vries given in his *Pictores Statuarii Architecti* of 1563. In its use

270

185. (top) Monument to the Countess of Devonshire, Ault Hucknall, Derbyshire (1627).

186. (bottom) A design by John Smythson, related to the monument (III/27).

of different coloured materials and its delicate low relief ornament it is reminiscent of the Bolsover keep fireplaces; it is crowned by five figures of very respectable quality (Plates 185–7).

The chimney-piece (Plate 189) at Clifton Hall, just outside Nottingham, has already been mentioned. It is set into a panel of ashlar framed by a moulding, a mannerism also used by John for the chimney-pieces in the Little Castle at Bolsover and at Welbeck, and for his father's monument.[31] The Clifton chimney-piece is in a handsomely decorated room which is one of the few survivors of an earlier house remodelled by Carr of York in the eighteenth century. The client was Sir Gervase Clifton, for whom Smythson also designed large but stylistically unambitious stables in 1632. There have disappeared, as has Smythson's banqueting house at Clifton, a charming little building in his mock castle manner.[32]

Among the Smythson drawings are a number of plans and designs for houses, by John. Some are for additions or alterations to existing houses. Among these are designs for Wyverton House, date 1615, Haughton House, dated 1618 (Plate 191), and Grove House, undated.[33] All three houses are in Nottinghamshire and

271

187. Design for a tomb, by Vredeman de Vries.

have been demolished or completely remodelled since the seventeenth century. Another curiously vernacular design, captioned 'the Newe Platt at Twyforde' (Plate 192) is probably for a farm in Leicestershire, which John Smythson held on lease from Sir Percival Willoughby, and ultimately bequeathed to Huntingdon.[34]

A plan for 'Mr Diball', dated 1622, is for a new building, and rather more distinctive (Plate 193). It is arranged with remorseless symmetry. The parlour and hall are twins, to either side of a narrow entrance lobby. Beyond, to either side of a courtyard, are two matching staircases, a kitchen matching a bakehouse and brewhouse, a larder matching a milkhouse, two more staircases, and matching rooms to either side of a central throughway on the axis of the entrance lobby.

273

188. (top left) Chimney-piece at Clifton Hall, Nottinghamshire (c. 1630).
189. (facing page) Design for a chimney-piece, from Dietterlin's *Architectura*.
190. (top right) John Smythson's adaptation from Dietterlin.

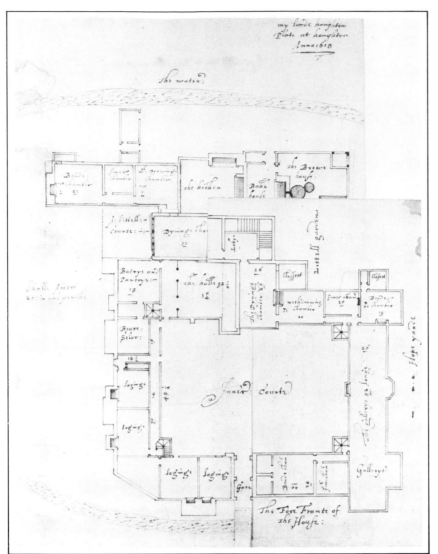

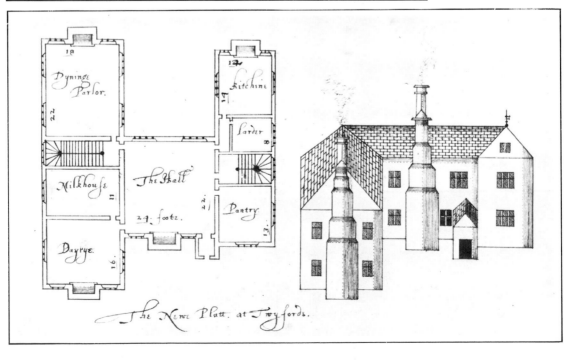

191. (left) Plan by John Smythson for additions to Haughton House, Nottinghamshire, 1618 (III/4).

192. (bottom). 'The Newe Platt at Twy forde', Leicestershire (III/14).

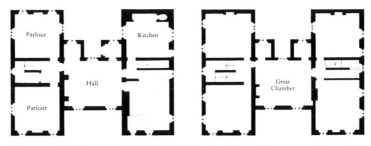

Fig. 22. Barlborough Old Hall, Derbyshire. The ground- and first-floor plans.

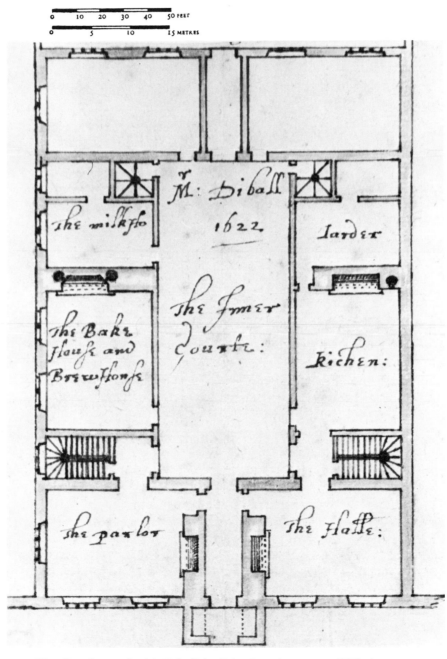

193. Plan for a house for Mr Diball, by John Smythson, 1622 (III/19).

194. The Old Hall at Wingerworth, Derbyshire, from an inlaid table-top of *c.* 1676.

Robert Smythson seems to have abandoned this kind of comprehensive symmetry after Wollaton. The elevation and basement plan of John Smythson's Slingsby suggests that its main floor was planned with similar symmetry, and that this kind of planning expressed his personal taste. On these and other grounds, another house, Barlborough Old Hall, can be attributed to him; so, more tentatively, can a long demolished house at Wingerworth.

Barlborough Old Hall survives, decayed but little altered except for its roofs. It is in the village of Barlborough, is dated 1618 on the porch, and was probably built as a subsidiary house of Sir Henry Savile, whose main seat was at Methley in Yorkshire.[35] The Methley Saviles had collaborated with Gilbert Talbot and, probably, Robert Smythson on the building of Heath School, Halifax; Barlborough is in the heart of the Smythson country; and the elegantly symmetrical plan of the Old Hall (Fig. 22) strongly suggests the hand of John Smythson, although he is unlikely to have had much to do with its detailing.

Its centrally-placed hall opens into matching porch and window bay; to preserve frontal symmetry the porch door is placed round the corner, in the

276

manner of Burton Agnes. These two projections were probably originally carried above the eaves line to form the matching turrets. Two such turrets, a symmetrical elevation, and surmounting battlements were the dominant features of Wingerworth Hall, a house built by the Hunloke family, which certainly shows the influence and perhaps more than the influence, of the Smythsons. It was situated a few miles from Hardwick, but survives only in the charming form of an inlay on a seventeenth-century table (Plate 194).[36]

Both Barlborough Old Hall and Wingerworth were comparatively low houses. At Carlton Hall in Yorkshire Bess of Hardwick's grand-daughter, Elizabeth Stapleton, built a tower-like house clearly influenced by the Little Castle at Bolsover.[37] It survives today, although substantially remodelled under the remorseless hand of Edward Welby Pugin. Two other tower houses suggest Bolsover and Smythson. Tupton Hall, near Chesterfield, was perhaps built in about 1610–20, added to in the 1660s, refenestrated in the eighteenth century, and demolished in the 1930s.[38] Stydd Hall, near Ashbourne, survives, but has been much altered.

The charming hunting-stand at Ledstone, in Yorkshire, is on the edge of the Smythsons' country; it would be nice to be able to link it with them, but evidence is lacking even of its date, let alone its designer.[39] Its cluster of turrets is reminiscent of the two turrets of the curious and delightful little building known as the Stand at Swarkeston, near Derby (Col. Plate XVI). This is the one remaining appendage of the vanished great house of the Harpurs, a family connected with the Cavendishes both by blood and by marriage. It cannot, from its heraldry,[40] date from before 1623, but it is reminiscent of the Bolsover keep: betwen two towers surmounted by little ogee domes is a two-storey battlemented centre, the lower part of which consists of an arcaded loggia with Tuscan columns supporting ogee arches similar to those of some of the keep fireplaces. It is probably the 'bowle alley house' for which the mason Richard Shephard was paid £111 12s. 4d. in 1630–2.[41] Although there are no John Smythson drawings connected with it, on the grounds of style, geography and family conection, it can reasonably be attributed to him.

John Smythson must almost certainly have been present at the time of the royal visit to Bolsover, and perhaps watched the masque. If so, his reactions may have been mixed, for one of its themes was a burlesque of the new pretensions of architecture. In the 'Dance of Mechanics' the surveyor is called Coronell Iniquo Vitruvius and he addresses his artificers in language that makes fun of that of the architectural theorists of the time: 'Well done my musical, arithmetical, geometrical gamesters; or rather my true mathematical boys! it is carried in number, weight, and measure, as if the airs were all harmony, and the figures a well timed proportion.' Though the recent building operations at the castle may have given the excuse for this part of the masque, Jonson is obviously taking the opportunity to take a poke at his old enemy, Inigo Jones.

One wonders what John Smythson, who aspired now to the dignity of Gentleman and Architect, thought of this ridicule of architects. He was not a highly educated man, and the allusions may have escaped him. Perhaps he had the laugh in the long run. For the buildings of Bolsover, never sophisticated, always stiff and eccentric, and now dirty, cracked and deserted, remain a delight and an inspiration, filled, as Sacheverell Sitwell writes, with 'a ghostly poetry that fires the imagination, that can never be forgotten, and that never cools'.

In the year of King Charles's visit, John Smythson died. His will survives, dated 5 November 1634, and proved on 3 December.[42] It is an interesting document, giving some idea of how well John had done out of his career, and in what way his employers had paid him. He states his profession in the new style, calling himself 'John Smithson, Architecter'. To his wife Margaret he left the use for life of his house and farm at Bolsover with its 'barns, stables, orcharde, gardens, Land, meadow and pastures'. Huntingdon was left farms at Twyford and Gadsby in Leicestershire, on leases granted to John by Sir Percival Willoughby of Wollaton, no doubt payment for the orchard and glass-house, and perhaps other designs or services; a farm at Skegby in Nottinghamshire, on a lease from Mr Lindley of Skegby, perhaps another payment in kind; the farm at Kirkby which Sir Charles Cavendish had leased to him in 1615; and the house and farm at Bolsover on his mother's death.

John, Huntingdon's obscure younger brother, got a rent on a lease of a farm in Newthorpe, some interests in demesne lands in Sutton-in-Ashfield, next to Kirkby, and the lease of a farm in Cossall, Nottinghamshire. There are minor bequests to his unmarried daughter, Elizabeth, and his various relatives.

The furniture and fittings of the house at Bolsover were ultimately to be divided between Huntingdon and John. Its main rooms are listed: Hall, parlour, Chamber over parlour, Kitchen, Middle Chamber, and Closet; some of these contained 'seling' and 'Waynscott'. The 'Library and Books', alas not named, and most of the furniture went to Huntingdon. John got the furniture in the Middle Chamber and Closet, 'together wth fre Liberty to use them as long as he is unmarried'.

The will ends with an appeal, stiff but not unmoving, which reflects perhaps, John's uneasiness at ill-feeling between his sons, and certainly loyalty, and affection for the two brothers who had treated him so well.

And lastly I beseech the right honble William Earle of Newcastle my most honoured Lord and Master and the right Wor.ll Sir Charles Cavendish Kt to be overseers and supervisours of this my last will, Unto whom I straigtlye charge my said two sonnes to be observant and to endeavour by gode assistance according to their honble example to lyve togeather in unyty, knowinge that as upon them soe upon all others keepinge unviolated the eternall bonde of brotherlie love God will contynually multiply and showre downe his blessinges.

278

HUNTINGDON SMITHSON

Huntingdon Smithson (as he seems always to have spelt his name) is a mysterious figure, for we know so little about him. He married, perhaps not till after his father's death, Isabel, daughter of Thomas Hall of Barlow Lees, Derbyshire, whose family were small gentry connected by marriage with the Newtons of Kirkby-in-Ashfield.[43] The initials H.S. 1629 on the 1629–30 building at Bolsover may be his. In 1632 he carried out three land surveys for Newcastle, of Ogle and Moralee-in-Haydon in Northumberland and Mansfield Park in Nottinghamshire. These form part of a great series of surveys of Newcastle's estates, most of which were made by William Senior.[24] On the Mansfield survey Huntingdon called himself 'Practioner of the Mathematiqs'. At this time he was living in the house at Kirkby-in-Ashfield which Charles Cavendish had leased to his father, as the Kirkby survey in the same group shows; his father had moved to a house at Bolsover. Perhaps by then he had taken over the post of bailiff to the Cavendish estates in that area from his father. He was also capable of acting as an architect, for according to the evidence of his epitaph in the church at Bolsover:

> *His skill in architecture did deserve*
> *A fairer tombe his mem'ry to preserve.*

No doubt he assisted his father, as his father had assisted Robert. When he was up at Ogle in 1632 he may have combined surveying with supervising the building of Newcastle's new house.

There were eight years to go between John Smythson's death in 1634, and the outbreak of the Civil War. If Newcastle engaged in any further building during these years one would have expected him to have employed Huntingdon as his architect. Such building would be more likely to earn Huntingdon a reputation for skill in architecture than any help which he may have given his father.

Three possibilities exist, only one of which is of much interest. The first is the addition of an extra storey above the hall in the terrace range, and other alterations to this end of the range. The relevant Bolsover drawing at Renishaw shows quite clearly that the hall was originally finished off with a battlemented parapet, similar to the parapet above the gallery. At some stage this parapet was replaced by an attic floor, lit by four scrolled gables, of the type drawn by John Smythson on his visit to London in 1619. Similar gables replaced the straight-sided ones originally surmounting the front to the courtyard. At the same time, or perhaps a little earlier, the gables on the terrace front were replaced by a parapet, and 'cannon' buttresses inserted underneath, to match the adjoining galley façade.

The second and much more important possibility is the long range at Bolsover containing the riding school and related accommodation, including, probably, stables. This range is decorated with long rows of stone dormers, each surmounted by scrolled gables similar to those above the hall, but smaller and rather more robustly modelled (Plate 196).

The third possibility is closely related to the second. Grimm's drawing of the west front of Welbeck (Plate 195), made in the eighteenth century, shows four bays to the left of the porch, lit by windows and dormers apparently identical to those on the riding-school range at Bolsover. These four bays look like the only completed part of a projected rebuilding involving the rest of the façade.

It is tempting to assign all three pieces of building to Huntingdon Smithson. The main objections are that the 1658 engraving after Diepenbeke shows the west front of Welbeck before the rebuilding of the four bays; and that none of the Diepenbeke engravings of Bolsover shows the riding-school range, although it was clearly relevant to the theme of *La Methode Nouvelle* and both riding school and stables at Welbeck were illustrated. But it seems likely that Diepenbeke's illustrations were made in Antwerp on the basis of drawings made in England in 1633 or thereabouts; in which case Diepenbeke would have been unable to show any buildings of later date, however relevant, because the necessary information would have been lacking.

If the riding-school range is by Huntingdon it both does him credit, and relates sufficiently closely to his father's work, even if lacking all his father's oddities. It is a robust and friendly row of buildings, agreeably diversified by scrolled gables and generous rustication. This rustication has none of John's idiosyncratic vermiculation. The two great doorways leading into the riding school and stables

280

are especially splendid (Plate 199); they are probably derived from doorways in Francini's *Architecture*, published in 1631 (Plate 198)[44].

There are no other buildings which can be attributed to Huntingdon Smithson; and except for one or two minor possibilities,[45] there appear to be no drawings by him in the Smythson collection, for the riding-school range or anything else. With him, sadly enough after the fireworks provided by Robert and John, the Smythson architecture seems to fizzle out. For, whatever his own talents may have been, he did not get a fair deal. He was a young man, little over thirty, when his father died. After only eight years, during three of which Newcastle was away in London, the outbreak of war put an end, for the time, to building. In 1644 the Royalist army was defeated at Marston Moor, and Newcasle fled to the Continent. Bolsover was forfeited to the Commonwealth and bought up for

196. Bolsover Castle. Looking from the Little Castle across the Fountain Garden to the riding-school range (c. 1635–40).

197. Inside the riding school, Bolsover.

198. (right) Design for a gateway, from Francini's *Architecture*.

its materials by a speculator, who started to demolish it. In this gloomy atmosphere of destruction and defeat Huntingdon Smithson fades away, dying in 1648, when he was at most forty-seven years old.

His will is a nuncupative, that is to say oral one, owing, to quote its own words, to his having been 'surprised by his sickness in his intellectuals'.[46] He left property valued at £960 16s., including unspecified books and mathematical instruments in his study worth £20. He was buried in the church at Bolsover, where his epitaph reads as follows:

Reader beneath this plaine stone buried ly
Smithsons remainders of mortality
Whose skill in architecture did deserve
A fairer tombe his mem'ry to preserve
But since his nobler gifts of piety
To God to men of justice and charity
Are gone to heaven a building to prepare
Not made with hands, his friends contented are
He here shall rest in hope till th' world shall burn
And intermingle ashes with his urne.
Huntingdon Smithson
Gent.
Obit IX bris 27 1648

199. (following page) One of the doorways in the riding-school range.

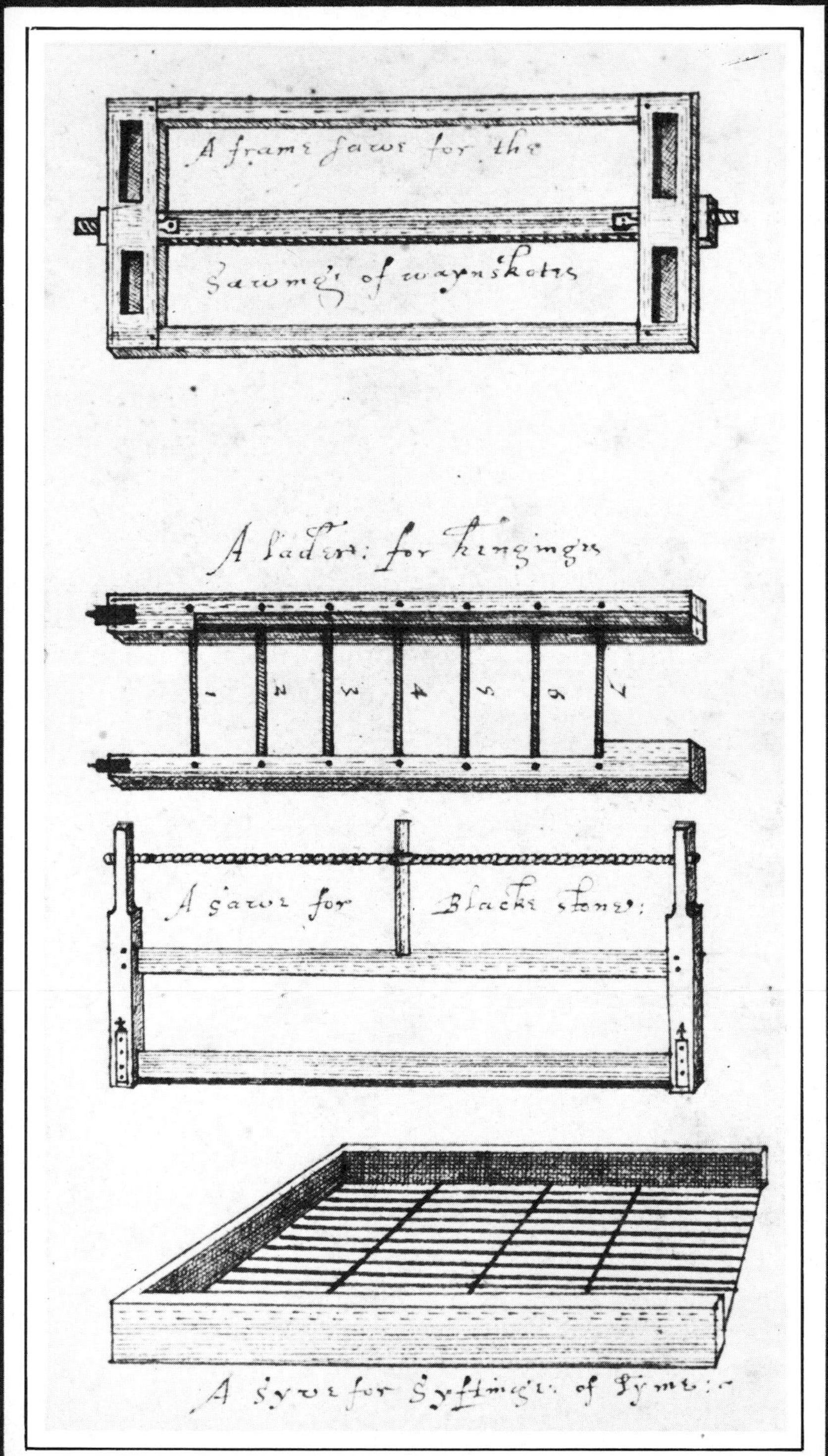

A frame sawe for the

sawmgs of waynskotes

A ladder: for hanginges

A sawe for   Blacke stone:

A syve for syftinge of lyme:-

8 Robert Smythson:
A Summing Up

HOWEVER obscure a figure Huntingdon may be, the buildings of his father, John, form one of the more curious and delightful side-alleys in the history of English architecture. But seen in the context of the time they are a provincial cul-de-sac, and had little influence on the architecture that surrounded or followed them. Robert Smythson is in a different class. Not only do the houses with which he can be connected include some of the most important and impressive of their period; they were also full of ideas, new or newly expressed, which were taken up and developed elsewhere in the country. There is little doubt that Robert Smythson was one of the creators of the Elizabethan style; and a final chapter is needed in which to try to estimate the nature and influence of what he achieved.

This is not easy to do, because his whole career is so full of question marks. Quite apart from the houses which are only attributed to him in any documented Smythson house, what is Smythson and what is not? How much was dictated to him by Bess of Hardwick, or Willoughby, or Thynne, or Charles Cavendish? How much was left to the initiative of the workmen? The designs he made – perhaps from the start incomplete or lacking in detail – were at the mercy of the patron's whim, or the inefficiency or independence of the men who carried them out. His employers did not see themselves as consulting a creative genius; they were employing a servant, to give form to their ideas, or provide ideas of his own which they would have no hesitation in expanding or adapting.

Yet however much is allowed for wastage there remains a hard core with a flavour and consistency that cannot be explained away. One Smythson house develops from another; at the back of every uncertainty is the feeling of an original mind and a strong imagination at work.

In Robert Smythson's drawings one gets as near as one can hope to his own conceptions, undistorted by time or chance. Taken as a group they are impressive in their variety, especially when one considers the background of the man who made them. Among them are original plans and elevations, survey drawings of houses, colleges, churches and gardens, designs for screens, chimney-pieces, beds, panelling, brewhouses, marble-cutting equipment, tombs, possibly fountains, and windows. The sources of inspiration include Vredeman de Vries, Serlio, and English medieval Gothic work. The designs for screens shows a real feeling for the sobriety, weight and restraint of Renaissance architecture; but Smythson was equally prepared to design rose-windows in a curious neo-Gothic style, and sketch Gothic detail and vaulting-plans; and his collection contained three late medieval drawings of remarkable interest.

The impression of variety continues when one considers just the plans, which form the most important section of the collection. Perhaps the dominant characteristic of these is a delight in pattern making such as appears elsewhere in, for instance, the rose-window drawings. The plans derive from a realisation that by taking a small number of basic types – the courtyard house, the rectangle and the H shape – and enriching them with different combinations of different types of

286

200. (preceding page) Designs for tools, by Robert or John Smythson (II/26).

projection – curved, polygonal or rectangular – an endless variety of outline could be achieved. Beautifully drawn out on a sheet of vellum or high-quality paper, and enriched with italic inscriptions and elaborately ornamented scales, these geometric plans are in themselves arresting and attractive; and they were no doubt felt to be such, quite apart from the qualities of the houses in which they may ultimately have taken form.

Inside the ingenious outline the variety continues. The elements are the same, offices, hall, parlour, staircase, great chamber, withdrawing chamber, long gallery and lodgings: the standard requirements of the Elizabethan gentry, which Smythson was in no position to alter. But the way in which they are arranged is full of surprises. The offices are in the basement or on the ground floor; the hall is along or across the centre, or to or down one side; the great chamber, withdrawing chamber and gallery are on the first or second floors, and have a variety of shapes, combinations and positions. The problem of fitting the necessary rooms, of every kind of size and use, under one roof and within the compact and decorative outline is tackled with considerable ingenuity. Nonetheless, awkwardnesses remain: bay windows which have an uneasy relation to the rooms behind them, mezzanine floors which are not as well lit as they might be, and other sacrifices of convenience which Smythson (and his patrons) were prepared to make for the sake of symmetry and originality of form.

There is one specific type of plan which Smythson has some claim to have originated, and which figures prominently in the architecture of the time. This is the compact non-courtyard plan of the Wollaton-Hardwick type, with the Hardwick feature of a cross-hall and, on occasion, the Wollaton feature of basement offices.

This plan had certain obvious advantages. It was a novelty; it was stylish; it was compact, convenient and economical. Although unsuitable for a house on the grandest scale, it was capable of considerable contraction and expansion. It served equally conveniently as the house of a successful court official, or the hunting-lodge or subsidiary residence of a great nobleman.[1]

Its compactness, as has been pointed out, had prototypes earlier in the sixteenth century and even before. Basement offices had probably been constructed at Longleat before Smythson came there. The cross-hall may have been suggested by Bess of Hardwick, rather than by her surveyor, and had been anticipated in the Banqueting House at Holdenby. Smythson's achievement was to have created a type-house. Type-houses have, almost inevitably, their prototypes and their debts to other sources; but they are buildings in which one or more concepts are crystallised and presented in so attractive a form that they become the object of widespread imitation.

Yet, in Smythson's case, just how widespread was this imitation? The pedigree is by no means fool-proof. Smythson himself does not seem, on the available evidence, to have used the cross-hall very often. Apart from Hardwick it appears only twice among his drawings, both times for schemes that were never carried out: the house at Blackwell-in-the-Peak, and the fancy Greek-cross plan (II/10). Manor Lodge, Worksop, can reasonably be attributed to him. A few other northern houses have, or had, cross-halls: Tissington Hall (*c.* 1609) and Renishaw Hall (*c.* 1625) in Derbyshire, possibly Constable Burton, Broughton and Sandbeck in Yorkshire.[2] These are buildings which one would perhaps hesitate to assign to Smythson, but which must have been influenced by his work.

There is no cross-hall at Fountains, Chastleton, Caverswell, Burton Agnes, or the designs for Slingsby and Welbeck. These all date, certainly or probably, from after Hardwick. Burton Agnes, with a courtyard, no basement, and relatively conventional hall, is less advanced from the planning point of view than Hardwick and Wollaton, designed ten and twenty years before. Wollaton, in the unromantic sphere of sanitation, was far in advance of Hardwick. Smythson had to come to terms with the conservatism of his northern patrons. The same conservatism was probably responsible for scotching other experimental originalities in his plans. The corridor-system of the Slingsby plan and of a plan related to it (I/19) are advanced for their date; at Barlborough an even more complete corridor-system was actually executed; but elsewhere in Smythson's work the lines of communications are comparatively rudimentary. The dramatic potentialities of the Hardwick staircases were never exploited in any of his other buildings.

Variants on the cross-hall plan, usually with basement offices, reappear in the first decade of the seventeenth century, in a group of houses built by southern patrons. These include Charlton House, Greenwich (1607), Somerhill, Kent (*c.* 1613), Sir George Coppin's house on the site of Kensington Palace, a vanished lodge built by Sir Robert Cecil in the park at Hatfield, and Plas Teg in Flintshire, built about 1610 by a highly successful London placeman, Sir John Trevor. Plans of Somerhill, the Coppin house and Hatfield lodge appear in Thorpe, together with a number of anonymous plans of the same type.[3]

What remains uncertain is the connection between these southern houses and the Smythson group. Two of Thorpe's anonymous plans are tracings from the 1601 or 1610 edition of Palladio's *Architecture*; these have been adapted for English use, but their cross-halls come from Palladio. Somerhill and Plas Teg are variants on these Palladian types. Did the southern surveyors in the early seventeenth century know of the Smythson cross-halls? Thorpe knew Wollaton, but there is no evidence that he knew Hardwick. It is possible that the two groups evolved quite independently, the Smythson group perhaps empirically (although influence from Palladio or du Cerceau is not impossible), the Thorpe or southern group ten or fifteen years later from Palladio. On the other hand, the Earl of Salisbury acquired a plan of Hardwick in 1608, and other southern builders may have done the same. The truth probably is that two separate forces converged upon these houses, Smythson and Palladio: it would perhaps be rash to suggest which came first, or which was the more important.

When one leaves this specific type and comes to the general field of Elizabethan and Jacobean architecture, the extensive gaps in our knowledge of the period make it hard to estimate Smythson's influence. As Sir John Summerson has pointed out, the Elizabethan age is one of experiment and the Jacobean of consolidation. The Elizabethans created types, and the Jacobeans evolved endless variations on them. Under Elizabeth a number of men were experimenting, probably to a considerable extent independently, though they were all heading in the same direction. Smythson was one of these, certainly one of the most important. Nearly all the qualities typical of Jacobean houses can be found in Smythson designs made before the end of the sixteenth century. But they can be found, too, in other Elizabethan houses with which Smythson is unlikely to have had any connection. Much more work needs to be done in classifying, dating and researching into Elizabethan houses – in particular, Elizabethan houses that have been demolished – before one can be over-confident in saying who was first with what idea. The fact that Smythson's drawings survive, and those of his contemporaries have for the most part disappeared, tends to give him an importance in our eyes that is perhaps exaggerated.

It is easy to forget how separate a world the North Midlands and North of England was under Elizabeth, who never herself penetrated them in all her many progresses. Locally, there can be little doubt that Robert Smythson was the dominant architectural influence from his arrival at Wollaton in 1580 until his death in 1614. Whenever, in this area, one finds a high or compact house, with basement offices, lavish fenestration, towers, bay windows, bold recession or a commanding site, one can assume that either Smythson or his example is at work. Ingestre in Staffordshire, Sheriff Hutton, Howsham and Marske in Yorkshire, Chipchase in Northumberland, and Gainford in Durham are examples of the latter class; and there are many more.

When one comes to houses outside the north, one is on less secure grounds in assessing Smythson's influence. It is true that up till 1580 he was in the south or south-west. But nothing is known of his work before Longleat, at Longleat he was one of a team, Wardour was only a conversion job, and his connection with Lulworth and Bradford-on-Avon is purely conjectural. Once he went up to Wollaton in 1580 there is no certain evidence that he was consulted about any southern buildings. There is evidence of a kind, however, in the case of Hatfield; the fact that Charles Cavendish provided a plan for it, ostensibly of his own devising but probably owing much to Smythson, suggests a way by which Smythson's influence may have penetrated to the south.

It is impossible to say with any exactitude how well known his northern houses were in the south. There is no reason to suppose that Fountains, Burton Agnes, or Pontefract were known at all outside their own area. On the other hand, Wollaton was certainly a famous building. Worksop and Hardwick were both known of and admired by Lord Salisbury, and Hardwick was praised in Camden's *Britannia*. Thorpe drew the elevation of Doddington, though he improved it with a number of fashionable London trimmings. It is at least probable that Thorpe visited Wollaton to draw the plan of it, and actually met Smythson; and Smythson was in London, certainly in 1609 and possibly in 1602.

So there is some evidence for southern knowledge of Smythson and his buildings after 1580. His importance in the south remains difficult to assess because – unlike the north – there were so many other influences at work, including the whole formidable body of the officials of the Queen's Works. However, one hypothesis can be put forward. There are two dominant Elizabethan and Jacobean types – complementary aspects of the effort to impress. There is the great courtyard house, spread out round one or more courts, with angle pavilions, subsidiary wings, and a lavishly symmetrical organisation of a number of elements over a large area. Kirby, Holdenby and Theobalds are notable Elizabethan examples; under James the line culminates with Audley End, and includes smaller (though far from small) houses such as Blickling, Bramshill and Knole. It is not a type with which Smythson had much to do, though he used it, in relatively simple form, in his designs for Lord Sheffield, and, more elaborately, in his design for Welbeck.

In contrast are the high compact houses, where the drama and swagger of the design is concentrated in one single dominating mass. The cross-hall type discussed earlier in this chapter form one department of these houses, but there are many others, with small internal courtyards or more conventional halls. Montacute is a typical example of the type in its least revolutionary aspect. All the notable Smythson houses fall inside this group; and although the evidence is far from conclusive, Smythson was probably more responsible than any other Elizabethan for developing it.

Many of these compact houses were heavily glazed; some were almost continuous glass all the way round. They were lantern-houses, and Smythson has a particular claim to have pioneered this aspect of Elizabethan architecture. At Kirby (started in 1570) the hall side of the courtyard was a continuous wall of glass, but the rest of the house was much less amply windowed. At Leicester's Building at Kenilworth (c. 1570–5) the tiers of many-lighted windows inspired Laneham to compare it to a lighthouse, but there were in fact considerable areas of wall between the glazing. The building of Holdenby probably started a year or two after the remodelling of Longleat. Longleat, unless a vanished prototype comes to light, can be claimed as the first of Elizabethan lantern-houses.

The houses that were erected on the basis of Smythson's plans were exciting and original creations, but it remains something of a problem to what extent he intended to achieve the effects which we admire in them. A typical Smythson plan when executed results in projections and recessions, and combinations of different cubic shapes that, as three-dimensional drama, can be enormously effective. But did Smythson realise this, or was he primarily concerned with the 'ingeniose device' as drawn out in the plan – that is with the construction of novel two-dimensional patterns and with the conceit of using these as a basis for building?

290

Perhaps it is impossible to give a final answer to this question, because the evidence is lacking. But when one surveys, not only Smythson's own work, but also the whole field of Elizabethan and Jacobean architecture it is hard not to see it as a gradual realisation of the dramatic potentialities of height and skyline, of grouping and recession, of the tower, the bay window and the gable. In this way it makes sense; one step leads to another; and one is not reduced to believing that one of the most original chapters in the history of English architecture was written by mistake. Smythson might have been unable to put into words what it was he was after; but his own buildings are evidence that, whether consciously or not, he had a wonderfully vivid dramatic sense.

As such he was not alone among his contemporaries, but he was certainly among the leaders of those who fashioned this aspect of the Elizabethan style. This was no small achievement, for the style was a remarkable one. Seen in its European context it is something of a phenomenon. In a certain sense (and certainly to a far greater extent than continental Renaissance architecture) the Elizabethan is a functional style: that is to say the elements of which it is composed, towers, windows, and gables, are functional in origin even if frequently used in a highly unfunctional way. Decorative detail is relatively unimportant; what is so impressive about many Elizabethan houses is the way in which they achieve a sensational effect with the minimum of decoration.

Their effect is sensational because of their sense of the dramatic, of the potentialities of grouping, skyline, and movement. In this they have something in common with the whole contemporary architecture of northern Europe. But the formula is seldom if ever so pure on the Continent, where classical prototypes pressed harder, and the fascination of detail often obscured the grand simplicity of the masses. In contrast there is a direct and single-minded pursuit of one concept about the best English buildings of the period. The bold recession of Wimbledon and Fountains, the glass walls and shifting towers of Hardwick, the cliff façade of Hatfield, the crystal clarity of Wootton, have no comparable equivalents on the Continent.

It is worth examining the fortunes of the style after it fell out of favour in the reign of Charles I. English architecture then veered back on a Renaissance tack, and aimed to achieve balance, restraint, proportion and scholarship; there is little sense of the dramatic or of movement in the architecture of either Jones or Wren. Aubrey's remark that 'under Elizabeth architecture made no progress but rather went backwards'[4] sums up concisely the opinion of an age which had a different sense of values. Elizabethan architecture was tried, and naturally found wanting, by the standards of the Renaissance.

But in 1731 Nicholas Hawksmoor could write that Wollaton showed 'some true stroaks of architecture',[5] for the climate of opinion had changed. There is a considerable amount in common between Elizabethan architecture and that of Hawksmoor and Vanbrugh, who believed, unlike their predecessors, in the value of imagination as well as reason, and brought drama and poetry back into architecture. They owed, of course, a great deal to the baroque architecture of the Continent, but they also borrowed something from the Elizabethans. Vanbrugh's own house at Claremont was built on a purely Elizabethan plan, and that of Seaton Delaval had a strong Elizabethan flavour. There are undoubted Elizabethan reminiscences, whether intentional or not, about the six towers, the bow windows, and the clerestoried hall at Blenheim, and the similar features at Eastbury. And smaller buildings, like the stable pavilions at Castle Howard and Gooseberry House in Whitehall, are really Elizabethan lodges or conceits expressed in eighteenth-century language.

The Palladians banished Vanbrugh and the Elizabethans into the outer darkness of bad taste, but the cult of the picturesque brought back a certain measure of appreciation of both styles. Adam's and Sir Joshua Reynolds's praise of Vanbrugh is well known; and Richard Payne Knight in his didactic poem *The Landscape* (1794) published facing engravings in which a classical house in a Capability Brown-type park was contrasted unfavourably with a house of Elizabethan type, seen as part of an 'undressed' landscape. Payne Knight's friend, Uvedale Price, in the second volume of his *Essays on the Picturesque* (1810) has an interesting comparison between Wollaton and Nottingham Castle. The former he describes as 'a house, which for the richness of its ornaments in the near view, and the grandeur of its masses from every point, yields to few, if any, in the kingdom'. The latter is 'a long, square house of the Italian style. . . . Such a building, on such high ground, and its outline always distinctly opposed to the sky, gives an impression of ridicule and disgust. The hill and town are absolutely flattened by it; while the comparatively low situation of Wollaton, is so elevated by the form of the house, that it seems to command the whole country round it.'[6] This passage is immediately followed by an enthusiastic appreciation of the architecture of Vanbrugh.

As early as 1789 George Byng, later Viscount Torrington, wrote a long and enthusiastic description of Hardwick: 'Such lofty magnificence! and built with stone, upon a hill! One of the proudest piles I ever beheld.'[7] A few Elizabethan and Jacobean houses are illustrated in the *Seats of the Nobility and Gentry* of this period, in W. Watts's collection of 1779, and W. Angus's of 1787. But there are many more in J. P. Neale's *Views of Seats* (1819-29) and Britton and Brayley's *The Beauties of England and Wales* (1801-15). By this time it was taken for granted that Elizabethan houses were worthy of interest, admiration, and even imitation. In his *Fragments on the Theory and Practice of Landscape Gardening* (1816), Humphry Repton says of the Elizabethan period: 'There is something so venerable and picturesque in many houses of this date, that I have always endeavoured to preserve as much of them as could be adapted to modern uses; and even in some cases advised new houses in that style of architecture.'

In the ensuing decades the lusciously romantic lithographs of Tudor and Jacobean houses published by Joseph Nash in the 1830s and 1840s helped to make the style popular; and a great many new Elizabethan houses were built, by Blore, Buckler, Salvin and others. These houses often seem to us to emulate the least attractive Elizabethan attributes: the ostentation, the crudity, the coarse and elaborate detail, which appealed to the new industrial rich as they had done to the new Elizabethan gentry. But the Victorians appreciated other qualities as well. Mentmore was modelled very closely on Wollaton, but has a skyline, visible for miles around, which is more reminiscent of Hardwick; and the entrance façade of Harlaxton is a dramatic work of art of the first quality.

Harlaxton is a useful symbol: for here is a mid-nineteenth-century building, based on Elizabethan prototypes, but approached through an entrance screen of colossal Vanbrughian grandeur. There is nothing unharmonious about the result. What is being suggested is that Elizabethan architecture was neither a bastard style nor an isolated oddity but one expression of a recurring English tradition: a poetic, romantic and anti-classical tradition. Seen in this context Robert Smythson appears as a major representative of one aspect of the English genius.

Yet how little is known about him. When one turns from the buildings to the man himself one is faced with an almost total blank. Where was he born? Who were his parents? Whom did he marry? What were his interests, if any, outside his trade? What books did he own or read? How welcome some brief personal reference would be; or, even more, some description as intriguing as Laneham's account of Captain Cox, the Coventry mason, with his library of romances and Gothic literature.[8] It would be pleasant to know, but rash to assume, that Smythson, whose Gothic roots were strong, owned a similar collection.

We know little enough about his relations with his patrons. His and Maynard's letter to Thynne is a mixture of obsequiousness, illiteracy and independence, as though they obscurely felt that they had claims to consideration, but did not expect these to be recognised and scarcely recognised them themselves. But this letter was written in the earlier stages of his career: no letter or document survives to show his relations with the Willoughbys, Talbots and Cavendishes when he had become a man of some reputation and property.

In view of his patrons there can be little doubt that he was a Protestant. On analysis they form a reasonably cohesive group: a Protestant group, a group that served and supported the Government, usually to their own financial benefit. They were vigorous, powerful, enterprising and aggressive. They exploited coal mines and hunted down recusants. With the exception of Francis Willoughby they were not intellectual. Few books, and those almost all unimportant, were dedicated to Smythson's patrons. The one exception – possibly significant – is a book of music, not of literature: George Wilbye's *Book of Airs*, dedicated to Charles Cavendish. Thynne came from humanist circles, but was himself no humanist. Willoughby had more intellectual pretensions, but cannot be connected with any intellectual circle of his time. Bess of Hardwick was not, one suspects, a reader.

It is worth commenting on the number and violence of the quarrels described or referred to in this book. Thynne was attacked by his neighbour, William Darrell. Henry Howard lived in a continuous whirlwind of squalid rows. Thomas Howard was accused of poisoning his wife and trying to disinherit his niece. Plots and quarrels dominated the life of Francis Willoughby. Bess of Hardwick fell foul of almost everybody: her son Henry, her grand-daughter Arabella, her husband, her tenants and her queen. Charles Cavendish was assaulted by the Stanhopes. Stephen Proctor was ambushed by his neighbours. Edward Talbot tried to poison his brother.

It was an age of violent social change, of which these quarrels were one symptom. The buildings it produced are often as violent as its quarrels, as tough as its quarrellers. These elements remain disturbing, even after the softening of three or four centuries. Smythson was a product of his age and a servant of his employers. He is, inevitably, a rough diamond among architects. The finer subtleties of detailing and planning are not to be expected of him. His work is full of ideas, but full also of loose ends, clumsinesses, gaps, and conceptions only half worked out. Wollaton, for all its originality, is a repulsive building. Hardwick, for all its magic, is a monument of ostentation and pride. Yet in spite of all uncertainties and shortcomings Smythson is one of the great geniuses of English architecture. As with the Elizabethan age as a whole, along with much that is vulgar, clumsy or hard, there is a boldness in his work that demands admiration and a poetry that can still set the imagination on fire.

APPENDIX I

The Letter from Smythson and Maynard to Thynne

I GIVE below the full text of this important letter, of which portions were quoted on pages 52 and 70. This is Robert Smythson's one known surviving letter, and it is worth noting that he signs it Smythson and not Smithson. The same spelling reappears on his monument at Wollaton. As in most surnames of this period numerous variant spellings appear in other documents, and among his descendants the spelling Smithson seems gradually to have gained the upper hand.

Wee houmble sowtte unto youre worshepe that yt wolde plese youe wt indeferense to here that wye shall saye unto youe at thes time as towching youre disspesorre allrede consaved aganste us for the which wye are sore yf wye could remede yt for wye have bene ride here to and offered oure sarvis evere sinse istere oure sellves and oure men the whech hathe bene to oure great lose for wye have not erned sense not halfe so mouche as wold pay for oure table and forther wye have sene that youe have not owsed other men so bout have lett them have worke anouthe and there mone at convenient teme when they wolde apoyt where as wye have not been so oused bout put frome oure worke and also oure mone kept from us the wheche ys to oure utter desscredit for that wye are not able to paye oure dettes and wye dowe persave that youe wolde have us to give oure attendanse here the which wye are not able to dowe after this sort but wye will and dowe take souche orders that your worshipe shall sofer no lose be ane thinge that wye have in hand for youe bout howe youre dessplesorre ys com upon us wye can not tell exsepe yt be for takynge of youre worke the which wye never ganed ane thynge bey yt bout yll wyll and displesoure the whech is aparent for before that teme wye were well paed the wheche wye calde not be never sens boutt therebye wye have lerned more exsperens then ever wye had before for those men that have takenge youre warke under us had overe mone and yet never contented and made us losours besyde bout for youer works wye thynk our selves better abelc to doue yt then thaye be for the ordenanse therof cam frome us as yore worshipe douthe knawe they ware nevere able to dowe yt the wheche ys lettle consedered of yore worshipe and mouche lesse of them who ought of doute to geve plase boutt for oure serves wye arrede to ofer unto youre worshipe so

295

that yt meght be acseptable for wye are sore thous to have your dessplesoure
yf yt wolde please youe to lett us to have the gyedenge of yt onlye wye wyll
dowe yt for youe better chepe then ane man hathe offered unto youe hithurto
for wye are not desyrous thous to leve yt exsept yt be youre plesoure and
ferthur yf youe have ane in youre worke that youe repose souche trouste unto
that ys able to make amende of yt then beseeche youe to dysscharge us in teme
that wye maye prepare for us and oure famele ells where for oure onlye trouste
mouste be in god for soure wye thynke that in all englande there ys none that
hath takeng in hand to sett outt the lyke worke that hathe resaved lesser profett
and lesser thankes than wye have done for wye have bene enstrowmentes to
searve other mens tornes for a great whele and oure own all waes unsarved
therfore wye beseche youve worshepe to conseder of oure estaste and lett us
have that ys ryght and wye desyer no more be youre houmble sarvantes to
command

Robart Smythson and alen maeneard

APPENDIX II

The Building Chronology of Bolsover Castle

THE reasons for dating the various portions of the castle are given here at greater length than in the main body of the text. It must be emphasised that much of the dating is hypothetical, for the building history is a complicated and confusing one, which will perhaps never become completely clear unless more evidence comes to light.

1. 1612-21. THE KEEP OR LITTLE CASTLE

The evidence suggests a straightforward history covering the years 1612-21, by the end of which the building was approaching completion, though the decoration of the interior was probably not finished until further into the 1620s.

a. The period covered by the surviving accounts:
    2 November 1612-12 March 1613/14.

In this period the medieval keep was demolished (demolition probably started before the surviving accounts begin), the basement was largely, if not entirely, completed, and work was started on the ground floor. This dating is based on the reasonable presupposition that the accounts refer to the building of the Little Castle. The payments cover vaults supported on two pillars for the great cellar, and on one for the kitchen and larder, and also mention a pantry, and kitchen stairs, back stairs, and cellar stairs. All this corresponds exactly with the basement of the Little Castle as it was built.

b. The remainder of Sir Charles Cavendish's life:
    March 1613/14-4 April 1617.

The one piece of evidence here is the chimney-piece in the hall, dated 1616. This chimney-piece is not (like the others in the Little Castle) an insertion, but an integral part of the main structure, so the date does not necessarily imply that the building had got beyond first-floor level in 1616.

c. Work done by Sir William Cavendish, 1617 to 1621 and later.
    (1) The main structure, if left incomplete at Sir Charles's death, must have been finished and roofed in.
    (2) The balcony window on entrance and garden fronts, and the panelling in

297

the Pillar Parlour. These are the direct result of John Smythson's London visit, 1618–19, and must date from after his return. Goulding assumed that the coat of arms on the entrance-front balcony (Cavendish impaling Ogle) showed that it dated from the time of Sir Charles Cavendish. This is clearly impossible. William Cavendish probably put up the shield in tribute to his father, whose conception the building was.

(3) The chimney-piece in the Pillar Parlour. The coat of arms is of Cavendish impaling Basset, with no coronet. It must date from after the marriage of William Cavendish to Elizabeth Basset (about 1618, according to the *Complete Peerage*) and (probably) before he was created Viscount Mansfield, on 29 October 1620. On the other hand, the two crests on the side of the chimney-piece are both surmounted by viscount's coronets. This suggests that the chimney-piece was started before and finished after the creation.

(4) The panelling in the Star Chamber. The panel painted with *Moses carrying the Tables of the Law* is dated 1621.

The surviving account and dates suggest a perfectly sensible if rather leisurely chronology for the Little Castle. It seems reasonable to assume that the forecourt with its four pavilions was built some time between 1614 and 1620, though there is nothing to show whether it was built before or after Sir Charles's death in 1617.

2. 1627–42. THE TERRACE RANGE AND THE FOUNTAIN GARDEN

a. Terrace Range, first stage, *c.* 1627–30.

This section deals with the canted wing at the north end of the terrace range (nearest the Little Castle) and the following portions of the long wing that stretches south from it along the terrace: on the west (terrace) front, the eleven windows of the basement and the first four windows of the two upper floors (corresponding to the first seven of the smaller windows of the basement); on the east (courtyard) front, the first two bays after the canted wing, and the hall range that follows on to the south, exclusive of the three gables that now surmount it.

The Renishaw drawings and Diepenbeke's engravings show a number of variations from the buildings as they are today. On the west front, running south from the canted wing, are four straight-sided gables in place of the present battlemented parapet; there are two similar gables in place of the present Dutch gables on the east front. These gables are shown differing from those of the canted wing in that they are straight sided and have chimney-stacks at their apices, but resembling them in having oval windows, and lantern finials at their bases. Beneath the gables on the terrace front there are no 'cannon' buttresses, such as today match up with those further to the south.

There are a few dates carved or painted on various parts of the fabric. No bills, accounts or building correspondence survive between the building accounts of 1612–14 and a few documents of the 1660s. There are a number of relevant

Smythson drawings, but none of them is dated. The series of seven drawings of the castle now at Renishaw are an important early record, but none is dated. They were almost certainly used as the basis for Diepenbeke's illustrations showing Bolsover in Newcastle's *La Methods Nouvelle*, published at Antwerp in 1658.

In the relevant Renishaw drawing the beginning of the hall range appears quite clearly, but is shown without the gables that surmount it today and provide an extra floor. Instead, it is crowned by a horizontal battlemented parapet, similar to that surmounting the gallery on the terrace front. Diepenbeke (in the illustration depicting '*Demy air par le droite*') mistook the rather crude perspective of the drawing and shifted the hall wall round ninety degrees, so that the hall disappears and its façade appears to be the end wall of the block to the north of it.

All this section seems to be of one build and has windows of similar detailing. Its masonry all has the same peculiarity of randomly-spaced blocks projecting slightly beyond the main masonry face to form studs. Some of the studs on the northern face of the canted wing are carved with the dates 1629 and 1630. There are similar studs on the so-called well-house (in fact a cistern-house) attached to the south-east section of the Fountain-Garden wall. This received water from springs to the north-east and south of the castle. Sir William Cavendish established a right of way for the pipe-line from the south in 1622, but according to an engraving in Pegge's *Bolsover* (1785) one of the four little conduit houses built along its line was dated 1627. The well-house probably dates from that year or shortly after.

John Smythson's ground-floor plan (III/1(4)) shows the main terrace range from (and including) the hall southwards, but omits the canted wing and the buildings between it and the hall. The dividing wall between the rooms shown by Smythson and the rest was clearly never meant to be external, for it is not thick enough. The portion not shown by Smythson would have had little point on its own and there are no straight joints at the junction. It seems likely that the whole range was envisaged from the start, even if the canted wing and the portion to the south of it were built first as the first section of a continuous building programme. All this suggests dates of *c*. 1629-30 for the canted wing and its attachment and *c*. 1631-3 for the hall, and for the basement beneath the hall and the north end of the gallery.

On stylistic grounds, quite apart from the inscribed dates 1629 and 1630, it is unlikely that the work dates from before 1620. The mouldings and rustication on the pediments of the gables are of a type that first appears in John Smythson's work at Bolsover on the balcony doorway in the Little Castle, which derives from the 1618/19 visit to London. Lantern-like finials, such as decorate the base of the gables, still survive on the Welbeck riding school of 1622-3, and are shown by Diepenbeke on the Welbeck stables of 1625.

b. *c*. 1630-3. The Venus Fountain, the building or remodelling of the Fountain Garden wall, the Stone Walk on the top of the wall and the original bridge from the Stone Walk to the canted block of the terrace range.

The Venus Fountain is carved with an earl's coronet, and cannot be earlier March 1628. The door leading out from the canted wing onto the bridge is dated 1633. There are Smythson drawings, attributable to John, for the fountain and the door from the Little Castle onto the Stone Walk.

It seems reasonable to suppose that 1633 is the date of the completion of the wall and Stone Walk, and that the Venus Fountain dates from the same few years. The Renishaw drawings show that the Walk originally had a battlemented parapet (since removed) similar to the parapets on the gallery and (originally) hall, but not to that on the Little Castle.

c. *c.*1633–5. The Terrace-Range gallery, and possibly the rest of the range south of the hall and parallel to the gallery.

The gallery as built is in the same position and of the same dimensions as the gallery shown in John Smythson's drawing. But whereas the gallery in the drawing is on the same level as the hall, as built it was several feet higher. This change meant that the kitchen and adjacent rooms in the basement beneath the north end of the gallery had to be raised. That the decision to raise them was taken after the lower walls had been built is suggested by the fact that their windows break through the string-course which continues the string-course above the basement windows to the north. Neither this upper portion of basement wall nor the gallery façade have the distinctive raised studs of the northern end of the terrace range. The detail of the gallery façade is quite different from that of the rest of the range, but relates closely to that of the door leading out from the Little Castle onto the Stone Walk.

The changes suggest that the gallery was built after the northern end of the range. It is tempting to attribute the greater elaboration and fancifulness of the gallery façade to the desire to provide something worthy of the royal visit in 1634. This would date the change to 1633, but, as argued on p. 265–6, the gallery is unlikely to have been completed in time to be used by the king. It is possible that the suite of rooms south of the hall were built at the same time as the gallery, but if so they were replaced in the 1660s, possibly after having been demolished or part-demolished in the 1650s. The chapel at the southern end of the range, shown in Smythson's plan, was probably never built.

d. Terrace Range. Minor alterations, *c.* 1635–42.

It was probably within these years that the parapet over the hall was replaced by an extra storey and by the existing three gables, the terrace formed and the north end of the façade to the terrace altered to bring it in line with the gallery. The architect for the work was presumably Huntingdon Smithson.

3. *c.* 1635–42. THE RIDING SCHOOL RANGE

No drawings or documentation for this survive. Stylistically, it could date from before, or just after the Civil War. The arguments for and against dating it to before the war are as follows.

Arguments against.

i. According to Vertue, it was built after the war, to the designs of Samuel Marsh. Vertue visited Bolsover in the early eighteenth century, and his information came from Lord Harley, who was married to William Cavendish's great-grand-daughter. But since he also attributes the gallery to the post-war period his dating must be suspect.

ii. The range is not shown in Diepenbeke's illustrations of Bolsover, published in 1658. But as suggested on p. 280 this could be because the Renishaw drawings, on which Diepenbeke's illustrations are clearly based, were made in the early 1630s. The fact that the drawings show no proper garden laid out round the Venus Fountain, and no terrace before the terrace range suggest that they may have been made before this phase of building at Bolsover was fully completed, that is in about 1633–4, supposing the suggested date for the gallery is correct. It is worth remarking that in 1634 Newcastle presented Charles I with an unspecified landscape by Alexander Kierincx (Trease, *Portrait of a Cavalier* p. 64). Kierincx was later to paint a series of views of Scottish towns, castles and palaces for Charles I, and it is just possible that the Bolsover series is by him.

Arguments for.

i. A range in the same position as the riding-school range is clearly shown in William Senior's survey, 'surveid in the yeares 1630, 1636 and 1637' according to the inscription on it. This is not conclusive, however, for the riding-school range could have replaced or perhaps partially incorporated an earlier range, demolished or made ruinous in the 1650s.

ii. In 1665 the gallery, which had lost the lead off its roof in the 1650s, was about to be re-roofed (Pwl 624). It is unlikely that Newcastle would have built a new riding-school before he repaired the gallery. The two projects could have been going on together, but if so the riding-school range would have been built at the same time as the new rooms on the courtyard side of the terrace range, designed by Samuel Marsh and stylistically much more up to date. This is improbable, and for the same reason it is even more unlikely that the riding-school range was built after 1665.

The evidence suggests, though it certainly does not prove, that the riding-school range was built before the Civil War but after 1634, to the designs of Huntingdon Smithson.

The Bolsover building chronology, as suggested so far, fits in comfortably with the building chronology of Welbeck, with an active period at Bolsover from 1612 to 1621, followed by a Welbeck period of approximately 1622–5, and then by another Bolsover period of approximately 1627–42. Moreover, the Robert Smythson wing at Welbeck was almost certainly built before 1612, and Vertue says that the garden arcades there were dated 1606. The impression given is that, as one might expect, extensive building works were never undertaken at Welbeck and Bolsover at the same time.

4. THE POST-RESTORATION PERIOD

According to the Duchess of Newcastle's biography of her husband (1667) Bolsover was 'half pull'd down' in the 1650s. This is clearly an exaggeration, but the roof was certainly taken off the gallery and possibly off other parts of the terrace range, and the rooms to the south of its hall may have been demolished.

Three documents in the Portland Papers at the University of Nottingham (Pwl 592-3, 624) and a letter from Newcastle to Andrew Clayton, now at Welbeck Woodhouse, give a little information about work done in the 1660s. £1460.9.6 was paid to Andrew Clayton, Newcastle's steward, for 'Bolsover Building' between 24 May 1663 and 13 May 1665. Work was still going on in 1666, when Joseph Jackson, a mason, was providing doors, chimney-pieces, and other details. Samuel Marsh was certainly providing designs for Newcastle by April 1665, and probably earlier. Notes by Clayton on the work done by Jackson in 1666 mention a 'special good carage wch the great columes was brought upon before Jackson came'. The great columns must be the two columns in the great doorcase from the courtyard into the terrace range, as they are the only monoliths at Bolsover. They must therefore date from before 1666. The new rooms to which this door gives entrance can confidently be dated 1663-6 and assigned to Samuel Marsh. Stylistically they relate closely to Nottingham Castle, which Marsh designed for the Duke of Newcastle in 1674.

Jackson and Clayton refer to the 'new building', the 'old new building' and the 'new old building'. 'The old new building' is definitely the northern end of the terrace range, and was probably so called because it was the old portion of the 'new building', that is of the terrace range where Marsh was building his new rooms. The 'new old Building' was probably the riding-school range, so called in contrast to the old building, that is the Little Castle.

In 1649 the parliamentary Council of State gave orders designed to make Bolsover indefensible. It is likely that the gates and gate-piers into the Great Court, the Fountain Garden, and the forecourt of the Little Castle were destroyed as a result of this order, and that the present gates and piers are all post-Restoration. The gate into the Little Castle forecourt is not that shown by Diepenbeke. The archway from the Stone Walk to the Terrace Range was certainly destroyed at this period, for Clayton records its rebuilding.

The opening which provides a viewing gallery into the riding school cuts crudely into the plasterwork frieze of the room behind it, and is probably post-Restoration. The Welbeck riding school originally had no viewing gallery, but one is shown in Grimm's drawing, made in the 1780s, and was probably the 'Ridinge House Chamber' for which Newcastle was giving instructions to Clayton in 1665. By then he seldom rode himself and preferred to 'take delight in seeing his Horses of Mannage rid by his Escuyers', as his wife relates in her biography.

302

APPENDIX III

The Smythson Family Tree and the Later Smithsons

THE TREE is based on those given by Knoop and Jones in their Bolsover Castle Building Accounts, derived from the Bolsover parish registers, and by Hunter in his *Familiae Minorum Gentium* (Harleian Society, vol. 39, p. 912), supplemented by information from wills, Wollaton Parish Register, and my own researches. Elizabeth Smythson's husband, John Roberts, was almost certainly related to the Thomas Roberts who worked at Wollaton and Hardwick, and whose will is in the Borthwick Institute (Prob. Reg. 33 f. 523). The later members of the family seem to have been invariably spelt Smithson.

JOHN SMITHSON II

Probably the John Smithson of Derbyshire who was admitted to Corpus Christi, Cambridge, in 1636 and ordained a deacon (Lincoln) in 1644. A John Smithson was vicar of Berwick-on-Tweed and hanged for the murder of his wife in 1672 (Venn, *Alumni Cantabrigenses*).

JOHN SMITHSON III

He practised as an architect like his father, grandfather and great-grandfather, and there are a few drawings in the Smythson collection which can be ascribed to him. Among these are designs for Bulwell in Nottinghamshire, probably made for the Byron family. This connection may be the reason why the Smythson drawings came into the possession of the Byrons. A Huntingdon Smythson admitted as a sizar at Trinity College, Cambridge, in 1670, may have been an otherwise unrecorded brother of William, John III and Charles.

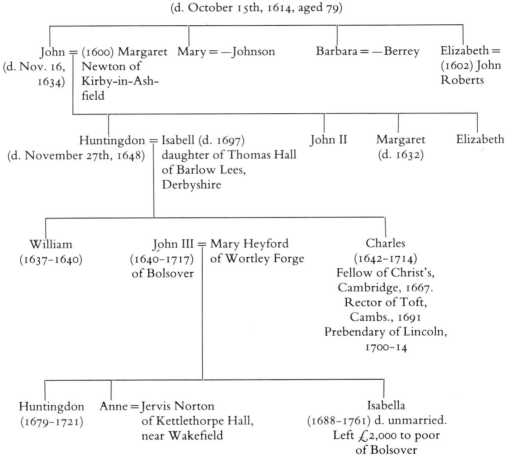

Robert Smythson
(d. October 15th, 1614, aged 79)

John = (1600) Margaret   Mary = —Johnson   Barbara = —Berrey   Elizabeth =
(d. Nov. 16,   Newton of   (1602) John
    1634)   Kirby-in-Ash-   Roberts
             field

Huntingdon = Isabell (d. 1697)   John II   Margaret   Elizabeth
(d. November 27th, 1648)   daughter of Thomas Hall   (d. 1632)
                     of Barlow Lees,
                     Derbyshire

William   John III = Mary Heyford   Charles
(1637–1640)   (1640–1717)   of Wortley Forge   (1642–1714)
                of Bolsover   Fellow of Christ's,
                                           Cambridge, 1667.
                                           Rector of Toft,
                                           Cambs., 1691
                                        Prebendary of Lincoln,
                                          1700–14

Huntingdon   Anne = Jervis Norton   Isabella
(1679–1721)   of Kettlethorpe Hall,   (1688–1761) d. unmarried.
                     near Wakefield   Left £2,000 to poor
                                           of Bolsover

NOTES TO THE TEXT

ABBREVIATIONS

B.M	British Museum	P.C.C.	Probate Court, Canterbury
D.N.B.	Dictionary of National Biography	P.R.O.	Public Record Office
D.O.E.	Department of the Environment	R.C.H.M.	Royal Commission on Ancient and
H.M.C.	Historical Manuscripts Commission		Historical Monuments
N.M.R.	National Monuments Record	V.C.H.	Victoria County History

INTRODUCTION

1. Sixteenth-century views of houses, other than surveys and design drawings, are almost exclusively of royal houses (as, indeed, are the views in *Plus Excellents Bâtiments*). See John Harris *The Artist and the Country House* (London, 1979) pp. 8-15 and *King's Works* IV, p. 9. The view of houses in surveys of property can vary from conventional symbols to reasonably accurate bird's eye views, e.g. Ralph Agas's survey of Toddington, Bedfordshire, made in 1581 (B.M. Add. MS 38065H) reproduced in *Country Life* CXXIX (23 March 1961) p. 638.

2. For Burghley see Calendar of State Papers (Domestic) LXXVII, 6 (1571). For Sidney see *Works* (Cambridge English Classics, ed. Feuillerat 1912-26) III, pp. 124-7. In commenting on the lines of Homer which he translates 'Qui multorum hominum mores cognovit et urbes', he says: 'When he saith cognovit urbes (if I be not deceaved) he meanes not to have seen townes, and marked their buildinges, for houses are houses in everie place, they doe but differ secundum magis et minus, but he intends the knowing of their religions, pollicies, lawes, bringing up of their children, discipline both for Warr and Peace, and such like.'

3. Further editions of Shute came out in 1579 and 1584. A facsimile edition, with a useful introduction by Laurence Weaver, was published in 1912. John Dee, in his preface to Henry Billingsley's translation of Euclid, *The Elements of Geometrie* (1570) includes a section on architecture, in which he refers to Vitruvius and Alberti, and quotes and translates the passages from their works relating to the qualifications of an architect. The relevant part of the preface is reprinted in Frances A. Yates, *Theatre of the World*, pp. 190-7.

4. Speech of Sir Nicholas Bacon at the opening of Parliament, 1571. B. M. Cottonian MSS, Titus, F. I, fols. 123-6.

5. A major exception is Sir Thomas Tresham, a Catholic in constant trouble because of his religion, who was also one of the most prolific, well-informed and original of Elizabethan builders.

6. William Harrison, *Description of England in Shakespeare's Youth*, ed. F. J. Furnivall (1877-1880) I, p. 238 (Book II, Ch. 12). This edition comprises the second and third books of Harrison's *Description of England*, which was originally printed at the beginning of volume I of Holinshed's *Chronicles* (1577) and reprinted in expanded form for the second edition of the *Chronicles* in 1586-7.

7. First Day's Exercise, B III. A little later it is revealed that Philoxenus, though an Italian, had had the good fortune to spend his youth in France and be converted to Protestantism.

8. Sir George Buck or Buc, *The Third Universitie of England*, Ch. 45, p. 986. Printed as an appendix to the 1615 edition of John Stow, *The Annales of England*.

9. Sir Thomas Elyot, *The Boke named the gouernour* (Everyman ed.) Bk. I, Ch. VIII, pp. 28-32.

10. Ben Jonson, *Works* (ed. Herford and Simpson), viii, p. 568, adapting a passage from Vives, the Spanish early sixteenth-century theorist. Quoted by D. J. Gordon, 'Poet and Architect: The Intellectual Setting of the Quarrel between Ben Jonson and Inigo Jones', *Courtauld and Warburg Journal* XII (1949), pp. 152-78, to which article I am indebted in this section and elsewhere.

11. See L. F. Salzman, *Building in England down to 1540* (Oxford, 1952), Ch. I, and M. Girouard 'Three Gothic Drawings in the Smithson Collection', *R.I.B.A. Journal*, November 1956, pp. 35-6.

12. Shute, *op. cit.*, f. B II-III. For Dee, see note 3. Frances Yates probably overestimates the influence of Dee's preface on London artificers.

13. For the Royal Works see *The History of the King's Works* (ed. H. M. Colvin) III: 1485-1660 Pt. I (1975) and IV: 1485-1660 Pt. II (1982).

14. For Somerset's building staff see the account of his cofferer, John Pickarell, 1548-51, B.M. Egmont MSS 2815.

15. See Mrs Baldwyn-Childe, 'The Building of Kyre Park, Worcestershire', *The Antiquary* XXI (1890).

16. For a full-length study of Elizabethan and Jacobean building methods and organisation, see Malcolm Airs, *The Making of the English Country House 1500-1640* (London, 1975).

17. Raphael Holinshed, *Chronicles of England Scotland and Ireland* (1807-8 ed.) IV, p. 434.

18. For Graves, Blagrave and Adams see *King's Works* III, pp. 90-5.

19. See the entry on Digges in the *Dictionary of National Biography*. It is possible that Fuller was confusing him with his son Thomas, also a mathematician, who was Surveyor in charge of remodelling Dover Harbour, 1582-4 (*King's Works* IV, pp. 757-61).

20. Harrison, *op. cit.* (see note 6) I, p. 267 (Bk. II, Ch. 15). For Henry VIII as a 'deviser' of buildings, see *King's Works*, IV, pp. 5, 375-7.

21. See p. 68.

22. John Strode's account book and notes, quoted John Hutchin, *History of Dorset* (3rd ed. 1861-73), IV, pp. 5-7. And see Arthur Oswald, 'Chantmarle', *Country Life* CVII (1950), pp. 1966-71.

23. *Richard Carew of Antony; the Survey of Cornwall etc.*, (ed. F. E. Halliday, 1953) p. 175.

24. See pp.183-4.

25. John Aubrey, *Brief Lives* and other selected writings (ed. Anthony Powell, 1949), p. 194.

26. Quoted *Dictionary of Architecture*, Architectural Publication Society (1852-92) III, p. 31, under 'Elizabethan Architecture'.

27. Salzman, *op. cit.* (see note 11), p. 5.

28. H.M.C., vol. 55 (Various Collections III), p. xxxiv.

29. John Summerson, 'The Building of Theobalds 1564-85', *Archaeologia*, XCVII (1959), pp. 107-26.

30. John Summerson, 'Three Elizabethan Architects', *Bulletin of the John Rylands Library* 40, No. I (September 1957), 218-19.

31. Parish register of Madeley, Salop, quoted H. A. Tipping, 'Condover Hall', *Country Life* XLIII (1918), p. 513.

32. For William Arnold see Arthur Oswald, *Country Houses of Dorset* (2nd revised and enlarged ed., 1959), pp. 25-30.

33. M. Girouard, 'The Development of Longleat House between 1546 and 1572', *Archaeological Journal* XVI (1959) pp. 206-8.

34. H. M. Colvin, *Biographical Dictionary of British Architects 1600-1840* (London, 1978), under Dinninghof.

35. For non-architectural activities of the Smythsons, see pp. 166-8, 279.

36. For Thorpe see John Summerson (ed.), *The Book of Architecture of John Thorpe*, produced as volume XL of the Walpole Society (1966).

37. For a slightly fuller account of the history of the Smythson Drawings see M. Girouard *The Smythson Collection of the Royal Institute of British Architects*, issued as volume 5 of *Architectural History* (1962), pp. 23-4.

38. The contents of the two volumes, and other contemporary architectural drawings of the period at Hatfield are catalogued in R. A. Skelton and John Summerson, *A Description of Maps and Architectural Drawings in the Collection made by William Cecil First Baron Burghley now at Hatfield House*, Roxburghe Club (1971). The catalogue only reproduces some of the architectural drawings, but there are facsimiles of all the contents of both volumes in the British Library Facs *372.

39. College of Arms, Talbot MSS, vol. P, f. 837 (5 August 1577). The lodge in question was probably at Handsworth, just outside Sheffield.

40. Girouard, 'Development of Longleat', pp. 216-17.

41. See the article on Cobham Hall, *Country Life* XV (1904), pp. 906-13.

42. See note 15. In 1613 Pitts also paid Robert Stickells, Clerk of the Queen's Works at Richmond, for a platt, probably for his London house.

43. See Laurence Stone, 'The Building of Hatfield House', *Archaeological Journal* CXII (1955), pp. 100-28.

44. Anthony Wells-Cole has established William Arnold's lavish use of ornament derived from de Vries at Montacute and elsewhere.

45. Source and copy are reproduced side by side in Summerson, 'John Thorpe and the Thorpes of Kingscliffe', *Architectural Review* CVI (1949), pp. 291-300.

46. Thorpe's plans T 34, 141 and 152 are based on tracings of the plans on pp. 52, 59 and 68 of Bk. II of the 1601 edition of Palladio. T 85 is derived from Palladio's Villa Valmarana (1601 ed., II, p. 59); the two are reproduced side by side in M. Girouard, *Life in the English Country House* (New Haven and London, 1978), p. 120.

47. See the appendix 'Books on art, perspective and architecture in English Renaissance libraries, 1580-1630' in Lucy Gent, *Picture and Poetry 1560-1620* (Leamington Spa, 1981). In the Smythson orbit, a Palladio first edition, belonging to Lord Shrewbury's daughter, Grace Cavendish, was recently sold in the London sale-rooms.

48. See p. 278.

49. Shute, *op. cit.* (ed. Weaver, 1912), pp. 7-9.

50. For Smith see article on Theydon Mount, V. C. H. Essex, IV, pp. 275-83.

51. See D. J. Gordon, *op. cit.* (note 10).

52. 'Description of a Masque' presented at the marriage of the Earl of Somerset and Frances Howard, *Works* (Oxford ed., 1909), p. 150, and n.p. 365. For Constantino see also Holles's letter book, B.M. Add. MSS 32, 464 f. 131.

53. See S. D. Kitson, 'Bernard Dinninghof', *Journal of British Society of Master Glass Painters* III (1929), pp. 55-8.

54. See D.N.B. and Whinney and Millar, *English Art 1625-1714* (1957), pp. 52-3 and Colvin, *Dictionary*.

55. Colvin, *Dictionary*.

56. See Christopher Hussey in his article on Raynham Hall, *Country Life* LVIII (1925), p. 748, and Norfolk and Norwich Architectural Society, *Norfolk Archaeology* XXIII, p. 99.

57. Oswald, *Country Houses of Dorset*, p. 28.

58. Airs, *English Country House*, p. 22.

59. T. W. Hanson, 'Halifax Builders in Oxford', *Trans. Halifax Antiquarian Soc.* (1928), pp. 235-317.

60. See Whinney and Millar, *op. cit.*, p. 34.

61. Summerson, *Architecture in Britain 1530-1830* (4th Ed. 1963), p. 20.

62. *A Letter whearin part of the Entertainment, untoo the Queenz Majesty, at Killingwoorth Castl ... 1575, is signified*, p. 65. Reprinted in J. Nichols, *Progresses of Queen Elizabeth* (1788), I. Laneham's letter also contains an interesting description of the garden at Kenilworth, with its fountain and birdcage.

63. First dayes exercise, A.I.

64. Emily Sophia Hartshorne, *Memorials of Holdenby* (1868), pp. 15-16.

65. Edmund Lodge, *Illustrations of British History* (1st ed. 1791), III, p. 336; College of Arms, Talbot MSS, Vol. L f. 122.

66. *Works* (ed. Feuillerat), I, p. 91.

67. Harrison, *Description of Britaine* (see note 6), Bk. I, Ch. 18, p. 109 of 1586 edition 'of the aire, soile, and commodities of this island'. This passage is not given in Furnivall's edition. He is in fact talking of foreigners, and regretting that the English climate prevented houses being so situated. But he clearly thinks the point of view a natural one; and

by the 1580s some Elizabethans were prepared to ignore the weather.

68. Harrison, *op. cit.*, I, p. 268 (from Book II, Ch. XV, 'Palaces belonging to the Prince').

69. For a convenient account of this characteristic as it appeared in literature see C. S. Lewis, *English Literature in the Sixteenth Century* (Oxford History of English Literature, 1954), especially pp. 270-1, 418-21. For the specific field of emblems and devices see Mario Praz, *Studies in Seventeenth-Century Imagery* (1939), I.

70. Printed among the conjectural poems in *Poems of Sir Walter Ralegh* (The Muses' Library, ed. Latham, 1951), p. 80.

71. From the *Arcadia*.

72. See note 22. I have never come across any contemporary evidence for the popular theory that E-plan houses were built in compliment to Queen Elizabeth.

73. It appears in Robert Smythson's plan of Wimbledon, Smythson drawings I/24.

74. The plan of Wothorpe was drawn by John Thorpe, T 56. See also J. A. Gotch, *The Old Halls and Manor-Houses of Northamptonshire* (1936), p. 8.

75. The plan is reproduced by W. H. Godfrey, *The English Almshouse* (1955), p. 48.

76. For Chilham see Christopher Hussey, *Country Life* LV, (1924), pp. 812-19. For Warmwell see Arthur Oswald, *Country Houses of Dorset* (revised and enlarged ed., 1959), p. 93-4, and Royal Commission on Historical Monuments, *Dorset*, II, pp. 327-9. The two Newhouses are illustrated in Airs, *English Country House*, pp. 10-11.

77. Quoted Mario Praz, *op. cit.*, p. 15.

78. George Puttenham, *The Art of English Poesie* (1589), p. 75.

79. Quoted Mario Praz, *op. cit.*, p. 52.

80. Quoted Mario Praz, *op. cit.*, pp. 54-5.

81. They are treated of in some detail in Chapter VI.

82. Calendar State Papers Dom. 1617, 70.

83. For Somerset's never completed house at Bedwyn Broil in Wiltshire, see J. E. Jackson, 'Wulfhall and the Seymours', *Wiltshire Archaelogical and Natural History Magazine* XV, p. 140. The article was reprinted as a separate book in 1875.

84. For Gresham and Clough see J. W. Burgon *Life of Sir Thomas Gresham* (1839), with an illustration of Bachcraig. See also M. Girouard, 'Bachcraig', *The Country Seat* (ed. Colvin and Harris, London, 1970), pp. 30-2, and Peter Howell, 'Houses in the Vale of Clwyd', *Country Life* CLXII (December 1977), pp. 1906-9.

85. William Camden, *Britannia* (first English trans., 1610): 'Where within our remembrance, Robert Corbet, carried away with the affectionate delight of Architecture, began to build in a barraine place a most gorgeous and stately house, after the Italians modell . . .'

86. Perhaps the London theatres should be placed in this classical group, for they were almost certainly influenced by Roman theatres, as described in Vitruvius and Serlio. The prototype was probably James Burbage's theatre in Shoreditch, built in 1576. See Yates, *Theatre of the World* (n. 3).

87. For a rather fuller treatment of the Gothic elements in Elizabethan architecture see M. Girouard, 'Elizabethan Architecture and the Gothic Tradition', *Architectural History*

6 (1963), pp. 23-40.

88. Roger Ascham, *The Schoolmaster* (written *c.* 1563-8), ed. Methuen's English Classics (1934), p. 29.

89. Idem, p. 74.

90. 'The Defence of Poesie', *Works* (ed. Feuillerat), III, p. 24.

91. Cumberland by Hilliard, Herbert and Mildmay by Oliver, Arundel in an anonymous picture at Hardwick dated 1584.

92. See Lytton Strachey, *Elizabeth and Essex* (Collected Works, London, 1957), pp. 34, 39.

93. See M. Girouard, *op. cit.* (see note 87).

94. *Works* (ed. Feuillerat), I, p. 15.

95 Given by John Aubrey, *Antiquities of Surrey* (1718), p. 15.

96. *Architecture in Britain* (4th ed.), p. 40.

NOTES TO CHAPTER I

The Longleat MSS drawn on for Chapter I are listed below, with the abbreviations by which they are referred to. For a fuller breakdown, see the first edition of *Robert Smythson*, pp. 73-4, and M. Girouard, 'The Development of Longleat House' (see n. 9), pp. 221-2.

> R.O.B. *The Records of the Building of Longleat.* Three gilt and leather-bound volumes into which, in the nineteenth century, Canon Jackson collected original bills, letters, etc., and excerpts copied from original documents.
> L.P. *Longleat Papers.* Mostly separate books of accounts, strapped several at a time into cardboard folders. Some are building accounts (including those covering 1568 to 1575, inclusive) or have sections covering building.
> T.P. *Thynne Papers.* Thynne correspondence and miscellaneous papers.
> *The Big Account Book.* Building Accounts from the fire (April 1567) to November 1568. A fair copy of the first half of L.P. Box LXVIII, Book 59, magnificently bound.
> *Seymour Papers.* A separate collection of MSS to do with the Seymour family, but containing some letters to John Thynne.

1. R.O.B. III, 61.

2. The Knollys family also owned Greys Court, near Henley, but their surviving work there (agreeable but unassuming) probably dates from the late sixteenth or early seventeenth century. See *Country Life* XCV (23 and 30 June 1940), pp. 1080-3, 1124-7.

3. In *A Relation of the Late Royall Entertainment given by the Right Honorable the Lord Knowles, at Cawsome House, neere Reading.* The Entertainment was by Thomas Campion. See Campion, *Works* (ed. P. Vivian, 1909), p. 78.

4. See the entry in his *Diary* for 8 June 1654.

5. Smythson or Smithson is not a common surname, but is found scattered all over England. The language of Robert Smythson's letter to Thynne (Appendix 1) suggests a North East, or North East Midlands origin, but far from conclusively so. (I am grateful to Dr Martin Wakelin for his opinion.) Research among wills has so far failed to find his origins, and no earlier Smythsons working as masons or artificers of other kinds have come to light.

6. Smythson drawings IV/1-3. See M. Girouard, 'Three Gothic drawings in the Smythson collection', *R.I.B.A.*

Journal, November 1956, pp. 35–6.

7. For John Thynne and his relatives William and Francis see the articles in the D.N.B., and for his relations with and work for Somerset, J.E. Jackson, *Wulfhall and the Seymours* (reprinted 1875 from volume XV of *Wilts Archaeological and Natural History Magazine*). No full-length study of Thynne has ever been published, though ample material is available in the Longleat MSS.

8. From a satire against Thynne written by his neighbour, William Darrell of Littlecote, in 1575, R.O.B. III, 213.

9. This section is a much compressed version of the detailed account in M. Girouard, 'The Development of Longleat House between 1546 and 1572', *Archaeological Journal*, CXVI (1961), pp. 200–22.

10. The payments for demolishing the old house are in *The Big Account Book* and L.P. LXVIII, Bk. 59.

11. Payment recorded both in *The Big Account Book* (back payment in June-July period 1568) and L.P. LXVIII, Bk. 59.

12. R.O.B. II, 121.

13. T.P. III, 206 v.

14. *Letters and Papers of Henry VIII* (ed. J. S. Brewer and J. Gardner) XIII, p. 2, No. 342.

15. Hill's very interesting will is in the Nottinghamshire Record Office (PRNW). It is part damaged and has no date; but the Worksop Parish Registers show that he was buried there on 3 October 1592. He owned property at Willington Street, Otham and Maidstone, and clearly came from that part of Kent. He had bedding, linen, brass, and pewter at Chilwell Hall, near Nottingham, where perhaps he rented lodgings. No wife or children are mentioned, and the bulk of his property was left to his nephews. 'Mr Robert Smythson' was appointed executor and left 20 shillings; John and Mary Smythson were left 10 shillings; 'Mr Smythson's daughters' were bequeathed 'all the brass and pewter that is mine at Chilwell Hall'. There is reference to a carpet 'that I had off William Styles', a craftsman who had worked at Wollaton, and to money owed to him by Richard Crispin, a carpenter who was at Longleat and Wollaton.

Hills may have been the route by which the drawing of Bishop Fox's Chantry Chapel in Winchester cathedral came into Smythson possession. Thomas Bertie, whom John Harvey considers the mason most probably responsible for the chantry, came from Bearsted, next door to Willington and Otham, that is to say from the same area of masons connected with the Kentish Rag quarries. (Harvey, *English Mediaeval Architects: a Biographical Dictionary down to 1550*, (London, 1954). No Smythson can be traced in this area, although there were Smythsons in the neighbourhood of Canterbury.

16. B.M. Egmont MSS 2815; R.O.B. I, 441, 465.

17. Hatfield Maps, I, Nos. 16 and 17 (B.M. Facs. *372 and *Vitruvius Britannicus* II, Plates 68, 69).

18. L.P. LXXXVII, Bk. 153, f. 11, and Bk. 154, *passim*.

19. Both payments in L.P. LXVIII, Bk. 60.

20. R.O.B. III, p. 189.

21. R.O.B. III, p. 197. The full text is given in Appendix I.

22. Compounded from the two lists given in R.O.B. III, p. 225 and T.P. XLIX (Box II), p. 315. But for 1575-80 I have had to rely on L.P. LXXXIX, Bks. 159, p. 161.

23. The cancelled will, L.P. III, 35. The second will P.R.O., P.C.C. Arundell, 44.

24. L.P. Bk. 179 B.

25. T.P. IV, p. 97; L.P. LXXXIX, Bks. 160 (I), p. 161.

26. The plan of Wickham Court was drawn by Thorpe (T175). See also *Country Life* XI (24 May 1902), pp. 656-62.

27. For Mount Edgcumbe and Michelgrove see pp. 97-100.

28. For Herstmonceux see *Country Life* LXXVIII (7 December 1935), especially p. 608.

29. For Richmond see *King's Works* IV, pp. 222-34.

30. See Thorpe's plan and annotations (T88) and the plan in *King's Works* V, p. 266, based on an eighteenth-century survey.

31. The planning and arrangement of Elizabethan and Jacobean country houses is treated at some length in M. Girouard, *Life in the English Country House* (1978), Ch. 4.

32. Inventory for 1574, T.P. L (Box III), f. 204; 1594, T.P. LIII (Box VII), f. 94; 1639, T.P. LXXIX (Box XXXII), f. 40.

33. For Wolfeton see Arthur Oswald, *Country Houses of Dorset* (1959), pp. 60-5, and 'Wolfeton House', *Country Life* CXIV (1953), pp. 414-18, 484-7; R.C.H.M., *Dorset* III, pp. 63-9. There is later work almost certainly by William Arnold.

34. See M. Girouard, 'New Light on Longleat: Alan Maynard, A French sculptor in England in the sixteenth-century', *Country Life* CXX (1956), pp. 594-7.

35. The possibility of Chalcot being connected with Longleat and the sixteenth century (rather than the late seventeenth as stated, for instance, in *Buildings of England: Wiltshire*) was first suggested to me by John Kenworthy-Browne. What survives is only a fragment; original stonework has either been re-used or its setting renewed; the door, alcove, panels, sash-windows and brickwork are eighteenth century. Chalcot was part of the Wiltshire estate of Sir Henry Vere and in the 1560s and 1570s was divided (it does not seem to be established how) between his three co-heiresses, one of whom married the first Lord Mordaunt of Turvey; in 1577 it was sold to George Tuchet, Lord Audley, and in 1585 to Henry and Nicholas Phipps. (Victoria County History, *Wiltshire* VIII (1965), pp. 97-8, 155.)

36. I am grateful to Anthony Wells-Cole for communicating the Veneziano and de Vries sources for this design to me. In my catalogue of the Smythson Drawings it was tentatively ascribed to John Smythson the younger (1640-1717), but its derivation makes a sixteenth-century date virtually certain. The draughtmanship is close to that of the copy of a de Vries term in the Smythson drawings (I/25(5)).

37. The possibility of a connection between Longleat and these two houses was not suggested in the first edition of *Robert Smythson*. The likely relationship of Longleat to Corsham was first suggested to me by Frederick J. Ladd, and is dealt with in some detail in his *Architects at Corsham Court* (Bradford-on-Avon, 1978), pp. 7-20; the du Cerceau design which may relate to the porch is illustrated by him in Plate 15.

38. For Smythe see A. L. Rowse, *The England of Elizabeth* (London, 1950), pp. 128, 331-2.

39. For Shaw House see *Country Life* XXVIII (3 September 1910, pp. 328-38, and Walter Money, *History of the Ancient Town and Borough of Newbury* (Oxford, 1887), pp. 204-6.

In the eighteenth-century Shaw belonged to the first Duke of Chandos, and there is a plan and elevation of this date in the Chandos papers in the Huntingdon Library, San Marino. I am most grateful to Mrs Weale and Miss Leamon, of Shaw House School, for help and information, and for pointing out to me the connection with John Dolman.

40. For Lovell's Berkshire property see his will, P.R.O., P.C.C. Brundenell 55, and the Calendar of the Patent Rolls (Edward VI), II, 423.

41. Part of Sherborne House in Gloucestershire seems to have been closely modelled on Longleat. The left-hand half of the U-shaped entrance front is decorated with three storeys of columns (Ionic, Corinthinan and Composite) and punctuated by projecting bays. The relationship with Longleat is obvious, but the scale is smaller, and the orders are of columns not pilasters. In the seventeenth century the other half of the entrance front was built on the same lines, but with different detail. The earlier portion must have been built by Thomas Dutton, who acquired Sherborne in 1551 and entertained Elizabeth there in 1574. He had dealings with Thynne, for he was bailiff of Thynne's manor of Buckland. Sherborne was extensively remodelled in 1829-34, but externally the remodelling followed the lines of the original. This is shown in an eighteenth-century watercolour belonging to Lord Sherborne. See M. Girouard, *Country Life* CXX (1956), p. 954, with illustrations.

42. Hertford to Thynne, T.P., I, p. 66. This letter is undated, but another (T.P., I, p. 43) in which Hertford asks Thynne 'to remember yr haste of my platt' is dated 3 September 1569.

43. Also in T.P., I, p. 66.

44. R.O.B., II, p. 117.

45. P.R.O., P.C.C. Arundell, 44.

46. Quotations from the *Oxford English Dictionary*.

47. Sir Christopher Hatton's Holdenby is a possible rival to Longleat's claim to be the first lantern house. It was approaching completion in 1579, but although the date when it was begun is not known it seems likely to post-date by a few years the commencement of the remodelling of Longleat in 1572. See M. Girouard, 'Elizabethan Holdenby', *Country Life* CLVIII (18 and 25 October 1975), pp. 1286-9, 1398-401.

48. R.O.B., III, p. 213.

NOTES TO CHAPTER 2

1. R.O.B., III, p. 219a.

2. For Wardour see the D.O.E., *Official Handbook* (first pub. 1968) by R. B. Pugh and A. D. Saunders. Mr J. R. Arundell owns a 1605 inventory, showing contents of great splendour (copy in V. and A. Furniture Dept.).

3. The building accounts existing cover these periods:
   Bk. 1. March to March, 1582-3.
   Bk. 2. November to November 1584-5.
   Bk. 3. March to March, 1586-7.
   Bk. 4. March to March, 1587-8.
   Bk. 5. March to November, 1588.
In addition the sheets headed 'The Account of Thomas Grassworth, servant to Sir Francis Willoughbie, knight, of money received and disbursed towards the charge of building', running from 1584-5, are mostly only a synopsis of the building accounts, but also contain some additional

payments; for instance, quarterly wages to Accres, the marble carver. These accounts, and all the Willoughby (Middleton) papers, are now deposited at Nottingham University Library. For a detailed study see P. E. Rossell, 'The Building of Wollaton Hall', Master's Degree Thesis, University of Sheffield, 1957.

4. For Francis Willoughby, see H.M.C. 69 (Report on Middleton MSS), especially pp. 504-610: 'An Account of the Willoughbys of Wollaton taken out of the Pedigree, old letters, and old Books of accounts, in my Brother Sir Thomas Willoughby's Study, Dec. A.D. 1702', by Cassandra Willoughby, later Duchess of Chandos, which contains extracts and information from many documents since lost. For modern studies see R. S. Smith, 'The Willoughbys of Wollaton 1500-1643 with special reference to mining in Nottinghamshire', Ph.D. Thesis, University of Nottingham, May 1964, and Alice T. Friedman, 'Wollaton Hall: Domestic Architecture and Daily Life in Elizabethan England', Doctoral Dissertation, Harvard University, 1980.

5. In the last years of his minority he was the ward of Sir Francis Knollys, another possible link with Smythson. See Friedman, *op. cit.*

6. For Willoughby's industrial activities, see J. V. Nef, *Rise of the British Coal Industry* (London 1954, II, pp. 12-13, and articles by R. S. Smith in *Trans. Thoroton Society of Nottinghamshire* LXV (1961), pp. 27-46, LXVI (1962) pp. 24-34; *Renaissance and Modern Studies* XI (1967), pp. 90-140.

7. Quoted by Cassandra Willoughby, *H.M.C. Middleton*, p. 582.

8. In Siberechts' view the three southern garden courts have been run together as one (this survives today, though with later balustrading) and the middle court to the east enlarged as a bowling-green. The middle court to the west has a building on the west side, possibly the 'bakehouse and brewhouse' shown by Smythson. None of the other out-buildings in the Smythson plan existed by 1697, if indeed they were ever built. John Harris has pointed out to me that the garden fountain painted by Siberechts, with jets playing from the circumference into the centre, is shown by Smythson. The pond is still there, complete with a lead pipe round the circumference pierced for jets, possibly a later replacement but following the original scheme. It would be interesting to know how the pressure for this elaborate fountain was achieved on Wollaton's hill-top site (payment of xixd. in September 1587 to Richard Smallwood 'for II dayes werke on making a cesprey for turning the water to the new house' may be relevant).

9. In the chapter on 'Digression of Air'. I owe this reference to Alice Friedman.

10. T 85. The Wollaton enclosed hall and prospect room have become a single-storey cross-hall with a very grand great chamber above.

11. For Wyatville's work at Wollaton see Derek Linstrum, *Sir Jeffrey Wyatville, Architect to the King* (Oxford, 1972), pp. 61-7.

12. For Accres at Chatsworth see Basil Stallybrass, 'Bess of Hardwick's Buildings and Building Accounts', *Archaeologia* LXIV (1913), p. 356.

13. The catalogue is in the Middleton papers (Mi., I, p. 17/1), and was probably made in the late 1680s. The library was then a large and very interesting one, which deserves research. It included some thirty sixteenth or early seven-

teenth century books on art, architecture, perspective and fortifications; as many of the entries are perfunctory, none is at all detailed and some pages seem to be missing, it is impossible to have an exact idea of all the contents. Numerous books listed in the catalogue can be identified in the catalogue of the sale of the Wollaton library, held at Christie's on 15 June 1925. Many of the books in the sale, including most of the architectural ones, were inscribed with the name or initials of Thomas Willoughby who succeeded to the Willoughby estates and baronetcy in 1688, and was created Baron Middleton in 1712; however, as the bulk of the books on art, architecture, etc. dated from the sixteenth or early seventeenth century and Thomas Willoughby is not known to have had any strong interest in architecture and was under twenty at the probable date of the compilation of the catalogue it seems likely that this part of the library was large collected by Sir Francis and Sir Percival. To what extent Robert Smythson was involved must remain a matter of surmise. The sale catalogue included Shute's *First and Chief Groundes* (1563 ed.) and a bound volume of engravings by or after Cock, Suavius, Floris and others, neither of which is identifiable in the seventeenth century catalogue. See Mary Welch, 'Francis Willoughby . . . a seventeenth-century naturalist', *Trans. of the Thoroton Society of Nottinghamshire* LXXXI (1977–9), p. 38.

14. I/25 (2), (4), (5), (6); III/27.

15. S. Serlio, Lib. I (1566 ed.) p. 15. See H. C. Desch, 'Timber Protection in Old Buildings', *Country Life* CXXIV (3 July 1958) pp. 10–11. The system was also employed in Robert Stickells' unexecuted design for a timber louvre at Lyveden New Bield (Summerson, 'Three Elizabethan Architects', *Bulletin of the John Rylands Library* 40 (1957), pp. 218–19).

16. This was, I think first pointed out by Nikolaus Pevsner, 'Double Profile' (a study of Wollaton), *Architectural Review*, March 1950.

17. The best account of Mount Edgcumbe is by J. M. Jope in *Studies in Building History* (ed. Jope, 1961), pp. 208–12.

18. This was pointed out to me by Mr John Harris. Early nineteenth-century elevations of Michelgrove still in the possession of the Shelley family show the date 1536 carved over the porch.

19. John Thorpe's perspective drawings (e.g. especially T.37–8 and T.50) almost certainly date from after 1590, and probably from after 1600. A remarkable bird's-eye view of Hull Manor House (L. R. Shelby, *John Rogers: Tudor Military Engineer* (1967), Plate 13) may date from the 1540s, but is a survey rather than a design and is drawn in very incorrect perspective; whereas Smythson and Thorpe carefully diminish their buildings towards a common vanishing point, and had probably studied contemporary books on perspective by du Cerceau or others.

20. Title given by Geymüller to a possibly unique copy in the Bibliotheque Nationale, Paris which has no title page. The comparison with the Wollaton plan (Middleton Mss Mi. DMF 11) had previously been published by D. N. Durant 'Wollaton Hall – a Rejected Plan' *Trans. Thoroton Society* LXXVI (1972) pp. 13–16.

21. H.M.C. *Middleton*, p. 429: 'for the platt maker's bord that came from London to measure groundes 12 May 1573, viii days.'

22. I am grateful to Alice Friedman for calling my attention to this provision of two great chambers.

23. The Waltham Forest design is reproduced in *King's Works* IV, p. 15. The plan of Nonsuch as recovered by excavation (idem, p. 197) suggests near-symmetrical King's and Queen's sides, with a common gallery.

24. See M. Girouard, *Life in the English Country House*, p. 114 and n. 81.

25. For the Ampthill plans see Thorpe, T. 267–8, 271–2, and Skelton and Summerson, *Hatfield Maps and Drawings* (see Introduction, n. 38). For Audley End and Hatfield see *Life in the English Country House* pp. 114–16; P. J. Drury, 'The evolution of Audley End 1605–1745', *Architectural History* 23 (1980), pp. 1–39.

26. For Melbury see A. Oswald, *op. cit.*, pp. 118–22 and R.C.H.M., *Dorset Vol. I West* (1952), pp. 164–7.

27. See Arthur Oswald, 'Tudor Outlook Towers', *Country Life Annual* (1957), pp. 84–7.

28. Marcus Binney 'Warwick Castle, III', *Country Life* CLXXII (16 December 1982) pp. 1952–5.

29. *King's Works*, IV, p. 208, fig. 21 and Plate 16.

30 At a Christmas feast in 1594. See John Stradling, *The Stori of the Lower Borowes of Merthyrmawr*, ed. Randall and Rees (S. Wales and Monmouth Record Society, 1932), p. 74

31. The Life of St Thomas of Canterbury from Jacob de Voraigne, *The Golden Legend* (1503). Sold with the bulk of the Wollaton library at Christie's, 15 June 1925.

NOTES TO CHAPTER 3

1. Hall's view is of the south front, and is engraved in Robert Thoroton, *Survey of Nottinghamshire* (1670). Buck drew the north and south fronts in the mid-eighteenth century by when the north front had been largely obscured by later additions. The originals are in the Gough Maps in the Bodleian library; the view of the south front was reproduced in volume III of Throsby's new edition of Thoroton (1790–7). Couse's engravings of the south front is very close to Buck's. All four are reproduced in M. Binney, 'Worksop Manor, I' *Country Life* CLIII (15 March 1973), pp. 678–82. By the time of Buck and Couse the fenestration of the south front had been altered and many of its irregularities removed. Hall's view is the earliest and most valuable, and corresponds closely to the Smythson survey; on the other hand his engraving of Wollaton, also in Thoroton, can be checked against the existing house and makes one hesitant about relying on him too closely.

2. Such knowledge as we have of the interior of Worksop comes from the Smythson survey plan (III/17) and a short *Description of Worksop Manor before the Fire* (Arundel Castle MSS, Sheffield City Library, W123) which gives the height of the hall. An inventory of 'goods at Worksop Lodge' taken on 20 July 1591 (Arundel Castle MSS, W122) lists a withdrawing-chamber and chapel, probably on the same floor as the great chamber, but on the whole is disappointingly vague in its nomenclature of rooms.

3. The main biographical source for the sixth Earl of Shrewsbury and the next generation of Talbots is the large collection of Talbot papers, divided into two since the seventeenth-century. See *A Calendar of the Shrewsbury Papers in the Lambeth Palace Library*, ed. E. G. W. Bill (London, 1966), and *A Calendar of the Talbot Papers in the College of*

Arms, ed. G. R. Batho (London, 1971). Both calendars are published jointly by the H.M.C. and Derbyshire Archaeological Society, and are referred to in the footnotes as *Shrewsbury Papers* and *Talbot Papers* respectively. Two further collections are now in Sheffield City Libraries. See Sheffield City Libraries, *Catalogue of the Arundel Castle Manuscripts ... with an Appendix of a Calendar of Talbot Letters (part of the Bacon Frank collection*, (Sheffield, 1965).

4. David Durant's *Bess of Hardwick; Portrait of an Elizabethan Dynast* (London, 1977) contains a full account of her quarrel with her husband, her building works and the creation of her fortune, based on a detailed study of original documents.

5. Edmund Lodge, *Illustrations of British History*, (2nd ed., 1838), I, p. XXIX.

6. *Shrewsbury Papers*, 700 f. 101.

7. *Talbot Papers*, L f. 122, quoted Lodge, *op. cit.*, III, p. 336.

8. *Talbot Papers*, G f. 308.

9. *Shrewsbury Papers*, 698 f. 87.

10. *Talbot Papers*, G f. 283.

11. *Shrewsbury Papers*, 698 f. 55.

12. *Vertue Note Books* VI (Walpole Society, XXX), p. 70.

13. John Leland, *Itinerary* (Toulmin Smith, ed. 1907), IV, p. 17.

14. Durant, *op. cit.* p. 107.

15. Summerson, *Architecture in Britain* (4th ed., 1963), p. 33.

16. For Elizabethan Chatsworth see Stallybrass, *op. cit.* (Ch. 2, n. 12) and M. Girouard, 'Elizabethan Chatsworth', *Country Life* CLIV (22 November 1973), pp. 1668-72.

17. For Richmond see *King's Works*, IV, pp. 222-34. The Royal lodgings there formed a compact free-standing block three storeys high and about 110 by 140 feet square, built round a small central court. It should perhaps be seen as an enormously grand version of medieval lodging towers such as at Tattershall, Raglan, Warwick and Henry VII's own tower at Windsor. The ground floor was occupied by household officials, and *King's Works* suggest that the King's and Queen's lodgings each occupied one half of the first floor. However, surviving drawings by Wyngaerde and Hollar both seems to show first and second floors of equal height with windows of the same size, suggesting that the royal lodgings were one above the other. If so, the Chatsworth arrangement, of household on the ground floor, the Shrewsburys on the first floor, and grand visitors on the top floor, probably derived from it, with the modification that the second floor was higher and grander than the first to allow for a royal visit.

18. In a bound volume of surveys of the Earl of Newcastle's estates, made in the 1630s. Microfilms of these are in Nottinghamshire County Record Office and Sheffield University Library.

19. John Jones, *The benefit of the ancient Bathes of Buckstones* (1572), p. 2.

20. The notebook of William Dickenson, Shrewsbury's bailiff at Sheffield, records payments in November 1574 to 'Turner and Rodes' for mason's work 'measured at the Tyrrett there' (Sheffield Library, MD 192 f. 168). Rodes was probably one of a family which also worked at Wollaton and Hardwick.

21. A contract survives (quoted Stallybrass, *op. cit.*) for plasterwork at a building known as the 'turrets in the mount', to be finished by April 1581. An inventory of 1601 shows that this was a different building from the Stand, but the contract (which mentions four turrets) suggests that the two buildings were similar, and probably close in date. The Chatsworth building accounts for 1577-80 survive, and have no mention of the Stand.

22. For Thorpe Salvin and the Sandfords see Joseph Hunter, *Deanery of Doncaster* (1828), I, pp. 309-11, with print and description. Considerably more of the house remained then than does now.

23. Francis Rodes was leasing property in Worksop from the Earl of Shrewsbury as early as 1568. *Dukery Records*, p. 339.

24. For Francis Rodes see D.N.B. For the Rodes pedigree see Hunter, *op. cit.*, p. 130.

25. See n. 16. At ground floor level the Chatsworth galleries may have taken the form of open arcades, as was certainly the case with their seventeenth-century successors.

26. The relationship between the corridor systems of Hengrave and Barlborough was first pointed out to me by Mr Lawrence Stone.

27. John Gage, *History of Hengrave* (1822), p. 184.

28. For a more detailed description of Barlborough see my account in *Archaeological Journal* CXVIII (1961), pp. 223-7.

29. In the Joint Record Office in the Public Library, Lichfield.

30. Great Houghton Hall, near Barnsley, is said to have been built by Francis Rodes for his fourth son Godfrey. The illustration in Louis Ambler, *The Old Halls and Manor Houses of Yorkshire* (London, 1913, p. 61, Fig. 98) suggests the possibility of Smythson involvement, but the house has unfortunately been demolished.

31. For Heath see *Country Life* XXII (1907), pp. 90-6 – an early and not very comprehensive article. Careful records of the house were made at the time of demolition by the Ministry of Works.

32. For North Lees see Rosamund Meredith, *Farms and Families of Hathersage Outseats* (1981), Part One, pp. 8-21. This (obtainable through Sheffield City Libraries) replaces and amends an earlier article by her published in *Derbyshire Life and Countryside* in 1965.

33. Quoted by Robert White, *The Dukery Records* (1904), p. 133. The original is now deposited in Sheffield City Libraries, Arundel Castle MSS, W 27.

34. *Shrewsbury Papers*, 707 f. 189.

35. Sheffield City Libraries, *Talbot Letters*, 2/128.

36. 'Eton, Roger Portington's man' was involved in the pulling down by Shrewsbury's servants of the Stanhope family's weir on the Trent in 1595. See H.M.C., *Salisbury*, V, p. 254. On 15 October 1597, Roger Portington signed a quit-claim to all right and title to Worksop Park (Arundel Castle MSS, WD 753). He married Mary, daughter of Hercy Sandford of Thorpe Salvin, and was knighted in 1603 (Joseph Hunter *South Yorkshire* (1828-31 and facsimile, 1974), I, pp. 213, 310).

38. Thomas Fuller, *The Worthies of England* (1st ed., 1662), p. 280.

39. Joseph Hunter, *Hallamshire* (1819), p. 71, and see Introduction, n. 39.

40. Sidney, *Works* (ed. Feuillerat 1912-26), I, p. 91.

41. Thoroton, *History of Nottinghamshire* (Throsby ed., 1797), III, p. 401.

42. Robert White, *Worksop, the Dukery and Sherwood Forest* (1875), p. 82.

43. For the Hewett family see also Joseph Hunter, *Deanery of Doncaster*, pp. 141–2, 304, and D.N.B. under Sir William Hewett.

44. Sir William Dugdale, *History of St Paul's Cathedral* (2nd ed., 1716), p. 67, with a transcription of the inscription.

45. For the pedigree of the Hewetts of Shireoaks I have preferred Robert White, *op. cit.* (see n. 42) to Burke's *Extinct Baronetage* (1844).

46. For the reconstructed plan and section of Shireoaks, and much help and information, I am indebted to Leo Godlewski.

47. For Doddington see Christopher Hussey, *Country Life* LXXX, pp. 356, 382, and R. E. G. Cole, *History of Doddington* (Lincoln, 1897). Repairs and alterations made in the last five years have revealed a certain amount of original detail, concealed beneath the Georgian overlay, and suggest that the Elizabethan interiors were exceedingly simple. Work on the parapet has proved that the lunettes shown in Kip's engraving of 1707 actually existed, and were not the artist's fancy (information supplied by Anthony Jarvis).

48. For Howley see T. D. Whitaker, *Loidis and Elmeto* (1816), p. 238 with illustration.

49. For Stonyhurst see H. A. Tipping, *Country Life* XXVIII (1910), pp. 534, 574.

50. Thoroton *Nottinghamshire* (1677), under Chilwell. Robert Smythson's old associate, the mason John Hill, seems to have had lodgings at Chilwell Hall at the time of his death in 1592 (see Ch. I, n. 15). It is possible that Smythson's plans were for an abortive Sheffield house in Nottinghamshire.

51. The engraving is in Scunthorpe Museum and Art Gallery, the drawing in the possession of the Sheffield family.

52. B.M., Add. MS 32464, f. 44.

NOTES TO CHAPTER 4

1. In fact William later bought the reversion of Chatsworth from Henry and it became the main seat of his descendants.

2. The relevant documents for the buildings at Hardwick are as follows:

Hardwick MSS 6. Building Accounts, 1587–99.

            7. Account Book of Countess of Shrewsbury, 1591–7.

            8. Account Book of moneys paid by Countess of Shrewsbury mostly to her House Steward, 1592–9.

The MSS are now in the muniment room at Chatsworth. Stallybrass, *op. cit.* (Ch. II, n. 9) contains a very capable account of these building operations, with many excerpts from the accounts. The accounts for the Old Hall have been edited by D. N. Durant and Philip Riden, *The Building of Hardwick Hall, Part 1* (Derbyshire Record Society IV, 1980); a second volume, covering the New Hall, is projected. The inventory attached to Bess's will (P.C.C., 23 Windebanck) is a valuable record of the original content and use and nomenclature of rooms at the two Hardwicks and Chatsworth. It has been edited (except, unfortunately, for the Chatsworth section) by L. Boynton and P. Thorn-

ton as 'The Hardwick Hall Inventories' (*Journal of the Furniture History Society* VII, 1971). For a detailed general guide to Hardwick, its contents and history see M. Girouard, *Hardwick Hall* (National Trust, 1976).

3. The first specific reference to 'the new foundations' is on 5 December 1590, but Durant interprets an increase in labourers on the pay roll between 26 October and 21 November as the result of the digging of the foundations. See Durant and Riden, *op. cit.*, p. xxvi.

4. Hardwick 7, f. 195.

5. The hall screen payment is in Hardwick 6, f. 205, and that for the chapel landing door, idem, f. 175.

6. B. of the fireplaces in Bk. VII.

7. A possible source of design-work at Hardwick may have been the painter John Balechouse (perhaps, to judge from his name, a German or Fleming) who first appears at Chatsworth in 1578, and becomes increasingly important at Hardwick. He continued to work there under William Cavendish for whom he seems to have supervised considerable but mysterious work carried out at Hardwick in 1608–12. See Durant and Riden, *op. cit.*, pp. xxiii–iv, and Girouard, *Hardwick Hall*, pp. 23, 38.

8. S. and D. Lyson, *Magna Britannia* V (Derbyshire, 1817), p. 42. The house would have been in an exposed but beautiful position high up in the Peak district and was perhaps intended as a hunting-lodge.

9. See Stallybrass, *op. cit.*, pp. 371–2.

10. Hardwick 7, f. 179a.

11. The Hardwick-type plan (I/8) suggests a design in which the staircases rose straight up round a central square newel, in the conventional Elizabethan manner, and the great chamber was over the great hall. It is possible that a similar arrangement was envisaged at Hardwick. The north staircase was certainly originally planned to rise into the little dining chamber; the beginning of a discontinued flight of steps survives in a cupboard. Such an arrangement, if continued to the second floor, would have made a gallery on the scale of the existing one impossible, unless the house was intended to be a storey higher.

12. Plan and elevation of the Holdenby banqueting-house were drawn by Thorpe (T. 182). It is shown on the survey of Holdenby made in 1587, but not on that made in 1580. It later came to be known as the Dairy House. See M. Girouard, 'Elizabethan Holdenby' (*op. cit.*, Ch I, n. 47), pp. 1398–9, where the Thorpe drawing and the relevant part of the 1587 survey are illustrated.

13. The hall at Hardwick Old Hall does not feature recognisably in the accounts, and may date from the period immediately before they start, in August 1587. Stallybrass assigns the hall to 1588. See Durant and Riden, *op. cit.*, pp. xiv–xv.

14. The High Great Chamber at Hardwick is much the biggest of known Elizabethan or Jacobean great chambers. Its grandeur, and that of the other second-floor rooms at Hardwick, suggests that Bess was planning for a special relationship with royalty, involving frequent visits. Such a relationship would have resulted had her grand-daughter Arabella Stuart succeeded Elizabeth as Queen, a possibility which certainly existed in the 1590s, but which Bess probably exaggerated.

15. For this ritual of serving meals see M. Girouard, *Life in the English Country House*, pp. 46–8.

16. The chapel was later divided horizontally into two and the lower half made into a steward's room. The sixth Duke of Devonshire's *Handbook to Chatsworth and Hardwick* (1845), p. 212, provides the evidence for the original arrangements.

17. The detailing of the kitchen columns suggest that the kitchen was originally planned to be on the same level as the hall.

18. Pevsner (*Buildings of England*, Derbyshire, p. 153) is of the opinion that these staircases cannot be Elizabethan, and were perhaps put in or reshaped by the sixth Duke of Devonshire some time in the first half of the nineteenth century. But it would have been an extraordinarily difficult job to insert staircases as complicated as these after the main structure had been built. And Torrington *Diaries* (ed. Byng, 1935-6) II, p. 33 refers to stone stairs as a curiosity of the house.

19. *British Architects and Craftsmen* (1945), p. 26.

20. For instance, Camden in the *Britannia*. On King's Chapel, Cambridge: 'a chapel ... which may rightly be counted one of the fairest buildings of the whole world'. And (perhaps more surprisingly) on the west front of Lincoln: '... that fore-front at the west-end which in a sort raiseth and allureth the eyes of all that come towards it'.

21. See Heathcote Statham, *Short Critical History of Architecture*, and Horace Walpole in his *Anecdotes of Painting*.

NOTES TO CHAPTER 5

1. The receipt was on a loose paper in the Wollaton building accounts for 1588; it was seen by P. E. Rossell but has since been mislaid. I owe this and the following three references to P. E. Rossell's thesis 'The Building of Wollaton Hall' (see Ch. 2, n. 3).

2. Middleton I, 8 (IV).

3. P.R.O. (1600-1), E 134/43.

4. Middleton 6/171/56. This is interesting evidence that Smythson was seeing William Cavendish and his mother early in 1602. There was no known building work going on at Hardwick or Owlcotes then. He may have been involved in the last stages of the house's decoration; alternatively, he may have been seeing them in connection with Willoughby's business interests.

5. See R. S. Smith, 'Huntingdon Beaumont, Adventurer in Coal Mines', *Renaissance and Modern Studies* I (1957), pp. 115-53, based on letters in the Middleton MSS at Nottingham University.

6. *Op. cit.*, p. 137.

7. *Op. cit.*, p. 139.

8. British Record Society (The Index Library), LVIII, *Nottinghamshire Marriage Licences*, I, p. 16.

9. The Newtons' house and land are shown on the survey of Kirkby in the volume of surveys of the Newcastle estates (for which see Ch. III, n. 18).

10. e.g. in a deed in the Portland collection (now in the Nottinghamshire County Record Office), D.D.P. 52. There are many other Newton deeds in the same collection.

11. His will is in York Registry, 33, f. 405. It is short and uninformative, but establishes his relationship with John, who is the main legatee.

12. See p. 255.

13. See Lawrence Stone, 'Inigo Jones and the New Exchange', *Archaeological Journal* CXIV (1957), pp. 106-22.

14. For Gilbert Talbot's involvement with Heath Grammar School see Thomas Allen, *A New and Complete History of the County of York* III (1831), pp. 240-1. See also T. W. Hanson (*op. cit.*, Introduction, n. 59), p. 253, and A. J. Pacey, 'Ornamental Porches of mid-Seventeenth-Century Halifax', *Yorkshire Archaeological Journal* XLI (1965), pp. 455-64.

15. For Pontefract and Edward Talbot see D.N.B. under Gilbert Talbot, seventh Earl of Shrewsbury, and George Fox, *History of Pontefract* (1827), pp. 353-5.

16. The date is shown in an eighteenth-century drawing by John Carter, B.M. Add. MSS 29929 f. 37, but has since weathered away. In 1586 the sixth Earl of Shrewsbury proposed to hand over all his estates, except Handsworth and Sheffield Manor, in return for a rent from his sons (*Talbot Papers*, G f. 335). If the handover took place Pontefract New Hall could have been started a year or two before 1590.

17. Hardwick MSS 7, ff. 55a, 58b, 60a; MSS 8, f. 48b.

18. Hardwick MSS 10 (a).

19. Hardwick MSS 7, ff. 188a, 196b; MSS 8, f. 51b.

20. John Chamberlain, *Letters written during the reign of Queen Elizabeth* (Camden Society, 1861), pp. 54-5. Reprinted *Elizabethan and Jacobean Prose: 1550-1620* (Penguin, 1956) p. 36.

21. In a manuscript *Account of the Manor of Kirkby, Notts*, written by Sir Richard Kaye, Bart., Vicar of Kirkby, at the end of the eighteenth century, B.M. Add. MSS 18552.

22. D. Knoop and G. P. Jones, *The Bolsover Castle Building Accounts, 1613* (1936), p. 8.

23. S. and D. Lysons, *Magna Britannia* V (Derbyshire, 1817), p. 182. Some courtyard walls, fragments of strapwork and an alcove survive.

24. Leeds University MS 295 (Wilson Collection), 242, Item 115.

25. See A. St. C. Brooke, *Slingsby and Slingsby Castle* (1904), pp. 140-67. The later house is discussed in Ch. VII, pp. 257-60.

26. See pp. 183-5 and n. 34.

27. Its interiors were redecorated with disastrous thoroughness in the mid-nineteenth century; at the same period the moat was emptied and the original balustraded parapet replaced by battlements.

28. For Mathew Cradock and his father, see the William Salt Archaeological Society, volume for 1920-2, pp. 6, 22. Mathew is described as the builder of the castle on his monument in Caverswell church. He should not be confused with his cousin and namesake, the Governor of Massachusetts.

29. Degges, *Observations upon the possessors of Monastery Lands in Staffordshire*, p. 6 (printed as an appendix to the 1717 ed. of Sampson Erdeswicke, *Survey of Staffordshire*).

30. A branch of the Cradocks, settled in Durham but apparently related to the Staffordshire Cradocks, built the Old Hall, Gainford, a compact small manor house of interesting plan which might be connected with the Smythsons. The house is illustrated and described in Pevsner's *Durham*, where it is dated 1604. See also R. Surtees, *History of Durham* IV (1840), pp. 8-13.

31. For Charles Cavendish and Welbeck see A. S. Turberville, *Welbeck Abbey and its Owners* I (1938), pp. 15-17. For

a plan of Welbeck as it was in 1750, which conclusively establishes the identity of the Smythson plan, see A. H. Thompson, *The Premonstratensian Abbey of Welbeck* (1938), p. 78.

32. The executed fragment of the Smythson plan for Welbeck is shown in two eighteenth-century drawings, reproduced in A. H. Thompson, *op. cit.*, pp. 106, 108, and in one of the illustrations to the Marquess of Newcastle's *Plus Excellent Methode*. The little domed turret, which features prominently in the illustrations, survived the eighteenth-century remodelling.

33. H.M.C., Portland MSS II (1893), p. 143.

34. H.M.C., Salisbury MSS XIX (1965), pp. 120–1.

35. *Talbot Papers*, L ff. 149, 151.

36. In Charles Cavendish's plan 'the one side may be a fit lodging for the King, the other for the Queen, and both to use the gallery', which is exactly the arrangement adopted at Hatfield. For Hatfield see Lawrence Stone, 'The Building of Hatfield House', *Archaeological Journal* CXII (1956), pp. 100–28, where, however, the Cavendish and Shrewsbury letters are not mentioned.

37. Such lobbies are also shown in Smythson plans II/1 and 4, but were not adopted at Hatfield.

38. Burton Agnes was fully described by Christopher Hussey, *Country Life* CXIII (1953), pp. 1804, 1886, 1972; he did not, however, know of the Smythson plan.

39. When he built a house at Whichnor, beginning it on 5 August 1584, Stebbing Shaw, *History and Antiquities of Staffordshire* I (1798), p. 125. The house was rebuilt at the beginning of the eighteenth century.

40. But it may have been removed when sash windows were inserted on this front in the eighteenth century.

41. There is a side entrance to the porch in Smythson II/5, a plan which seems to relate to Pontefract New Hall; so it is likely that the final arrangement at Burton Agnes was due to Smythson rather than Griffiths.

42. For Chastleton, see Margaret Dickins, *A History of Chastleton* (Banbury, 1938), and P. Mainwaring Johnston, *Country Life* XLV (1919), pp. 90, 116. The circular garden at Chastleton has an intriguing resemblance to Lord Bedford's garden at Twickenham, the plan of which was taken by Robert Smythson in 1609 (I/20 and Plate 92). See the plan of the Chastleton garden in the *Country Life* article.

43. The roofscape at Chastleton is most carefully designed, with an exquisitely symmetrical arrangement of roofs, chimneystacks, gables, dormers, and towers, worth comparing with the carefully-drawn roof-plan of Smythson II/2.

44. For Sheldon and Jones see Dickins, *op. cit.*, pp. 19–20, 23, 25. For Weston, see the engraving and account in Dugdale *The Antiquities of Warwickshire* (new ed. 1732), pp. 582–5. It is just worth mentioning that the bailiff of Bess of Hardwick's Oxfordshire estates was called Edward Jones, and that her principal property there was the manor of Bampton, the next door town to Witney, where Walter Jones' father had settled. (Durant, *Bess of Hardwick*, p. 182.) No Edward Jones, however, appears on the early-seventeenth-century Jones pedigree preserved at Chastleton.

45. Printed in volume XXV (1856) of the Chetham Society, pp. 125–74.

46. For Gawthorpe see J. M. Robinson, 'Gawthorpe Hall', *Country Life* CLVIII (4 and 11 September 1975), pp. 558–61, 630–3.

47. Christopher Hussey, *Country Life* LXX (1931), pp. 180–6.

48. There are plans for three storeys of a house for Sheriff Hutton, Yorkshire, by Bernard Dinninghof, datable *c.*1618, which are obviously connected with Fountains; they show a house with a recessed centre, the sides higher than the centre, and two staircases in projections at the back. It is possible that Dinninghof also provided plans for Fountains. On the other hand this Sheriff Hutton design has none of the resemblances to Wollaton, or subtleties of level, that appear at Fountains, and it is more likely that Fountains was a Smythson house, which Dinninghof was influenced by. The plans are in the Temple Newsam MSS. Collections now in Leeds Central Library. One of them was reproduced by Kitson, *op. cit.* (see Introduction, n. 53).

49. It is described in a contemporary account (B.M. Harl. MSS 6853, f. 450) as 'A very beawtyfull house newely built, the like whereof for bewty and good contrivinge is not in the North, the buyldinge cost newe 3000 li. notwthstandinge the opportunitie of stone gott at hand out of the Abbey walles.' This comes from an undated letter containing particulars of the Fountains Abbey estate written by Timothy Whittingham to an unnamed prospective buyer. According to R. Surtees, *History of Durham* II (1820), p. 330, Whittingham bought Fountains in 1622 and sold it in 1625.

50. For Proctor and Fountains see E. M. Walker, *Stephen Proctor, the Builder of Fountains Hall* (Ripon, 1952) and John Lyon, 'New Light on the Gunpowder Plot', *History Today* IV, 4 (April 1954). Proctor acquired the Fountains property in 1597, and put up the infant Prince Charles and his retinue for a night in 1604, facts which make one a bit suspicious of the traditional date of the Hall.

51. V. C. H. Yorks, *North Riding* II, pp. 74–5 (under Topcliffe).

52. See Arthur Oswald, *Country Life* CXXXII (1962), pp. 840, 900, 1020, where the possible connection of Smythson with the Hall was first discussed.

53. For a fuller account of Wootton see M. Girouard, *Country Life* CXXV (1959), pp. 522, 596. Since the *Country Life* articles the eighteenth-century interiors have been remodelled, the internal framing replaced by concrete, the exterior sand-blasted and extensively added to, the glazing altered, and the surroundings re-landscaped. The house is illustrated as before the changes.

NOTES TO CHAPTER 6

1. John Nichols, *Progresses of King James I* (1828), II, p. 49.

2. Many contemporary descriptions of tournaments and pageants are quoted in John Nichols, *op. cit.* above, and *Progresses and Public Processions of Queen Elizabeth* (2nd improved ed., 1823), and also in Robert Withington, *English Pageantry* (1918–20). Pioneer post-war studies, to which I am much indebted, are Frances A. Yates, 'Elizabethan Chivalry: the Romance of the Accession Day tilts', *Journal of the Warburg and Courtauld Institutes* (1958), pp. 86–103, XX (1957), pp. 4–25, and Roy C. Strong, 'The Popular Celebration of the Accession Day of Queen Elizabeth I', *idem*, XXI, pp. 86–103 and 'Elizabethan Jousting Cheques in the

Possession of the College of Arms', *The Coat of Arms* V, Nos. 34 and 35.

3. For Lee and the Accession Day Tilts see especially Frances A. Yates, *op. cit.* above.

4. Nichols, *Queen Elizabeth* II, pp. 312-29.

5. Idem, III, pp. 41-50.

6. Sir Philip Sidney, *The Countesse of Pembroke's Arcadia* (1590 ed.), Bk. II, Ch. 21 (ed. A. Feuillerat, 1922), pp. 282 ff.

7. Campion, *Works* (ed. P. Vivian, 1909), p. 17.

8. For European chivalric pageantry of this period see *Fêtes de la Renaissance*, edited by Jean Jacquot for Centre National de la Recherche Scientifique (Paris, 1956, 1960), and Frances A. Yates, *The Valois Tapestries*, Studies of the Warburg Institute, 23 (1959).

9. Edited and the illustrations reproduced by H. A. Lee, Viscount Dillon, *An Almain Armourer's Album* (1905).

10. Nichols, *James I*, II, p. 287.

11. Idem, II, p. 361.

12. Idem, II, p. 609.

13. Idem, II, pp. 707-18.

14. See Withington, *op. cit. passim*.

15. Idem, I, p. 113.

16. Idem, II, p. 115.

17. Idem, II, p. 198.

18. Yates, *The Valois Tapestries* (see note 8), p. 61.

19. Withington, *op. cit.*, I, p. 216, and Nichols, *Queen Elizabeth*, III, pp. 101-21, where the whole of the contemporary tract describing the entertainment is reprinted, and the engraving reproduced.

20. *Fêtes de la Renaissance*, I, plate XVII and pp. 191-203 (article by J. Vanuxem).

21. Nichols, *James I*, II, p. 361.

22. See B.M. Royal MS 17 CXXXV, 'A description of the severall fireworks ...' with illustrations.

23. Yates, *The Valois Tapestries* (see n. 8), p. 53.

24. For Cranborne see especially Arthur Oswald, *Country Houses of Dorset* (1959), pp. 123-7.

25. For Longford see Christopher Hussey, *Country Life* LXX, pp. 648, 696, 724.

26. *Faerie Queene*, Bk. II, Canto IX, Stanza XXII.

27. H. Avray Tipping, *English Homes; Late Tudor and Early Stuart* (1929), p. 204. For Carew see D. J. C. King and J. C. Perks, *Archaeological Journal* CXIX (1964), pp. 270-305.

28. These walls are illustrated in the article by Christopher Hussey on Hazelbury, *Country Life* LIX (1926), p. 279.

29. The Ware Park garden has gone, but was described by John Chamberlain in 1606; it was an example of mock-modern rather than mock-medieval fortification (*Letters of John Chamberlain* I, ed. N. E. McClone (Philadelphia, 1939), p. 235). It may be the garden shown in a plan at Hatfield (Skelton and Summerson, *op. cit.* (see Introduction, n. 38), p. 85). For the Audley End garden see P. J. Drury, *op. cit.* (Ch. 2, n. 25), p. 21 and Plate 22A. Here the triangular and circular bastions of the garden wall were echoed in the entrance range by triangular and semi-circular bay-windows and circular turrets, clear indication of deliberate castle references in the architecture as well as the garden. For Lismore see the article by M. Girouard in *Country Life* CXXXVI (6 August 1964), pp. 336-40. The garden has bastioned walls as at Hazelbury and was laid out by the Earl of Cork in 1626-7.

30. See Nikolaus Pevsner, *Buildings of England*, North Somerset and Bristol (1958), p. 274.

31. For Lulworth see R.C.H.M. Dorset II (1970), pp. 146-8; Joan Berkeley *Lulworth and the Welds* (Gillingham, 1971); Arthur Oswald *Country Houses of Dorset* (2nd ed., London, 1959), pp. 127-30.

32. Quoted *Lulworth and the Welds* p. 24.

33. According to the 2nd edition of Hutchins, *History of Dorset* (ed. R. Gough and J. B. Nichols, 1796-1815) the foundations were laid in 1588 and the house finished in 1609. The precise dates suggest documentary evidence which has since disappeared. Henry Howard, second Viscount died in 1590 when the manor of East Lulworth became the life property of his widow. She married again, but is said to have lived in 'bankeroute and famished povertie' and is unlikely to have had the resources for building. A situation involving the starting of work and its discontinuance for ten years is quite possible.

34. For Ruperra (alternatively spelt Rhiwpurra) see J. R. Phillips *Concise History of Glamorgan* (1879) p. 84, and RCHM (Wales) *Glamorgan* IV Pt I pp. 262-8.

35. *Arundel Castle Manuscripts* (see Ch. 3, n. 3), p. 144, SD 411, 887.

36. Matthew Arundell of Wardour was a cousin of Henry Howard's; in 1577 the Privy Council, which was much concerned about Howard's profligacy and debts, appointed him head of a commission of four to look after Howard's affairs in Dorset, in line with the settlement of his debts laid down by Act of Parliament in 1576 (P.R.O. State Papers Domestic, CXI, 9). He remained financially embarrassed even after his father's death in 1582, but the numerous references to his debts in contemporary state papers cease in January 1587.

37. For the likelihood of Arnold being involved with Lulworth see *Country Houses of Dorset*, pp. 128-9. Arnold's father had worked as a joiner at Longleat in the 1550s; at Wolleton Manor he succeeded the Longleat craftsmen; and the influence of Longleat is strong in two buildings with which he was almost certainly involved, Montacute and the Hall, Bradford-on-Avon. But no evidence for any direct connection between him and Smythson has come to light. Sir Francis Willoughby had considerable estates in Dorset (H.M.C., *Middleton, passim*), and it is not impossible that Smythson travelled south to Dorset on business connected with them.

38. The dedication commends 'your excellent skill in Musicke, and your great love and favour of Musicke'.

39. For Charles Cavendish see A. S. Turberville, *Welbeck Abbey and its Owners* I (1938), pp. 36-42.

40. John Aubrey, *Natural History of Wiltshire* (ed. John Britton, 1847), p. 88, where a number of the devices are described.

41. Nichols, *James I* III, p. 969.

42. Idem, p. 472-3.

NOTES TO CHAPTER 7

1. For Bolsover see P. A. Faulkner, *Bolsover Castle* (Department of the Environment Official Handbook, 1972). Although detailed and interesting this needs to be read with caution, since it tends to state as fact what can only be surmise. From the dating point of view Bolsover sets com-

plex and sometimes insoluble problems, which are discussed in Appendix II, at greater length than seemed desirable in the main text. The dates suggested here are not always in agreement with the Official Handbook. Among other publications R. W. Goulding's pamphlet, *Bolsover Castle* (5th and enlarged ed., 1928), is still useful. See also Samuel Pegge, *Sketch of the History of Bolsover and Peak Castles* (1785), reprinted John Nichols, *Bibliotheca Topographica Britannica*, 1790.

2. The accounts were printed, with notes, by D. Knoop and G. P. Jones, *The Bolsover Castle Building Account, 1613* (issued in advance of *Ars Quatuor Coronatorum* XLIX, Part I, 1936).

3. This room is unconvincingly described as the servants' hall in the Official Handbook.

4. It is perhaps just worth noting the curious resemblance between some of the simpler Bolsover chimney-pieces and Turkish chimney-pieces of the sixteenth and seventeenth centuries, for instance in the Baghdad Pavilion (1638) and the bedroom of Murad III (reigned 1574-95) in the Seraglio at Istanbul. This is probably coincidence, although a link between Istanbul and Derbyshire is provided by Charles Cavendish's elder brother Henry, who was there in 1589. See Fox (Henry Cavendish's servant), *Mr Harrie Cavendish His Journey to and from Constantinople 1589*, Camden Miscellany, 17, 1940.

5. In Book IV. See the facsimile of the 1619 edition (Gregg Press, 1964), p. 185.

6. The plan is preserved among the Middleton Papers in Nottingham University Library (5/165/130). It is endorsed 'A plott for the glasse house, July 30, 1615, John Smythson'.

7. She left him a small legacy in her will, of which there is a copy among the Portland Papers in Nottingham University Library, PWI/393-4 (Misc. 32).

8. *Vertue Notebooks II*, Walpole Society XX (1932), p. 32.

9. Nottinghamshire County Record Office, D.D.P., 15/52.

10. Nottingham University MSS PWI/331.

11. Apart from his wife's well-known biography, six chapters are devoted to him in volume I of A. S. Turberville, *Welbeck Abbey and its Owners* (1938). A full-length biography by Geoffrey Trease *Portrait of a Cavalier* (London, 1979) sets out to attack the view of him as an ineffective dilettante, put forward in Clarendon's *History of the Rebellion*, and generally accepted since.

12. *Walpole Society* XX (Vertue Note-books II) (1932), p. 32.

13. For these early works of Jones see John Harris *Catalogue of the Drawing Collection of the R.I.B.A.: Inigo Jones and John Webb* (1972), p. 13.

14. A practical rather than stylistic trophy from this southern visit was an Italian type of shuttered casement window, which he saw at Arundel House and drew in careful detail (III/7(4)). These windows seem to have been fitted in the Terrace range at Bolsover, but none survive there, though one can be seen (unlikely to be connected with John Smythson) at Beckley Park, near Oxford.

15. The agreement is in the Warwick Castle archives in Warwickshire County Record Office CR 1886/2831.

16. For Vertue see n. 12. The drawing is one of a series of Welbeck by Grimm, B.M. Add. MSS 15545, ff. 64-9.

17. A fine hammer-beam roof survives above the ceilings of the present chapel and library. Curiously enough this is not the roof shown in the Smythson and Grimm drawings, but appears to be a mid-nineteenth-century replacement.

18. Part of a survey of all the Cavendish estates, made *c.* 1629-40, mainly by William Senior. There are colour-transparencies of all the maps in Nottingham University Library and Nottinghamshire County Record Office.

19. For other examples see Roy Strong, *The Renaissance Garden in England* (London, 1978), pp. 53, 125-34.

20. The panelling is of the same pattern as the incomplete panelling in the Star Chamber at Bolsover. Winifred, Duchess of Portland, told Mr Brown, the former custodian at Bolsover, that it had been removed from Bolsover to Welbeck.

21. John Hodgson, *History of Northumberland*, Part II, I (1827), p. 379, quotes from an account of the castle written by Robert Fenwick in 1664, which appears to be describing a medieval building. It is possible that a re-building of the old moated castle was planned, but never carried out. According to Hodgson 'not a vestige of the castle was remaining in June 1827'.

22. Clarendon, *Autobiography* (1857 ed.) I, p. 250.

23. The two-coloured effect which this difference of stone must have produced may have been inspired by the colour scheme of the Banqueting House in Whitehall, as it was before the mixture of Portland, Northamptonshire and Oxfordshire stone was replaced by Portland stone alone in the late eighteenth century.

24. The vaults of the two biggest rooms (probably the kitchen and cellar) have collapsed, but one of them is shown still vaulted in a charming watercolour by Cotman in the Worsley collection at Hovingham Hall.

25. The appointment was a caretaker one, during the minority of his nephew William, third Earl of Devonshire, who was not to come of age, however, until October 1638. It is just possible that the cannon motif on the terrace range refers to a Lord-Lieutenant's principal role, as commander of the county militia.

26. Sir Osbert Sitwell bought them from a dealer, after the war. It seems likely that Diepenbeke's illustrations of Ogle, Bothel and Welbeck were made from similar drawings, which may come to light.

27. The Masques are printed in Jonson's *Works* (ed. Herford and Simpson, 1925-50) VII, pp. 787 and 805.

28. I am most grateful to Anthony Wells-Cole for drawing my attention to this Dietterlin source.

29. Account-book of William Cavendish, Chatsworth archives, Hardwick MS 29 f. 581.

30. Ibid., f.665.

31. Compare also the framed coat of arms above the porch at Wootton Lodge (Plate 126) where John may well have worked with his father.

32. For Clifton see *Country Life* LIV, pp. 246-54, where, however, a mistaken attempt is made to relate the house to John Thorpe's plan of Clifton Hall, Warwickshire.

33. Barbara Neville of Grove married Sir John Meres of Aubourn Hall, Lincolnshire, an attractive but puzzling house, or fragment of a house which seems to show some Smythson influence. See *Country Life* CXXI (1957), pp. 286-9.

34. In his will (see n. 42) they are described as 'farms called Twyfords and Gadsbyes in Nottinghamshire'. Notting-

hamshire must have been written by mistake for Leicester-shire where Twyford and Gadsby are both villages at which the Middleton papers show that the Willoughbies owned property.

35. A fireplace in a first-floor room carries the arms of Savile impaling Garth, that is of Sir John Savile, one of the founders of Heath Grammar School (see Ch. V n. 14) and his first wife, Jane Garth. Sir John died in 1607, and as the house seems to be of one date, it was probably built by his son, Sir Henry Savile.

36. The table is in the Victoria and Albert Museum, but was originally at Wingerworth Hall. I am most grateful to Mr David G. Edwards for drawing my attention to it. The inlay includes the Hunloke and Tyrwhitt crests, and was probably made to commemorate the marriage of Sir Henry Hunloke to Katherine Tyrwhitt in 1676.

37. See M. Girouard, 'Carlton Hall I', Country Life CXLI (1967), pp. 176-80, where a drawing by Buck (B. M. Lansdowne MS 914 f. 41), showing the house before Pugin's remodelling, is reproduced. The remodelled seventeenth-century block now has a staircase tower at one corner, rather in the manner of the Little Castle at Bolsover, but this seems to be a nineteenth-century addition.

38. Tupton is a puzzling house. According to family tra-dition, it was built in 1611 and added to by Thomas Glad-win in the 1660s; his name and that of his wife Helen were incorporated in the balustraded parapet. At some period the house was reduced in size. Photographs of it shortly before its destruction (unfiled prints in National Monu-ments Record) show a three-storey parapeted block, five bays wide, with five storeys of small windows in the two outer bays and three storeys of bigger windows in the three central ones; the photographs clearly show the original arrangement, although the fenestration had been altered at one end, probably in the eighteenth century. The result looks like a self-contained house of c. 1620, very much in the Smythson manner. I am grateful to David G. Edwards and Peter Reid for information about Tupton. Nothing seems to have been written about Stydd, which was brought to my attention by Peter Leach; there are photo-graphs in the National Monuments Record. Another demolished house which deserves research is Tankersley Hall, north of Sheffield, on a property which belonged to the Earls of Shrewsbury. An eighteenth-century engraving in the Sheffield Central Libraries shows a long thin house with towers and battlements. The house was brought to my attention by Leo Godlewski; a few ruined fragments survive.

39. The Ledstone tower is usually attributed to Sir John Lewis and assigned to the 1660s.

40. It bears the Howard and Harpur coat of arms, in reference to Sir John Harpur and his wife, Elizabeth, daughter of Henry Howard, third son of the first Earl of Suffolk. The date of the marriage does not seem to be known, but Sir John Harpur was still a King's Ward in 1623.

41. See Colvin, Biographical Dictionary of British Architects, under Shephard.

42. P.R.O., P.C.C. Seager 110.

43. See Joseph Hunter, Familiae Minorum Gentium (Har-leian Society Publications Nos. 37-40, 1894-6) II, p. 567; III, p. 912. Isabel's sister, Ann, married William Newton of Kirkby. Her mother was the daughter and co-heiress of Matthew Beresford of Newton Grange, Derbyshire. A brother, Charles, married firstly Abigail Bellamy, through whom he acquired the estate of Kettlethorpe in Lincoln-shire, and secondly Anne, daughter of Sir Thomas Trol-lope, Bart., of Casewick, Lincolnshire. Two other brothers were Turkey merchants; one of them, Richard (1612-65), who afterwards inherited Barlow Lees, lived, according to Hunter, 'some years in Turkey where he was a merch^t and improved his fortune. Amongst other things he brought home horses which were sold to the Duke of Newcastle.'

44. Francini was a Florentine; it was in about 1635 that Newcastle became a patron of the Florentine sculptor, Francesco Fanelli (Francis Haskell Patrons and Painters (1980) p. 178).

45. A miscellaneous Smythson drawing which might pos-sibly be by Huntingdon is the design for a wall tomb with kneeling figures, IV/13.

46. Will and inventory are in Birmingham Probate Re-gistry.

NOTES TO CHAPTER 8

1. For an interesting discussion of this type of plan see Eric Mercer, 'The Houses of the Gentry', Past and Present V (1954), p. 11.

2. G. Jackson Stops 'Tissington Hall, I', Country Life CLX (15 July 1976), pp. 158-61; M. Binney, 'Constable Burton', Country Life CXLIV (28 November 1968), pp. 1396-9; M. Girouard, 'Sandbeck Park, I', Country Life (XXXVIII (7 October 1963), pp. 879-83.

3. For Coppin's house see P. A. Faulkner, 'Nottingham House: John Thorpe and his relationship to Kensington Palace', Archaeological Journal CVII (1950), pp. 66-77; for Plas Teg. P. Smith, Flintshire Historical Society Publica-tions 18 (1960), pp. 157-62, and the article by M. Girouard, Country Life CXXXII (1962), pp. 134-7. The Thorpe plans are: Somerhill, T. 202; the Coppin house T. 94; Hatfield Lodge, T. 253.

4. In his MS, Chronologia Architectonica. See H. M. Colvin 'Aubrey's Chronologia Architectonica' in Concerning Ar-chitecture (ed. J. Summerson, 1968), p. 4.

5. Quoted Geoffrey Webb, 'The Mausoleum at Castle Howard', Walpole Society XIX, p. 126.

6. Uvedale Price, Essays on the Picturesque (1810) II, p. 210.

7. The Torrington Diaries, ed. C. Bruyn Andrews, (1935) II, p. 30.

8. See John Nichols, Progresses of Queen Elizabeth, 1823 ed., I, pp. 449-55.

LIST OF ILLUSTRATIONS

COLOUR PLATES

Between pages 56–59
I. Detail from the painting of Longleat House, Wilt-shire, by Jan Siberechts (Oscar Johnson).
II. A view on the roof at Longleat (Edward Piper).

Between pages 90–95
III. Design for a bay-window, probably for Longleat (RIBA, Smythson I/XX).
IV. Wardour Old Castle, Wiltshire. The north front (Edward Piper).
V. Wollaton Hall, Nottinghamshire. Detail from the painting by Jan Siberechts (Yale Center for British Art, Paul Mellon Collection).
VI. Wollaton Hall. Looking from the roof to one of the towers (Edward Piper).

Between pages 126–131
VII. The Hunting Tower, Chatsworth (Edward Piper).
VIII. Barlborough Hall, Derbyshire (Edward Piper).
IX. Manor Lodge, Worksop, Nottinghamshire. The rear façade (Edward Piper).
X. Design by Robert Smythson for an unidentified house and the hall screen at Worksop Manor (RIBA, Smythson II/11 and I/26).

Between pages 162–165
XI. Hardwick Hall, Derbyshire. A distant view (Edward Piper).
XII. Burton Agnes Hall, E. Yorkshire. Looking along the entrance front (Peter Burton).

Between pages 228–231
XIII. Little Castle, Bolsover, Derbyshire. Chimney-piece in the Star Chamber (Edward Piper).
XIV. Bolsover Castle, Derbyshire. The Venus Fountain (Edward Piper).

Between pages 262–265
XV. Drawings made by John Smythson on his visit to London, 1618–19 (RIBA, Smythson III/6).
XVI. Swarkeston, Derbyshire. The Stand (Edward Piper).

BLACK AND WHITE PLATES

1. Drawing of a summer house in Chelsea, by Robert or John Smythson (RIBA, Smythson I/9).
2. Design by Robert Stickelles for a lantern for Lyveden New Bield, Northamptonshire (British Library, Add. MS 39831 ff. 3–4).
3. Design by John Thorpe for an unidentified house (Soane Museum, Thorpe T86).
4. Diamond-shaped poem (George Puttenham, *Art of English Poesy*, 1589).
5. An emblem (Geoffrey Whitney, *A Choice of Emblemes*, 1586).
6. Design for a circular house (Redrawn from Thorpe drawing T145–6).
7. A geometric plan (RIBA, Smythson II/10).
8. One of a book of designs, probably for garden layouts (British Library, Harl. MS 5308).
9. A design for a round window (RIBA, Smythson II/34).
10. Bachegraig, Denbighshire.
11. Bishop Gardiner's chantry, Winchester Cathedral (NMR).
12. A chimney-piece at Longleat House, Wiltshire (*Country Life*).
13. Wenceslas Hollar. Richmond Palace, Surrey (Ashmolean Museum, Oxford).
14. Burghley House, Cambridgeshire (*Country Life*).
15. Longleat House, Wiltshire, the entrance front (*Country Life*).
16. Wimbledon House, Surrey (Engraving after H. Winstanley).
17. Holland House, London (Ilchester, *Home of the Hollands*, 1937).
18. Design for a chimney-piece perhaps for Longleat House, Wiltshire (RIBA, Smythson IV/10).
19. The ground and first-floor plans of Longleat, from plans at Hatfield House, Hertfordshire (Marquess of Salisbury. Photo Courtauld Institute).
20. On the roof at Longleat (*Country Life*).
21. Another view on Longleat roof (Edward Piper).
22. Alan Maynard's design for the façade at Longleat (Marquess of Bath. Photo Courtauld Institute).
23. The doorway at the top of the staircase at Wolfeton Manor, Dorset (RCHM).
24. The stone staircase at Wolfeton (*Country Life*).
25. Design for a classical façade, by Maynard (Marquess of Bath. Photo Courtauld Institute).
26. Chalcot House, Wiltshire (Edward Piper).
27. An early eighteenth-century drawing of the entrance front, Corsham Court, Wiltshire (Lord Methuen).
28. The porch at Corsham (Edward Piper).
29. Shaw House, Berkshire (John Piper).
30. The Strand façade of Old Somerset House, London (1547–52) (DOE).
31. One of the bay-windows at Longleat House, Wiltshire (*Country Life*).
32. Looking along the south front at Longleat (*Country Life*).
33. Design by Robert Smythson, possibly for the gate-

house at Wollaton (RIBA, Smythson II/12).

34. Wardour Old Castle, Wiltshire. The entrance front (*Country Life*).
35. Wardour Old Castle. Doorway and staircase in the inner court (Edward Piper).
36. Wardour Old Castle from the south (*Country Life*).
37. Wollaton Hall, Nottinghamshire. The entrance front (Gotch, *Architecture of the Renaissance in England*, 1894).
38. Robert Smythson's original design for Wollaton and its outbuildings (RIBA, Smythson I/25(1)).
39. Design for a Huguenot chapel (Jacques Perret, *De Fortifications et Artifices ... Architecture et Perspective*, 1601).
40. Smythson adaptation (I/25(4)) of de Vries, for the panels of Wollaton screen (RIBA, Smythson I/25(4)).
41. Base of a Doric column (Vredeman de Vries's, *Variae Architecturae Formae*, 1563).
42, 43. De Vries metopes copied for use at Wollaton.
44, 45. Doric entablatures, from de Vries.
46. The hall screen, Wollaton (*Country Life*).
47. Design for Wollaton screen (RIBA, Smythson I/25(7)).
48. Wollaton. The hall (*Country Life*).
49. Doric chimney-piece (Serlio Architettura et Prospettiva, Lib. 4).
50. Wollaton. The hall chimney-piece (*Country Life*).
51. Prior Overton's tower, Repton, Derbyshire.
52. Mount Edgcumbe, Cornwall, as drawn *c*. 1735 by Edmund Prideaux (J. C. Prideaux-Brune).
53. Michelgrove, Sussex, shortly before demolition in the early nineteenth century (John Harris).
54. One of the corner towers at Wollaton (Gotch, *Renaissance Architecture in England*, 1894).
55. Design for part of Wollaton (RIBA, Smythson I/25(2)).
56. A plan in the Willoughby papers (Lord Middleton. Photo University of Nottingham Library).
57. Plan and elevation of a house (J. A. du Cerceau, *Petits Habitations, c.* 1555).
58. Two anonymous plans in the library at Longleat (Marquess of Bath. Photo Courtauld Institute).
59. Melbury House, Dorset. The hexagonal prospect tower (RCHM).
60. Design by Robert Smythson, probably for the hall screen, Worksop Manor, Nottinghamshire (RIBA Smythson II/14).
61. Worksop Manor. The south front, from an early eighteenth-century drawing by Samuel Buck (Thoroton (Throsby ed.), *City and County of Nottingham*, 1790-7).
62. Worksop Manor, from a drawing by Robert Hall (Thoroton, *City and County of Nottingham*, 1677).
63. A survey plan of Worksop by John Smythson (RIBA, Smythson III/17).
64. A needle-work view of old Chatsworth (*c.* 1551-75), now at Hardwick Hall (*Country Life*).
65. Queen Mary's Tower, Sheffield Manor (Sheffield City Libraries, Yorkshire).
66. Thorpe Salvin, Yorkshire (Edward Piper).
67. Barlborough Hall, Derbyshire (1583-4). A detail of the entrance front (Edward Piper).

68. Heath Old Hall, Yorkshire (*c*. 1585). The entrance front (NMR).
69. A drawing by S. H. Grimm of the north front at Barlborough (H. H. Robinson. Photo Courtauld Institute).
70. The Jezebel chimney-piece, formerly in the great chamber at Heath Old Hall (*Country Life*).
71. North Lees Hall, Derbyshire (Edward Piper).
72. Manor Lodge, Worksop, Nottinghamshire. Rear view (*Country Life*).
73. Manor Lodge, Worsop. Front view (Edward Piper).
74, 75. Shireoaks Hall, Nottinghamshire. Front and rear views (Edward Piper).
76. Doddington Hall, Lincolnshire. The entrance front (Edward Piper).
77. Doddington Hall. A detail of the entrance front (*Country Life*).
78. Design for a house for Lord Sheffield (RIBA, Smythson I/18(3)).
79. Lord Sheffield's house at Normanby, Lincolnshire, from a survey drawing of *c.* 1700 (Sir Reginald Sheffield).
80. Howley Hall, Yorkshire (T. D. Whitaker, *Loidis and Elmeto*, 1816).
81. Design for Bess of Hardwick's monument in All Saints' Church, Derby (RIBA, Smythson I/6).
82. Hardwick Old Hall, Derbyshire, from a drawing by S. H. Grimm (British Library).
83. Two designs for chimney-pieces (Serlio, *Architettura et Prospettiva*, Lib. VII).
84. Hardwick Hall, Derbyshire. One of the long-gallery chimney-pieces (NMR).
85. Robert Smythson's variant plan for Hardwick (RIBA, Smythson I/8).
86. Designs for Blackwell-in-the-Peak, Derbyshire (RIBA, Smythson I/1).
87. Hardwick Hall, Derbyshire, from the south (NMR).
88, 89. Two views of Hardwick from the south-west (*Country Life*).
90. Hardwick Hall. The entrance front (Edwin Smith).
91. The Banqueting House, Holdenby, Northamptonshire, as drawn by John Thorpe (Soane Museum, Thorpe T182).
92. Hardwick Hall. The first flight of the great staircase (*Country Life*).
93. Hardwick Hall. The last stage, and the door to the High Great Chamber (*Country Life*).
94. Hardwick Hall. From the first to the second floor (*Country Life*).
95. Hardwick Hall. The chapel landing (NMR).
96. Late medieval design for a tower (RIBA, Smythson IV/3).
97. A Smythson design for vaulting (RIBA, Smythson II/25).
98. Robert Smythson's drawings of Westminster Abbey, 1609 (RIBA, Smythson I/15).
99. Robert Smythson's design for a round window, 1599 (RIBA, Smythson II/33).
100. Lord Bedford's house at Twickenham, Middlesex (RIBA, Smythson I/20).
101. The New Exchange, the Strand, London (RIBA, Smythson I/11).

102. New Hall, Pontefract, Yorkshire. The main front in 1885.
103. The side façade of New Hall (NMR).
104. A Smythson plan related to New Hall (RIBA, Smythson II/5).
105. The 'hour-glass' plan, by Robert Smythson (RIBA, Smythson II/4).
106. Upper-floor plan of an unidentified house (RIBA, Smythson II/1).
107. Plans for three storeys of an unidentified house (RIBA, Smythson II/2).
108. Robert Smythson's unexecuted plan for Slingsby Castle, Yorkshire. The basement plan (RIBA, Smythson I/19(1)).
109. Slingsby Castle. The ground-floor plan (RIBA, Smythson I/19(2)).
110. Caverswell Castle, Staffordshire (Plot, *Natural History of Staffordshire*, 1686).
111. The south front of Welbeck Abbey, Nottinghamshire, in the early eighteenth century (Turberville, *Premonstratensian Abbey of Welbeck*).
112. Robert Smythson's plan for rebuilding Welbeck (RIBA, Smythson I/23).
113. Burton Agnes Hall, Yorkshire (Gotch, *Renaissance Architecture in England*, 1894).
114. Robert Smythson's plan for Burton Agnes (RIBA, Smythson I/2).
115. Burton Agnes. The long gallery (*Country Life*).
116. Chastleton House, Oxfordshire. The long gallery (Edward Piper).
117. Chastleton House. The main façade (Edward Piper).
118. Chastleton House from the east (*Country Life*).
119. Gawthorpe Hall, Lancashire. The entrance front before Barry's alterations (*Country Life*).
120. Gawthorpe Hall. The east front (*Country Life*).
121. Fountains Hall, Yorkshire. Looking along the main front (*Country Life*).
122. Fountains Hall. The main front (*Country Life*).
123. The Hall, Bradford-on-Avon (Edward Piper).
124. Wootton Lodge, Staffordshire. The distant view (*Country Life*).
125. Wootton Lodge. The main façade (*Country Life*).
126. Wootton Lodge. The view from the terraces (*Country Life*).
127. A design for a fountain by John Smythson (RIBA, Smythson III/25(3)).
128. Bolsover Castle, Derbyshire, seen from the valley (DOE).
129, 130. The south-west and north-west façades of the Little Castle, Bolsover, from drawings probably made in the 1630s (Reresby Sitwell).
131. The Little Castle, Bolsover. The hall (DOE).
132. The Little Castle, Bolsover (DOE).
133. The Little Castle, Bolsover. A pendant in the pillar parlour (Edward Piper).
134. Tilting armour worn by Sir Henry Lee of Ditchley (Victoria and Albert Museum, London).
135. Prince Henry exercising with the lance, from an engraving.
136. Lord Herbert of Cherbury, from the miniature by Isaac Oliver (National Trust).
137. The pageant castle erected for the Queen's entertainment at Elvetham, Hampshire, in 1591 (Nichols, *Progresses of Queen Elizabeth*, 1823).
138. The Magician's Castle, erected as a centre-piece for the fireworks display held to celebrate the marriage of Princess Elizabeth to the Elector Palatine in 1613 (British Library).
139. Cranborne Manor, Dorset (*Country Life*).
140. Longford Castle, Wiltshire. The great chamber (*Country Life*).
141. Lulworth Castle, Dorset, from an eighteenth-century engraving showing the central tower.
142. Lulworth from the south-east (RCHM).
143. Ruperra Castle, Glamorgan (National Monuments Record, Wales).
144. Bolsover Castle, Derbyshire. Design by John Smythson for the gallery doorway in the terrace wing (RIBA, Smythson III/1(5)).
145. The Little Castle, Bolsover. The forecourt and entrance front (NMR).
146. The Little Castle, Bolsover. The south-east front (DOE).
147. The Little Castle, Bolsover. The Marble Closet (DOE).
148. The Little Castle, Bolsover. The Scullery (NMR).
149-56. Eight chimney-pieces in the Little Castle (149-52, DOE; 153, Edward Piper; 154-6, NMR).
157. Four designs for chimney-pieces (Serlio, *Architettura et Prospettiva*, Lib. IV and VII).
158. Bolsover Castle. A design by John Smythson related to the Marble Closet (RIBA, Smythson III/1(2)).
159. Bolsover Castle. Variant design by John Smythson for the hall chimney-piece in the Little Castle (RIBA, Smythson III/1(3)).
160. Panelling at Theobalds, Hertfordshire (RIBA, Smythson III/13).
161. Chimney-piece at Arundel House, London (RIBA, Smythson III/6).
162. Gate at Arundel House and house by New Exchange (RIBA, Smythson III/6).
163. Italian gate and window at Arundel House, drawn by John Smythson (RIBA, Smythson III/7(1)).
164. The balcony over the entrance to the Little Castle (DOE).
165. Welbeck Abbey, Nottinghamshire. John Smythson's design for the Riding School (RIBA, Smythson III/15(3)).
166. Welbeck Abbey. The interior of the Riding School, from the drawing by S.H. Grimm (British Library. Photo Courtauld Institute).
167. Welbeck Abbey. The stables (Duke of Newcastle, *Methode Nouvelle pour dresser les Chevaux*, 1657).
168. Welbeck Abbey. John Smythson's plan and elevation for the stables (RIBA, Smythson III/15(5)).
169. Welbeck Abbey. Design for one of the water pavilions in the garden (RIBA, Smythson III/24).
170. A chimney-piece designed by John Smythson at Welbeck (Mark Girouard).
171. The monument to Robert Smythson (d. 1614) in the church at Wollaton (NMR).
172. Ogle Castle, Northumberland, from the view by Diepenbeke (Duke of Newcastle, *Methode Nouvelle pour dresser les Chevaux*, 1657).

173. Slingsby Castle, N. Yorkshire (NMR).
174. Slingsby Castle. John Smythson's elevation (RIBA, Smythson III/12(1)).
175. The basement plan of Slingsby, from a drawing of *c.* 1700 at Hovingham Hall, Yorkshire (Sir Marcus Worsley, Bart.).
176. Bolsover Castle, Derbyshire. The Little Castle and Terrace Range, from the view by Abraham Diepenbeke (Duke of Newcastle, *Methode Nouvelle pour dresser les Chevaux,* 1657).
177. Bolsover Castle. John Smythson's plan for the terrace range (RIBA, Smythson III/1(4)).
178. Bolsover Castle. The terrace range from the courtyard (DOE).
179. Bolsover Castle. Looking along the terrace (Edward Piper).
180. Bolsover Castle. The entrance to the long gallery in the terrace range (NMR).
181, 182. Designs by John Smythson for the door from the Little Castle to the Stone Walk, and the balcony over the gallery door (RIBA, Smythson III/1(7-8)).
183, 184. Two designs for windows (Wendel Dietterlin, *Architecture,* 1598).
185. Monument to the Countess of Devonshire, Aulb Hucknall, Derbyshire (Mark Girouard).
186. A design by John Smythson, related to the Aulb Hucknall monument (RIBA, Smythson III/27).
187. Design for a tomb, by Vredeman de Vries.
188. Design for a chimney-piece (Wendel Dietterlin, *Architecture,* 1598).
189. Clifton Hall, Nottinghamshire. Chimney-piece in the Great Chamber (*Country Life*).
190. Design for chimney-piece adapted from Dietterlin (RIBA, Smythson III/28).
191. Plan by John Smythson for additions to Haughton House, Nottinghamshire, 1618 (RIBA, Smythson II/4).
192. 'The Newe Platt at Twy forde', Leicestershire (RIBA, Smythson III/14).
193. Plan for a house for Mr Diball, by John Smythson, 1622 (RIBA, Smythson III/19).
194. Wingerworth, Derbyshire. The old hall from an inlaid table-top of *c.* 1677 (Victoria and Albert Museum, London).
195. Welbeck Abbey, Nottinghamshire. The west front, from the drawing by S. H. Grimm (British Library).
196. Bolsover Castle, Derbyshire. Looking from the Little Castle across the fountain garden to the riding-school range (DOE).
197. Inside the riding-school, Bolsover (DOE).
198. Design for a gateway (Francini, *Architecture,* 1631).
199. Bolsover Castle, Derbyshire. One of the doorways in the riding-school range (NMR).

200. Designs for tools, by Robert or John Smythson (RIBA, Smythson II/26).

TEXT FIGURES

All plans drawn to the same scale, except Figs. 2 and 20

Fig. 1. Wollaton Hall. The ground-floor and first-floor plans.
Fig. 2. Mount Edgcumbe, Cornwall. The ground-floor plan (Jope, *Studies in Building History*).
Fig. 3. Barlborough Hall, Derbyshire. The ground-floor plan.
Fig. 4. Heath Old Hall, Yorkshire. The ground-floor plan.
Fig. 5. Manor Lodge, Worksop, Nottinghamshire. Ground and first-floor plans
Fig. 6. Shireoaks Hall, Nottinghamshire. Ground and first-floor plans.
Fig. 7. Doddington Hall, Lincolnshire. The ground-floor plan.
Fig. 8. Hardwick Old Hall, Derbyshire. The ground-floor plan. (Stallybrass, *Archaeologia* LXIV (1913)).
Fig. 9. Hardwick Hall, Derbyshire. Ground, first and second-floor plans.
Fig. 10. New Hall, Pontefract, Yorkshire. The ground-floor plan (R.C.H.M., England).
Fig. 11. Burton Agnes Hall, E. Yorkshire. The ground-floor plan.
Fig. 12. Chastleton House, Oxfordshire. The ground-floor plan.
Fig. 13. Gawthorpe Hall, Lancashire. The ground and first-floor plans.
Fig. 14. Fountains Hall, Yorkshire. The section.
Fig. 15. Fountains Hall, Yorkshire. The ground-floor plan (Ambler, *Old Halls and Manor Houses of Yorkshire*).
Fig. 16. Wootton Lodge, Staffordshire. The ground-floor plan.
Fig. 17. Lulworth Castle, Dorset. The ground-floor plan (R.C.H.M., England).
Fig. 18. Ruperra Castle, Glamorgan. The ground-floor plan (R.C.H.M., Wales).
Fig. 19. The Little Castle, Bolsover, Derbyshire. The section.
Fig. 20. Bolsover Castle, Derbyshire. The ground-floor plan.
Fig. 21. The Little Castle, Bolsover, Derbyshire. Basement and first and second-floor plans (D.O.E.).
Fig. 22. Barlborough Old Hall, Derbyshire. The ground and first-floor plans.

INDEX OF NAMES AND PLACES

Accres, Thomas, carver, 87, 88, 147
Adam, Robert, architect, 292
Adams, James, mason, 146-7
Adams, Robert, 8
Agas, Ralph, 305 n.1
Agincourt, battle of, 217, 218
Akroyd family, 17, 171
Alberti, architect, 10, 14, 15
Alciati, Andrea, *Emblematum Liber*, 24
Ampthill, Bedfordshire, royal house at, 104
Amsterdam, 17
Ancaster, 84
Anet, Chateau de, 90, 97
Angus, W., *Seats of the Nobility and Gentry*, 292
Annesley Woodhouse, Notts., 246
Antony, Cornwall, 9
Antwerp, 30, 247, 258, 281, Rubens' house at, 269
Ariosto, *Orlando Furioso*, 209, 215
Aristotle, 5
Arnold, William, mason architect, 10, 11, 17, 44, 198-9, 221, 228
Arthur, Prince, son of Henry VII, 218
Arundel, Thomas Howard, Earl of, 35, 212, 231-2, 251
Arundell, Sir Matthew, of Wardour, 78, 82, 100, 228
Ascham, Roger, *The Scholemaster*, 34
Ashby, Thomas, carver, 249-50
Ashmore, Robert, waller, 176
Aston Hall, Warwickshire, 36, 291
Aswellthorpe, 15
Aubourn Hall, Lincolnshire, 316 n.33
Aubrey, John, 9, 232, 291
Audley End, Essex, 11, 36, 104, 141, 225, 290, 291
Audley, George Tuchet, Lord, 308 n.35
Ault Hucknall, Derbyshire, 279, Pl. 185

Bachegraig, Denbighshire, 30, pl. 10
Bacon, Sir Francis, 9, 10, 30; *Essay on Agriculture*, 17
Bacon, Sir Nicholas, 3
Baldersby Manor, Yorkshire, 197
Balechouse, John, 312 n.7
Bampton, Oxfordshire, 314 n.44
Barbaro, Daniel, 88
Baret, James, *Alvearie or Quadruple Dictionarie*, 16
Barlborough Hall, Derbyshire, 120-5, 179, 199, Pls. 67, 69, Col. Pl. VIII Fig. 3; Barlborough Old Hall, 276-7, Fig. 3
Barlow Lees, Derbyshire, 279
Barnby-on-the-Don, Yorkshire, 133
Barry, Sir Charles, at Gawthorpe, 191
Bartoli, Daniello, *De' Simboli trasportati ai morale*, 25
Bath, stone from, 50
Beamsley Almshouse, Yorkshire, 25
Beaumont, Sir Henry, of Coleorton, 166
Beaumont, Huntingdon, coal-speculator, 166-7, 246
Beckley Park, Oxfordshire, 316 n.14

Bedford, Earl of, his house at Twickenham, 309 n.42, Pl. 100
Bedwyn Broil, Wiltshire, 29, 41
Bellin, Nicholas, 3
Bentley, John, 17
Berners, Lord, 70
Bernini, 4
Bertie, Thomas, mason, 308 n.15
Berwick, 7, 44; Earl of Dunbar's house at, 19, 113
Bess of Hardwick, *see* Talbot, Elizabeth, Countess of Shrewsbury
Bisham Abbey, Berkshire, 107
Blackwell-in-the-Peak, Derbyshire, 148, Pl.86
Blagrave, Thomas, Queen's Surveyor, 9
Blenheim Palace, Oxfordshire, 292
Blickling, Norfolk, 17, 36, 290
Bluom, Hans, 88
Boccador, 3
Bolsover, Derbyshire, the Smythson house at, 278, 279; Huntingdon Smithson's monument in church at, 283
Bolsover Castle, Derbyshire, 36, 131, 137, 162, 175, 181, 185, 206-10, 228, 231, 234-47, 249-51, 260-69, 279, 280-1, Pls. 128-33, 144-56, 158-9, 164, 176-82, 196-7, 199, Col. Pls. XIII, XIV, Figs. 19-21, building chronology of, 297 302
Bolton Castle, Yorkshire, 140
Bosville Family, 136
Boyton Manor, Wiltshire, 197
Bradford-on-Avon, The Hall, 62, 197-9, Pl. 123
Bramante, 3, 72
Bramshill, Hampshire, 290
Brentford, Sir John Thynne at, 49
Bristol, 50
Britton and Bayley, *Beauties of England and Wales*, 292
Broughton Hall, Yorkshire, 288
Buck, Sir George, *The Third Universitie of England*, 5
Buck, Samuel, draughtsman, 110, Pl. 61
Buckingham, Duke of, 17
Buckland Abbey, Devon, 42
Bugge, original name of Willoughby family, 83
Bullant, Jean, 2, 15
Burghley Lord, *see* Cecil, William
Burghley House, Cambridgeshire, 14, 25, 30, 34, 72, 117, 133, 141, 152, 183, Pl. 14
Burlington, Earl of, architect, 10
Burton, Robert, *Anatomy of Melancholy*, 86
Burton Agnes, Yorkshire, 169, 185-8, 277, Pls. 113-15, Col. Pl. XII, Fig.11
Butterwick, Lincolnshire, 141
Buxton, Derbyshire, 112, 117-18, 154
Byron, Lord, 11-12
Byron family, 167

Calwich Abbey, seat of Sir Richard Fleetwood, 204
Cambridge, 17, 83; King's College Chapel, 162, 170

Camden, William, topographer, 2, 84, 86, 313 n.20
Campion, Thomas, 17, 40, 213, 215
Caprarola, 36
Carew, Richard, of Antony, 9, 28
Carew Castle, Pembrokeshire, 225
Carleton, Sir Dudley, 28
Carlton Hall, Yorkshire, 277
Carter, John, drawing of Pontefract, 174
Casewick, Lincolnshire, 317 n.43
Castle Howard, Yorkshire, 292
Castle Rising, Norfolk, 235
Cataneo, 15
Cavell, Richard, steward at Longleat, 46
Cavendish, Anne (née Keighley) Countess of Devonshire, 270, Pl. 185
Cavendish, Sir Charles, son of Bess of Hardwick, father of Duke of Newcastle, 9, 10, 123, 144, 148, 168, 170, 175, 179, 182-5, 228, 231-3, 239, 244, 260, 278; reputation as architect, 183-5
Cavendish, Sir Charles, younger brother of Duke of Newcastle, 257-9
Cavendish, Henry, 1st son of Bess of Hardwick, 144, 316 n.4.
Cavendish, Sir William, 1st husband of Bess of Hardwick, 34, 112, 117
Cavendish, Sir William, 2nd son of Bess of Hardwick, later 1st Earl of Devonshire, 144, 166, 175, 176, 197, 270, 312 n.7
Cavendish, Sir William, eldest son of Sir Charles, Viscount Mansfield, Earl and Duke of Newcastle, 24, 159, 183, 232, 242, 244, 246-8, 260, 265-6, 278, 279, 281; *Book of Horsemanship (La Methode Nouvelle)*, 145n, 184, 247, 262, 281, 314 n.32, 317 n.43, Pls. 167, 172, 176
Caversham, near Reading, 40
Caverswell Castle, Staffordshire, 181-2, 199, 228, Pl.110
Caxton, William, 70
Cecil, Robert, 1st Earl of Salisbury, 9, 13, 113, 181, 184, 221, 226
Cecil, Thomas, 1st Earl of Exeter, 133
Cecil, William, Lord Burghley, 2, 5, 10, 13, 19, 25, 30, 34, 35, 40, 50, 112
Chalcot House, Wiltshire, 63, Pl. 26
Challuau, Château de, 56, 92
Champernowne, Sir Arthur, 9, 28,
Chamberlain, John, 28
Chandos, 1st Duke of, 309 n. 39
Chantmarle, Dorset, 9, 25
Chapman, John, stone-carver, 44, 45, 68
Charles I, King, 4, 215, 265-6
Charleval, Château de, 97
Charlton House, Greenwich, 173, 288
Chastleton, Oxon, 188-91, 196, Pls. 116-18, Fig. 12
Chatsworth, 32, 87, 112, 115-16, 119, 120, 123, 125, 138, 144, 147, 154, 311 n.17, Pl.64; Hunting Tower at, 119, Col. Pl. VII
Chaucer, Geoffrey, 76
Chaunce, John, surveyor, 8

Chaworth, Sir George, 19, 113
Chenonceau, Château de, 90
Chilham, Kent, 25
Chilwell Hall, Nottinghamshire, 308 n.15
Chipchase Castle, Northumberland, 199, 289
Chrispian, Richard and Stephen, carpenters, 49, 87, 308 n.15
Cicero, 68
Claremont, Surrey, Vanbrugh's house at, 292
Clarendon, Edward Hyde, Earl of, *Autobiography*, 258
Clifton, Sir Gervase, 270
Clifton Hall, Notts., 269, 270, Pl. 189
Clough, Richard, agent to Sir Thomas Gresham, 30
Cobham Hall, Kent, 14
Coke, Rev. D'Ewes, owner of Smythson drawings, 12
Colt, Maximilian, Flemish sculptor, 14
Condover Hall, Salop., 10
Coningsby, Thomas, jousting, 212
Constable Burton, Yorkshire, 288
Cooke, Lady, 249
Cope, William and Anthony, of Hanwell, 140
Copped Hall, Essex, loggias at, 152
Coppin, Sir George, 288
Corbett, Robert, in Salop., 30
Corsham Court, Wiltshire, 65-6, Pls. 27-8
Corsley, near Longleat, 45, 46
Coryat, *Crudities*, 17
Cossall, Nottinghamshire, 278
Cotehele House, Cornwall, 107
Cotes, Richard, of Worksop, 126
Cotton, Charles, *Wonders of the Peak*, 116, 117
Courtenay, Sir William, 78
Cox, Capt., Coventry mason, 293
Cradock, Mathew, of Caverswell, 182
Cradocks, of Gainford, 313 n.30
Cranborne Manor, Dorset, 10, 36, 221, Pl.139
Cumberland, Earl of, 35, 212

Daniel, Thomas, *The Civil Wars*, 168, 217
Darrell, William, of Littlecote, satire on Sir J. Thynne, 52, 76
Da Vinci, Leonardo, 3
Dee, John, 7
Degges, Sir Simon, *Monastery Lands in Staffs.*, 182
De Keyser, Hendrick, 17
De l'Orme, Philibert, French architect, 2, 15, 88
Derby, All Hallows, monument to Bess of Hardwick, 169, Pl.81
Descartes, 247
Devonshire, Countess of, *see* Anne Cavendish
Devonshire, 1st Earl of, *see* William Cavendish
de Vries, Vredeman, 13, 14, 15, 30, 65, 90, 255, 270, Pls. 41, 44-45, 187
de Witt, Giles, Flemish craftsman, 14
Diball, Mr, plan for, 273
Dickenson, William, bailiff to Earl of Shrewsbury, 114, 311 n.20
Diepenbeke, Abraham, 247, 252, 257, 262, 281, Pls. 167, 172, 176

Dietterlin, Wendel, *Architectura*, 13, 266-9, Pls. 183-4, 188
Digges, Leonard, 9
Digges, Thomas, 306 n.19
Dinninghof, Barnard, glass painter, 11, 17, 314 n.48
Ditchley, Oxfordshire, entertainment at, 213
Dobson, William, 9
Doddington Hall, Lincolnshire, 137-9, Pls. 76-7, Fig. 7
Dodsworth, Roger, antiquary, 179
Dolman family, 68
Dormer, Sir Robert, tomb at Wing, 29
Drayton, Michael, *The Baron's Warres*, 217
Dublin, Trinity College, 13
Du Cerceau, Jacques Androuet, 2, 13, 15, 28, 59, 66, 88, 90, 97, 101, 104, 154, 180, Pl. 57
Dudley family, 83
Dugdale, Sir William, 136
Dunbar, Earl of, at Berwick, 19, 113
Dunne, Angell, grocer, 106
Dutton, Thomas, 309 n.41

Eastbury House, Dorset, 292
Edgcumbe, Sir Richard, 99, 100
Edge, William, mason, 17
Edward VI, 3
Elizabeth I, Queen, 3, 4, 29, 104, 112, 113, 212-13, 216, 218
Elizabeth Stuart, Princess, marriage to Elector Palatine, 219, Pl. 138
Elvetham, Hampshire, 218, Pl. 137
Elyot, Sir Thomas, *Boke named the Governour*, 6
Erasmus, 74
Escorial, Spain, 13
Essex, Countess of, marriage to Earl of Somerset, 215
Essex, Earl of, 35, 212
Euclid, *Elemente of Geometrie*, 7
Evelyn, John, 40, 70
Exeter, 1st Earl of, *see* Cecil, Thomas

Felbrigg Hall, Norfolk, 199
Fleetwood, Sir Richard, of Wootton, 204
Florence, Uffizi gallery, tapestries in, 215
Fontainebleau, 97, 221
Fosbery, mason, 46
Fountains Hall, Yorkshire, 192-7, 199, 291, Pls. 121-2, Figs. 14-15
Foxe, *Sermons*, 74
Francini, *Architecture*, 281, Pl. 198
François I, of France, 3
Francquart, Jean, *Premier Livre d'Architecture*, 248
Froissart, *Chronicles*, 70, 74
Fuller, Thomas, *The Worthless of England*, 9

Gadsby, Leicestershire, 278
Gainford, Old Hall, Durham, 289, 313 n.30
Gardiner, Bishop, his chantry, *see* Winchester Cathedral
Gaunt, Adrian, French joiner, 44, 45, 46, 49, 62, 68
Gawthorpe Hall, Lancashire, 177, 191-2, 199, 228, Pls. 119-20, Fig. 13
Gerbier, Sir Balthasar, Dutch diplomatist, architect to Duke of Buckingham, 17
Gidea Hall, Essex, loggias at, 152

Giocondo, Fra, 3
Giovio, Paolo, *Dialogo delle Imprese militare a amorose*, 27
Gladwin, Thomas, 317 n. 38
Gonerson, Arnold, joiner, 44
Gonerson, William, *see* William Arnold
Goujon, Jean, 2
Gower, George, portraitist, 84
Graves, Thomas, Queen's Surveyor, 8
Great Houghton Hall, Yorkshire, 311 n.30
Green, Ralph, Queen's musician, 197
Greenwich, the Queen's House, 28
Grenville, Sir Richard, 42
Gresham, Sir Thomas, founder Royal Exchange, 30, 41
Greves, Giles, stone-mason, 113, 114
Greville, Fulk, poet, later 1st Baron Brooke, 5, 212, 249
Grey, Lady Jane, 83
Greys Court, Oxfordshire, 307 n.2
Griffiths, Sir Henry, of Burton Agnes, 185, 187, 190, 204
Grimm, Samuel Hieronymous, artist, 251, Pls. 69, 166, 195
Grombald, William, mason, 10
Grove House, Nottinghamshire, 271
Gryffyn, William, mason, 146

Hadrian, emperor, 9
Halifax, Heath Grammar School, 171, 276, 317 n.35
Hall, John, of Bradford-on-Avon, 153, 197, 199
Hall family of Barlow Lees, 279
Ham House, Surrey, 170
Hampton Court, Middlesex, 3
Hancock, Walter, Shropshire mason, 10, 11
Handsworth, near Sheffield, 107, 112, 134, 306 n.39
Hardwick, Derbyshire, The Old Hall, 117, 144-5, 153, 154, work by John Smythson at, 270, Pl. 82, Fig. 8; The New Hall, 13, 25, 49, 61, 74, 112, 116, 123, 145-62, 166, 172, 188, 189, 196, 289, 291, 293, 312 n.7, Pls. 84-5, 87-90, 92-5, Col. Pl. XI, Fig. 9; plan of, sent to Hatfield, 184; George Byng, Lord Torrington, on, 292
Hardwick, Notts., 246
Harlaxton, Lincs., 293
Harpur, Sir John, of Swarkeston, 277
Harrison, John, surveyor, 132
Harrison, William, *Description of England*, 9, 20, 28
Harvey, Gabriel, friend of Spenser, 108
Haselbury, Somerset, 50
Hatfield House, Herts., 9, 13, 14, 25, 36, 173, 181, 184, 218, 291; lodges at, 134, 288
Hatton, Sir Christopher, 5, 19, 30
Haughton House, Notts., 271, Pl. 191
Hawksmoor, Nicholas, architect, 291
Hawthorne, Henry, Queen's Surveyor at Windsor, 10
Hazelbury Manor, Wilts., 225
Heath Grammar School, *see* Halifax
Heath Old Hall, Yorkshire, 120, 125, Pls. 68, 70, Fig. 4
Hengrave Hall, Suffolk, 123, 125, 181
Henrietta Maria, Queen, 265-6
Henry II, of France, 210
Henry VII, 32, 104, 217, 218

Henry VIII, 3, 9, 10, 20, 28, 32, 40, 44, 104, 217
Henry Stuart, Prince of Wales, 17, 215, 219, Pl. 135
Herbert, Lord, of Cherbury, 35, Pl. 136
Herstmonceux, Sussex, 56
Hertford, Earl of, son of Duke of Somerset, 9, 68, 218
Hewett family, 122, 135-7
Heydon, Sir Henry, of West Wickham, 56
Hill (or Hills), John, mason, 49, 87, 133
Hill Hall, Essex, Sir Thomas Smith at, 30
Hilliard, Nicholas, miniaturist, 20, 24
Hobbes, Thomas, 247
Hodgkyns, John, mason, 49
Holbein, 20
Holdenby, Northants, 5, 19, 30, 34, 97, 104, 141, 152, 183, 290, 309 n.41; Banqueting House at, 153, Pl. 91
Holinshed's Chronicles, 9
Holleman, Gerard, sculptor, 14
Holles, Sir John, 141
Holt, Thomas, carpenter, 17
Honnecourt, Villard de, designer, 13
Horsey, Sir John, 42
Hovingham Hall, drawings at, 258
Howard, Frances, 212
Howard, Henry and Thomas, 2nd and 3rd Viscounts Bindon, 226-8
Howley Hall, Leeds, 142, Pl. 80
Howsham, Yorkshire, 199, 289
Hull, Yorkshire, manor at, 310 n.19
Hunloke family, 227

Ingestre, Staffs., 289

James I, King, 174, 215
Jessop, William, of North Lees, 126
John of Padua, 3, 68
Jones, Edward, 314 n.44
Jones, Inigo, 4, 15, 16, 17, 28, 36, 166, 171, 249, 250, 251, 277, 291
Jones, Dr John, The benefit of the ancient Bathes of Buckstones, 118
Jones, Walter, of Chastleton, 188, 190
Jonson, Ben, 17, 216, 231, 247, 277; The King's Entertainment at Welbeck, 265; Love's Welcome at Bolsover, 266, 277
Justinian, Emperor, 9

Kaye, John, of Heath Old Hall, 125
Kenilworth Castle, Warwickshire, 19, 34, 44, 224, 290
Kettlethorpe, Lincolnshire, 317 n.43
King, John, mason, 49, 51-2
Kip and Knyff, Britannia Illustrata, 2, 116
Kiplin, Yorkshire, 25
Kirby, Richard, surveyor to Sir Thomas Smith, 15
Kirby Hall, Northamptonshire, 14, 30, 34, 72, 152, 290
Kirkby-in-Ashfield, Nottinghamshire, 168, 171, 175, 246, 278; Smythson house at, 278, 279
Knight, Richard Payne, The Landscape, 292
Knole, Kent, 36, 290
Knollys, Sir Francis, 40, 309 n.5
Knyvett, Sir Thomas, 15
Kyre Park, Worcestershire, 8, 14
Kytson family, of Hengrave, 123

Labacco, 15

Lacock Abbey, Wiltshire, 44, 107
Lake House, Wiltshire, 197
La Muette, Château de, 56
Laneham, Robert, 19
Langley, mason, 114
Layer Marney, Essex, 32
Lee, Sir Henry, of Ditchley, 212-13, 216, Pl. 134
Leeds, Dukes of, 136
Leicester Abbey, 270
Leicester, Earl of, 44
Leland, John, Itinerary, 114
Le Moine, Pere, S.J., on devices, 27
Lennox, Duke of, 210. 215
Lescot, Pierre, architect of the Louvre, 2, 72
Lewis, John, master carpenter, 44, 49, 62, 68
Lewis, John, the younger, 87
Lindley of Skegby, 278
Lismore Castle, Ireland, 225
Lodge, Edmund, Illustrations of British History, 112
London
    Robert Smythson's visits to, 166, 167, 169-71; John Smythson's visit to, 248-50; Angel Dunne's house, in City, 106; Arundel House, 249, 250, 251, 316 n.14, Pls. 161-3; Campden House, 11; Chelsea, summer-house in, Pl. 1; Gooseberry House, Whitehall, 292; Holborn, houses in, 249, Col. Pl. XV; Holland House, 11, 36, 173, Pl. 17; Kensington, Sir George Coppin's house, 288; Middle Temple Hall, 44, 90; New Exchange, Strand, 171, Pl. 101; Northampton House, 170; Royal Exchange, 30; St James's Palace, Riding School, 171; Somerset House, 8, 29, 41, 45, 56, 59, 66, 70-2, 170, Pl. 20; Strand, Col. Cecil's house, 249; Theatres in, 307 n.86; Westminster Abbey, 170, Pl. 98, Henry VII's Chapel, 162, 170; Westminster Hall, masque in, 218; Whitehall, Banqueting House, Elizabethan, 4, 8, of Inigo Jones, 171, 249, 252, 316 n.23
Longford Castle, Wiltshire, 25, 28, 30, 223-4, 244, Pl. 140
Longleat House, Wiltshire, 8, 9, 13, 30, 34, 40-76, 80, 88, 97, 101, 115, 117, 157, Pls. 12, 15, 18-22, 31-2, Col. Pls. I-III; plans for house in library at, 104-5, 162, 192, 228, Pl. 58
Longly, John, mason, 113
Lovell, Christopher, mason, 49, 87, 88
Lovell, Humphrey, Queen's Master Mason, 40, 68
Ludlow Castle, Shropshire, 108
Lullington Manor, Somerset, 44
Lulworth Castle, Dorset, 162, 177, 185, 225-8, Pls. 141-2, Fig. 17
Lumley Castle, Durham, 140
Lumley, Lord, 184
Luther, Martin, 76
Luttrell, Sir John, 24
Lyminge, Robert, artificer at Hatfield, 14, 17
Lyveden New Bield, Northamptonshire, 10, 25, 310 n.15, Pl. 2

Mackworth Castle, Derbyshire, 90
Madrid, Château de, 56
Maidstone, Kent, 49

Mallery, Richard, 146
Mansfield, Viscount, see Cavendish, William
Mansfield Park, Nottinghamshire, 279
Marlowe, Christopher, 108
Marsh, Samuel, designer, 262, 302
Marske Hall, Yorkshire, 289
Mary I, 3, 29
Mary Stuart, Queen of Scots, 111, 114, 119
Mason, Richard, mason, 133
Maune, Château de, 97
Maynard (Maeneard), Alan, French sculptor and colleague of Robert Smythson, 44, 45, 49, 51, 52, 54, 62-5, 70-76, Pls. 22, 25; letter to Thynne, 295-6
Melford Hall, Suffolk, 34
Melbury House, Dorset, 105-6, Pl. 59
Mentmore, Beds., 293
Mercer, mason, 51-2
Merser, Edward and Valentine, masons, 49
Methley Hall, Yorkshire, 276
Michelangelo, 266
Michelgrove, Sussex, 56, 100, Pl. 53
Mildmay, Sir Anthony, jousting, 35
Monkton Deverill, Wiltshire, 50
Montacute, Somerset, 10, 14, 25, 225
Montgomery, Earl of, 210, 232
Moore, Gabriel, mason, 9
Moralee-in-Haydon, Northumberland, 279
Mordaunt, Lord, of Turvey, 308, n.35
Moreton Corbet, Shropshire, 30
Morgan, Sir Thomas, steward to Earl of Pembroke, 228, 232
Morte d'Arthur, 34, 209
Mount Edgcumbe, Cornwall, 56, 97-100, 102, 105, 107, Pl. 52, Fig. 2
Mount Hall, Essex, 16
Mulgrave, Earl of, see Edward, Lord Sheffield
Mulgrave, Yorkshire, 141

Nash, Joseph, lithographer, 292
Nayll, Henry, mason, 146
New Bield, Lyveden, see Lyveden New Bield
New House, Goodrich, Herefordshire, 25
New House, Wiltshire, 25
Newcastle, Duke and Earl of, see Cavendish, William
Newthorpe, 278
Newton family, of Kirkby, 168, 279
Nonsuch Palace, Surrey, 3, 104
Nonsuch, the Earl of Worcester's house at, 170
Norden, John, topographer, 2
Normanby, Lincolnshire, 141-2, Pl. 79
North Lees Hall, Derbyshire, 125-6, Pl. 71
Northumberland, John Dudley, Duke of, 29
Northumberland, Henry Percy, 9th Earl of, 11, 15
Nottingham Castle, 247, 292
Nunney, Somerset, 44, 62

Oatlands Palace, Surrey, 107
Ogle, Baroness, wife of Sir Charles Cavendish, 232, 246
Ogle Castle, Northumberland, 257, 279, Pl. 172
Osborne, Edward, related to Sir William Hewett, 136
Owlcotes, Derbyshire, 112, 171, 175-6, 206

Oxford, Edward Harley, Earl of, 114
Oxford, 17; Christ Church, 244; Wadham College, 10

Padua, John of, 3, 68
Palladio, Italian architect, 13, 14, 15, 88, 104, 288
Paradise of Dainty Devices, 22
Paris, 218; Louvre, the, 72; pageants in, 218, 219
Peacham, George, *Compleat Gentleman*, 17
Peake, Robert, 17
Peele, George, *Polyhymnia*, 212-13
Pembroke, Henry Herbert, 2nd Earl of, 108
Pembroke, William Herbert, 3rd Earl of, 210, 228, 231-2
Perret, Jacques, *Fortifications et Artifices*, 86, Pl. 39
Petworth, Sussex, 15
Pevsner, Sir Nikolaus, 147
Phipps, Henry and Nicholas, 308 n.35
Pierrepont family, at Owlcotes, 175
Plas Teg, Flintshire, 288
Plumtree family, wallers, 176
Pontefract, Castle, 112; New or Old Hall, 171-5, 189, Pls. 102-4, Fig. 10
Portington, Roger, 133
Poulett, Lord, of Walton Castle, 225
Pratt, Sir Roger, architect, 9, 166
Preston, Sir Richard, at pageant, 215
Price, Uvedale, *Essays on the Picturesque*, 292
Primaticcio, Francesco, architect to François I, 3
Proctor, Sir Stephen, of Fountains Hall, 197
Pugin, Edward Welby, 277
Puttenham, George, *Art of English Poesy*, 21, 25, Pl. 4
Pytts, Sir Edward, at Kyre, 8

Raglan Castle, Monmouthshire, 311 n.17
Ralegh, Sir Walter, 5, 21, 228
Raphael, 3
Renishaw Hall, Derbyshire, 288; drawings at, 262, 279, Pls. 129, 130
Repton, Humphry, *Landscape Gardening*, 292
Repton, Derbyshire, Prior Overton's Tower, 90, Pl. 51
Reynolds, Sir Joshua, 292
Rhiwperra, *see* Ruperra
Richmond Palace, Surrey, 32, 56, 117, 153, Pl. 13
Robynson, at Worksop, 113
Rodes, Sir Francis, of Barlborough, 122-3
Rodes, Godfrey, 311 n.30
Rodes, John and Christopher, stone-masons, 87, 88, 146; Rodes, at Sheffield, 311 n.20
Rodminster Lodge and A. Maynard, 62
Rome, Farnese Palace, 5, 269; Vatican, Belvedere, 72
Rosso, 3
Rothwell, Northants. 10, 30
Royal Works, the, 7, 8, 9, 10, 11, 44
Rubens, 4
Rufford Abbey, Notts., 112, 244
Ruperra Castle, Glamorgan, 225, 228, Pl. 143, Fig. 18
Rushton, Northants., Triangular Lodge, 25
Rutland, Earl of, 1

St Osyth's, Essex, 107

Salisbury, Robert Cecil, 1st Earl of, 9, 13, 113, 181, 184, 221, 226
Sambin, Hugues, 2
Sandbeck Hall, Yorkshire, 288
Sandford, Elizabeth, 122
Sandford, Hercy, of Thorpe Salvin, 119, 311 n.36
Sandys, George, *Relation of a Journey*, 17
Savile, Edward, 171
Savile, Sir George, 171
Savile, Sir Henry, 276
Savile, Sir John, of Howley Hall, 141
Savoy, Duke of, 247
Seaton Delaval, Northumberland, 292
Senior, William, surveyor to Duke of Newcastle, 255, 279
Serlio, Sebastiano, 3, 13, 14, 15, 17, 28, 30, 59, 68, 88, 90, 147, 154, 242, 307 n. 86, Pls. 49, 83, 157
Servi, Constantino de, architect to Prince Henry, 17
Seymour family, 83
Shakespeare, William, 15; *Henry V*, 217; *Midsummer's Night Dream*, 59
Shaw House, Berkshire, 65, 66-8, Pl. 29
Sheffield, Edward, 2nd Lord, Earl of Mulgrave, 140-2; house designed for, 140, 290, Pl. 78
Sheffield Castle, Yorkshire, 112; Manor, 112, 119, 131, Pl. 65
Sheldon, Ralph, 190
Shelley, Sir William, of Michelgrove, 100
Shephard, Richard, mason, 277
Sherborne Abbey, Dorset, 62
Sherborne House, Gloucestershire, 309 n.41
Sheriff Hutton, Yorkshire, 289, 314 n.48
Shireoaks, Nottinghamshire, 134-8, 228, Pls. 74-5, Fig. 6
Shrewsbury, Countess of, *see* Talbot, Elizabeth
Shrewsbury, 5th Earl of, *see* Talbot, Francis
Shrewsbury, 6th Earl of, *see* Talbot, George
Shrewsbury, 7th Earl of, *see* Talbot, Gilbert
Shrewsbury, 8th Earl of, *see* Talbot, Edward
Shute, John, 29, *The First and Chief Groundes of Architecture*, 2, 7, 14, 15, 16, 310 n.13
Shuttleworth, Laurence, of Gawthorpe, 191
Siberechts, Jan, 84, 309 n.8
Sidney, Sir Philip, 2, 5, 34, 35, 108, 209, 212, 215, 305 n.2, *Arcadia*, 20, 34, 35, 134, 213
Sitwell, Sacheverell, on Hardwick, 157; on Bolsover, 278
Skegby, Nottinghamshire, 278
Slaugham, Sussex, loggias at, 124, 152
Slingsby Castle, Yorkshire, 179; unexecuted design for, 123, 169, 179-81, 228, Pls. 108-9; executed design for, 257-60, 276, Pls. 173-5
Smallwood, Richard, 309 n.8
Smith, Abraham, stone-carver and plasterer, 147
Smith, Sir Thomas, ambassador and scholar, 16, 30, 40, 45
Smithsons, the later, 303
Smithson, John, son of Huntingdon, 303
Smythe, Thomas, 65
Smythson family, neglect of, and reason for, 2-3; their drawings, 11-13; their importance, 38; and the Gothic tradition,

162; their family tree, 303-4; spelling of their name, 166-7, 279, 283, 295, 303
Smythson, Elizabeth, unmarried daughter of John, 278
Smythson or Smithson, Huntingdon; birth, 167; origins of name, 167; initials at Bolsover, 262; legacies from John, 278; marriage, 279; as land-surveyor, 279; living at Kirkby, 279; death and will, 282
Attributed works: at Bolsover, 279-81; at Welbeck, 280
Smythson or Smithson, Isabel (née Hall), wife of Huntingdon, 279
Smythson, John, first appearance of, at Wollaton, 87; at Hardwick, 148; connection with Huntingdon Beaumont, 167; early career summarised, 168; likely collaboration with father, 168, 169; marriage, 168; work for Willoughbys, 167, 246, for Cavendishes, 246; visit to London, 247-51; house at Kirkby, 246, at Bolsover, 278, 279; farm at Twyford, 273, 278; death, will, and property, 278; use of pattern-books, 242, 244; attitude to design, 269
Works:
Documented: Bolsover, Little Castle, 234-45, Terrace Range, 260-9; Clifton, 269, 271; plan for Mr. Diball, 273; Grove, 271; Hardwick, 270; Haughton, 271; Leicester, 270; Ogle, 257; Slingsby, 257-60; Twyford, 273; Welbeck, riding-school, 251-2, stables, 252-5, garden buildings, 255, house, 255-6; Wollaton, orchard and glass-house, 167; Wyverton, 271.
Attributed: Ault Hucknall, Devonshire monument, 270-1; Barlborough Old Hall, 276-7; Shireoaks, 137-8; Wollaton, monument to Robert Smythson, 256.
Possible connection: Aubourn, 316 n.33; Carlton, 277; Caverswell, 182; Stydd, 277; Swarkeston, the Stand, 277; Tupton, 277; Wingerworth, 277
Smythson or Smithson, John, younger brother of Huntingdon, 278, 303
Smythson, Margaret (née Newton), wife of John, 168
Smythson, Robert, possible origins of, 307 n.5; arrival at Longleat, 40; his team of masons, 49; letter to Thynne, 52, 70, 295-6; move to Wollaton, 82; non-architectural work for Willoughbys, 166-8; visits to London and south, 167, 168, 169-71; surveys Warwick Castle, 149; death and will, 168, 313 n.11; monument in Wollaton church, 82-3, 168, Pl. 171; use of pattern books, 63-5, 66, 90, 102, 147; knowledge of perspective, 101; characteristics of his buildings, 187-8; work and influence discussed, 286-94;
Works:
Documented: for Sir Francis Knollys, 40; Longleat, 45-54, 68-76; Wardour, 78-82; Wollaton, 82-108; Worksop Manor, 115; Lord Sheffield, house for, 140-1; Hardwick, 147-9; Blackwell-in-the-Peak, unexecuted, 148; Derby, Shrewsbury monument at, 169; unidentified plans, 176-9; Slingsby, Yorkshire, unexecuted, 179-81; Welbeck, 182-3; Burton Agnes, 185-7.

Smythson, Robert—*cont.*
  Works—*cont.*
  Attributed: Corsham, 65–6; plan in library, Longleat, 105; Barlborough, 120–3; Manor Lodge, Worksop, 131–2; Shireoaks, 137–8; Doddington, 138–9; Normanby, 141–2; Pontefract, 171–3; Kirkby-in-Ashfield, 171, 175; Owlcotes, 171, 175–6; Caverswell, 181–2; Fountains, 192–7; Wootton, 199–204; Little Castle, Bolsover, 234, 239.
  Possible connections: Shaw House, 65; Hunting Tower, Chatsworth, 119; Heath Old Hall, 125; North Lees, 126; Heath Grammar School, 171; Chastleton, 183–91; Gawthorpe, 191–2; the Hall, Bradford-on-Avon, 197–9; Lulworth, 225–8.
Soane Museum, 11
Somerhill, Kent, 288
Somerset, Edward Seymour, Duke of, Lord Protector, 8, 29, 40, 44, 49, 59
Somerset, Robert Carr, Earl of, marriage to Countess of Essex, 215
South Wingfield Manor, Derbyshire, 112
South Wraxall Manor, Wiltshire, 62
Southampton, Earl of, jousting, 210
Spenser, Edmund, 5, 209, 215, 224; *Faerie Queene*, 34, 209, 213
Spicer, William, Queen's Surveyor, 10, 44, 45, 51, 68, 76, 224
Stanhope family, 168, 175, 311 n.36
Stapleton, Elizabeth, niece of Sir Charles Cavendish, 277
Stickells, Robert, Clerk of the Works at Richmond, 10, 306 n.42, 310 n.15
Stockton House, Wiltshire, 197
Stoke, Somerset, 50
Stone, Nicholas, 17
Stonyhurst, Lancashire, 141
Stotte, Robert, joiner, 114
Strangways, Sir Giles, of Melbury, 105
Strelley family and coal-pits, 167, 168
Strode, Sir John, of Chantmarle, 9, 25
Stuart, Arabella, 156, 312 n.14
Stydd Hall, Derbyshire, 277
Styles, William, mason, 87, 88, 308 n.15
Suffolk, Henry Grey, Duke of, 83
Summerson, Sir John, 17, 115, 289
Sutton-in-Ashfield, Nottinghamshire, 278
Sutton Scarsdale, Derbyshire, 209
Swarkeston, The Stand, Derbyshire, 277, Col. Pl. XVI
Symondes, John, at Kyre Park, 14
Symons, Ralph, 17
Syon House, Middlesex, built by Duke of Somerset, 8, 29, 41, 44, 59

Tailor, Thomas, Registrar of Lincoln, 138
Talbot, Alethea, married Earl of Arundel, 231
Talbot, Edward, later 8th Earl of Shrewsbury, of Pontefract, 171
Talbot, Mary, married 3rd Earl of Pembroke, 228
Talman, William, at Chatsworth
Tankersley Hall, Yorkshire, 317 n.38
Tasso, *Gerusalemme Liberata*, 215
Tattershall Castle, Lincolnshire, 311 n.17

Theobalds House, Hertfordshire, 5, 10, 28, 30, 97, 117, 141, 152, 183, 290; panelling copied at Bolsover, 249, 250, Pl. 160; stables at, 171
Thornbury Castle, Glos., 32, 125, 199
Thoroton, *History of Nottinghamshire*, 135
Thorpe, John, surveyor, 11, 13, 14, 24, 25, 68, 86, 290, Pls. 3, 6, 91
Thorpe Salvin, nr. Sheffield, 119–20, 122, 154, Pl. 66
Thynne, Francis, antiquary, 41
Thynne, Sir John, built Longleat, 9, 10, 30, 40–61 *passim*, 68–76, 78
Thynne, Sir John, the younger, 53
Thynne, William, Comptroller to Henry VIII, 40, 41
Tissington Hall, Derbyshire, 288
Tixall, Staffordshire, 34
Toddington, Bedfordshire, 305 n.1
Torre, Richard, at Worksop, 113, 133
Torrigiano, emplyed by Henry VIII, 3
Torrington, George Byng, Lord, *Diaries*, 292
Toto de Nanziato, 3
Townshend, Sir Roger, 17
Tresham, Sir Thomas, 10, 15, 30, 231, 305 n.5
Trevor, Sir John, 288
Trollope, Sir Thomas, Bart., 317 n.43
Tupton Hall, Derbyshire, 277
Tutbury, Staffordshire, 112
Twickenham, Middx., the Earl of Bedford's house at, 309 n.42, Pl. 100
Twyford, Leicestershire, 273, 278, Pl. 192

Upham, Upper, Wiltshire, 62

Valois tapestries, Uffizi, 215
Vanbrugh, Sir John, architect and playwright, 291–2, 293
Van Dyck, 4, 247
Veneziano, Agostino, 65
Verneuil, Château de, 101
Vertue, *Notebooks*, 11, 114, 246, 249, 255
Verulam House, Herfordshire, 9
Vignola, 15, 88
Villard de Honnecourt, 13
Vincent, mason, 51–2
Vitruvius, 6, 16, 88, 307 n.86
Vives, Spanish philosopher, 305 n.10

Walden, Lord, 215
Walpole, Horace, *Anecdotes of Painting*, 11
Waltham Forest, Essex, royal house at, 104
Walton Castle, Somerset, 225
Warde, John, waller, 176
Wardour Castle, Wiltshire, 78–82, 90, 125, 160, 224, 228, Pls. 34–6, Col. Pl. IV
Ware Park, Hertfordshire, 225
Warmwell, Dorset, 25
Warwick, Earl of, 11
Warwick, St Mary's, 249
Warwick Castle, 106, 149, 311 n.17
Watts, W., *Seats of the Nobility and Gentry*, 292
Welbeck Abbey, Nottinghamshire, 169, 170, 182–3, 228, 231, 244, 246, 251–7, 260, 262, 265–6, 280, 290, Pls. 111–12, 165–70, 195

Wells Cathedral, stairs at, 160
West Wickham Court, Kent, 56
Weston House, Warwickshire, 191
Westwood, Worcestershire, 107
Weymouth, Lord, 53
Wheeler, John, Stourbridge ironmaster, 201
Whetstone, George, *Heptameron of Civil Discourse*, 5, 19
Whichford, Warwickshire, 191
Whichnor, Staffordshire, 314 n.39
Whitehead, Anthony, mason, 191
Whitney, *Choice of Emblemes*, 24, 26, 27, Pl. 5
Whittingham, Sir Timothy, 197, 314 n.49
Whitwell Manor House, Nottinghamshire, 255
Wilbye, John, madrigalist, 231, 293
Willoughby, Sir Francis, of Wollaton, 30, 32, 82–4, 88, 108, 166, 315 n.37
Willoughby, Henry, 166
Willoughby, Sir Percival, of Wollaton, 88, 166–7, 246, 273
Willoughby, Sir Thomas, 1st Lord Middleton, 310 n.13
Wilton, Wiltshire, 228, 232
Wimbledon House, Surrey, 25, 36, 162, 168, 169, 170, 291, Pl. 16
Winchester Cathedral, Gardiner Chantry, 29, Pl. 11; Fox Chantry, 40
Windsor, Lord, jousting, 212
Windsor, 7; Henry VII tower, 125, 311 n.17; St George's Chapel, 10, 28
Wing, tomb of Sir Robert Dormer at, 29
Wingerworth Hall, Derbyshire, 277, Pl. 194
Wolfeton Manor, Dorset, 61, 62, 315 n.37, Pls. 23–4
Wollaton, Nottinghamshire, Hall, 14, 32, 49, 74, 82–108, 113, 115, 145, 146, 149, 152, 162, 166, 188, 192, 193, 221, 246, 259, 262, 288, 293, Pls. 33, 37–8, 40, 42–3, 46–8, 50, 54–5, Col. Pls. V, VI, Fig. 1; Hawksmoor on, 291; Uvedale Price on, 292; coal pits at, 166–8; monument to Robert Smythson in church, 168, 234, Pl. 171
Wolsey, Cardinal, 3
Woodlands Manor, Mere, Wiltshire, 62
Woodstock, Oxon, entertainment at, 213
Wootton Lodge, Staffordshire, 107, 199–204, 291, Pls. 124–6, Fig. 16
Worcester, 188
Worcester, Earl of, his house at Nonsuch, 170
Worksop, Nottinghamshire, 49, 126, 133; Manor Lodge, 131–3, 135, 153, Pls. 72–3, Col. Pl. IX, Fig. 5; Manor, 66, 74, 110–15, 117, 119, 120, 123, 125, 132, 134, 138, 144, 145, 149, 154, 157, 162, 186, Pls. 60–3, Col. Pl. X
Worthe, Roger, 117
Wothorpe, Northamptonshire, 25
Wotton, Sir Henry, 17, 247
Wyatville, Sir Jeffry, 48, 50, 87
Wyverton House, Nottinghamshire, 271

Zutphen, Battle of, 108

SUBJECT INDEX

Accommodation, analysis of, in the Elizabethan country house, 59–60
Amateurs in architecture, 9–11; Sir Charles Cavendish as architect, 183–5
Architect, the idea of the, 6–7, 16–17, 18
Architectural books, *see* Pattern books
Architectural drawings, Elizabethan and Jacobean, 9–14; at Hatfield, 13, 49–50, Pl.19; by Maynard, 62–3, 70, Pls. 22, 25; by the Smythsons, 11–13, 286–7, and *passim*; by Thorpe, 11–12, 25, 86, 153, 288, 289, Pls. 3, 6, 91; by others, 9–11, 45, 68, 101–2, 249, 310 n.15, 314 n.48, Pl.2; aesthetic pleasure in, 287
Architectural drawings, late Gothic, in the Smythson collection, 40, 162, Pl. 96
Artisan class, the, 10–11, 15, 17, 162; non-architectural activities of, 10–11

Balconies, 249, 250, 259, 265, Col. Pl. XV, Pl. 164
Banquet, the, 48–9
Banqueting houses, 48–9; Clifton, 271; Hardwick, 157; Holdenby, 153, Pl. 91; Longleat, 48–9, Pls. 20–1; Welbeck, 255, Pl. 169; Whitehall, 249, 252, 316 n.23
Bowling-alley house, 277
Building accounts and contracts, at Bolsover, 234; Chatsworth, 117, 311 n.21 Gawthorpe, 191; Hardwick, 144, 146, 312; n.2 Longleat, 45, 51, 307; Owlcotes, 176; Wollaton, 82, 309 n.3; Worksop, 113

Castles, Elizabethan and Jacobean, *see* Sham-castles
Chivalry, *see* Sham-castles *and* Tournament
Compact house-plan, the 56, 97–100, 115–20, 287–8, 290
Corridors, 123, 179–80
Cross-halls, 131, 153–4, 170, 287–8

Design of Elizabethan and Jacobean houses, who responsible for, 8–14, 15, 28
Devices, 21–4, 25–7, 212, 232, Pls. 4,5,8; in architecture, 24–8, 108, 290, Pls. 6,7,9

Elizabethan and Jacobean architecture, later attitudes to, 291–3

Employers, their influence in design, 9–10, 28; their philistinism, 5–6; their quarrels, 294

Flemish architecture, the influence on England, 30–2, 249; at Bolsover, 249; Wollaton, 90; *and see main index, under* de Vries
Foreign architects and craftsmen in England, 14, 17, 44, 314 n.48
Fountains, 113, 266, 309 n.8
French architecture, its influence on England, 28–9; at Corsham, 66; Longleat, 44, 56, 59, 62, 72; Wollaton, 90, 97, 101–2; *and see main index, under* du Cerceau
French architecture, influenced by England, 86

Gables, Flemish, 90, 249, 255, 262
Gardens, 97, 113, 170, 180–1, 246, 255, 309 n.8., 314 n.42 Pls. 38, 100; fortified, 225, 266, Pl. 190, Col. Pl. XIV
German architecture, influence of, at Bolsover and Clifton, 266–9, 271
Glass, Elizabethan passion for, 19, 32–4, 72, 101, 110, 290, 309 n.47
Gothic architecture and the Middle Ages, their influence on the Elizabethans and Jacobeans, 20–1, 32–5, 160–2, 198–9, Pls. 13, 14; on the Smythsons, 162, 170, 244, Pls. 96–8; at Barlborough, 123, 125; Bolsover, 234, 242, 244; Caverswell, 181–2; the Hall, Bradford-on-Avon, 198–9; Hardwick, 160–1; Lulworth and Ruperra, 255; Slingsby, 259; Wardour, 82; Welbeck, 251, 256–7; Wollaton, 90, 97–100; *and see* Sham-castles
Great Chamber, function of, 59; provision of two, at Wollaton and elsewhere, 104
Greek inscription, at Shaw, 68

Italian architecture, influence on England, 3–4, 17, 36, 59, 72, 247–8, 269, 316 n.14; *and see main index, under* Francini, Palladio, Serlio, Veneziano

Libraries, architectural, in the 16th and early 17th centuries, 15; of the Willoughbys, 88, 310 n.13
Lodges, 13, 107, 133–4; Blackwell, 148; Holdenby, 153; Lulworth, 226; Manor

Lodge, Worksop, 133–4; Mt. Edgcumbe, 107; Wootton Lodge, 199–201; Worksop Manor, called a lodge, 134
Loggias, 152

Middle Ages, their influence, *see* Gothic architecture
Model, made for Longleat, 46

Parlour, function of the, 60
Pattern, Elizabethan fondness for, 20, 25
Pattern-books, 14–15, 88; *and see in the main index*, under de Vries, Dietterlin, du Cerceau, Francini, Francquart, Palladio, Perret, Serlio, Shute, Veneziano
Payment to craftsmen, methods of, 8; at Longleat, 51; Wollaton, 87; *and see* Building accounts and contracts
Perspective, 101, 310 n. 19
Prospect rooms and towers, 105–7, 110, 119, 157
Protestantism, 4–5, 36, 84, 86, 108, 197, 293

Railway, at Wollaton, 167–8
Renaissance architecture, Elizabethan attitude to, 18
Roofs, open timber, at Bolsover, Pl. 197; Longleat, 62, 90; Welbeck, 251, Pl. 166; Wollaton, 90, Pl. 48

Sham-castles, Elizabethan and Jacobean, in pageantry, 217–19, Pls. 137–8; in architecture, 206–9, 219–31, 232; *and see* Gothic architecture
Staircases, 19; especially noteworthy, at Barlborough, 124; Burton Agnes and Chastleton, 188; Hardwick, 157–60, Pls. 92–5; Wardour, 82, Pl. 35; Wolfeton, 61, Pl.24; Wollaton, 85
Stone, supply of, to Longleat, 50, 197; Wollaton, 82, 84
Surveyor, 8–9, 148–9

Theatre, Elizabethan, 307 n.86
Topographical drawing, Elizabethan and Jacobean, 2; of Bolsover, 262, Pls. 129–30
Tournament, the Elizabethan and Jacobean, 210–16, 231–2, Pls. 134–6
Turkey, possible influence of, at Bolsover, 316 n.4

Hardwicke for hugenes, Worsope for height,
Wellbecke for use, and Bolser for sight.
Worsope for walles, Hardwicke for Hall,
Welbecke for brew-house, Bolser for all.
Welbecke a parish, Hardwicke a Court,
Worsope a gallas, Bolser a Fort.
Bolser to Feast, Welbecke to ride in,
Hardwicke to thrive, and worsope to bide in.
Hardwicke good house, Welbecke good keepinge,
Worsope good walkes, Bolser good sleepinge.
Bolser new built, Welbecke well mended,
Hardwicke concealld, and worsope extended.
Bolser is morne, Welbecke day bright,
Hardwicke high noone, Worsope good night.
Hardwicke is noon, Welbecke will last,
Bolser will be, and worsope is past.